MYTH AND
PHILOSOPHY

SUNY Series, Toward a Comparative Philosophy of Religions
Frank E. Reynolds and David Tracy, Editors

MYTH AND PHILOSOPHY

Frank Reynolds
and
David Tracy, Editors

State University of New York Press

Published by
State University of New York Press, Albany

For information, address State University of New York Press,
State University Plaza, Albany, N.Y., 12246

Library of Congress Cataloging-in-Publication Data

Myth and philosophy / Frank E. Reynolds and David Tracy, editors.
        p. cm. — (SUNY series, toward a comparative philosophy of
religions)
        ISBN 0-7914-0417-X. — ISBN 0-7914-0418-8 (pbk.)
        1. Myth. 2. Religion—Philosophy—Methodology.   I. Reynolds,
Frank, 1930 -.   II. Tracy, David.   III. Series.
BL304.B856   1990
200¹. 1—dc20   89-48910
                                                                    CIP

10 9 8 7 6 5 4 3 2 1

For Chris Gamwell
The Dean who conceived the original idea
and
mobilized the necessary resources

CONTENTS

Myth, Philosophy, and Exegesis

Myth, Philosophy, and Secularization

Introduction

Frank E. Reynolds

The time is ripe for the development of a new approach to the philosophy of religion. Among philosophers interested in religion, there is a growing recognition of the importance of the structure and content of actual religious traditions, both Western and non-Western. At the same time, many scholars in more empirically oriented disciplines such as the history of religions and anthropology are becoming increasingly intrigued by the philosophical aspects and implications of the religions they study.

The *Toward a Comparative Philosophy of Religions* series, which this volume initiates, will explore the possibilities inherent in this new situation. Over the next few years, this series will publish a number of books that consider a variety of issues in the comparative philosophy of religions and a variety of types of philosophically relevant data. Some of these volumes will be collections of essays; others will be individually authored books. Authors will include philosophers as well as philosophically oriented scholars from related disciplines such as theology, the history of religions, and anthropology.[1]

David Tracy and I have chosen to inaugurate this series with a collection of essays on *Myth and Philosophy* for two closely related reasons. We are convinced that a philosophy of religions that has pretensions to a truly global perspective must give a very high priority to the exploration of the various ways in which these two modes of discourse have been related in the past, and how they might be related in the future. We are also convinced that "myth and philosophy" is a topic that will be of immediate and obvious interest to the whole range of scholars to whom the series is directed.[2]

The twelve essays that are included in this initial volume are divided into two groups. The first, which goes under the rubric of "Philosophical

1

Perspectives," contains three papers that defend the notion that the philosophy of religions should and can become global in its orientation; that it should and can become comparative in its approach; and that it should and can be grounded in the empirical study of actual religious traditions including, though not limited to, their philosophical expressions. Each essay addresses the relevant issues in its own distinctive way.

David Tracy sets the stage for the series as a whole, and for this volume in particular, by revisiting the origins of the modern effort to develop a philosophy of religion. Tracy reviews the ground-breaking work of Hume, Kant, and Hegel, the three great figures of the late eighteenth and early nineteenth centuries who are generally recognized as the founding fathers. In his "return to the origins" Tracy demonstrates that each of these highly creative philosophers of religion, unlike most of their more recent successors, give strong expression to global, comparative, and empirical concerns. Thus Tracy maintains that what must be done to reinvigorate the philosophy of religions today is not a wholesale rejection of the heritage that it has received from its past. What is needed, rather, is a retrieval—in a new mode commensurate with late twentieth-century sensibilities and resources—of the kind of vision that animates and informs the work of the founders.

The other two essays that are included in this section of the volume set forth constructive strategies for taking up Tracy's challenge. Charles Taylor, in his essay on "Comparison, History, Truth," makes the case for a globally oriented comparative approach that depends on empirical research carried forward in a hermeneutic mode. In spelling out his position, Taylor draws on the work of Hans-Georg Gadamer, and highlights and develops Gadamer's metaphor of philosophic and religio-historical interpretation as a process of "conversation."

Paul Griffiths takes up Tracy's challenge in a very different way. Entitling his essay "Denaturalizing Discourse," Griffiths sets forth a strategy for a globally oriented and comparative approach that pursues empirical study in a manner that is firmly rooted in the tradition of analytic philosophy. Griffiths distinguishes two different types of religious language, both of which appear cross-culturally. The first type, which characteristically operates within specific cultural contexts, he labels "naturalized discourse." The second type, which characteristically seeks to establish claims to truth on more rationalized and universally defensible grounds, he identifies as "denaturalized discourse." According to Griffiths, both types of religious discourse should be studied, and should be studied comparatively. But from his perspective the comparative analysis of denaturalized religious discourse—since it is more explicitly "philosophical" in character—is of special interest and importance for philosophers of religions.

In Part II of the volume there is a shift from essays that focus more directly on the discussion of theoretical and methodological issues to essays that deal more extensively with actual historical data. To be sure, the authors of the essays included in Part II share the same kinds of theoretical and methodological interests that are the explicit focus of the essays in Part I. Moreover these scholars are equally concerned with broad-ranging issues such as the nature and diversity of the human imagination and human rationality. In the present context, however, they have chosen to contribute the kind of essays that pursue these more general interests and issues through studies of particular religious expressions (especially mythic and philosophic expressions) embedded in particular historical situations.

In addition to their common concern to contribute to a new kind of philosophy of religions that is globally and comparatively oriented, the eight authors whose essays have been selected share a general perspective concerning the "myth and philosophy" topic. They all affirm that myth and philosophy (categories whose exact referents are very much at issue) are two different but broadly overlapping modes of discourse that have been, and still remain, related to one another in a variety of ways. On the one hand, they reject the notion—still very potent in contemporary academic culture—that philosophy is intrinsically superior to myth. On the other, they are seeking for ways to interpret the relationship that takes the distinctive characteristics and contributions of both myth and philosophy seriously into account.

Within Part II, the first section entitled "Myth and Philosophy: Similarities and Differences" contains three essays that make three very important and closely related points that are basic to refiguring the way in which we think about the relationship(s) between myth and philosophy. Arthur Adkins' paper on "Myth, Philosophy, and Religion in Ancient Greece" begins this process of simultaneous deconstruction and reconstruction by providing a new look at the development of Greek intellectual life during the middle centuries of the first millennium BC. On the deconstructive side, Adkins' discussion thoroughly discredits the all-too-prevalent notion that what was involved in the movement from Homer and Hesiod to Plato and Aristotle was a move from a naively mythic orientation that was prereflective and arbitrary to a truly rational philosophical orientation that has banished mythic modes of thought to the periphery. On the reconstructive side, Adkins presents a fascinating account of an intellectual development that leads from a myth*ology* that involves its own modes of rationality and reflection, to a mode of philosophical discourse in which the processes of *de*mythologizing and *re*mythologizing coexist.

Thomas Kasulis' discussion of Kūkai, the classic founding figure of the Japanese philosophical tradition, also has both deconstructive and reconstructive implications. The common Western prejudice which

Kasulis' essay implicitly but very effectively deconstructs is the notion that philosophy, by its very nature, must take a critical attitude toward "archaic" modes of religious expression in general, and mythic modes in particular. By focusing on Kūkai, Kasulis provides us with a powerful example of a philosopher of the very first rank who adopts and develops highly sophisticated philosophical categories and methods that he employs very effectively to express, to explain, and to defend the "truth" and efficacy of myth (and of other so-called archaic modes of expression as well).[3]

The essay that may have the most radical implications for restructuring our thinking concerning the relationship(s) between myth and philosophy (and certainly the one with the most intriguing title) is Gregory Schrempp's "Antinomy and Cosmology: Kant Among the Maori." This essay, like the preceding contributions by Adkins and Kasulis, challenges a common Western prejudice concerning myth and philosophy. This time the target is the very persistent modern Western notion that philosophy is sophisticated and profound in contrast to myth which is primitive and naive. Stated in a more positive mode, and in more specific terms, Schrempp's argument is that Kantian philosophy and Maori mythology express clearly analogous understandings concerning the rational necessity of two very similar (and logically inconsistent) notions of the origins of the cosmos. To put Schrempp's basic point more simply, the same kind of very profound and highly sophisticated cosmological insight that Kant generated and expressed in a philosophic mode, the Maori generated and expressed in a mythic mode.

The six remaining essays in the collection fall rather neatly into three pairs that depict three distinctive kinds of relationship between myth and philosophy. The first pair examine texts in which elements that we think of as mythic, and elements that we think of as philosophic, are tightly integrated within a more inclusive poetic frame. Laurie Patton, in her essay on the Ṛg Vedic "Hymn to Vāc," considers two radically opposed interpretations proposed by two highly respected Vedic scholars: one who approaches the hymn as a mythic text and one who opts for a philosophic analysis. In her discussion, Patton exposes the inadequacy of both interpretations and sets forth her own alternative. She makes a very convincing argument that in this famous and highly erudite hymn, undifferentiated mythic and philosophic elements are encompassed within a creative poetic vision that transcends them both.

The companion essay by Hossein Ziai focuses on the writings of Suhrawardī, a famous Iranian mystic of the twelfth century. In Ziai's account of Suhrawardī's didactic exposition of the mystic "Path to Illumination," he highlights the sophisticated use of philosophical allusions (Suhrawardī, is clearly a knowledgeable connoisseur of Greek philosophy), and the equally sophisticated use of mythic themes. But Ziai also demonstrates that these philosophical and mythical elements are so intimately interwoven that they can hardly be separated; and that they both are integrated in a distinctive mode of soteriological rhetoric that share more affinities with poetry than it does with philosophy as such.

The next set of essays addresses the issue of myth and philosophy as it emerges within religious traditions that center on the exegesis of sacred texts. Focusing on rabbinic Judaism, Howard Eilberg-Schwartz challenges the tendency to see logic, which is closely associated with philosophy, as antithetical to myth. Eilberg-Schwartz shows how the distinctive logic of the rabbis is enmeshed in the Torah-myth, a set of assumptions about what the Torah (Scripture) is and how it should be interpreted. These foundational assumptions and practical rules validate, and in turn are validated by, the particular criteria of rationality that the rabbis utilize. It is Eilberg-Schwartz' basic contention that, since myth and logic are intimately connected, criteria of rationality are relative to specific historical contexts.

Francis X. Clooney, working with Indian Vedic and Vedāntic materials, also describes a situation in which there is a close relationship between the mythology and mythic authority of a sacred corpus of texts, and the development of an exegetical tradition that generates an authentically philosophical mode of thought (in his case, a full-blown philosophical theology). Clooney demonstrates that Vedānta—as the name itself implies—quite explicitly presents itself as an exegesis of Vedic texts. And he uses very specific examples to illustrate various ways in which Vedānta was actually influenced by its mythic/Vedic heritage, both in terms of its formal structure and its specific philosophical contents.

The final pair of essays, both contributed by Winston Davis, bring us back to our own historical situation in the modern West. Davis' subject is the Western version of the myth of natural law and the secularization of that myth that has occurred in the theories of modern political and social philosophers from Hobbes to the present. Focusing on two closely related lines of development, the two essays provide a fascinating, richly documented account of the way in which the once-dominant myth of natural law has been challenged and weakened, and of the various mythically oriented and philosophically oriented efforts that have been made to amend it, to reinterpret it, or to replace it completely.

In addition to their descriptive value, Davis' essays—perhaps more than any of the others included in Part II—present an explicitly normative viewpoint as well. In "Natural Law and the Study of Myth in a World Without Foundations," Davis identifies himself rather closely with the modern tendency to utilize philosophically oriented rational reflection to ground and criticize principles of social order and practice. In "Natural Law and Natural Right: The Role of Myth in the Discourse of Community and Exchange," he highlights the value, even the necessity, of recourse to mythic modes of thought and justification. Taken together, the two essays clearly convey Davis' prescriptive conviction that appropriate mythic resources and appropriate philosophic resources must both be marshalled (and maintained in tandem and in tension) in order to provide a sound basis for human flourishing in a modern, democratic society.

The *Toward a Comparative Philosophy of Religions* series, including this first volume on *Myth and Philosophy*, has been generated by a multiyear project sponsored by the Divinity School, University of Chicago. In 1986 the original initiative was taken by Dean Franklin I. Gamwell. At that time Dean Gamwell asked Stephen Toulmin (who later moved to Northwestern University and became a "special consultant") and David Tracy to join with me to serve as co-directors of a project designed to explore new ways of pursuing the philosophy of religions. Important seed money was personally contributed by two alumni of the Divinity School—E. J. Tarbox and Michael Busk. For the past three years generous funding has been provided by the Booth Ferris Foundation.

In order to generate the necessary conversations among interested philosophers and theologians on the one hand, and historians of religions and anthropologists on the other, the project has convened six semiannual conferences. Each conference has been attended by approximately thirty participants from approximately ten different universities in Europe and North America.[4]

All but two of the essays included in this volume were originally presented at one of the six semiannual conferences; and the two others (the first by Tracy and the last by Davis) have been written in response to conference discussions. All of the papers have been revised in order to assure a clear focus on a core of crucial issues identified by the group as a whole.

Despite the richness and diversity of the essays that constitute the present volume, many perspectives, many insights, and much very intriguing data put forward in the six conferences could not be included. Thus we plan to offer, as the third volume in our *Toward a Comparative Philosophy of Religions* series, another collection of essays that will explore the topic that we considered in the later phases of our discussion. This collection, which builds on the foundations already established through our deliberations and debates concerning "myth and philosophy," will appear under the title *Discourse and Praxis* (forthcoming from the State University of New York Press, 1992).

Notes

1.   The second volume in the series will be Lee H. Yearley, *Aquinas and Mencius: Theories of Virtues and Conceptions of Courage* (forthcoming from State University of New York Press in the fall of 1990). Volumes 3 through 7 are already "in process."

2.   The editors wish to express their very special thanks to Francisca Bantly for her highly efficient help in the publication process, and for her excellent work in preparing the index. We are also grateful to Laurie Patton for her willingness to contribute whenever her assistance was needed.

3.   Those interested in a fascinating and directly relevant comparison between a Greek understanding of language that became very influential in the history of Western philosophy, and Kukai's understanding of language, should consult Kasulis' earlier article on "Reference and Symbol in Plato's Cratylus and Kukai's Shojjissogi" published in *Philosophy East and West*, vol. 32, no 4 (October, 1982).

4.   A large amount of the credit for the success of the project during its first three-year phase must go to the four student assistants who have been involved. In the early stages of the project Sheryl Burkhalter, the Project Assistant for year one, handled the details of organization and hospitality with great skill and grace. What is perhaps even more important, she and Robert Campany produced "Summary Reports" of conferences one and two that brought order out of chaos and paved the way for the far more cohesive discussions that followed. In the later stages Francisca Bantly, the Project Assistant for years two and three, managed the administrative burden with a happy combination of competence, good humor, and personal flair. In addition, she and Laurie Patton wrote superb "Summary Reports" for conferences three through six. (The set of six "Summary Reports" is being edited by Francisca Bantly. It will be published by the Divinity School, University of Chicago, and will be available from the Dean's office in early 1990.)

Part I

Philosophical Perspectives

Chapter 1

On the Origins of Philosophy of Religion: The Need for a New Narrative of Its Founding

David Tracy

I. Introduction: The Problem of Origins in Philosophy of Religion

To understand the possible new relationships of philosophy of religion and history of religions it is helpful to recall the aims of the founders of both. More exactly, it is crucial to note that both disciplines are modes of inquiry that emerged in the modern West. Both have precursors in Western culture and alternative forms for inquiry in the other great cultures.[1] A fuller account of comparative philosophy of religion and history of religions would need to consider both precursors and alternatives. Otherwise, Western philosophers would find themselves trapped once again—in more subtle but no less limiting ways—to only Western models of philosophy or only Western models of history of religions.[2]

A part (but only a part) of that larger project is to rethink the development of the discipline of philosophy of religion in the modern West.[3] For that development, the founding moment of modern philosophy of religion demands attention. In this essay, therefore, I shall provide some initial reflections on that founding in order to suggest a new approach to comparative philosophy of religion for the present: a present where the promise of a comparative philosophy of religion in direct and critical collaboration with a comparative history of religions is beginning to bear fruit. From either a philosophical or a history of religions perspective, the insistence on the need to rethink—both philosophically and historically—this history of the emergence of both disciplines in the modern West and their often troubled relationships may prove important. However, the limitations of the present essay must be stated frankly. First, there is the major limitation of lack of attention to the alternative formulations of both philosophy of religion and history of religions in other cultures and the less limiting but still real lack of attention to the premodern 'precursors' of these disciplines in the West itself. Second, there is the limitation of a lack of attention (in this paper at least) to the other two disciplines which have influenced the modern developments of both philosophy of religion and history of religions: viz., theology (especially Christian theology) and anthropology (especially social and cultural anthropology).[4]

We shall observe some of the interrelationships and tensions occasioned by the presence of Christian theology as a conversation partner to both modern philosophy of religion and history of religions. On the whole, however, this discussion would demand a separate study clarifying the models for Christian theology itself in the modern period (e.g., *Glaubenslehre*, or confessional theology, or philosophical theology or public theology).[5] The debates within Christian theology are sufficiently complex in the modern period since Schleiermacher developed his model of *Glaubenslehre* to demand such separate treatment. The same kind of complexity—indeed conflict of interpretations—is equally present in the crucial disciplines for understanding the 'other' in the modern West: viz., anthropology and history of religions.

These severe limitations only reinforce the modesty in execution yet utility in aim of the present attempt: to clarify the founding of the discipline of philosophy of religion in the modern West in order to see what 'comparative' interests were present in that founding.

Philosophy of religion, as an autonomous and modern discipline, emerges principally in Hume, Kant, and Hegel.[6] As much as in several other issues in philosophy, a great deal of contemporary philosophy of religion is still determined by the programs of these founders: sometimes by critical reaction against the founders; sometimes by refinement of their positions; usually by some combination of both. Unfortunately, there has been too little attention given to the 'comparative religion' interests of the founders—interests which, as we shall see below, are present in these pre-history of religions founders of philosophy of religion.

As initiated by Hume, Kant, and Hegel in their very different ways, philosophy of religion was to be an autonomous discipline, either distinct from (Hegel) or separate from theology (Hume and Kant). To prove autonomous, philosophy of religion must not be placed within a theological context. The work of such 'precursors' to modern philosophy of religion as Clement of Alexandria, Origen, Anselm, Augustine, Maimonides, Aquinas, and Scotus are all construed in modern philosophies of religion as developing valuable philosophical arguments (e.g., on the existence of God or the nature and attributes of God). However, those arguments, by their placement within a theological context, render their strictly philosophical character sometimes difficult to interpret (witness the continuing debates on Anselm and Aquinas) and, therefore, often difficult to assess on exclusively philosophical grounds.[7] Even Hegel, that most theological of the philosophical founders, is not an exception here. For Hegel's insistence on the *Aufhebung* provided by the *Begriff* of the philosophical concept in relationship to the *Vorstellung* of religion insists upon a transformation of all traditional theology into the new theological philosophy of the Hegelian system.[8]

A respect for, yet distance from, their patristic and medieval theological precursors seems clear in the founders' attempts to establish a modern and autonomous philosophy of religion. Their relationships to their more immediate modern philosophical seventeenth-century precursors is more complex. In one sense, Spinoza and especially Leibniz may be viewed as the true founders of a modern philosophy of religion. Indeed, Leibniz hoped that a philosophical account of religion could help undo the horrors of the interconfessional conflicts which ravaged Central Europe in the Thirty Years' War. Moreover, Leibniz's great interest in the reports of the Jesuit missionaries from China impelled him (as it did such later *philosophes* as Voltaire and Diderot) to genuinely comparative interests.[9] The emergence of notions of 'natural religion' among the Deists are analogous to Spinoza's earlier transformation of traditional theological concepts into strictly philosophical ones. Both provide clear and influential precursors for the founders of modern philosophy of religion.

Little would be lost and much gained by allowing the story of the 'founding' of philosophy of religion to begin in the seventeenth century—or, indeed, in such sixteenth-century skeptical humanists as Montaigne, or in such Christian humanists as Ficino and della

Mirandola. However, the most influential formulations of what became philosophy of religion in the modern West may still be found in the representative texts and emphases of Hume, Kant, and Hegel. In that sense, they represent the truest, as clearest, founding of an autonomous philosophy of religion.

The story of the 'emergence' of that discipline has been oft-told, of course, but told, I believe, too partially, even wrong-headedly. For insofar as modern philosophy of religion involves two distinct tasks, it is crucial to distinguish those tasks as carefully as possible. In general terms, the tasks are that of philosophical elucidation and justification.[10] The philosopher is bound, first, to elucidate the meaning and structure of the religious phenomenon as a phenomenon understood philosophically. Often but not always this attempt at elucidation will occur under the rubric of a 'concept' of religion which is either presumed or argued to possess universal characteristics. Sometimes this concept of religion will be claimed to possess 'sui generis' characteristics that render it either distinct from or (the stronger claim) grounding to other human activities like art and morality.[11] At other times (especially in the contemporary philosophy of religion influenced by Wittgenstein), there will be a denial of the philosophical utility of any universal concept of 'religion' in favor of delineating the structure and meaning (often the grammar) of the distinct but related ('family-resemblances') 'religious' language-games disclosing distinct but related 'religious' forms of life.[12]

Whatever the conclusions of the philosophical task of 'elucidation', however, it should be acknowledged as a philosophical, as distinct from a purely historical-empirical, work. For however informed by empirical-historical work, the philosopher of religion is, above all, concerned to clarify either the 'concept' of religion implied by all the historical manifestations of the religions or, alternatively and more modestly, to clarify analytically either the 'grammar' of a particular religious language or to provide a descriptive, i.e. eidetic or hermeneutic, phenomenology of religion and the religions.[13]

In every case, however, the task of philosophical elucidation may be distinguished from the task of philosophical justification. In principle, a philosopher could provide a philosophically persuasive elucidation of religion without undertaking the task of justification. The debates over the philosophical (as well as strictly historical) utility of various candidates for a universal concept, or, more modestly, definition of religion, are merely the clearest instance of the need to distinguish these two tasks.[14] For whatever the results of particular philosophical debates on justification (e.g., is religion a responsive or projective phenomenon?; is it grounding to or merely disclosive of other human cultural activities?),[15] the question of justification should be kept distinct from the question of elucidation. Some contemporary philosophical positions argue against any attempt at justification at all as, in effect, a philosophically muddled 'foundationalism';[16] in more usually (at least with the 'founders') the two tasks are distinguished, but both are undertaken.

In the context of this distinction between elucidation and justification, one may look anew at the narrative of the emergence of philosophy of religion in the founders. As that story is usually told, the story is one of various candidates for 'justification' (positive or negative) on 'religion' philosophically construed. There can be little doubt that the drive to 'justification', with the important exception of some contemporary descriptive phenomenologists and some analytical philosophers of religion, is a crucial component in the larger narrative of Western philosophy of religion.

But it is just as important to try to see the narrative anew from the viewpoint of elucidation; and, especially, to see what comparativist elements are present in particular elucidations. One need not deny that the comparativist elucidations of the founders were undertaken with an overriding interest in philosophical justification. This is clearly the case with Kant and even, though in significantly modified forms, with Hume and Hegel. In all these cases, however, the distinct elucidating procedures may, even when part of a larger justificatory schema, be distinguished and narrated on their own. For even in those philosophers who believe that the fuller task of philosophy of religion should include the demands of justification (as Hume, Kant, and Hegel clearly do and as I admit I do)[17] an interpreter nevertheless may distinguish these two tasks in order to see what comparativist elements may have been present, either deliberately or subconsciously, in the philosophical elucidation of 'religion' or the 'religions'.

Such a new interpretation may provide a more complex narrative than the usual one on modern philosophy of religion. It may help to open even the justification enterprise to more comparativist demands. At the least, a new narrative of the origins of philosophy of religion may clarify how the 'founders' did in fact possess 'comparativist' interests, however inadequately those interests were executed by contemporary standards. This new narrative of origins could provide a new way to interpret the 'origins' of philosophy of religion so that the interdisciplinary and comparativist demands of contemporary philosophy of religion are encouraged. Such is the modest aim of the present and necessarily brief narrative on the origins of philosophy of religion: a narrative which will emphasize how the founders' philosophical elucidation of the religious phenomenon had comparativist aims, even when these aims were often overshadowed by a concern with justification.

II. The Founders: Hume, Kant, Hegel

A: David Hume

The need for a new narrative of the emergence of philosophy of religion is nowhere more clear than in the case of David Hume. As usually presented, Hume was interested solely in the issues of justification of philosophical arguments on miracles and the existence of God. Except for the new skeptical orientation to his thought, Hume's position is usually interpreted less as beginning a new approach to the question of religion than as a continuation (with new, because largely negative, results) of the traditional disputes in philosophical theology on the classical arguments on the existence of God, as well as the arguments on the nature and attributes of God and the arguments on miracles.

To be sure, Hume does analyze the 'arguments' of his predecessors and especially the 'design-arguments' of his eighteenth-century contemporaries. But there are also novel moves in Hume's approach to religion—moves which merit far more attention than they ordinarily receive.

On one reading, Hume is concerned solely with the issue of rational justification—hence the emphasis in most interpretations of Hume on religion solely in the *Dialogues Concerning Natural Religion*.[18] But even the *Dialogues* should not be read simply as a series of 'arguments' proposed by the participants (Philo, Cleanthes, Demea) as those arguments may be clarified by contemporary analytical philosophers. This conceptual analysis approach to the interpretation of Hume, although clearly valid to clarify the individual arguments as valid or invalid arguments, misses the larger structure and thereby underlying concerns of Hume's refashioning of how to approach arguments on religion. By returning to the dialogue form to place all the arguments of the dialogue partners,[19] Hume intended to challenge purely formal analyses of religious topics. For Hume, purely formal arguments disallow, especially on the subject of religion, an analysis of the characters, intentions, or, as Hume would prefer it, the 'passions' informing all the individual arguments. For Hume, religion is the kind of subject on which formal arguments must have a crucial but not the sole role. The arguments of the *Dialogues* are both formal and substantive and thereby concerned with both logical validity and contextual and rhetorical claims to plausibility. By their rhetorical placement in the *Dialogues*, the arguments also disclose how particular human beings characteristically reflect upon religious claims. In Hume, rhetoric is more encompassing than dialectic for reflection on religion: hence the need not merely for arguments but for arguments placed in the wider rhetorical setting of a dialogue. Too often Hume's dialogical approach to religion is read as a failure to distinguish 'logic' and 'psychology.'

Sometimes this may be the case but, more usually, Hume's choice of the dialogue form deserves far more attention than 'conceptual analysis' allows. For the dialogue form, from Plato to Hume, demands interpretive attention to the interests, dramatic setting, and passions of the characters.[20] On 'religion', Hume suggests, such a wider mode of inquiry is crucial. Otherwise, the philosopher will ignore how religion functions as a passionate human interest and concern and thereby how human beings actually reflect upon religion critically.

Moreover, Hume's choice of Cicero's *De natura deorum* as the model for his own dialogue on religion also discloses what can only be called his genuinely comparativist interests. Like Cicero, Hume clearly considers religion to be a topic which demands some understanding of other positions in order to understand one's own. One can formulate this 'dialogical' principle of inquiry in later, explicitly hermeneutical terms which are not Hume's but nicely illuminate his own practice of inquiry on religion: to understand as complex, puzzling, difficult, and culturally important a topic as religion, the philosopher must find a mode of self-understanding that reaches self-understanding by understanding-interpreting some genuine 'other'.[21] Just as Cicero approached the issue of religion rhetorically rather than dialectically by writing a dialogue where a Stoic, an Academic, and a Skeptic speak to one another, so Hume writes not an argumentative essay but a rhetorical dialogue where a moderate skeptic (Philo), a design-argument Newtonian (Cleanthes), and an a priori orthodox theist (Demea) must speak to one another. Hume's brilliant stroke, moreover, is to compose his dialogue with such pervasive irony[22] that readers, to this day, cannot tell exactly what Hume's own opinion is: recall the ironic suggestiveness in Hume's portrait of the not very bright narrator, the curiously inconclusive 'conclusion' of the dialogue and the use of irony by all the speakers, especially Philo. In Hume's ironic hands, the dialogue form is not an extended monologue nor a single argument but rather a sustained and implicitly comparativist conversation among genuine others. This is clearly the case with Cicero on religion and just as clearly so with the radically ironic David Hume.

At the same time, it must be admitted that, in the *Dialogues*, Hume's principal but not sole interest is in the question of theism (and the rational grounds or lack thereof for that belief). This remains the case despite the fact, as Hume's title would suggest, that the principal interest of the dialogue is not in theism but in 'natural religion'. But here is where the usual reading of Hume by philosophers of religion most needs challenge. For Hume wrote not only the *Dialogues Concerning Natural Religion* with their dialogical and implicitly comparativist concerns with issues of justification on philosophical theism, he also wrote the equally interesting (but too seldom studied) 'companion' text, *The Natural History of Religion.*[23] Here too, to be sure, Hume's interests are again largely those of justification. Yet in the *Natural History*, far more than in the *Dialogues*, an interpreter can see how Hume's concern with justification demands extended elucidation—and that with an explicitly comparativist twist.

In one sense, in the *Natural History* Hume continues his general philosophical concern with the relationships between the 'understanding' and the 'passions' in order to clarify the several meanings of 'natural religion' and, indeed, religion more broadly. In another sense, Hume's entire approach may be interpreted as an early comparativist analysis of the possible 'origins' of religion in human nature. Influenced by Hobbes, Bayle, and his own wide reading in classical Western sources (especially Roman) as well as his fascination with contemporary accounts of Western explorers in the 'New World', Hume fashioned, in this fascinating text, a kind of philosophically construed cultural anthropology. Hume believed that he could elucidate the question of religion (or religions) by clarifying the 'origin' of religion in human nature. With the resources available to him and with his own historical skills as a noted historian of his period, Hume turned into a kind of comparativist philosopher-anthropologist in order to try to elucidate the origin of religion in the human passions of 'fear' and 'hope'. His eighteenth-century prejudices on 'savages' are as clear as are the relative limitations and classically oriented range of the Western religious data he analyzes. But Hume's obvious limitations of scope are far less interesting to a contemporary philosopher than his insistence, throughout the study, that a philosophical analysis of religion cannot rest content with issues of justification by rational argument alone but must elucidate the shifting meanings of 'religion' in terms at once comparative and philosophical. For Hume, the philosophical attempt to find the 'origins' of religion in the human passions of fear and hope[24] can only succeed if one can provide some comparativist analysis of the roots of both 'popular' religion and 'philosophical' religion.

On this reading, then, philosophy of religion emerges in Hume as an implicitly comparativist enterprise: both in Hume's insistence on the need for the dialogue form[25] in the *Dialogues* for addressing issues of justification, and, even more so, in his philosophically construed elucidation of the origins of religion as certain human passions are manifested in the historical religions. Both the implicitly comparativist, because dialogical, form of the *Dialogues* and the explicitly comparativist interests of the *Natural History*·largely drop from sight in the more familiar readings of Hume's contributions to philosophy of religion as an autonomous discipline. But the 'truncated' versions of Hume as philosopher of religion will no longer serve—either as an adequate reading of Hume's philosophy or as an understanding of the comparativist interests in modern Western philosophy of religion as that discipline was first formulated by its founders.   ·

B: Immanuel Kant

With Kant, the situation is more complex. There is no clear distinction in Kant between the task of elucidation and the task of justification.[26] Although Kant approached the questions of religion (especially the question of God) in all three Critiques as well as in his major work on religion, *Religion Within the Limits of Reason Alone*, his overriding interest (as befits his attempt at a critical philosophy) was on the question of a critical justification of the implicit or explicit cognitive claims of religion. At the same time, Kant's interest in comparativist issues was surprisingly strong:[27] as one learns from reports of his frequent courses in Eastern religions in the summers; his lifelong interest in geography; his fascination with the reports of explorers; his interesting observations on Persian religion in his typology on Zoroaster and Job in the *Opus Posthumum*; and, above all, in his insistence, in *Religion Within the Limits of Reason Alone*, that his philosophical analysis of religion applied not only to Christianity but to all the religions.[28]

The debates on the interpretation of Kant on religion continue unabated.[29] For the present purposes of interest in the presence or absence of comparativist concerns in Kant, the following concerns are relevant. First, Kant's use of the category 'limit-concept' (that which can be thought but not known) has proved one of the most fruitful Western philosophical categories not only for the task of justification but also for the task of the elucidation of the peculiar logic of religious language as religious.[30] Second, the still more familiar interpretation of Kant as, in effect if not in design, reducing religion to morality seems at best a partial reading—and one displaying too little concern for how Kant actually elucidated both morality and religion in direct but distinct relationship to one another. Kant's famous definition of religion as 'to recognize the demands of duty as divine commands'[31] does not render religion merely an exemplification of morality, nor does his construal of religion (rather than morality) as 'justified hope'. Above all, one must note Kant's concern (especially in the *Critique of Practical Reason* but throughout many texts) to show how the postulates of practical reason—freedom, immortality, and God—open critical morality to a moral religion (more usually, a 'moral theism'). A *moral* theism, for Kant, must meet the demands of morality but is not reduced to them. Moreover, religion, as justified hope, responds, above all, to the third of the three famous Kantian questions: 'What can I know? 'What ought I do? What *may* I hope for?' The question of religion is the question of hope. It is a question where 'may', not the ethical 'ought' prevails. But that 'may' of religious hope can be a rational 'may,' not, *pace Vaihinger*, simply a fictionalism of 'as if'.[32]

The moral finitude of human being opens rational morality to struggle to attain what cannot be attained in this finite life: the *Summum Bonum*.[33] This finitude relates the ever striving autonomous self not only to the categorical imperative but to virtue and happiness—and thereby implicitly to religion as a justified (because moral) hope for a virtue worthy of happiness. The Third Critique (that preferred text of the Romantics) opens the questions of religion still further:[34] by the analyses of the possible relationships of nature and freedom in aesthetic and teleological judgment; by the analyses of the symbol (which gives us more to think about than any concept can encompass); and by the analysis of the sublime as distinct from the beautiful. All these Kantian emphases in the 'unifying' Third Critique (as the Romantic successors of Kant were right to see) undo any Kantian temptation to pure moralism by providing new modes of inquiry on the crucial roles of symbol, art (the beautiful and the sublime), and religion as endowing moral finitude with reasonable hopes for a teleological unity of nature and freedom.

On this reading, therefore, Kant's philosophy of religion is not confined to the famous arguments on the existence and nature of God (of the First Critique), nor to the moral argument for God as a postulate of practical reason (in the Second Critique). Rather the Kantian philosophy of religion moves forward through the architectonic of all three Critiques to address the question of the justification of the claims of religion (especially theistic religion) in ever wider terms. After completing the three Critiques, moreover, Kant was able to turn deliberately and critically to two explicit tasks: both a more complete critical justification and a more detailed elucidation of religion (especially, but not solely, the Christian religion) in his major work on religion, *Religion Within the Limits of Reason Alone* (henceforth *RWLR*).[35]

In sum, the philosophical task of critical justification (which is the principal aim of Kant's critical philosophy from his first work to his last) leads inexorably to the need for a fuller elucidation of a concept of religion. That concept, on Kantian grounds, should be faithful to the different historical manifestations of religions and not only to Protestant Christianity. And yet one must be cautious here. For Kant's concept of religion is, at one and the same time, a conclusion to his critical philosophy directed, above all, to questions of critical justification and a conclusion (in *RWLR*) to his attempt at the philosophical elucidation of the Christian religion.[36]

The use in modern philosophy of religion of Western concepts of 'religion' (for example, Schleiermacher's concept or Hegel's or Kant's) has proved an ambiguous heritage from the very beginning. The central question is not easily resolved in the case of Kant, Hegel, or Schleiermacher: how much their candidates for a definition of religion can be viewed as either the result of genuine, if, by contemporary standards, inadequate historical-comparative study and philosophical elucidation of that study or, alternatively, how much their concepts of 'religion' are imported from their studies of the Christian religion.[37] In Kant's case, the hermeneutical issue is particularly acute. On the one hand, there is the fascinating information that Kant actually taught 'Oriental religions' and geography; there are, furthermore, his frequent references to religions other than Christianity and his claim (in *RWLR*) that his concept could elucidate and be tested by other than the Christian religion.[38]

On the other hand, one cannot but judge Kant's reflections on the role of history, more exactly on the role of historical research for both philosophical elucidation and critical justification, unclear at best. His interest in history was real, and his appeals frequent.[39] But how such historical-comparative work influenced Kant's philosophical elucidation of religion is unclear. For Kant, unlike Herder, his former student, and Hegel, his successor, the fact that both reason and religion have a history seemed true but relatively unimportant. It has remained unimportant for many critical, transcendental philosophers following Kant.

And yet this is clearly not the whole picture nor the only possible legacy for comparativist purposes of Kant's philosophical interpretation of religion. What is both intriguing and puzzling about Kant's analysis of historical religion (or, as he phrases it, 'revelational religion') in *RWLR* is his suggestive use of the analogy of the schematizing of the categories in his critical epistemology of the First Critique.[40] The intent of the analogy is clear: just as Kant needed the concrete schemata of the imagination in his epistemology to show the mutual adaptation between the general categories of the understanding and sense perceptions, so too Kant needed the revelational-historical forms of religion (image-history-community) to show the mutual adaptation between moral theism (the 'natural religion' resulting from critical philosophy) and the historical, revelational religions.

The difficulties for the philosophical elucidation of the religions by means of the ingenious Kantian analogy are also clear: for how strict, finally, is the analogy? Moreover, Kant's actual elucidation of religion (directed, above all, to the question of radical evil as construed by Christianity) means that the elucidation of the central historical realities (image, community, and history) is so influenced by the task of a critical justification of the Christian religion (focused, above all, on Kant's interpretation of the 'Kingdom of God') that it is often extremely difficult to sort out Kantian philosophical elucidation from Kantian philosophical justification.[41] Nevertheless, Kant's appeal to this analogy of schematization as concretization suggests both historical and comparativist interests in principle even though, often enough, these interests are not in fact employed when Kant uses the schema of concretization to elucidate the historical religions.

But even granted these not inconsiderable difficulties, the hermeneutical complexity of interpreting Kant on religion is increased if one relates (as I believe one should) Kant on 'symbol' in the Third Critique with Kant on 'religious image' in *RWLR* rather than interpreting *RWLR* only in the light of the first two Critiques.[42] In sum, the exact role of history (and implicitly, therefore, of history of religions) in Kant's philosophy of religion remains a puzzle. If the proper analogy to history in Kant is to his political philosophy as well as to what might be named "the philosophy of history" in his minor writings, then *RWLR* encourages far more attention to history of religions than even Kant's own use of the analogy of the schematizing of the categories suggests. But this must remain, for the moment, merely a possible path of interpretation for the possible comparativist elements in Kant. For my part, I do not believe that Kant ever successfully integrated his genuine interest in history with his philosophy of religion. Perhaps Kant's overwhelming interest in the task of critical justification for philosophy of religion united to the ambiguities in his use of historical materials in his philosophical reflections on image, community, and history occasioned Kant's atypical failure to make clear distinctions here. This is odd since Kant attained the greatest Western expertise in making fine distinctions since Aristotle.[43]

But whatever the truth of this interpretation of Kant's ambiguities on both history and comparison, this need not mean that the usual Neo-Kantian (or other transcendental) readings of Kant on the possible relationships of philosophy of religion and history of religions suffice.[44] Rather, one can see in Kant's entire enterprise, culminating in *RWLR* and in the Zoroaster-Job typology of his *Opus Posthumum*,[45] an ever more encompassing attempt to move away from a concern solely with the critical justification of Western theistic beliefs to a more historical and, at least in principle, comparativist interest in elucidating the historical (revelational) religions in the critical light of the Kantian analogy of the schematism.

Herder would develop Kant's opening to the religions as historical and cultural totalities in new and more promising terms than Kant's own. Hegel, moreover, would rethink this opening in more strictly philosophical terms than Herder's. Although in Hegel, as we shall see below, these still remain important ambiguities in the relationships between his elucidation and justification of a 'concept' of religion and the elucidation of 'determinate (i.e., historical) religions', the central Kantian ambiguity ceases: for, in Hegel, history (and, therefore, history of religions with a comparativist thrust) must, in principle, be accorded full rights in any Hegelian philosophy of religion. In that sense Paul Ricoeur's self-description as a philosopher who returns to Kant through Hegel makes eminent sense: a return *through* Hegel is a return through a philosophical-hermeneutical concern with the historical forms of both reason and religion (as in Ricoeur's own *Symbolism of Evil*);[46] a return *to* Kant is a return to more modest critical aims after the collapse of Hegelian claims on both the 'consummate religion' and the absolute system.[47] To this puzzling journey of Hegel, the final 'founder' of modern philosophy of religion, we now turn.

C: G. W. F. Hegel

In Hegel, a philosophical interest in what can be called the history of religions first emerges in explicit terms among the founders of modern Western philosophy of religion. This emergence, however,—as the recent research in and publication of Hegel's different *Lectures on the Philosophy of Religion* (1821, 1824, 1827, 1831) show—was a gradual and never finally resolved one. The issues, however, are there from the very beginning of Hegel's reflections on religion, as his youthful concern with the 'positivity' of religion in his *Early Theological Writings* amply demonstrates.[48] In both of his two great philosophical texts (*The Phenomenology of Spirit* and *The Science of Logic*), moreover, Hegel's concern with the necessary manifestation in historical forms of Spirit to spirit is prominent.[49] In either of the two distinct 'entries' (the phenomenological and the 'logical') to Hegel's philosophy of Absolute Spirit, philosophical analysis of religion is undertaken. Indeed, Hegel is the first great modern philosopher to make historicity and thereby the reality of concrete ('determinate') historical forms central to his philosophy. Hegel's philosophical elucidation of religious forms, to be sure, is placed within and partly controlled by the grand dialectical schema of his philosophy of Absolute Spirit.[50] For example, the concrete religions are rendered in Hegelian terms throughout his work. Thus the religions are named not by their more usual 'historical' names (Buddhism, Hinduism, Greek religion, Judaism, Christianity, African religions, etc.) but by philosophical descriptions of what Hegel construes as the essence of each (the religion of sublimity or expediency or beauty or magic, etc.).

What is fascinating about Hegel's philosophy of religion from the beginning to the curiously ambiguous end, however, is his overriding concern to affirm the necessity for philosophical attention to the historical forms of religion: minimally to 'test' the 'concept' of religion; at its best, to formulate that concept itself. The concern for justification is rendered most clearly in the two distinct entries to his philosophy—the phenomenology of consciousness of *The Phenomenology of Spirit* and the onto-theology of *The Science of Logic*.[51] Even there, however, religion cannot be understood simply abstractly as a concept, but only as a concept that develops from and is always dependent upon the dialectics of the concrete historical forms of representation. This Hegelian dialectical principle is defended throughout his philosophy insofar as consciousness must dialectically express itself in determinate negations and determinate *Aufhebungen* if it is to reach the truly concrete universal in an adequate *Begriff*.

It is a travesty to Hegel, I am persuaded, to read him as if, in his later systematic work, he had abandoned his earlier historical interests for the deductive onto-theology of his system of Absolute Spirit.[52] To be sure, Hegel never meant by historical study (even in the *Early Theological Writings* on positivity) what, for him, would be a merely empirical, passive description of historical religions. His search is more accurately described as hermeneutical: i.e., the acknowledgment that even in the description of historical realities (including historical religions) we ourselves as historical interpreters are always already involved.[53] Therefore, if we are to claim to be engaged in truly historical interpretation (or, to use the terms of this essay, if we are philosophically to elucidate the meaning and structure of historical religion), we must also understand ourselves as the historical selves we actually are (for Hegel, in and for Spirit) in order to understand the historical other at all. If this hermeneutical principle is united to Hegel's insistence (from the *Phenomenology* forward) that we only understand ourselves in dialectical relationship to some other, the hermeneutical turn to history in Hegel is clear—as is the implicit philosophical insistence that all understanding is (dialectically) comparativist.

The oft-noted (sometimes with surprise by more empirical historians) success of Hegel in naming certain essential characteristics in the historical religions is directly dependent on this Hegelian hermeneutical understanding of the historical task. By abandoning the 'Romantic empathy' model of many of his contemporaries and by criticizing the philosophical and hermeneutical naiveté of a merely empirical model for historical study, Hegel fashioned a phenomenology of religion that, at its best, was successful in elucidating the meaning and structure of some concrete historical forms of religion. In more contemporary terms, Hegel, at his elucidatory best, was developing a comparative hermeneutics of the historical religions *avant la lettre*.[54]

And yet one must always add the qualifier 'at his best'. At his worst, Hegel could feel free to ignore historical context (e.g., Egyptian religion), ignore internal developments and differences in distinct strands of a religious tradition (e.g., Buddhism and Hinduism), and ignore (except for Christianity—the 'consummate' religion) the religions as living religions (e.g., Judaism).[55] This series of devastating Hegelian limitations for a hermeneutic of the history of religions is not dependent solely on the relative inadequacy of the historical sources at Hegel's disposal nor on the fact that 'history of religions' as a self-conscious discipline had yet to emerge. Hegel's problem is, rather, largely dependent on three crucial ambiguities in his philosophy of religion. First, by his own standards, Hegel never satisfactorily conceived of the relationship of empirical historical work to his own philosophical concept of the necessary historicity of all the manifestations of Spirit—including reason and religion. Second, Hegel often distinguished but just as often conflated (as Kant did before him) the abstract

philosophical tasks of elucidation and justification. Here, Hegel's philosophy of Absolute Spirit both drove him to extraordinary phenomenological,
hermeneutical, and thereby comparativist insights into certain essential
characteristics of particular religions, even as the very same philosophy
sometimes impeded his ability to dwell upon historical details, contexts,
and differences. Third, this dual set of problems occasioned the mounting
trouble Hegel had in relating the typologies of his philosophical elucidation of the determinate religions to the philosophical elucidation and justification of the dialectical schema he used in his 'concept of religion' and his
account of Christianity as the 'consummate religion'.[56]

Thanks to the remarkable research and interpretations of Jaeschke
and Hodgson, one can now witness these ambiguities in detail in the
various lectures on religion of Hegel's later years.[57] Hegel's constant
need to reorder the 'religions' in section II of his Lectures (on 'determinate religion') and his need (e.g., on Buddhism) to read more and
rethink his earlier interpretations are testimonies to both his philosophical and historical integrity and his larger problem. It may well be the
case, as Hodgson avers, that Hegel was most concerned in his last years
with rethinking the crucial section on determinate religions and, in that
sense, with history of religions. But it is also the case that Hegel never
lived to work out the exact relationships of his typologies (or, even with
Jaeschke, the geography) of his philosophical elucidation of the determinate religions to the larger dialectical schema of philosophical justification dominant in the first section ("The Concept of Religion") and
the third and final section ("The Consummate Religion"). In fact, that
dialectical schema pervades even the presentation of the typological-elu-
cidatory analyses of 'Determinate Religion'.

The ambiguities in Hegel's great attempt at a philosophy of religion, however, have much to teach us even today. It is difficult, for
example, to see how any persuasive claim to develop a concept of religion in Hegel's sense could succeed (if it can at all) without following
rather than preceding an analysis of the 'determinate', historical religions.[58] Such a post-Hegelian philosophical enterprise of elucidation
need not retreat to a purely empirical, passive, and philosophically
naive understanding of historical work in order to allow for the necessity of philosophical reflection on the self-other relationship in all historical as hermeneutical understanding. Hegel's hermeneutical
instincts informed all his philosophical elucidation of the historical
forms of the 'determinate' religions. In my judgment, these instincts
are sound on general hermeneutical grounds. His larger dialectical

justification schema (articulated in his two great works, the *Phenomenology* and the *Science of Logic*) remain unpersuasive to all who do not accept Hegel's 'absolute standpoint'.

Whether one can affirm aspects of Hegel's work (e.g., the master-slave dialectic, or the insights into Greek religion) without the absolute standpoint which is, for Hegel, both the *telos* of the entire *Phenomenology* and the self-manifesting and self-disrupting origin of the *Logic*, is the most troubling philosophical issue of all. At least that is the case for all the 'middle' or 'left-wing' post-Hegelians who cannot accept the denial of our finitude seemingly entailed by the Hegelian absolute standpoint and at the same time cannot deny the persuasiveness of many—very many—moments in the Hegelian journey to and from Absolute Spirit.[59] But whatever the fate of Hegel's larger justification schema (and its implicit imperialism),[60] the example of Hegel persists as a paradigmatic early modern example of the need to distinguish a philosophical elucidation of the religious phenomenon even in the midst of an overriding philosophical concern with questions of rational justification. Perhaps, as Foucault suggests, all later post-Hegelians who believe that we have finally removed Hegel from our midst may find ourselves at the end of our own line of inquiry surprised to find Hegel standing there again—smiling and knowing.

III. Conclusion: The Lessons of the Founders

On the interpretations proposed above, it is a fruitful task to return to the origins of philosophy of religion as an autonomous discipline and reflect anew on the projects of the founders. Neither the discipline of history of religions nor the discipline of anthropology were available to any of the founders. Moreover, their principal task, in continuity with the philosophical theologies of the Western tradition, can be described as the task of assessing the grounds for rational belief (or justification) of Western theism. In each case, however, their interests in the questions of theism were united to an attempt to develop a philosophy that would be autonomous—i.e., stand on its own ground free of traditional theological paradigms. This aim at methodological autonomy allowed these first modern philosophers of religion to reconceive even the question of God as first a question of religion.[61] Hence, they attempted to elucidate on philosophical grounds the essential characteristics, the meaning, and structure of 'religion'. This task of philosophical elucidation ordinarily took the form, among the founders, of defending either some general concept of the 'origins' of all religions in certain basic human passions (Hume), or the need for relating the rational concept of morality to a concept of moral religion concretized in image, community, and history (Kant), or a concept of 'religion' that could be dialectically related to the historical manifestations of the 'determinate religions' (Hegel).

By the present criteria of either history of religions or philosophy of religion, no one of these enterprises can be deemed a success. By present criteria, the founders' philosophical elucidation of religion both failed to relate the particular 'concept' of religion to careful historical accounts of the religions and too often conflated the task of Western philosophical justification with the task of elucidation. Nevertheless, the mixed discourse of the founders merits a new reading. For from the horizon of contemporary interests in a comparative philosophy of religion, one can observe that the comparativist interests of the founders were, despite the usual narrative, neither secondary nor *ad hoc*. Hume wrote two treatises on religion: one concerned principally with issues of justification from a dialogical and implicitly comparativist perspective; and one concerned principally with issues of explicitly comparativist elucidation. Kant was led, by the logic of his own work throughout the three Critiques, to affirm the need for the concretization of religion in particular images, communities, and histories; and thereby opened his philosophy, in principle, to historical and comparativist concerns. Hegel tried, from his earliest *Theological Writings* through the series of revisions of his *Lectures on the Philosophy of Religion* to think through again and again how to elucidate in comparativist terms (and not only justify) the philosophically construed historical religions.

The intellectual crises that occurred after this first 'founding' of philosophy of religion as a modern Western enterprise—first historicism and then positivism—intervened so radically as to render almost forgotten the earlier attempts of the founders at comparativist philosophical elucidation. Furthermore, the development of those Western disciplines concerned principally with the problem of 'other', including other religions (viz., history of religions and anthropology), has enriched and shifted the possible form needed by a comparative philosophy of religion beyond anything the founders imagined. In the twentieth century, therefore, there occurred what might be named a second 'founding' of philosophy of religion: nonpositivist and nonhistoricist, but welcoming of the results of history of religions and anthropology for the now necessarily interdisciplinary task of philosophy of religion. The story of this second founding[62]—in William James and the American experiential and pragmatic traditions; in the later Wittgenstein and the new analytical philosophies of 'language-games', 'forms of life', and 'family resemblances'; in the emergence of both eidetic phenomenology and hermeneutic phenomenology—is another narrative that needs to be retold. If the narratives of both foundings of philosophy of religion were rethought, then we might begin to understand how contemporary attempts to develop a comparative philosophy of religions in critical conversation with history of religions and anthropology need not simply forget the programs of either the first or second founders, nor simply repeat them.[63] Rather the entire narrative of philosophy of religion in the modern West needs rethinking and retelling if both the 'roots' and the 'fruits' of that curious modern Western invention, philosophy of religion, is one day to play a properly interdisciplinary and intercultural role.

Notes

1.   A helpful survey of precursors and some non-Western models may be found in Eric J. Sharpe, *Comparative Religion: A History* (London: Duckworth, 1975). One should also consult the relevant articles (with bibliographies) in the *Encyclopedia of Religion* (Mircea Eliade, Editor in Chief) (New York: Macmillan, 1987), as well as Jan J. Waardenburg, *Classical Approaches to the Study of Religion*, 2 vols. (The Hague: Mouton, 1973-74).

2.   Two recent examples by Western scholars of the creative use of both Western and non-Western materials (e.g., on reason) may be found in Wendy Doniger O'Flaherty, *Other People's Myths: The Cave of Echoes* (New York: Macmillan, 1988) and Lawrence E. Sullivan, *Icanchu's Drum: An Orientation to Meaning in South American Religions* (New York: Macmillan, 1988).

3.   See James Collins, *The Emergence of Philosophy of Religion* (New Haven: Yale University Press, 1967).

4.   On Christian theology, see Ninian Smart, John Clayton, Patrick Sherry, and Steven F. Katz, *Nineteenth Century Religious Thought in the West*, vols. 1, 2, and 3 (Cambridge: Cambridge University Press, 1985). On anthropology, see Michael Banton, ed., *Anthropological Approaches to the Study of Religion* (New York: Praeger, 1966).

5.   Each of these models is distinct and would require separate treatment. For examples of each, see John Marquarie, *Twentieth Century Religious Thought: The Frontiers of Philosophy and Theology* (London: SCM, 1963) and Claude Welch,

Protestant Thought in the Nineteenth Century vol. 1 (1799-1870) and vol. 2 (1870-1914) (New Haven: Yale University Press, 1972 (1) and 1985 (2)).

6.   This claim is admirably sustained in James Collins, *The Emergence of Philosophy of Religion*, op. cit.

7.   On Aquinas, see David Burrell, *Aquinas, God and Action* (Notre Dame: University of Notre Dame Press, 1979); on Anselm, see John Hick and Arthur McGill, eds., *The Many-Faced Argument* (New York: Macmillan, 1967).

8.   Inter alia, see Emil Fackenheim, *The Religious Dimension in Hegel's Thought* (Bloomington: Indiana University Press, 1967) and James Yerkes, *The Christology of Hegel* (Missoula: American Academy of Religion Dissertation Series, 1978). Several studies have also appeared in the State University of New York Series of Hegelian Studies, especially Quentin Lauer, *Hegel's Concept of God* (Albany: SUNY Press, 1982). An important study of the terms *Vorstellung* and *Darstellung* in Kant, Hegel, and Heidegger may be found in Eric Crump, *Imagination, Representation and Faith: Foundations for a Revised Representational Christology* (University of Chicago Dissertation, 1989).

9.   This 'ecumenical' side of Leibnitz's enterprise is emphasized in Stephen Toulmin, *Beyond Modernity*, forthcoming, 1990.

10.   See Wayne Proudfoot, "Philosophy of Religion," in *The Encyclopedia of Religion* (Mircea Eliade, Editor in Chief), vol. 2, op. cit, 305-311.

11.   Inter alia, see Joachim Wach, *The Comparative Study of Religion* (New York: Columbia University Press, 1958); Mircea Eliade, *Patterns of Comparative Religion* (London: Sheed and Ward, 1958). A recent philosophical challenge to 'sui generis' concepts may be found in Wayne Proudfoot, *Religions Experience* (Berkeley: University of California Press, 1985), especially 1-48.

12.   A valuable 'sorting-out' of these Wittgensteinian categories may be found in Fergus Kerr, *Theology After Wittgenstein* (New York: Blackwell, 1986). An alternative reading is D. Z. Phillips, *Faith and Philosophical Enquiry* (New York: Schocken, 1971).

13.   It will be noted that phenomenologists, whether eidetic or hermeneutical, usually do attempt some common notion (under rubrics like 'essence' or 'definition') of religion, whereas Wittgensteinians are doubtful of all general definitions and, therefore, confine their attention to 'family-resemblances' and 'forms of life'.

14.   For a historical account of Western concepts of religion up to the early nineteenth century, see Michel Despland, *La Religion en Occident* (Montreal: Fides, 1979).

15.   The modern hermeneutics of 'retrieval' of religion as 'sui generis' in the tradition of *Religionwissenschaft* from Otto through Eliade and Kitagawa interpret religion as a 'responsive' category. The modern hermeneutes of 'suspicion' from Feuerbach to Marx and Freud explain religion as a 'projective' category. The general philosophical issue, in hermeneutics, may be reformulated as the relationship of 'understanding' and 'explanation' as in Paul Ricoeur, *Interpretation Theory* (Fort Worth: Texas Christian University Press, 1976). An alternative analytical philosophical account may be found in Wayne Proudfoot, *Religious Experience*, op. cit. In Proudfoot's interpretation of hermeneutics (41-73), there is a curious failure to analyze the hermeneutical distinction of 'understanding' and 'explanation' as *both* realities are demanded for the fuller task of interpretation.

16.   On 'foundationalism', see William P. Alston, "Two Types of Foundationalism," *Journal of Philosophy* 73 (1976), 165-85.

17.   In a contemporary philosophy of religion, the question of justification would demand a comparative analysis of Western and non-Western notions of philosophical justification. Contemporary Western debates on 'rationality' are relevant here: inter alia, see Bryan Wilson, ed., *Rationality* (Oxford: Basil Blackwell, 1970) and Martin Hollis and Steven Lukes, eds., *Rationality and Relativism* (Cambridge: MIT Press, 1982).

18.   David Hume, *Dialogues Concerning Natural Religion*, ed. N. K. Smith (Indianapolis: Bobbs-Merrill, 1963).

19.   For an analysis of the relationship of the wider category of dialogue to argument, see David Tracy, *Plurality and Ambiguity: Hermeneutics, Religion, Hope* (San Francisco: Harper & Row, 1987), 1-28.

20.   On Plato, see Paul Friedlander, *Plato: An Introduction* (Princeton: Princeton University Press, 1969), 154-71 and Hans-Georg Gadamer, *Dialogue and Dialectic: Eight Hermeneutical Studies in Plato* (New Haven: Yale University Press, 1980); Herman Sinaiko, *Love, Knowledge and Discourse in Plato* (Chicago: University of Chicago Press, 1965); Kenneth Seeskin, *Dialogue and Discovery: A Study in Socratic Method* (Albany: SUNY Press, 1987); David Tracy, "Argument, Dialogue and the Soul in Plato," *Witness and Existence: Essays in Honor of Schubert M. Ogden*, eds. Philip E. Devenish and George L. Goodwin (Chicago: University of Chicago Press, 1989), 91-106. On Hume, it is important to observe that even his first great work, *A Treatise on Human Nature*, is too often read only in its epistemological parts in Part I without sufficient attention to Hume's extensive discussion of the 'passions': see *A Treatise of Human Nature* (Oxford: Oxford University Press, 1951).

21.   The Hegelian influence in hermeneutics here is clear; see Hans-Georg Gadamer, *Truth and Method* (New York: Seabury, 1975) and Michael Theunissen, *The Other: Studies in the Social Ontology of Husserl, Heidegger, Sartre and Buber* (Cambridge: MIT Press, 1984).

22.   See John Vladimer Price, *The Ironic Hume* (Austin: University of Texas Press, 1965) and the representative essays in V. C. Chappell, ed., *Hume: A Collection of Critical Essays* (Garden City: Doubleday, 1966), 361-424; A. Jeffner, *Butler and Hume on Religion* (Stockholm: Aktiebolaget Tryckmans, 1966); Anthony Flew, *Hume's Philosophy of Belief* (New York: Humanities Press, 1961).

23.   David Hume, *The Natural History of Religion*, ed. H. E. Root (London: Black, 1956).

24.   Ibid., 28-49.

25.   The dialogue form is implicitly comparativist insofar as it always demands some other for self-understanding. Even reflective monologues are, in that sense, dialogical. The use of the dialogue form renders clear this hermeneutically comparativist nature of all human understanding. In my judgment, Hume's is one of the most successful dialogues in the Western tradition.

26.   Kant, of course, is an expert in distinction and engages often in particular elucidations—but almost always in the context of his larger critical philosophy.

27.   See James Collins, *The Emergence of Philosophy of Religion*, op. cit., 167-211.

28.   Immanuel Kant, *Religion Within the Limits of Reason Alone* (New York: Harper, 1960).

29.   Among the most valuable studies, see Michel Despland, *Kant on History and Religion* (Montreal: McGinn-Queen's University Press, 1973); Emil Fackenheim, "Immanuel Kant," in *Nineteenth Century Religious Thought*, vol. 1, op. cit., 17-40; G. E. Michalson, *The Historical Dimensions of a Rational Faith: The Role of History in Kant's Religious Thought* (Washington: University Press of America, 1977); A. W. Wood, *Kant's Moral Religion* (Ithaca: Cornell University Press, 1970); idem., *Kant's Rational Theology* (Ithaca: Cornell University Press, 1978).

30.   Inter alia, see Ian Ramsey, *Religious Language: An Empirical Placing of Theological Terms* (New York: Macmillan, 1963); Paul Ricoeur, "The Specificity of Religious Language," *Semeia* 4 (1975): 107-45; David Tracy, *Blessed Rage for Order* (New York: Seabury, 1978), 92-94 and 146-171. Whether this Western limit-language analysis of religious language is applicable outside its Western context is an open question for a contemporary comparative philosophy of religion.

31.   Immanuel Kant, *The Critique of Practical Reason and Other Writings in Moral Philosophy* (Chicago: University of Chicago Press, 1949), 232.

32.   For Kant's own use of 'as-if' see his *The Doctrine of Virtue* (New York: Harper, 1964), 162-63. The exact meaning and import, in different Kantian contexts of the 'as-if' qualifier remains a controverted question in Kant scholarship—and not one necessarily resolved by Hans Vaihinger's fictionist interpretation in Hans Vaihinger, *The Philosophy of 'As If': A System of the Theoretical, Practical, and Religious Fictions of Mankind* (New York: Harcourt, Brace, 1935).

33.   On the debates on the *Summum Bonum*, see James Collins, *The Emergence of Philosophy of Religion*, op. cit., 150-52; 182-84; Emil Fackenheim, "Immanuel Kant," op. cit., 19028; J. R. Silber, "The Importance of the Highest Good in Kant's Ethics," *Ethics* 73 (1963), 179-97.

34.   It is unfortunate, in my judgment, that so many interpretations of Kant on religion ignore the *Third Critique*. The central analyses suggested in that text (especially on symbol) point to resources in Kant which help to illuminate both his unifying aim in the *Third Critique* and his unifying and humanizing understanding of religion in *RWLR*—which, after all, comes chronologically after all three critiques were completed and not after *The Critique of Practical Reason* alone. In sum, in terms of reception, I align myself with those (e.g., Schelling to Heidegger and Gadamer) who insist on the importance of the Third Critique for understanding Kant's full philosophical position. To be sure, *RWLR* is not a fourth critique but does assume the position of all three of the critiques in order to be understood. Whether Kant's *Critique of Judgment* (New York: Hafner, 1951) succeeds in its unifying intent is a more difficult question. But that is the intent: the *Third Critique* does, minimally, supply the kind of resources for philosophy of religion suggested in my text (especially on symbol and on the possible relationships of the 'sublime' and the 'religious').

35.   The debates on Kant's interpretation of Christianity may be found in Karl Barth, *Protestant Thought from Rousseau to Ritschl* (London: SCM Press, 1959) and Josef Bohatec, *Die Religionsphilosophie Kants in der 'Religion innerhalb der Grenzen der blossen Vernunft'* (Hamburg: Hoffman und Campe, 1938).

36.   Kant consistently understood this enterprise to be distinct from any theology: see Bohatec, op. cit., for examples of the theologians Kant read and commented upon.

37.   In Schleiermacher, the concern for defining 'religion' in the *Glaubenslehre* and even the *Speeches* is more theological than critical-philosophical in contrast to both Kant and Hegel who remain consistently philosophical in their approaches to religion. On Schleiermacher, see B. A. Gerrish, *Tradition and the Modern World: Reformed Theology in the Nineteenth Century* (Chicago: University of Chicago Press, 1978); idem., *The Old Protestantism and the New: Essays in the Reformation Heritage* (Chicago: University of Chicago Press, 1982), 196-208; idem., "Friedrich Schleiermacher" in *Nineteenth Century Religious Thought in the West*, op. cit., 123-56. The influence of Schleiermacher's Christian theological (rather than philosophical) concept for defining religion complicates the reception and reinterpretation of Schleiermacher by such phenomenologists of religion as Rudolph Otto. Schleiermacher was also, of course, a philosopher. However, his major work and influence on discussion of definitions of 'religion' in modernity comes principally, not from his philosophical work, but from his theological work in *The Christian Faith* and even (in an admittedly more modified sense) in *The Speeches*. An interpretation of Schleiermacher, therefore—crucial as it is for understanding the relationships of history of religions and Christian theology in the modern period (e.g., in Ernst Troeltsch) and important as his influence has proved in some philosophies of religion (e.g., Rudolph Otto)—is not appropriate for this essay on the founders of philosophy of religion. Here the crucial figures remain Hume, Kant, and Hegel, just as Schleiermacher remains the major founder of modern Christian theology. For the historical context of the important conflicts of Hegel and Schleiermacher, in philosophy and theology, see Richard Crouter, "Hegel and Schleiermacher at Berlin: A Many-Sided Debate," *Journal of the American Academy of Religion* 48 (March 1980), 19-43.

38.   It is important here to recall that both the two major modern disciplines concerned with the 'others' and often (but not always) with explicit comparison (history of religions and anthropology) emerge subsequent to the 'founding' of both philosophy of religion (Hume, Kant, Hegel) and modern Christian theology (Schleiermacher). All four thinkers read rather widely in the scholarly texts and translations of other religions available to them. None, of course, could foresee the work of Max Müller (who may serve as the first explicit historian of religion).

39.   See Michel Despland, *Kant in History and Religion*, op. cit.; and G. E. Michaelson, *The Historical Dimensions of a Rational Faith: The Role of History in Kant's Religious Thought*, op. cit.; in Kant, see *On History*, ed. L. W. Beck (Indianapolis: Bobbs-Merrill, 1963).

40.   Immanuel Kant, *Critique of Pure Reason* (New York: Macmillan, 1933), 180-87; 210-12; 546-47; *Critique of Practical Reason*, op. cit., 177-79; *RWLR*, 58-59. Note, especially, Kant's care to avoid anthropomorphism in his use of the schematism of analogy in *RWLR* in fidelity to the use of the schematism of the first two Critiques.

41.   On the influence of the Jewish-Christian formulation of the question of radical evil for Kant, see Emil Fackenheim, "Kant and Radical Evil," *University of Toronto Quarterly* 23 (1953-54), 339-52; Paul Ricoeur, "The Symbol: Food for Thought," *Philosophy Today* 4 (1960), 206-07. In Kant, see *RWLR*, 129-38.

42.   I do not claim that Kant explicitly undertakes this comparison of 'symbol' (in the *Critique of Judgment*) and image (in *RWLR*). However, *pace* Collins, with Ricoeur, this seems a fruitful place for further Kantian reflection on not merely the 'humanizing' (Collins) role of religion but also the unifying and excessive role of the symbol (as distinct from the concept) in the Kantian philosophy of religion.

43.   In an odd chronological reversal, my own reading relates Kant (with his architectonic and careful distinctions) as more akin, in philosophical spirit, to the great Western master of argument and distinction, Aristotle; just as Hegel's more daring speculative concerns make him more akin to Plato: thus, Kant: Aristotle:: Hegel: Plato. Plato, after Aristotle, is a puzzling, but, I hope fruitful path for further reflection.

44.   The most distinguished Neo-Kantian interpreters here remain Hermann Cohen and Ernst Cassirer.

45.   Immanuel Kant, *Opus Posthumum*, op. cit., 21-27.

46.   Paul Ricoeur, *The Symbolism of Evil* (Boston: Beacon, 1967).

47.   On Hegel, besides the works cited in n. 8, also see Peter C. Hodgson, "George Wilhelm Friedrich Hegel" in *Nineteenth Century Religious Thought in the West*, op. cit., 81-121; Charles Taylor, *Hegel* (Cambridge: Cambridge University Press, 1975); Stephen Crites, *In the Twilight of Christendom: Hegel vs. Kierkegaard on Faith and History* (Chambersburg: American Academy of Religion Studies in Religion, 1972); Mark C. Taylor, *Journeys to Selfhood: Hegel and Kierkegaard* (Berkeley: University of California Press, 1980). The most important new source of the study of Hegel in religion is the extraordinary work of scholarship of all the Hegelian manuscripts (Hegel's notes and student notes) of the 1821, 1824, 1827, and 1831 lectures in Berlin on the philosophy of religion. The English edition is: Peter C. Hodgson, ed., *Hegel: Lectures on the Philosophy of Religion*, 3 vols. (Berkeley: University of California Press, 1984 [1], 1987 [2], 1985 [3]). Of particular interest for the present study is volume 2, *Determinate Religion*, where we can witness Hegel's amazing flexibility and imaginative and speculative reconstructions of his categories for interpreting the historical religions philosophically. It is clear, from these volumes, that Hegel was prepared to rethink his interpretation of every religion and their relationships to one another throughout his career. This work (published in German, Spanish, and English by an international committee of scholars led by Walter Jaeschke, Ricardo Ferrara, and Peter Hodgson) renders useless for scholarly interpretations of Hegel the earlier synoptic editions of Hegel's *Lectures on the Philosophy of Religion*. For important debates on the significance of this project, see Walter H. Sonser and James Yerkes, *Papers of the Nineteenth Century Theology Working Group: AAR 1987 Annual Meeting* (Berkeley: Graduate Theological Union, 1987).

48.   G. W. F. Hegel, *Early Theological Writings* (Chicago: University of Chicago Press, 1948). On the young Hegel in religion, see Adrien Peperzak, *Le Jeune Hegel et la vision morale du monde* (The Hague: Nijhoff, 1960).

49.   The approach of volume 1, *Introduction and the Concept of Religion: Lectures on the Philosophy of Religion*, op. cit., illustrates how Hegel employed his entire philosophy of Spirit to develop a concept of religion. In Hegel's view, a concept of religion entails a concept of God. Indeed, in the philosophy of Spirit, religion is God's self-

consciousness in finite spirit: hence, the need for both the *Phenomenology* and the *Logic* to understand religion thus conceived as that relationship.

50.   The qualifier 'partly' is important, as is the use of the descriptive adjective 'dialectical' rather than 'developmental', for the schema. On the one hand, the concept of religion (of volume 1) and therefore Hegel's entire philosophy of Spirit—does inform and partly control the categories employed for interpreting the determinate religions of volume 2. On the other hand, as the shifts in the manuscripts show, Hegel was fully open to rethinking *which* categories in his philosophy were most helpful for understanding each historical religion. On the first factor, therefore, I agree with the critiques of Frank E. Reynolds and Merold Westphal. On the second factor, however, the interpretations of Walter Jaeschke and Peter C. Hodgson are persuasive: hence my use of the *via media* phrase 'partly controlled'.

51.   The *Science of Logic* (New York: Macmillan, 1951) along with the *Encyclopedia of Philosophy* (New York: Philosophical Library, 1959) are far more influential on Hegel's 'concept' of religion and his analysis (in volume 3) of Christianity as the 'consummate religion' than the more consciousness-oriented phenomenology of the *Phenomenology of Spirit*. Note, for example, the use of the Hegelian understanding of the divine inner life in volume 3 and Hegel's use of the classical arguments on God in both volumes 1 and 3.

52.   See Walter Jaeschke, "Between Myth and History: On Hegel's Study of the History of Religion," in *Papers of the Nineteenth Century Theology Working Group*, op. cit., 59-71.

53.   Note Hans-Georg Gadamer's reappropriation of Hegel (in contrast to Schleiermacher and Dilthey) for contemporary hermeneutics (even one like Gadamer's, which disallows Hegel's absolute standpoint) in *Truth and Method*, op. cit., 146-50.

54.   An example of Hegel 'at his elucidatory best' is his analysis of Roman religion as the 'religion of expediency' in volume 2, *Determinate Religion*, op. cit., 498-507 (Lectures of 1824).

55.   For a good critique of Hegel on Hinduism, see Merold Westphal, "Hegel, Hinduism and Freedom" in *Papers of the Nineteenth Century Theology Working Group*, op. cit., 88-100. Hegel's interpretations of Buddhism are especially ill informed and badly conceived. His failure to understand Judaism as a living religion is especially obvious—as is his lack of effort to understand Islam at all. His attempts to rethink both Buddhism and the 'place' and meaning of Judaism, however, in his later lectures remain indicative of the openness-in-principle of his philosophy of religion: see the essays of Reynolds and von der Luft in *Papers of the Nineteenth Century Theology Working Group*, op. cit., 100-23.

56.   Those relationships are, to be sure, often difficult to determine with exactness, given Hegel's constant rethinking of his categories for interpreting the determinate religions.

57.   Especially informative is the listing of Hegel's 'sources' for his interpretations on volume 2, *Determinate Religion*, op. cit., 3-13.

58.   Hegel's 'concept' of religion is determined by his philosophy of Spirit. It is less 'tested' than 'applied', but with amazing freedom, imaginativeness, and occa-

sional playfulness in his interpretations of the 'determinate religions'. Whether such a universal philosophy of religion can succeed, even in principle, seems highly doubtful.

59.   On these typologies (first introduced by D. F. Strauss), see Karl Löwith, *From Hegel to Nietzsche: The Revolution in Nineteenth Century Thought* (New York: Holt, Rinehart and Winston, 1964) and Emil L. Fackenheim, *The Religious Dimension in Hegel's Thought*, op. cit., 75-112.

60.   The Hegelian imperialism here is multifaceted: culturally Western, religiously Christian, and philosophically idealistic.

61.   In Hegel's case, it would be equally accurate to state dialectically that the question of religion is first the question of God, since religion is, for Hegel, God's own self-consciousness in finite spirit; more exactly, that relationship *is* religion.

62.   I hope, in the future, to provide a companion study to this one on what I claim is this 'second founding' of philosophy of religion—a founding necessitated not only by the changes in philosophy and culture (especially historicism and positivism), but also by the emergence of history of religions and anthropology as well as in the increasing autonomy (from theology) of philosophy of religion.

63.   The major difference would be the necessarily interdisciplinary nature of the task of any genuinely comparative contemporary philosophy of religion.

Chapter 2

Comparison, History, Truth

Charles Taylor

There are a number of connected issues which seem to recur in interdisciplinary discussions between philosophers, anthropologists, historians, and students of religion. One might speak of them as "zones of puzzlement," within which we tend to lose our bearings and talk at cross-purposes. Somewhat rashly, I would like to explore four of these areas in this paper. I start by listing them, not necessarily in any logical order.

1. The boundary between myth and science is a troublesome one for anthropologists and students of religion. Is myth only what 'they' (the people studied) do, and not what 'we' (scholars) engage in? Or is this an outrageously presumptuous and ethnocentric assumption?

2. Another recurring problem concerns whether or how any understanding we propose of a religion or a society at a given moment of time needs to be embedded in a view of history. The extreme case of this kind of embedding, of course, is something we see in Hegel or Marx: the very intelligibility of any society or culture is bound up with the place it occupies in a certain line of development, itself defined by definite "stages." In full flight from this (and with good reason), some of us might want to deny that any embedding in a broader historical picture is necessary for understanding. But the issue is whether something of the kind always and necessarily haunts us, even when we want to repudiate it.

3. There are a set of problems about comparison. These inevitably arise for any group of people engaged in understanding a culture/religion which is not theirs. How does the home culture obtrude? Can one neutralize it altogether, and ought one to try? Or is one always engaged in some, implicit if not explicit, comparison when one tries to understand another culture? If so, where does one get the language in which this can be nondistortively carried out? If it's just one's home language, then the enterprise looks vitiated by ethnocentrism from the start. But whose language, if not ours? And isn't the language of science "our language"? We get back here to no. 1: maybe science is our "myth," so that all we're doing is encoding others' myths in ours, etc.

4. Does understanding necessarily raise issues of truth? To understand another culture, does one have (implicitly or explicitly) to be making or relying on judgments about the truth or validity of the claims made by people in that culture? Or can one duck the issue, as most of us who consider Hegel-type syntheses as outrageously presumptuous would dearly like to do?

These "zones" are obviously related. In fact, even I had trouble keeping them apart at times. They have a common origin in a continuing malaise. We are engaged in a family of enterprises (I include philosophers as consumers if not producers of such studies) which originally defined themselves as offering sober, rational discourse about ways of life/discourses which often lacked those qualities. This discourse supposedly had another manner of access to its objects than they had to themselves. It had the benefit of reflective and rational understanding. It was 'science' (in the broad sense, like German 'Wissenschaft'—this has nothing to do with the crazy claims to model human on natural science). From this standpoint, all the areas of puzzlement above clear up without remainder. The boundary myth/science expresses this difference of access; the scientific discourse offered the medium of comparison. *Of course*, it offered judgments of validity. It was itself a discourse of greater validity. And clearly, all this went along with a certain understanding of growth in history, since the culture in which science flourishes itself has grown out of earlier, less favored cultures. The others are "behind" us.

We have trouble believing this now; for the well-known reasons. We have big doubts about some of the "scientific" claims (these are quite independent of doubt about positivist and reductivist claims about the language and methods of natural science, but plainly these also have had an influence). And we find the kind of satisfied ethnocentrism that the older view embodies both unbelievable and somewhat discreditable.

But at the same time, the discourse we use is continuous with that of our forebears. We write books and treatises like Frazer, with claims supported by not totally dissimilar canons of evidence and argument. We can't just repudiate this rational and sober discourse—not sincerely anyway, because it's what we still speak; and feel we ought to speak, when it comes to that. We argue and trip each other up according to the same canons of argument, even when we're supporting theses like the nondistinction of science and myth which would seem to make nonsense of these canons. It's very painful and confusing.

My whole way of thinking of these issues has been very much influenced by Gadamer (with some input, I have to admit, from Hegel as well), and so I'm naturally tempted to start off on this gamut of questions from the bottom, with some mixture of 3 and 4.

I think a crucial insight is the one that animates Gadamer's critique of Dilthey. The aim of understanding should not be to surmount or escape our own point of view, in order to 'get inside' another. We do often talk this way, and sometimes harmlessly. But there are a set of assumptions which this language suggests, which are very wrong. The reason why it rings all the wrong bells with us is something to do with our natural science tradition. Since the seventeenth century, the progress of natural science has been inseparable from our separating ourselves from our own perspective, even from the human perspective as such, in order to come as close as possible to "the view from nowhere," to use Nagel's phrase.[1] This starts with the sidelining of 'secondary' qualities in the seventeenth century, and continues through our detachment from the most fundamental features of the experienced world, with the acceptance of such things as curved space. The aim is to identify and then neutralize those features of the way the world appears which depend on our particular make-up. Science is only concerned with what is beyond these.

But this procedure is impossible in human science. It gets nowhere, and that for a reason of principle. If the aim of human sciences is to make people intelligible, and not just to predict their behavior (and we have ample proof that the range of the merely predictive sciences is very narrow in human affairs),[2] we have to rely on a kind of understanding of human affairs which sets the forms and limits of intelligibility. Each one of us has such an understanding from our home culture, and it is woven very deeply into our lives, because we don't mainly use it to make people intelligible in theoretical contexts, but to understand and deliberate about our own motives and actions, and those of the people we deal with every day. Indeed, much of our understanding is quite inarticulate; it is in this sense a form of 'preunderstanding'. It shapes our judgments without our being aware of it.

But that's what we have to draw on to make other people intelligible, because this sets the forms and standards of intelligibility for us. The idea that I should pursue human science by attempting to neutralize this understanding in me, as I must pursue physics by neutralizing my Euclidean intuitions about space, is obviously crazy. This wouldn't make a foreign culture any more accessible. On the contrary, it would just dissolve the field of human action into meaningless motion. This would fit the program of a strict behaviorism (which no one has ever really practiced, be it said), but would be against the very thrust of any more promising science.

This might seem to lock us into ethnocentric prisons. But as Gadamer points out, the fortunate thing about human beings is that this understanding can change. And one of the important sources of this learning can be meeting foreign cultures. In terms of the motives that I recognize as understandable, the Aztecs act pretty weirdly. The normal behavior, in any case, of priests and rulers, includes things like ripping people's hearts out, which I would expect only from psychopaths. Unless I want just to rule the whole society out as pathological, which conflicts with other evidence, I have to face a challenge.

I meet this challenge by altering and enlarging my human understanding, remaking its forms and limits. This means that I articulate things that were purely implicit before, in order to put them into question. In particular, I articulate what were formally limits to intelligibility, in order to see these in a new context, no longer as inescapable structures of human motivation, but as one in a range of possibilities. That is why other-understanding changes self-understanding, and in particular prizes us loose from some of the most fixed contours of our former culture. The very questioning we are engaged in here is an instance of this. The sober and rational discourse which tries to understand other cultures has to become aware of itself as one among many possibilities in order properly to understand these others. But then it no longer goes without saying that one ought to subscribe to its canons.

This offers a model for how in principle ethnocentrism can be overcome, while showing how it will be very difficult in practice. The latter follows immediately from the fact that the exigencies of understanding the other may require us to relativize features of our own self-understanding which we cherish. Some levels of understanding of some others will be resisted fiercely if unconsciously. But the thing can be done. It comes about, however, through a quite different route than that suggested by the natural science model.

What emerges from this model is that other-understanding is always in a sense comparative. That is because we make the other intelligible through our own human understanding. This is always playing a role, and can't just be put out of action. The more we think we have sidelined it or neutralized it, à la natural science model, the more it works unconsciously and hence all the more powerfully to ethnocentric effect. In a sense we only liberate the other and "let them be" when we can identify and articulate a contrast between their understanding and ours, thereby ceasing in that respect just to read them through our home understanding, but allowing them to stand apart from it on their own. But the necessary condition of that is that the understanding we personally have as students of the other has grown beyond what I've just called the "home understanding," because in making this contrast we have identified, articulated, and shown to be one possibility among others, what we previously felt as a limit.

If this account is right, then the great leaps in other-understanding take place through (perhaps implicit) comparisons, or contrasts. The hope that one can escape ethnocentrism reposes on the fact that these contrasts transcend and often incommode the previous home understanding. But we might object: the new understanding is also 'ours' in an important sense. It belongs to the community of scholars who are usually confined to the home culture (and in the case of history, or the study of past religions, this condition is insurmountable). The new understanding will also have limits. These will now define the common background against which the contrast is understood. Maybe this still distorts the other, maybe it still commands an ethnocentric reading.

There is no answer in principle against these charges. They are probably very often correct. On my account, there is no way to go except forward; to apply, that is, further doses of the same medicine. We must try to identify and place in contrast the new limit, and hence "let the other be" that much more effectively. This process may go on indefinitely, but that doesn't make the earlier stages without value: severe distortions may be overcome at any of them.

But, in a sense, understanding on this Gadamer view is always, in one way, from a limited perspective. When one struggles to get beyond one's limited home understanding, one struggles not towards a liberation from such understanding as such (the error of the natural science model) but towards a wider understanding which can englobe the other undistortively. Gadamer uses the image of a conversation, where in face of mutually strange reactions the interlocutors strive to come to some common mind (eine *Verständigung*—this expression has the right semantic reach to link understanding and common purpose). Of course, in many cases of study, the other can't talk back. But the image of the conversation conveys how the goal is reaching a common language, common human understanding, which would allow both us and them undistortively to be. But this means that our understanding of, say, the Romans could never be considered an objective reading in the sense striven after by natural science. This latter tries for a perspective-free account of the subatomic particles, for instance. What we get if successful is an understanding which allows us not to distort the Romans. Some other culture or age would have to develop a rather different language and understanding to achieve their own undistortive account of the Romans. The aim is fusion of horizons, not escaping horizons. The ultimate result is always tied to someone's point of view.

Let us imagine the ideal case, here not of historical but of contemporary intercultural language. Suppose a group of Christian and Muslim scholars with great effort and ecumenical understanding elaborated a language in which their differences could be undistortively expressed, to the satisfaction of both sides. This would still not be an objective, point-of-viewless language of religion. The effort would have to be started all over again if either wanted to reach an understanding with Buddhists, for instance.

Of course, in each case, something is gained; some narrowness is overcome. But this leaves other narrownesses still unovercome. The Gadamer perspective allows us the idea of reason of an omega point, as it were, when all times and cultures of humanity would have been able to exchange and come to an undistortive horizon for all of them. But even this would still be only de facto universal. If it turned out that one culture had been left out by mistake, the process would have to start again. The only possible ideal of objectivity in this domain is that of inclusiveness. The inclusive perspective is never attained de jure. You only get there de facto, when everybody is on board. And even then the perspective is in principle limited in relation to another possible understanding which might have arisen. But all this doesn't mean that there is no gain, no overcoming of ethnocentrism. On the contrary, it is overcome in inclusiveness.

How does this broader understanding arise? It comes, I want to claim, in comparisons or contrasts, which let the other be. Contrasts are crucial. But they come out in the broader understanding, which in turn comes from our articulating things which formerly were just taken as given. So the contrast is in a language of our devising. That was the ground of an objection above, that it is always we who are devising the language in which the other is understood. But here I want to come at that objection from another angle.

It seems to me that it is not entirely true that the contrast is made by our (broader) language. In a sense, the contrast can be said to precede the devising of the language. First, I argued above, there is a challenge because others don't really make sense against our home understanding. The challenge can just remain at the level of the strange and bewildering. But this is almost impossible to sustain. In fact, we almost always proceed to another stage, we find a way of placing the strange practice as corresponding to one (some) of ours. Even the gut Spanish reaction to the Aztecs, which saw their religion as of the devil, is an instance of this. The contrast was simple: we worship God, they worship the devil. Understanding is complete. We pass to action.

In other words, we place the strangeness opposite some bit of our lives, as it were. The challenge has a specific form, and we can go to work on it to try to make sense of the difference. Sometimes the way we place it impedes understanding. Our location of it reflects some limit we can't get around, and which would have to be overcome to understand them. Thus Frazer categorized magic and religion as modes of attempted control of the world. Magic works by finding impersonal connections; religion by propitiating and inducing the intervention of superhuman personal beings. These are thus lined up with each other, and with our own religion and also, of course, our technology. Seen this way, the contrast seemed to turn just on how much one knew and understood about the workings of the universe. Magic had to be placed quite differently before it could be better understood. (I'm not sure we've yet placed it adequately.)

But what I want to draw from this is that the intuition of contrast is in a sense primary. It is the challenge given a shape, when it has ceased to be something just bewildering and frightening (though it may still be both). We have a feel for the contrasts long before we think we understand, or have developed a language of contrast understood. In that sense, too, comparison seems basic to understanding.

I've been discussing issue 3, but now I'd like to turn to 4. It seems to me that some validity claims are inseparable from understanding. Gadamer makes this point very forcefully too. In fact, you understand another against the background of the surrounding reality. You see someone waving his hands wildly. You then look closer, and you see that some nasty flies are swarming around him. His action becomes intelligible against his background. People can only be understood against the background of their (presumed) world. It may be that closer scrutiny reveals no flies, but he tells you that he is warding off flies. Here too, his action becomes (more) intelligible. There is, of course, something else here to explain.

This story gives in simplified form the predicament of the explainer. It shows, I think why there can't be explanation without judgment of truth or validity. We understand him against his world. But we cannot but have our view about the contents of this world. Where his view differs from ours, we start to explain him in terms of illusion; and we identify something else to explain. Where the flies are real, the explanation stops there. Our account is shaped throughout by what we understand to be the reality of the case.

We come across a myth of the origin of the world at the hand of giants. We try to interpret this myth, to explain the power it had in this culture, why it became their origin myth. But of course, we never consider that there might have been giants. I am not complaining of the narrowness of our perspective, just pointing out that our whole search for an explanation presupposes that there weren't giants. If there were, then the myth has a quite different and much simpler explanation. In this way, our sense of reality is decisive for our understanding of these people. We know there aren't any flies, and that structures our entire quest.

This point is obscured because we feel our superiority to, say, Frazer, who seemed to be saying that earlier people were just mistaken about magic. They made the understandable but erroneous leap from noting similarity between two things to postulating some kind of influence of one on the other. Unfortunately, they just got it wrong. When we begin to place magic differently, and we see it for instance as an interpretation of the moral significance of things, and their relation to human purposes, we see it all in a quite altered light. These people no longer seem just wrong, inferior to us in knowledge. Now there are things that they know how to do, perhaps ways to come to terms with and treat the stresses of their lives, ways which we seem to have lost and could benefit by. The balance of superiority is not all on one side.

We feel more satisfied with this interpretation, first because it seems to make them more intelligible. If they were trying to find the best instruments for their purposes, in the way modern people do with technology, then they look very dumb, too dumb to be believable. They didn't need a course in statistics to see that the rate of success with some of these cherished *nostra* was quite low. By imputing to them purposes which are somewhat less intelligible to our contemporary home understanding, which require more work and stretching on our part, we make them, overall, more comprehensible.

But we also feel more satisfied with this account because it is less crassly ethnocentric. This reason isn't entirely detachable from the first, because we also think it implausible that one people should be constitutionally superior to others, but it also has a moral thrust which is independent.

So far so good. But it would be a mistake to think that this means that we are no longer making judgments of truth where Frazer was. We are still operating out of our conception of reality just as he was. Ours resembles his in that we don't really think that dances have any effect whatever on rain. But it differs from his in that we recognize other essential human purposes. We see how important it is for human beings to make sense of their world, to find some meaning in the things they experience. Even disease can be more easily repelled by the organism where the person can make sense of it all, and can mobilize his energies against it. High Victorian rationalists had trouble with this kind of thing—as do lots of people today, of course, including much of the medical profession—and this led to a too-narrow identification of what was going on in these practices. They were wrongly "placed." But this is still an understanding of the actions and beliefs of the people concerned in the light of what we recognize as reality. This has been slightly enlarged, and that is all to the good. But it's still operative.

It is all but unimaginable what it might be to operate without such a conception. True, one can study religions, for instance, and be genuinely agnostic about the existence of God. But some discriminations are still working. Thus the religion in question will have different theological expressions, different canonical statements. The student will inevitably be making some discrimination between them; all can't be taken as equally central and serious. How discriminate? One might just decide to go by the majority, or what the power centers opted for. But even this may be indeterminate, unless one has some sense of what is a more insightful or crasser statement of the religion. And to the extent that one did go completely on the basis of some such conforming criterion, one would be in effect operating on the assumption that religious formulations were not rankable on any internal criterion, on their richness or depth or inherent plausibility.

This is, of course, a view which no believer in the religion could share, and would betray a reductive view of religion, one which recognizes no good grounds that can be given for belief.

Of course, the sense of reality of the student doesn't have to be that standard in his home culture. Here the discussion above about comparison is relevant. I may be jogged out of a High Victorian view about human purposes, come to recognize the importance of finding a meaning in what happens to us, just because I am bothered and challenged by this phenomenon of magic. In the process, I place this phenomenon differently, come to recognize the ways in which we also find meaning in what happens, and see through the contrast how these aren't the only ones. My language and understanding will have been extended.

But this discussion adds an important nuance to the result of the previous one. There I was saying that making the other intelligible requires a language or mode of human understanding which will allow both us and them to be undistortively described. But from what has just been said, this has to be understood as compatible with our understanding them as, in important respects, wrong about their world. We can't say that understanding them without distortion means showing them to be unmistaken in any important respect. It does mean getting at the meanings things had for them in a language which makes them accessible for us, finding a way of reformulating their human understanding. But this may have to be in an account which also portrays them as being out of touch with important facets of reality.

I have been talking about problem areas 3 and 4. Now I'd like to turn to 1 and 2. And maybe I should start by saying something about 1, the boundary myth/science, or myth/rational discourse. This is naturally a place at which we feel strongly the basic dilemma, or cross-pressure that I described above. This distinction is a way of ranking discourses. We see ourselves as having climbed out of 'myth' (let this for the moment stand duty for all the not-yet-rational forms) into science or reason. In the course of this, something was supposedly gained, some clarity, self-conscious control of thinking, greater capacity to grasp truth, or something of the sort.

But ranking discourses seems to entail ranking societies or cultures, according to the discourses that they make possible or are hospitable to. So to put reason above 'myth' seems to be putting, e.g., the modern West above tribal Africa, or pre-Captain Cook Tahiti. But we are averse to this kind of ethnocentric ranking, for reasons I just gestured at earlier. This can lead us to relativize this distinction, or to make it somehow nonhierarchical. For instance, we can say that rationality is our 'myth', thus different from but on the same footing as theirs.

The dilemma or conflict arises, because we can't really treat reason in this way. It represents certain *standards*; otherwise it is no concept of reason at all. Rational and sober discourse constitutes a demand on us, which we try to meet. We argue with each other in the light of its canons, and blame each other for not living up to these in our arguments: 'you're being illogical,' 'you're not being consistent,' 'that's a sloppy argument.' In our actual practice we can't treat the distinction rational/less rational as a nonhierarchical one, because it defines how we ought to think.

We find ourselves in a sort of bind. We embark on the comparativist enterprise, or the study of other religions, because of some deep intuitions about the equal value of cultures. I think this has been a theme throughout the long history of concern and study of other cultures in the West, even though it was subordinate in the earlier, triumphalist period. But the various Jesuits in the sixteenth and seventeenth century who tried to assimilate to Indian or Chinese culture in order to convert these peoples, instrumentally as they may have acted, had already separated off the superiority of the Christian faith, about which they had no doubts, from any purported superiority of Western culture, which they were putting in question. True, there arose between them and us lots of progress theories which reduced everyone else to stepping stones to ourselves as the definitive culture. But this other intuition has always been there, and has motivated much of the work in other-cultural studies, to which the West has given itself more than any previous society.

In any case, today this intuition of equal value seems almost an axiom. So that we suspect ourselves of being still in an ethnocentric trap when we find ourselves believing a depreciating story. The conflict comes, because the intuition of equal value leads us to engage in an enterprise, cultural studies, which is a discourse with rational canons, hence to value this; while at the same time we note that it wasn't in the repertory of many cultures. Indeed, we might state the conflict more sharply: whatever it is which has pushed this Western culture to study others, at least nominally in a spirit of equality (it is because this is the spirit we recognize as legitimate that orientalists feel calumnied by the attacks of an Edward Said), is missing in lots of other cultures. Our very valuing of this equality seems to mark a superiority of our culture over some others.

This is one form of the dilemma which has been frequently noted, of Western universalism. There is a paradox in the view which, wanting to value others, values, say, Khomeinist Iran, which precisely rejects this value root and branch. Can we value them, precisely in their rejection of all other-valuing?

What seems to emerge from this is that the axiom of equality can't be worked out by making the distinction reason/not-yet-reason a simple nonhierarchical difference, at least not if we want to go on reasoning, as we do. I think that this is the wrong move.

But moves of this kind, e.g., 'reason is our myth,' can seem plausible, because we are vague about what we mean by reason. I won't exactly conquer vagueness, but I think that one can clarify things a little by extracting a core sense out of the tradition which comes to us from the Greeks. Taking reason back to 'logos', I think we can find the core demands it makes on us in a certain notion of articulacy. Socrates always wanted to make his interlocutors say what they thought, bring out the intuitions they were implicitly acting by. But this articulacy sees itself as under certain disciplines: the descriptions given must a) check out by the best means of validation recognized at the time for descriptions of their type, and b) they must be consistently applied. If this situation is described as 'F', then so must other like ones be. You can't deny 'F' to them without pointing out a relevant difference. Socrates trips up his unfortunate interlocutors by showing how their first-off articulations of 'justice', 'piety', and the rest, when applied across the board, generate utterly unacceptable results, like giving a homicidal maniac back his sword.

From this we can generate canons of reasoning, as Aristotle does. But beyond any formal statement of these canons, are the demands of argumentative rigor. Rationality ought to be considered as applying primarily to discourses, and derivatively to texts or statements. I mean by 'discourses' here the interchanges which generate texts. Whatever failings any particular text exhibits, it's part of rational discourse if it's seen as vulnerable to attack on the basis of the above standards, and if its authors see themselves as having to defend/amend it in the light of this attack.

Now there are two views about the scope of these demands, each of which generates in some form the temptation to take our distance from rationality, or to consider it just one set of possible demands among others. One of these draws its boundaries too broad, the other too narrow.

The first incorporates the changing principles of inference which different cultures and intellectual communities come to accept. Requirement a) above referred to the 'best means of validation recognized' in a given society. These change. The way people argued about issues of natural science before the Galilean revolution was very different from the way they argue after. Roughly speaking, where the whole background to understanding of the natural world was based on the notion that it bodies forth in some way the order of Ideas, certain inferences become just obvious and unchallengeable. So some Paduan philosophers 'refuted' Galileo's discovery of the moons of Jupiter by reasoning thus:

> There are seven windows given to animals in the domicile of the head. . . . What are these parts of the microcosmos? Two nostrils, two eyes, two ears and a mouth. So in the heavens as in a macro-cosmos, there are two favorable stars, two unpropitious, two luminaries, and Mercury undecided and indifferent. From this and from many other similarities in nature, such as the seven met-als, etc., which it were tedious to enumerate, we gather that the number of planets is necessarily seven.[3]

It raises a smile today, and it reminds us of the philosophers in Brecht's play about Galileo, but it made a great deal of sense within that whole out-look. If you take off from the basis that the list of things reflects the order of Ideas, then this kind of reasoning is very powerful. The same can be said for the argument of *qal va homer* which is discussed in chapter 9.

Now if you include these deep-lying views about the nature of things, which underlie our principles of inference in the category of rationality, then it seems that there are several such, and that there is no such thing as a universal standard. But I am suggesting that we should distinguish these views and principles from the demands which I stated above, which while not accepted as important in every culture are nev-ertheless not themselves differently conceived from culture to culture.

The second wrong view makes reason too narrow. It is a form of articulacy, I argued above. This is often forgotten, and we concentrate only on the demands made on articulacy, viz., a) and b) above. It seems then that we sufficiently answer these demands by avoiding any *infrac-tion* of them, whether we manage to articulate anything significant in the process or not. Various modern procedural conceptions of ratio-nality have tended in this direction. Reason is a matter of applying some canonical procedure, or avoiding inconsistency, or remaining up to some standard of rigor in one's inferences. The issue of how articu-late this allows one to be about important matters is left completely aside. In the end, some of the most important things are not talked about at all in the name of reason. Pushed to an extreme we would find our safest refuge against illogic in saying nothing—playing it safe, with a vengeance.

Needless to say, this departs crucially from the original Platonic conception. You really know something when you can 'logon didonai', give a 'logos' of it. It is important that this meet the constraints of reason, but it is also important that it be articulated. Aristotle really speaks for the full demands of reason when in the famous passage of *Ethics* I.3, he advises us "to expect that amount of exactness in each kind which the nature of the particular subject admits" (1094b25).

Now the too-narrow definitions of reason have bred a certain dissatisfaction with it, a sense that the important things have to violate its canons to be expressed. And this too has contributed to our frequently downgrading reason, and seeing it as just one myth among others. But I think that if we set aside both these mistaken views, the too broad and the too narrow, we identify something which we cannot so easily repudiate, which indeed, informs what we recognize as our best practice when we try to study any culture, ours or others'.

Of course, if we look back at the account of the comparative enterprise above, which consists in enlarging our human understanding so that we can make the other undistortively intelligible, we have to admit that this task doesn't necessarily call for rational discourse. Perhaps someone could do this very effectively by writing a novel about some strange culture. Golding's *The Inheritors* does a remarkable job of taking us outside our normal understanding of things in presenting an imaginative reconstruction of what a clan of Neanderthalers might have been like. Suppose they really had been like this; then perhaps this novel would be more effective in one sense in enlarging our understanding to meet them than many a monograph. But we are committed to the specific enterprise of enlarging this understanding by sober and rational discourses. And what we gain by this is the self-consciously critical stance which allows us to learn from our mistakes and to ground our conviction that one account is better than another. Maybe this enterprise is doomed to very meager success in comparison to literature. But it is clearly our enterprise, and this amounts to a commitment to rational discourse.

I'd now like, very reluctantly and hesitantly, to tackle issue no. 2: to what extent, if any, does our understanding of other cultures require that we embed them and us in a view of history? Hegel represents what we are fleeing from. But can we flee from all of it? Let me break down his view into components in order to get at this question.

Hegel's theory of history a) makes crucial use of Aristotle's concept of potentiality. What are *an sich* unfolds *für sich* in history; we have it in us from the beginning to become what we later become. b) This unfolding potentiality is the same for all human beings, even though some societies don't seem to get as far along in the process as others: at least at the moment of their historical flourishing they don't (it's not clear that Hegel rules out a second appearance of, say, China as a modern state, under European influence, of course). There is in other words, a single line of unfolding potentiality, and c) this unfolds in fixed stages, where each is the precondition of what follows.

Now clearly we find b), and hence c), difficult to credit, for reasons that I mentioned above and will probably return to later below. But can we do altogether without some variant of a)? Let's take this case of reason, which I was trying to describe in the immediately preceding pages. If we don't take our distance from it, and thus refrain from reducing it to an indifferent distinction (where the difference rational/not-yet-rational involves no ranking)—and I have tried to argue that we can't authentically do so—then don't we have to read its arising in history as a gain? This, of course, has been one of the reasons for the widespread admiration of the Greeks in post-Renaissance culture, that they pioneered the definition of the demands of rationality in our tradition. They brought about an important gain for human beings, brought to light and developed an important capacity. Can we really separate ourselves from this admiration and the judgments it's founded on? I think we can't. And by this I don't mean just psychologically can't, like I'm unable to experience certain smells without nausea. I mean rather that granted the things we do, strive after, the standards we consider binding on us, we couldn't authentically deny this admiration.

But then doesn't that amount to saying in some sense that we see rationality as a human potentiality, which the Greeks to their credit developed? We see it as a capacity which needed to be brought to fruition. Moreover, if we consider certain changes in history, of which the development of rational discourse is an example, we see another pattern reminiscent of Hegel: once they come about, they are more or less irreversible. Of course, they could be reversed by some massive disruption of human society, due to some natural or manmade catastrophe. But normally speaking, people don't want to go back on them. They become permanent and inescapable aspirations. There are other examples: perhaps the rise of city-dwelling is one, the invention of writing, and various kinds of technical advances as well.

These are often grouped under the title 'civilization', and made the object of an ineluctable progress story. The ineluctable part is more dubious, as is Hegel's assumption b) about the single track of human potentiality, but the important insight here is what I call the ratchet effect. History seems to exhibit some irreversible developments. Of course, some of these may have nothing to do with what we could define as human potentiality: we might so pollute the planet that we would have drastically to alter the way we live, and this might be irreversible. But I am talking about changes which seem irreversible because those who go through them can't envisage reversing them, because they become standards for those who come after them: the way, for instance, that even for the barbarians who have destroyed them, cities retain their prestige, as the locus of a higher form of life, and come thus to be reconstituted.

I am arguing that some notion of potentiality is needed to make sense of these changes. At the very least, they are changes such that those who have undergone them tend irresistibly to *define* them as development, or evolution, or advance, or realization of the properly human. Hence at least local history has a shape; there is a before and after, a watershed. By 'local' I mean something rather broad-scale. The Greeks and we are in one 'locality', and I am saying that we have to read their development of rational discourse as a gain whose standards now define us. History, in this civilization, and in this respect, had a direction.

This is true, incidentally, of more than rationality. For instance, one of the important features of modern culture is its universalism, the premise that all human beings count and have rights; another is its lower tolerance of avoidable suffering or death, which motivates the vast campaigns for famine or flood or earthquake relief, which are surely without precedent in history. It is hard not to read these as gains, and to see a Torquemada as existing before a watershed.

This has not prevented the twentieth century from witnessing crimes that would have made Torquemada blanch with horror—the holocaust, the killing fields. This may seem to call into question the rise in humanitarian standards I'm imputing to our age. I haven't got space to go into it here, but I think that these two developments, higher standards and unprecedented gruesomeness, are paradoxically and perversely connected. And in any case, their coexistence in the same age is reflected in the fact that these great crimes were kept secret.

But if we have to admit advance, at least 'locally', what does this do to what I have called the "axiom of equality"? This is badly named, I agree. It seems to imply some kind of likeness, homogeneity of cultures. Whereas what is crucial and difficult to recognize is just the opposite, how different they are. But what I was trying to get at with the term is the insight that all cultures allow for human flourishing. Consequently, what is ruled out is a reading of another culture which identifies its difference from us purely privatively: they lack what we have.

But isn't this what you have to do when you think in terms of potentialities, and define changes as advances, or developments? Weren't the prephilosophical Greeks deprived of something? Of course. But here's where we have to separate clearly Hegel's assumptions a) and b). To speak of potentialities doesn't mean to suppose a unitary set. We can and increasingly do recognize diverse lines of possible development, some of which seem incompatible with each other, at least at first blush. This, of course, has been salient in various post-Romantic traditions, which have regretted the passing of earlier forms of life, relegated by Progress, the Enlightenment, Industrialization, Disenchantment, or whatever. It is wrong to think that we have to choose between two readings of history, as Progress or Decline, fulfillment or loss. The most plausible view seems to be that it contains some element of both.

In other words, we should be able to think about the conflicts between the requirements of incompatible cultures on analogy to the way we think about conflicts between nonjointly realizable goods in our lives. When we find we can't maximize both freedom and equality, for instance, we don't immediately conclude that one of these isn't a real good. This is precisely the mark of the ideological mind, one that is convinced a priori that there can be only one system of goods. People with this mindset feel forced to tell us that one or the other goal isn't to be sought, or that, really, getting one will bring you the other (equality is true freedom, or free markets will bring you perfect equality).

But if we keep our heads, we recognize that the world can be nasty enough to put us in a dilemma, give us a tough choice, that genuine goods can conflict. Let us say that reason tends to sap and dissipate other valuable things in human life, like our attunement to the world, or our sense of community. This is not by itself a reason not to consider it a good—though it may be to make an all-things-considered judgment that it oughtn't to be fostered (if such a judgment could really be acted on, which I doubt for the reasons given above). Nor is it a good ground, having espoused reason, to consider the things it saps as without value.

Precisely the aim of the comparative exercise is to enable us really to understand the other undistortively, and hence to be able to see the good in their life, even while we also see that their good conflicts with ours. Its point is to get us beyond seeing them just as the transgressors of our limits, to let them be in the way our original home understanding couldn't, because it couldn't accommodate their meanings; to allow us to see two goods where before we could only see one and its negation.

The idea here is that what is true of a single life—viz., that con-flict doesn't invalidate or relativize the goods which clash, but on the contrary genuine conflict presupposes their validity—should hold of the opposition between cultures as well. But there might seem to be an important disanalogy. When we have a conflict in life, we feel justi-fied and called on to make a choice, to sacrifice or trade off one good for another. In the intercultural context, we might feel that this is pre-sumptuous. But this is based on a confusion. There are generally good reasons why we shouldn't *intervene* in the life of another culture or society, even to effect something which would be good if it came about spontaneously. But this doesn't mean that we have no right to make all-things-considered *judgments* about what ought to be sacri-ficed for what. Have we any doubt that the Jews and Moriscos ought not to have been expelled from Spain, even though this increased the homogeneity of the society, which in that day was considered an unquestioned good? Would we not welcome the discontinuance of sati? or of human sacrifice? (I hope these are rhetorical questions.)

Of course, these judgments are *ours*, and the suspicion can arise, even as it did with our contrastive understanding, that it is still too ethnocentric. There is no general-purpose measure which can guaran-tee us against this. We just have to try again, and meet the challenges as they come. But what is important to recognize is that successfully meeting them might reverse some of our present judgments; it wouldn't make judgment itself somehow impossible or inappropriate.

Nor does moral thinking have to confine itself to determining sacrifices or trade-offs. The conflicts don't all have to be taken as ineluctable, or as incapable of mitigation. Just as with the case of free-dom and inequality, within a general recognition of the difficulty of combining them, we can nevertheless strive to find forms which can combine them at higher levels, so we can strive to recover in some form some of the goods which reason, or urbanization, or disenchant-ment, in short which 'civilization' has relegated.

What seems to be emerging here is a rather hazy picture of his-tory in which our understanding will be embedded. It rejects altogeth-er the Hegelian single line of development, but it retains something like the notion of potentiality. This structures at least local history into a before and after, and allows us to speak of advance. But because potentialities are diverse, and frequently at least by our present lights and capacities incompatible, the gains will also involve losses, and the goods of different cultures will clash. But this shouldn't frighten us into a relativization of goods, or a disclaimer of the universal relevance of our own goods, about which we could never be sincere anyway.

It does point us to a future of humanity in which the kind of undistorted understanding of the other aimed at by what I have been calling "the comparativist enterprise" will be increasingly valuable. Not only to avoid political and military conflict where possible, but also to give people of every culture some sense of the immense gamut of human potentialities. This will serve not only to enlighten their judgments where goods clash, but also help where imagination and insight are capable of mediating the clash, and bringing two hitherto warring goods to some degree of common realization.

We can hope to advance in this direction, to the extent that the community of comparativists will increasingly include representatives of different cultures, will in effect start from different 'home languages'.

Understanding the other undistortively, without being led to deprecate or relativize the goods one still subscribes to: this can confer another important benefit. Most of the great religions or secular Weltanschauungen are bound up with a depreciatory view of others in contrast to which they define themselves. Christianity relative to Judaism as "merely" a religion of law, or relative to Buddhism and Hinduism as religions unconcerned for the world, depreciatory stories abound. These stories form part of the support system for faith everywhere. The contrasts are real; and so to come to understand the view against which one's own is defined, and hence to see its spiritual force, must bring about a profound change. The depreciatory story is no longer credible; this prop to faith is knocked away. Where the faith was nourished exclusively by the story it will wither. But where not, it will be free to nourish itself on better food, on something like the intrinsic power of whatever the faith or vision points us towards. In this sense, comparative understanding lets our own faith be too. It liberates ourselves along with the other.

Notes

1.   T. Nagel, *The View from Nowhere* (New York: Oxford University Press, 1985).

2.   I tried to draw the boundaries between these two kinds of science in "Peaceful Coexistence in Psychology," in *Human Agency and Language* (Cambridge University Press, 1985).

3.   Quoted from S. Warhaft (ed), *Francis Bacon: A Selection of His Works* (Toronto: University of Toronto Press, 1965) 17.

Chapter 3

Denaturalizing Discourse: Ābhidhārmikas, Propositionalists, and the Comparative Philosophy of Religion

Paul J. Griffiths

§1 Prolegomena

The enterprise of constructing a new intellectual discourse—the comparative philosophy of religion—must include some consideration of what is involved in bringing together the usually normative discipline of philosophy with the usually descriptive and analytic discipline of the history of religions. A number of theoretical issues arise here, including: the nature of the comparative enterprise; how philosophers use myth (more than they think); how historians of religion use normative philo-

The ideas expressed in this paper are a direct result of my participation in the University of Chicago Divinity School's colloquia on "Religion(s) in History and Culture" from 1986 to 1989. I am grateful to Frank Reynolds and David Tracy for organizing these colloquia and for making possible my participation in them. I am indebted also to Phil Quinn for providing me with a provocative and entertaining set of comments on an earlier draft; to Steven Collins for perceptively pointing out the central weaknesses in the paper; to Charles Hallisey, whose detailed reading of an early draft has led to some important changes; and to Peg Harker, who gave me useful suggestions and considerable help.

sophical discourse (not as self-consciously as they should); how important the institutional settings and cultural contexts of both (indeed all)
intellectual practices are; what can be learned by looking at examples of
the discourse of intellectuals from cultures other than the Western-academic; what the intellectual history of Western-academic culture reveals
about the practices and values of those who want to engage in the discourse of the new discipline under consideration; and how the complex
of categories derived from all this (myth, theory, narrative, practice,
power) may best be clarified and used in the service of our own ends.

For the sake of convenience the first person plural will be used in
the remainder of this study to refer to those who wish to engage in an
intellectual practice called "the comparative philosophy of religion."
Self-consciously engaging in such a practice requires that we tell each
other what we take to be important parts of the story of the complex
cultural and intellectual history that has made us what we are, and that
makes it seem worthwhile for us to engage in the comparative philosophy of religion. It is a small part of that story that I wish to tell in this
paper. It begins, inevitably, with Aristotle; proceeds in a manner that I
shall outline in very cursory fashion in the third part of this paper; and
culminates in the intellectual practices of a significant majority of contemporary anglophone philosophers. The underlying values of the
intellectual practices that constitute this story are radically ahistorical;
in so far as truths can be enunciated within the parameters of this story
they are presented in a decontextualized, abstract, fleshless discourse, a
discourse that pretends to stand nowhere solid, to be located nowhere
specific, and to have its utterance by any thinking subject as an accidental property rather than an essential one. Such truths, if true, are true
atemporally and universally; some of them, at least, can be both known
and expressed; and the chief epistemic duty for each knowing subject is
to maximize her stock of such true beliefs. Mystery is not positively valued, either cognitively or aesthetically; revelation and its reception is
typically not given pride of place as a reliable doxastic practice.

This part of our own (Western-academic) intentional world is far
too important to be left in the tacit limbo to which historians of religion often consign it. The Aristotelian emphasis on logic and propositions, and with it the Fregean language of pure thought (on which
more in §3), are too deeply embedded in our collective psyche to be
left undisturbed. This should be especially true for historians of religion, for if there is one kind of discourse which they have traditionally

ignored—despite the tremendously important part that it has played and continues to play within almost all religious communities—it is precisely the kind of discourse that issues in universalized normative claims and is typically self-consciously denaturalized in style (in a sense to be explained more precisely in §2). What is to be said of this kind of theoretical discourse by historians of religion? What part might it have to play in the new intellectual discourse that we are trying to construct?

To ask the same question in a slightly different way: what are the relations between broadly descriptive discourse and broadly evaluative discourse, between discourse which attempts to analyze by describing and discourse which gives explicit allegiance to the establishment of universalizable norms? Let's call the first kind "descriptive historical discourse." This is concerned with the causes of historical phenomena and the interrelations among them; in its ideal type this discourse issues in collections of descriptive natural-language sentences indexed to particular historical or sociocultural settings.[1] Examples might be: *myths M1 and M2 function normatively in community A* or *members of community Z typically take the proposition p to be true.* Collections of sentences of this kind would account for a very large proportion (though not all) of those constituting the discourse produced by historians of religion and anthropologists. The second kind of discourse is explicitly normative; it is concerned with judgment and truth and issues in collections of natural-language sentences whose scope is universal, for example, *everyone should abide by the norms of conduct set up by myths M1 and M2;* or *the truths assented to by those in community A who take seriously myths M1 and M2 are in fact true;* or *proposition p, typically assented to by members of community Z, is in fact true.* Such collections of sentences will account for a good deal (though not all) of what we might want to call "philosophical discourse." The key differentiating characteristics of the two types of discourse are normativity and universalizability. These are present in the second kind of discourse and absent in the first. Neither kind of discourse ever occurs in its ideal-typical form, but approximations can often be found.

The contrast between the descriptive and the normative can be put differently. Suppose we adopt for a moment the language of the propositionalist mythos (to which I shall return in §2 and §3). We might then say that the beliefs, practices, myths, and so forth, of any community—including the Western-academic—have propositional contents. That is, they explicitly make, or entail, large numbers of both metaphysical and axiological claims, claims about what is the case and what is of value, claims that (usually) may be true or false. The object of the descriptive discourse characteristic of the historical disciplines is ideal-typically *not* these propositional contents; rather, it is the etiology, form, and function of the cultural practices that have or embody such contents in particular contexts. By contrast, the object of the discourse characteristic of the philosophical disciplines is, ideal-typically, precisely these propositional contents themselves.

It may be useful at this point to state the most extreme position that can be taken on the question of the relations between these two kinds of discourse. It is that the relevance of the deliverances of the first kind of (indexed descriptive-historical) discourse to the truth or falsity of the judgments enshrined in the second kind of (universalized philosophical-normative) discourse is precisely zero.[2] This position claims that historical-descriptive statements of any and all kinds, where 'historical, is construed broadly in the sense given in the preceding paragraph, cannot be intrinsically related in any interesting sense to normative claims. No story that can be told about the specific intentional world or particular historical development of a community that asserts some universal philosophical-normative claim can contribute either positively or negatively to the likelihood of that claim being true. This extreme position, if taken seriously, leads to a radical disjunction between the philosophical-normative enterprise and the historical-descriptive one.

It may perhaps be the case that some anglophone philosophers shaped by the tradition that stems from early twentieth-century Cambridge would want to assert such a radical disjunction; it may perhaps also be the case that some anthropologists and historians of religion with relativistic tendencies would want to end up with such a disjunction simply because they think that all universalized normative discourse (and so most of philosophy, Western or Eastern) is false just because it tries to universalize its norms. But I do not think that either group can defend such an extreme position. Philosophy, even in the hands of its most hardheaded analytical practitioners (Roderick Chisholm, W. V. O. Quine, et al.) is more historical than the disjunctive picture allows; and cultural relativism, at least in its more extreme forms, is self-referentially incoherent. The question then remains: if there is some kind of noncontingent connection between the deliverances of the historical-descriptive disciplines and those of the normative disciplines, what kind of connection is it? What, to return to our starting point, is the nature of the connections between the discourse of historians of religion and that of philosophers? What relevance, to take a specific example, have the findings of historians of Buddhist thought to the question of whether Buddha has any essential properties?

I don't propose to answer these questions here, but I do want to pursue a possibly fruitful way of exploring them, a way, moreover, which might make the category 'denaturalized discourse' of use to historians of religion as a tool for the kinds of descriptive-historical analysis they are typically interested in. I should like to consider, descriptively, the kinds of discourse that are typically used by religious communities to engage in the task of arguing for and demonstrating the truth of certain claims (claims about the truth of certain doctrines and the rightness of certain ways of action) to which they, or at least their intellectual representatives, wish to give assent. I shall consider these kinds of discourse as intellectual practices. As such they are necessarily located in institutional structures, influenced by sociocultural determinants, and so forth; but I shall also show that they are determined by their own inner logic to extract themselves from their natural locations and contexts, to *denaturalize* themselves.

It is often suggested that (what I am calling) the attempt to denaturalize discourse—on which more in §2—is a unique characteristic (and a reprehensible one) of Western intellectual culture since Descartes; that the idea of the mind as a central processing unit,[3] theoretically separable from all sociocultural determinants, and, concomitantly, the very idea that the production of a denaturalized discourse is a possibility, belongs exclusively to us and not to them—and so much the worse for us. I shall argue that the historical part of this thesis is false: that the attempt to denaturalize discourse and to see such discourse as playing a vital part in the establishment of those non-community-specific truths—of which all religious communities claim to possess some examples—can be found in many cultures. (I hesitate to say in all, since to say that would be to make an empirical claim which neither I nor anyone else is qualified to make.) I shall argue, that is, for the validity and usefulness of the category 'denaturalized discourse' as a tool for the kinds of comparative cross-cultural analysis with which those interested in the comparative philosophy of religion are concerned, analyses which are the very lifeblood of the history of religions.

In what follows I shall attempt to state more clearly what is meant by denaturalized discourse (§2), that is, to delineate, both formally and functionally, what sort of a thing this is; to explore, briefly, the place that such discourse has held within the intellectual history of

the West (§3); to take an example of an attempt to denaturalize discourse from another time and place—the development of Buddhist
scholasticism in India—and to explore its form and function in its context (§4); and to conclude with some suggestions as to the applicability
of the concept of denaturalized discourse as a tool for cross-cultural
analysis, and as to the implications of the use of this type of discourse
for the development of a proper understanding of the relations
between philosophy and the history of religions. I intend, that is to
say, to offer some comments on the ways in which denaturalized discourse typically enters into and informs the intellectual life of religious communities in different cultures.

§2 Denaturalized Discourse: A Formal and Functional Analysis

Epistemology, anglophone philosophers have been fond of saying in the last few decades, badly needs to be naturalized. That is,
briefly and much too crudely, the intellectual discipline which was traditionally concerned with defining knowledge and establishing criteria
for recognizing its occurrence, with separating mental events that have
cognitive content from those that do not, and with explaining how it is
that one can come to make such nice discriminations—this discipline
needs to be seen not as abstract and a priori, but rather as naturalistic
and descriptive. So, classically, W. V. O. Quine on the necessity for
naturalizing epistemology:

> epistemology still goes on, though in a new setting and a clarified
> status. Epistemology, or something like it, simply falls into place
> as a chapter of psychology and hence of natural science. It studies
> a natural phenomenon, viz., a physical human subject. This
> human subject is accorded a certain experimentally controlled
> input—certain patterns of irradiation in assorted frequencies, for
> instance—and in the fullness of time the subject delivers as output
> a description of the three dimensional external world and its his-
> tory. The relation between the meager input and the torrential
> output is a relation that we are prompted to study for somewhat
> the same reasons that always prompted epistemology . . .[4]

What, precisely, is being rejected here and what advocated? What
is a denaturalized epistemology in contradistinction to a naturalized
one? And why do Quine and his followers think that the latter is

preferable to the former? To enter fully into all of this would require a complete history of twentieth-century anglophone epistemological theory, something that I am neither competent to do nor especially interested in doing. For the purposes of this study, three important contrasts can be drawn between a naturalized epistemology and a denaturalized one; these contrasts can then be applied to a formal and functional analysis of denaturalized discourse.

First, a denaturalized epistemological theory is typically normative: it is concerned to establish what ought to count as knowledge (and why), and is thus centrally involved with questions of justification. It tends also to be foundationalist in that it looks for certain and indubitable foundations (impressions, ideas, sensibilia, etc.) upon which all knowledge is based. The normative distinction between what is knowledge and what is not is then often made by establishing the proper relations between these foundations and an instance of knowledge, and seeing whether a particular putative instance of knowledge bears the required relations to the foundations. A naturalized epistemological theory is, by contrast, typically descriptive and explanatory: it is concerned to delineate accurately the psychological and cultural processes that lead to the acquisition of (what is called) knowledge by a particular subject or group in a particular culture. It is not concerned with justification, but rather with the explanatory elucidation of a process, and is typically not foundationalist.[5]

Second, a denaturalized epistemological theory is typically regarded by its constructors as universalizable: it is seen as applicable to all subjects in all places at all times. Indeed, the goal of universalizability motivates the construction of the theory and is inextricably linked with the normative thrust of such theories. Naturalized epistemological theories are much less concerned with universalizability. Some versions would be regarded by their constructors as universalizable, but only if the descriptive analysis of the psychological process in which they typically issue is seen, for reasons peripheral to the production of the naturalized epistemology itself, as an essential property of all human knowers. Even where this occurs, though, it is not constitutive of naturalized epistemological theories in the way that it is of denaturalized ones. Naturalized epistemologists, especially those with interest in and knowledge of sociocultural variables, are comfortable with specificity and multiplicity in ways that denaturalized ones are not. The thrust towards universalizability is thus not integral to naturalized epistemology in my sense, though it may often be contingently associated with it. It is, by contrast, essential to denaturalized epistemology, just because of the normative thrust of the latter.

Third, a denaturalized epistemological theory is typically abstract, stated in something as far from a natural language as it is possible to get. For example, it is not uncommon to find statements of a denaturalized epistemological theory in the following forms: "S knows p iff (1) p; (2) sBp; and (3)EsBp."[6] Abstraction could scarcely go further. Naturalized epistemological theories on the other hand tend to be concrete, expressed in full and grammatical natural-language sentences, and concerned to give a full-blooded description of complex natural processes. It may seem that the kind of abstraction present here is more like shorthand than anything else. But there are important differences. The symbols of shorthand systems are, by definition, translatable into words or sentences in natural languages without semantic difficulty. This is not true for the abstractions of the user of denaturalized discourse. The only way to make the translation between the denaturalized discourse of the philosopher and semantic items in a natural language is to stipulatively disambiguate the semantic items in such a way that they are not any longer items in any natural language.

I do not wish to enter here into the complicated question of whether and to what extent a denaturalized epistemology is possible, and whether and to what extent a completely naturalized epistemology is capable of being both coherent and interesting.[7] I'd like instead to use this series of contrasts to clarify what is meant by 'denaturalized discourse'. It should be clear that the first two contrasts, those concerned with normativity and universalizability, issue in the third: a tendency to use a certain kind of discourse. The thrust toward a universally applicable normative theory of what knowledge is requires, when engaged in seriously, an abstract form of discourse, a form of discourse whose ideal type would be a set of symbols and syntactical principles of combination utterly detached from any natural language and equally accessible (or inaccessible) to the users of all. This provides the beginnings of both a formal and a functional analysis of denaturalized discourse.

More fully, denaturalized discourse is almost always (perhaps always) linked with an attempt to clean up the messy ambiguity of ordinary language used in ordinary contexts. Polysemy, multivalence, the stuff of poetry and the language of love: these are not values for a user of denaturalized discourse. This is usually because the contexts within which such discourses are developed and applied are judged to be unreal, consisting in apparent or constructed objects rather than real ones. The *lebenswelt*, the constructed world of lived experience in which we have our being is, of course, exceedingly messy. We always say more than we mean and less than we hope; we use language to evoke sentiment, to inspire to action, to manipulate, and to meditate. All of this is discourse in context, naturalized discourse that glories in specificity, growing from and shaping particular human needs in particular cultural contexts.

Denaturalized discourse is everything that this is not. It is normative and universalizable in its claims, formal and abstract in its style, concerned to disambiguate and make possible precise description of or reference to what there really is. It usually goes with an austere ontology: if the messy confusion of any given intentional world is best shaped and expressed by the equally chaotic richness of naturalized discourse, then it seems evident that a user of denaturalized discourse will see the world reflected and described by such discourse as correspondingly austere, whether it be the world of God's changless attributes or the ever-changing universe of unanalyzable propertyless *svalakṣaṇāni* reflected by the denaturalized discourse of the Buddhist scholastic.

In sum: formally, a denaturalized discourse is one that, in its ideal-typical form, shows no evidence of rooting in any sociocultural context; exhibits no essential connections with any natural language; and is completely unambiguous. Functionally, a denaturalized discourse is aimed primarily at making available to its users what really exists, a function that, from the viewpoint of a user of such discourse, cannot be performed by ordinary, nondenaturalized, discourse. What "making available" means can be unpacked in a variety of ways, depending largely upon the ontology with which a particular instance of such discourse is combined. For some, "making available what really exists" may be understood in terms of reference to what really exists; for others in terms of removing cognitive blocks to the direct experience of what really exists; and so forth. But the fundamental impulse is the same in every case.

Given this preliminary formal and functional analysis of denaturalized discourse in its ideal-typical form, it should be stressed that such discourse never in fact occurs. It is quite impossible to completely denaturalize discourse, though one might, I suppose, asymptotically approach such a goal. Nevertheless, the formal and functional characterization I have given of denaturalized discourse may, following Weber, enable approximations to it to be recognized when encountered, and may thus have heuristic value.

§3 Denaturalized Discourse in the West

The idea that one needs to denaturalize discourse in order to express truth is already clearly evident in Aristotle, who judged that among sentences (*logoi*), only those in the indicative mood are propositions (*apophan-*

tikoi logoi), and only these latter can be bearers of truth and falsity. Other kinds of discourse—and the example to which Aristotle adverts is that of prayer—are to be investigated and used by rhetoricians or poets, not by philosophers.[8] They do not, as we would say, possess truth-value, though they may very well (perhaps always do) entail claims that do possess such value. It's important to notice that there's a difficulty involved in claiming that particular indicative-mood natural-language sentences are capable of truth or falsity; if one makes this move then one must also say that sentences in quite different natural languages (say, Greek and Sanskrit) can have the same truth-value, the same truth-conditions, and, indeed, express the same thing. And if completely different sets of phonemes can indeed express the same thing, they must have the truth-value they have not in virtue of being the organized sets of phonemes they are, but rather in virtue of that which they refer to, express, or resemble. For Aristotle, it seems, natural-(Greek)-language sentences in the indicative mood have the truth-value they have in virtue of the mental events (*noēmata, pathēmata*) of which they are resemblances (*homōiomata*).[9] The truth of natural-language sentences[10] thus derives from their resemblance to complex mental events that in turn resemble, or somehow hook into, *realia*.

The significance of this picture for our purposes is clear: in order to be capable of being true, linguistic expressions must be denaturalized and decontextualized. First they must be reduced from the chaotic complexity of mood and context in which ordinary language use consists to simple declarative sentences; then they must be denaturalized even more by seeing them as resembling, reflecting, or referring to something altogether nonlinguistic—thoughts, abstract entities, or simply *realia*. This basic picture I should like to call the "propositional mythos." It is a dramatic story, or, perhaps better, image of what there is and how language relates to it. It explains the impulse towards symbolic non-natural-language discourse and the rejection of ordinary language already adverted to. The perfectly denaturalized language, towards which the Aristotelian propositional mythos propels us, is no language at all but rather a universe of disembodied *noēmata*, changelessly reflecting reality.

To generalize: the Western intellectual traditions from Aristotle until the twentieth century have been heavily influenced by this propositional mythos. This is true even when as has not infrequently happened, the mythos has been rejected.[11] There are some terminological changes (and confusions), but the basic picture remains clear. For most medieval thinkers, by and large, *propositio* referred to a type of natural-language sentence or utterance (*oratio*) capable of truth or falsity. It was clearly recognized that a particular proposition's truth or falsity consists in its relationship to some state of affairs or other, and that truth or falsity are thus relational properties subject to change as either of the relata which they relate change.[12]

But by the nineteenth century it had become clear that this was confusing, both terminologically and conceptually. Propositions, when understood as natural-language sentences in the indicative mood, had always been taken to be objects of judgment, entities to which one could either give or withhold one's assent. And yet, as I have already suggested in my brief remarks on Aristotle, there would seem to be an equivocation here. If one gives one's assent to the natural-language sentence *the attainment of the awareness of all modes of appearance is free from defilement by any obstacle*, is the object of one's assent that sentence or the state of affairs to which it refers? If the former one has the problem of underdetermination: many (infinitely many) natural-language sentences are capable of referring to (expressing) the state of affairs referred to (expressed) by the English sentence *the attainment of the awareness of all modes of appearance is free from defilement by any obstacle*.[13] Is it necessary to make a separate act of assent to each? And is it desirable to say that the object to which one assents when one assents to the Sanskrit sentence *sarvākārajñatāvāptiḥ sarvāvaraṇanirmalā* is other than that to which one assents *the attainment of the awareness of all modes of appearance is free from defilement by any obstacle*?

One might, to avoid these difficulties, then wish to say that the object of one's assent is not any natural-language sentence, but rather the states of affairs to which such sentences make reference. But if this move is made, the notion of truth becomes both linguistically and conceptually odd; states of affairs—such as the attainment of all modes of awareness being possessed of a certain quality—are not themselves true or false but simply obtain or do not obtain. It makes no sense to predicate truth or falsity of them. If, then, the object to which one assents when one assents to a proposition is neither a natural-language sentence nor a state of affairs, what is it? A *tertium quid* is needed.

For Aristotle, the *tertium quid* was, implicitly at least, the *noēmata*. For Western logicians it became, after J. S. Mill and Bolzano, something rather different: the *Satz an sich*, as Bolzano puts it, the *propositio redivivus*, an abstract entity that can (like a natural-language sentence) express a state of affairs, and yet is itself capable of expression by an infinite number of natural-language sentences. These abstract entities generally came to be known as propositions; and while there has been and continues to be a good deal of debate on their exact nature and on whether one needs to postulate the existence of anything so ontologically odd in order to develop a satisfactory theory of belief and reference,[14] something much like the propositional mythos sketched in the immediately preceding paragraphs continues to underly a great deal of contemporary anglophone philosophizing.[15]

A classical formulation—and a splendid encapsulation of what I intend by the term *denaturalized discourse*—of the propositional mythos and the kind of discourse to which it leads is the following from Gottlob Frege:

Whenever anyone recognizes something to be true, he makes a
judgment. What he recognizes to be true is a thought. It is impossible to recognize a thought as true before it has been grasped. A
true thought was true before it was grasped by anyone. A thought
does not have to be owned by anyone. The same thought can be
grasped by several people. Making a judgment does not alter the
thought that is recognized to be true. When something is judged
to be the case, we can always cull out the thought that is recognized as true; the act of judgment forms no part of this.[16]

Notice the depersonalization of "thoughts" (*Gedanke*) here. They
need not be "owned" by anyone in order to exist, neither need they be
articulated or conceptualized. They are abstract entities, ideally
expressed by denaturalized discourse. *Gedanke* is Frege's version of the
tertium quid. In his first major work, the *Begriffschrift* (1879), his goal
was to develop a "formalized language of pure thought modeled upon
the language of arithmetic"[17] a language that could appropriately reflect
the conceptual content—or, better, the propositional content—of assertions.[18] This is precisely denaturalized discourse; only by using this kind
of discourse, thought Frege, can a proper understanding of truth and
falsity be arrived at. Frege thus provides an excellent example of the
dominating influence of the propositional mythos upon modern philosophical thinking; and his own influence upon the great names in the
anglophone philosophy of the twentieth century (Russell, Wittgenstein,
Carnap, Tarski, Quine) is very great.

This is not to say that the propositional mythos and the denaturalized discourse that goes with it dominates even contemporary anglophone philosophy without being questioned and modified. There are
many debates about the status and necessity of propositions, as well as
about the account of what it is to believe that typically goes with the
propositional mythos.[19] But since I do not need, for the purposes of this
paper, to explore in any detail either the historical vicissitudes of the
kind of denaturalized discourse that has issued from the propositional
mythos in the West, or the systematic difficulties involved with the normative claims entailed by accepting such a mythos, it will suffice to note
that there are plenty of both.

I do, however, wish to argue that this mythos, this picture of what
it is to believe and of how one can make assertions with truth-value, has
been and remains of great influence upon Western thinkers concerned
to make normative claims of any and all kinds, and that this fact explains
the imperative philosophers seem to feel to denaturalize their discourse.

To recapitulate the essentials of the propositional mythos: propositions are mind-independent and language-independent entities that have as essential and atemporal properties the truth-values they have. Any particular proposition can be expressed by an infinitely large number of natural-language sentences. There is a broad range of attitudes that individual subjects may have towards these abstract entities. These attitudes will include belief, disbelief, trust, confidence, hatred, and so forth. Naturally, these propositional attitudes (as they are called) are usually directed not in the first instance to propositions *an sich*, but rather to natural-language sentences that express them. While this state of affairs is inevitable, given the essentials of the propositional mythos, propositionalist philosophers typically want to make these natural-language intermediaries—the sentences of their own discourse—approach as closely as possible to their totally denaturalized objects. Hence denaturalized discourse.

So much for the etiology of denaturalized discourse. The importance of recognizing this phenomenon for historians of religion is, I suggest, threefold. First, there is its significance as a genre. Denaturalized discourse has easily recognizable genre-characteristics, characteristics which, as I shall later suggest, may make it of considerable use in comparative cross-cultural analysis, and thus also in the delineation of what the comparative philosophy of religion might look like. Second, considering denaturalized discourse as the ideal type of philosophical discourse serves as a heuristic for the pointed normative question with which this paper began: for if the presuppositions underlying the propositional mythos turn out to be defensible, then the basic question with which we began must be answered with the extreme negative position already mentioned. That is, there can be no noncontingent connection between denaturalized philosophical discourse and the discourse of historians of religion. There is a paradox here: if historians of religion want to claim that the presuppositions upon which the propositional mythos are based are not defensible, it would seem that the only terms in which they can make such a claim are those of the very mythos which they want to reject. I shall return to this point later. Third, historians of religion need to accommodate this kind of discourse into their theorizing about religion, to recognize the importance that it has held among élite intellectuals within religious communities both Eastern and Western; for it seems beyond dispute that such intellectuals have typically resorted to denaturalized discourse in constructing and defending the universalizable doctrinal norms of their communities.

§4 Abhidharma: A Formal and Functional Analysis

Denaturalized discourse is not confined to the West; neither, as I shall try to show, is it necessarily combined with a propositional mythos of the Fregean type. In this section I shall outline the development of one example of denaturalized discourse in a non-Western cultural and intellectual context, and shall try to say something about its form and function in its context. The example I have chosen is the discourse which Indian Buddhist scholastics came to call "*abhidharma*."

§4.1 Abhidharma as a Technical Term

The meaning of the Sanskrit term *abhidharma* is parasitic upon the meaning of *dharma*, and the latter is, notoriously, semantically polyvalent in all Indian contexts, but perhaps most especially in Buddhist contexts.[20] No simple answer can therefore be expected to the question of the semantic range of *abhidharma* considered as a technical term, though I think it true to say that the senses of *dharma* to the fore in the term *abhidharma* are almost always the doctrinal, both in the general sense (*dharma* as *buddhadharma*, the set of true propositions taught by Buddha), and in the specific ontological sense (*dharmas* as the irreducible existents of which the cosmos is made up). Formally the term consists of a nominal item (*subanta—dharma*) with a prefix (*upsarga—abhi*); the prefix usually has a directional sense, and ranges over the English 'towards', 'concerned with', or 'about'; alternatively it may have an intensive sense: 'full', 'complete', or 'transcendent'. This latter sense explains such Western translations as "Dharma spécial," "Super-Doctrine," "profonde loi," and "Further-Dhamma."[21] "Metaphysics" is an English translation commonly used by some, a translation which, if taken in its Aristotelian sense to refer to an intellectual enterprise which deals with the question of being-qua-being, that is, with the question of ontology (what there is in the world) as well as with the metaquestion of what it means to exist at all, certainly preserves some of the more important connotations of *abhidharma*. The former directional sense of the prefix *abhi-* explains such translations as "über den Dhamma" and "concerning the doctrine."[22] But since usage is always more important then etymology (even for *ābhidhārmikas* who frequently felt compelled to buttress their usage by constructing fake etymologies), I shall now turn to some examples of how Buddhists have understood and used the term. I should stress that what follows is by no means a complete survey. Almost every systematic Buddhist text from every school has something to say about *abhidharma*; the examples I have chosen are meant on the one hand to provide something of a diachronic perspective, and on the other to concentrate upon the more illuminating discussions. I shall begin with some comments upon the meaning(s) of the term in the Pali canonical collection, and proceed from there to an analysis of the semantic range of the term in 'classical' *abhidharma* texts (especially the *Abhidharmakośa* and its commentaries) and in one *Mahāyāna* text (the *Mahāyānasūtrālaṅkāra* and its commentaries).

The Pali term *abhidhamma* occurs most frequently in the early texts of the Pali canonical collection as one member of a pair—the other being *abhivinaya*—in the locative case.[23] Thus, for example, we find the following passage in the *Majjhima Nikaya*:

> Sir, a monk who has gone to the forest should yoke himself to abhidhamma and abhivinaya. There are those who will question such a monk about abhidhamma and abhivinaya, and if, Sir, he is unable to give an answer when questioned about abhidhamma and abhivinaya, they will say of him: "What's the good of this venerable one who has gone to the forest and who, living alone in the forest as he pleases, cannot answer when questioned about abhidhamma and abhivinaya?" Therefore, Sir, a monk who has gone to the forest should yoke himself to abhidhamma and abhivinaya.[24]

Abhidhamma, along with *abhivinaya*, is clearly something which a monk is supposed to know about, but contexts such as these do not provide much help in deciding what the content of such knowledge is. The most natural way to take the compounds in this context, and in many others like them, is as meaning very generally 'what pertains to doctrine' (*abhidhamma*) and 'what pertains to monastic discipline' (*abhivinaya*) respectively.[25] This paired usage of *abhidhamma* and *abhivinaya* accounts for the vast majority of the occurrences of the term *abhidhamma* in the earlier strata of the Pali canonical collection.[26]

There are, though, some instances of the term *abhidhamma* being used in these texts without being paired with *abhivinaya*, and these are rather more useful for my purposes. Most often such usages are in connection with some debate or discussion (*kathā*) about a particular doctrinal issue. The locus classicus for this is the *Kintisutta* of the *Majjhima Nikaya*,[27] in which the Buddha lays down rules for making peace between groups of monks who have opposed interpretations of *abhi-*

dhamma, who differ as to its spirit (*attha*) and its letter (*byañjana*). The *abhidhamma* about which the monks differ is spelled out precisely in the text: it is the thirty-seven practices which aid the production of awakening (*bodhipakkhiyadhamma*), a standardized list of *dhammas* about which I shall have a little more to say when I come to discuss the *mātṛkā* below. Here, then, we appear to have a fairly precise usage of *abhidhamma*: it refers to a particular way of summarizing, through a list, the doctrine (*dhamma*) in general.[28] Debates or discussions about doctrine, then, are not infrequently linked to specific sets of doctrinal formulae and labelled *abhidhammakathā* in the *Suttapiṭaka*.[29] It is important to note that even in cases such as this there is no reference to texts; rather, the compound *abhidhammakathā* can consistently be interpreted as discussions about or discourses on what pertains to the doctrine, though with the awareness that "what pertains to the doctrine" is beginning to have a more specific reference: it is beginning to mean precisely those stereotyped sets of numbered formulae by means of which the doctrine was remembered, recited, and handed on. This will be important when I come to say more about the historical developments underlying the composition of classical *abhidharma* texts.

In conclusion: the term *abhidhamma* in the earlier strata of the Pali canonical materials does not refer to a body of texts, nor, for the most part, to a precisely defined set of ideas. It means simply "what pertains to doctrine" and is linked frequently to debates about the meaning of doctrine and to questions about specific doctrinal issues. There is also a noticeable and growing connection between the term and particular doctrinal lists and formulae; the term *abhidhamma* comes in some texts to refer straightforwardly to these lists, and in this development can be seen the beginnings of the development of *abhidharma* as a genre with its own defining characteristics.

The idea that *abhidharma* is, in essence, an intellectual discipline and discourse devoted to the conceptual analysis of doctrinal lists and of the *realia* reflected by those lists comes more and more to the fore as Buddhist scholastic philosophizing developed in India. So, in the scholastic compendia of the early centuries CE, it is often said that *abhidharma* is a discourse that collects *dharma* (understood now both as doctrine and, in the plural, as those *realia* that constitute the cosmos) together, orders it (them), and analyzes it (them).[30] These trends are especially evident in the *Abhidharmakośa*,[31] a systematic *abhidharma* text from (perhaps) the fourth century CE, and the definitions of the term given at the beginning of this text summarize most of the important aspects of the term's semantic range by that period:

What then is this abhidharma? *Abhidharma is flawless insight together with its accompaniment* (v. 2a).[32] Here, "insight" means the analytical investigation of dharmas. "Flawless" means without defilement. "With its accompaniment" means with its retinue. So it has been said that there is an undefiled abhidharma consisting of five aggregates. This is abhidharma in its ultimate sense.[33]

In this first part of his definition the text tells us what *abhidharma* is "in its ultimate sense" (*paramārthika*). We are told first that it is "insight" (*prajñā*) itself a *dharma*, one of the irreducible categories of existents into which the world is analyzed. Drawing upon the commentaries of Yaśomitra and Sthiramati upon this passage, as well as upon other passages from the *Abhidharma kośabhāsya*, we learn that "insight" is a synonym here for "discernment" (*mati*), one of the ten mental qualities that exist to some extent and in some manner in every moment of mental existence.[34] When analytical investigation (*pravicaya*) of *dharmas*—what there is in the world—occurs, this quality of understanding becomes "flawless" (*amalā*) or "undefiled" (*anāsrava*), and becomes the dominant quality in the mental life of the practitioner.[35] *Abhidharma* is thus identified with a particular mental quality, and with those other qualities that accompany it—for example, undefiled qualities from any of the five aggregates (*skandha*) which comprise the person.[36] This explains the reference to the "undefiled abhidharma consisting of the five aggregates." All of this, we are told, is *abhidharma* considered in its ultimate sense: in brief, *abhidharma* is that analytical activity of the mind which gives its practitioner access to what there really is in the world (i.e., *dharmas*).

But there is also a conventional (*sāṅketika*) sense in which the term can be understood, and this is explained in the next element of the definition in the *Abhidharmakośa*:

> In its conventional sense, though *[abhidharma] is that [insight] and that treatise which are conducive to the attainment of this [flawless insight]* (v. 2b). "Insight" means that defiled insight which consists of hearing, reflection, and meditation, and which is dependent upon birth. It also refers to what accompanies that [defiled insight]. "That treatise" refers to the [treatise] which is aimed at the attainment of that undefiled insight; this is also called abhidharma because it is a requisite for [the attainment of] this [undefiled insight].[37]

Here, in the secondary or conventional meaning of *abhidharma*, we find a reference to both "defiled insight" (*sāsrava prajñā*) and to "treatise" (*śāstra*), both of which are regarded as necessary prerequisites for the attainment of the flawless insight which has already been identified as *abhidharma* proper. The defiled insight "consists in hearing, reflection, and meditation" (*śrutacintābhāvanāmayī*), a standard Buddhist way of classifying and ordering the stages through which the doctrine is appropriated and understood. First one hears about it, then one reflects upon its meaning, and finally one meditates upon that meaning in order to completely appropriate and internalize it.[38] This kind of insight is defiled because it is, of necessity, preliminary and imperfect, and this explains also in what sense it is "dependent upon birth": the kind of preliminary (and thus defiled) insight possible for any given individual depends in large part upon the state or condition in which that individual is born—for one thing, it is necessary to be born in a physical condition that enables one to at least hear the dharma, and this means avoiding rebirth in any of the hells, or as any kind of sentient being for whom hearing with understanding is not possible.[39]

The reference to "treatise" in this second part of the definition of *abhidharma* in our text is the first real indication that the term was understood to refer to anything literary. Yaśomitra explains here that "treatise" means "*abhidharma* treatise," and that it can be understood to refer more specifically to the seven canonical *abhidharma* treatises of the Sarvāstivāda school.[40] Sthiramati says that all treatises are composed of linguistic bits and pieces that make communication possible, and that since this is so they have the power to clarify the meaning (*artha*) of *abhidharma*, and are thus to be understood as requisite for the attainment of *abhidharma* proper.[41] It seems, then, that we should understand any text—including the *Abhidharmakośa* itself and any and all of the canonical texts of the Sarvāstivāda — as at best instruments, perhaps necessary conditions, for the attainment of that flawless insight which is *abhidharma* proper. I shall return to this point when I come to consider more closely the question of *abhidharma* as a type of discourse.

The *Abhidharmakośa* concludes its definition of *abhidharma* with an etymological analysis of the term:

> Etymologically speaking, this [abhidharma] is a dharma because it bears its own defining characteristic. This abhidharma, then, is a dharma directed towards the ultimate dharma—Nirvāṇa—or towards the defining characteristic of any [particular] dharma.[42]

I have already shown that *abhidharma* is considered by our text to be a mental *dharma*—undefiled insight—and that this in turn is identical with the analytical investigation of those *realia* which make up the cosmos. Here our text applies the specifically Vaibhāṣika understanding of what a *dharma* is, to *abhidharma* considered as a *dharma*. A *dharma* is something which, of necessity, has a unique defining characteristic, something which marks it off from every other existent, and in the first part of his etymological discussion our text simply says that *abhidharma* is a *dharma* in just that sense. It too has its own unique defining characteristic, the characteristic which belongs to undefiled insight. Then, because of the fact that *abhidharma* considered in the ultimate sense consists in analytical investigation of *dharmas*, it must also be understood as something which directs itself towards the defining characteristics of any *dharma* other than itself,[43] including, finally, the ultimate *dharma* which is *Nirvāṇa* itself.

In summary: our text distinguishes two senses of *abhidharma*: in the first and highest sense *abhidharma* is pure insight, both in the sense of the experiential event itself, and in the sense of the knowledge that results from such an event. In the second and lower sense *abhidharma* is the activity of preliminary analysis of what exists, as well as the texts and discourses in which this activity is preserved and expressed. *Abhidharma* in the highest sense is valued very highly by the traditions represented in our texts: without it, salvation is not possible.[44]

There should be, if what I have said about denaturalized discourse is to have any purchase upon the enterprise of the *ābhidhārmika*, one who engages in *abhidharma*, a connection between *abhidharma* considered as a metaphysical enterprise—the attempt to list, categorize, define, and relate to one another all the existents there are—and the kind of discourse used to further this goal. And to that question, to *abhidharma* as genre, I now turn.

§4.2 Abhidharma as a Discourse

It is important to remember that, while all schools have their canonical *sūtra* and *vinaya* texts largely in common, this is not true of the canonical texts called "*abhidharma*." It is almost certain that there were a number of different canonical *abhidharma* collections composed in a variety of middle Indic languages in India between the third and first centuries BCE. It is also clear that while these works had much in common as regards both style and substance, there were also

significant differences among them, differences explained largely by
the fact that they developed in isolation from one another, as part of
different scholastic traditions.[45] The historical details of this process
are complex and obscure; for the purposes of this paper it will suffice
to note that, of these canonical *abhidharma* collections, only two survive in their entirety, that belonging to the Sarvāstivādins, from
Kāśmir, and that belonging to the Theravādins in Śrī Laṅkā. Each of
these collections comprises seven separate works,[46] though only the
Theravādin collection survives complete in an Indic language—in this
case Pali. The Sarvāstivādin texts survive complete only in Chinese,
though there are fragments in Tibetan and Sanskrit. In the comments
that follow I shall be concerned mostly with evidence from the
Theravādin tradition since I am not competent to discuss the Chinese
evidence. How then did these canonical *abhidharma* texts come into
being, and what kind of discourse is typically found in them?

I've already noted that the earliest uses of the term *abhidharma* link
it with doctrinal debates and expositions, and often with specific numbered lists of concepts. Buddhism has delighted in such numerical lists
from the very earliest times (four truths, eight-membered path, twelve-
membered chain of dependent origination), largely for mnemonic purposes, and the development of the canonical *abhidharma* texts appears to
have been very closely linked to the elaboration of these lists, an elaboration which occurred in a number of different ways. I shall focus upon
two of these methods for elaboration: simple enumeration and question-and-answer, both closely connected with the development of
mātṛkā (Pali *mātika*), conveniently translated by the cognate English
term *matrices*: summary lists of important doctrinal terms.

At the beginning of the *Dhammasaṅgaṇi*, the first, and in many
ways the most important book of the Theravādin *abhidhammapiṭaka*,
we find a short list of terms arranged in triads and dyads called *abhidhammamātikā* "the matrix of *abhidhamma.*"[47] This list is somewhat like
a table of contents, not only for the *Dhammasaṅgaṇi*, but also for the
entire Theravādin canonical *abhidhamma* collection; more will be said
of it below, but for the moment it's sufficient to notice that this developed list (consisting of 22 triads and 100 dyads) is largely made up of
terms drawn directly from *sutta* texts (earlier texts purporting to contain the discourses of the Buddha), though nowhere are those texts
arranged in this way. For example, the first triad of the *abhidhammamātikā* is: *dhammas* that are positive (*kusala*); *dhammas* that are negative (*akusala*); *dhammas* that are neutral (*avyākata*). When this triad is

given detailed exposition in the body of the *Dhammasaṅgaṇi*, these headings are used as the basis for an attempt to place every *dhamma*, every existent, under one of these headings. Similarly for each of the other triads and dyads: each of them provides a different way of cutting the cake, of ordering and analyzing the existents (*dhammas*) of which the world is comprised. This *abhidhammamātikā* at the beginning of the *Dhammasaṅgaṇi* is the most developed and comprehensive form of matrix available in the Theravāda materials. There are, however, scattered through the *sutta* and *vinaya* texts, a number of less comprehensive matrices, or organized doctrinal lists, and it is from these, common as they are to all schools, that all canonical *abhidharma* texts grew.

There are references in the discourses to monks who are "versed in the matrices" (*mātikādhara*). Such statements are usually connected with statements to the effect that one should question (*paripucchati*) and interrogate (*paripañhati*) such monks, and that they will then dispel doubt about dubious doctrinal issues (*Kaṅkhāṭṭhāniya dhamma*), and will open up (*vivarati*) the meaning of the doctrine.[48] It is not easy, however, to find explicit statements in the discourses as to exactly what 'matrix' meant at this stage of development; it certainly did not mean the very developed matrix found at the beginning of the *Dhammasaṅgaṇi*. The earliest fairly explicit definitions of *mātṛkā* that I've been able to find come not from the discourses but from the vinaya of the Mūlasarvāstivādins,[49] and from two Chinese versions of the *Aśokāvadāna*.[50] In these texts the term is linked explicitly to the list of thirty-seven 'aids to awakening' which I've already had occasion to mention, and this is important since I have already shown that there is a strong link between this basic list and the early senses of the term *abhidhamma*.[51]

Other scholars have subjected the history of this list and its relation to the canonical *abhidharma* texts as they now stand to detailed study; this paper is not the place to offer a review of that work.[52] I shall simply assume, on the basis of it, that, at a very early period in the history of Buddhist thought (certainly within a century of the Buddha's death, and in some cases long before that), numerical ordered lists (*mātṛkā*) of items of doctrine were developed and formalized as mnemonic aids. These lists were the earliest form of *abhidharma*. They were gradually expanded, interwoven, and systematized until, probably by the second century of Buddhist history, statements by monastic teachers as to the relationships between these lists and the characteristics of their members began to be accepted as authoritative. It is very probable that from the beginning the matrices were used primarily as mnemonic aids and were always accompanied by oral exposition; no doubt certain forms of oral exposition, certain ways of relating elements in the matrices to one another, became standardized and were passed on from teacher to pupil. In these standardized forms we have the kernels of the canonical *abhidharma* texts. The expansion of these kernels into the texts as they now stand took longer, and in the texts as we now have them there is clear evidence of intellectual interests far more extensive than the development of mnemotechnical aids.

In the canonical *abhidharma* texts we find attempts first to explain the meanings of the terms found in the matrices, and second to provide a comprehensive and consistent explanation of the connections operative among these terms. The basic intellectual impulse behind these developments was the desire for comprehensiveness and consistency: the compilers of the canonical *abhidharma* texts wanted to account for, list, and categorize every existent, and then to explain (comprehensively) all the relations that can obtain among the various kinds into which existents are classified. These enterprises are undertaken by simple enumeration and by question-and-answer.

To take an example from the *Vibhaṅga*: one of the elements in one of the matrices underlying this work is the list of the five aggregates (*khandha*) which comprise the person. These are physical form (*rūpa*), sensation (*vedanā*), conceptualization(*saññā*), motivations (*saṅkhārā*), and consciousness (*viññāna*). In the matrices as they occur in the discourses these terms receive either no explanation at all, or a very brief formalized statement as to their meaning. In the *Vibhaṅga* they receive sixty-nine pages of close discussion (even in an edition that omits some of the stylized repetitions). The method is one of question-and-answer throughout. First, the basic question is asked: "What is the aggregate of physical form?" The initial answer is given by listing all the terms that can properly be applied to that aggregate (eleven in this case—such things as "past" (*atīta*), "future" (*anāgata*), and so forth). The same question is then put about each of these eleven—"What is X?"—and answers are given largely by listing synonyms. For example, in answer to the question "What is past material form?" the text says: "Past material form is material form which is past, ceased, dissolved, changed, terminated, disappeared."[53] When all the terms in question have been listed and elucidated in this way, the text turns to a numerical analysis of the aggregates, listing all the senses in which each aggregate can be considered unitary (e.g., the aggregate of physical form is unitary because it is caused, because it is the object of attachment; it is dual because it is both distant and proximate—and so forth), and so on up through the numbers until all the senses in which physical form is elevenfold are listed. Finally, all the dyads and triads listed as *abhidhammamātikā* at the beginning of the *Dhammasaṅgani* are applied by question-and-answer to each of the five aggregates, using the following form: "Of the five aggregates, how many are positive, how many negative, how many neutral?"

The method should now be clear. It should also be evident that this way of doing metaphysics, while it certainly has the advantages of clarity and comprehensiveness, tends to produce very long and very repetitive works. Every possible option must be considered, enumerated, listed, and analyzed. The example given in the preceding paragraph should have suggested that the historical links between the canonical *abhidharma* texts and the oral expositions of *mātṛkā* which underlie them come across very clearly in the extensive use of question-and-answer found in the texts. What we have here is perhaps the most extensive and consistently worked out instance of metaphysical catechesis in the history of the world, and if a genre-label for these texts is desired this seems not inappropriate: canonical *abhidharma*, for the most part, is metaphysics done through catechesis. It is also denaturalized discourse; that is, its users were, quite self-consciously, reducing the complexity and ambiguity of everyday discourse to something as close as possible to a list of terms connected with an (implicit) existential quantifier, lists that, given the syntax of the Indic languages used for this discourse, are entirely verbless.[54]

There is, naturally, a close connection between the development of this kind of denaturalized discourse and the metaphysical beliefs of those who used it. Buddhist metaphysics is, for the most part, an analytical and reductionist pursuit; it is interested not in wholes but in parts, not in chariots but in wheels, floors, and seats, not in persons but in form, sensation, and consciousness. This is apparent from the beginning, long before the full flowering of canonical *abhidharma*. Such an analytically reductionist metaphysical enterprise necessarily raises certain pressing questions: how far can the analytical reduction go? Are there basic constituents, unanalyzable categories, with which the reduction will end? If so, what are they and what are they like? The Buddhist answer, at least until Nāgārjuna, was that there are indeed basic constituents (*dharmas*), and that the object of metaphysics is simply to list these and to elucidate the relationships obtaining among them and the functions which can properly be attributed to them. It is difficult to imagine a genre more intimately reflective of the substantive views expressed through it than the Buddhist denaturalized discourse which is canonical *abhidharma*.

In sum: *abhidharma*, considered as a discourse, an intellectual practice, is a splendid instance of denaturalized discourse. It is, though, connected with and expressive of a metaphysic quite different from that of the propositional mythos that fostered denaturalized discourse in the West. But its function is the same: to make available to its users what there really is and, in so doing, to make claims about what there really is that are universalizable. It is, formally and functionally, close to the ideal type of denaturalized discourse.

§5 Conclusions

Denaturalized discourse is an intellectual practice. Just as every first-order ethic has a metaethic, so every practice has a metapractice, a reason for which its practitioners practice it. The metapractice of those who use denaturalized discourse is that they want to make assertions of both fact and value that have universal application. Using denaturalized discourse is not the only way of doing this, but it is the paradigmatic, perhaps the ideal, way for intellectual virtuosi in all cultures; it is perhaps the only possible practice when the goal in mind is not simply to make a statement of the universalizable facts and norms espoused by the community, but also, in making that statement, to make it evident to those outside the community that these facts and norms do have universal applicability.

Religious communities typically do want to make available through the discourse they use that which really exists; they want to make it available—to refer to it, describe it, remove obstacles to its apprehension—both to their members and to those outside the community. This is a goal usually thought to have soteriological significance. Hence, the élite intellectual representatives of religious communities will often engage in the production and application of various forms of denaturalized discourse.

Like Hilary Putnam, like our *ābhidhārmikas*, and like the intellectual representatives of most religious communities at most times, I do not think that discourse can ever be fully naturalized if the metapractice of those producing it includes the goal of making available to all human beings those realities and truths which are of universal application. If universalized normative claims are to be made, one dimension of making them will be the construction of a denaturalized discourse in and through which they are stated and argued for. But neither do I think that discourse can ever be fully denaturalized and continue to exist as discourse. That goal is only approached asymptotically.

Given these considerations, the challenge for us—for those interested in constructing a comparative philosophy of religion—is to clarify what our metapractice is. Do we do what we do in order to purse and set forth the kinds of universal truth lusted after by the users of denaturalized discourse? If so, our discourse will cease to be constitutively comparative, and will instead become one more player in the field. Its play may be more fully informed of the range of possibilities than is usual, and from such fuller information it can only benefit; but it will be concerned centrally with elucidating and defending norms, and must, as such, enter into explicit competition with other, opposed, norms. If this route is taken, the comparative aspects of the enterprise are contingent to it, not essential; and I cannot see how to make them other.

Alternatively, our metapractice may be classificatory; we may want to see how and in what ways different religious communities at different times have developed and used denaturalized discourse, to do for the connections between types of discourse and ontological systems what a similar set of colloquia has already attempted to do for cosmogonies and ethical systems.[55]

Both goals have their value; but the paradox, to which I have already adverted several times, is that the axiology informing the second metapractice—the classificatory one—is private and community-specific. It is grounded, if it can be grounded at all, in a revelation of norms to some particular practice-constituted community. And if it is to be explicated, made attractive, and defended to those outside the intentional community that engages in it, this can only be done by laying bare (notice, already and inevitably, the denaturalizing metaphor) the ontology that underlies and informs its axiology and its metapractice: and this will, because it must, involve a descent into the very denaturalized discourse that the classificatory and descriptive-analytical metapractice seeks to treat solely as an object. Here too, then, our practice becomes a player in the field; here too it is forced to enter its axiology and its ontology as one among many options, and to defend them against opposition. This can be avoided, it seems, only at the (high) cost of fideism and relativism. We can avoid denaturalized discourse only if we are prepared to reduce the comparative philosophy of religion to a practice requiring much energy and a taste for the exotic, as well as considerable leisure and a tenured academic position, and to tacitly deny that it has claims on anyone outside the community of those with such tastes and such positions.

Denaturalized discourse thus forces itself upon us, both as an object of our study and as a vehicle for the expression and justification of our metapractice. This paper can itself be understood as clearing the ground for a (denaturalized) statement and defense of the normative enterprise in which we are really engaged; and it will be evident to the careful reader that its comparative dimensions, while important, are contingently related to its theme.

Notes

Works frequently cited in the notes have been identified by the following abbreviations:

AK	Abhidharmakośa
AKBh	Abhidharmakośabhāṣya
AKK	Abhidharmakośakārikā
AKT	Abhidharmakośaṭīkā
AKV	Abhidharmakośavyākhyā
AN	Anguttaranikāya
DN	Dīghanikāya
MN	Majjhimanikāya
PT	Peking Tanjur (bstan-'gyur)

1.   I have in mind here something like what Max Weber meant by the term. His comments on it are (as usual) sufficiently full of insights to warrant extensive quotation (Weber speaks here in the context of his attempt to develop a typology of religious world-rejections): "The constructed scheme, of course, only serves the purpose of offering an ideal typical means of orientation. it does not teach a philosophy of its own. The theoretically constructed types . . . make it possible to determine the typological locus of a historical phenomenon. They enable us to see if, in particular traits or in their total character, the phenomena approximate one of our constructions: to determine the degree of approximation of the historical phenomenon to the theoretically constructed type. To this extent the construction is merely a technical aid which facilitates a more lucid arrangement and terminology. Yet, under certain considerations, a construction might mean more. For the rationality, in the sense of logical or teleological 'consistency', of an intellectual-theoretical or practical-ethical attitude has and always has had power over man however limited and unstable this power is and always has been in the face of other forces of historical life." Weber, "Religious Rejections of the World and Their Directions," 323-324.

2.   Unless, of course, the referent of the judgment in question is itself a historical event or is inextricably linked with one in some interesting fashion. Of this

kind, presumably, would be *Jesus Christ was born of the Virgin Mary*, or *Buddha visited Kapilavastu*.

3.   See Shweder, "Cultural Psychology: What Is It?" for some discussion of this view.

4.   Quine, "Epistemology Naturalized," 68.

5.   It should be noted that many of those who claim to have naturalized epistemology à la Quine have not thereby abandoned normative claims. This is true of Quine himself: see, inter alia, "What Price Bivalence?" and *Roots of Reference*. Quine wants to (normatively) distinguish among theoretical systems according to their utility in predicting observations. This is a (scientistic) claim to normativity, based as it is upon the ontology of the natural sciences. Many other so-called naturalized epistemologists also use normative criteria of similar kinds, on which see Putnam, *Realism and Reason*, 244-247. It remains true, though, that a strict naturalization of epistemology would require an abandonment of all universalizable normative claims other than the strictly contingent kind adverted to in the next paragraph.

6.   Freely adapted from the many examples given in Shope, *Analysis of Knowing*. This example might be freely translated thus: "A particular knowing subject knows a particular proposition if and only if: (1) that proposition is true: (2) the subject in question believes that it is true; (3) the subject's belief that the proposition is true has a certain desirable epistemic status." It should be clear that the descent to symbolism has at least the advantage of brevity, though probably no others; certainly not that of literary elegance.

7.   On these questions see especially Putnam, *Realism and Reason*, 229-247, and the extensive bibliography in Shope, *Analysis of Knowing*.

8.   *On Interpretation* 16a-17a, McKeon, *Basic Works*, 40-42. Aristotle's discussion at the beginning of the *On Interpretation* is heavily indebted to that in the *Sophist* (especially 262A-C), Hamilton and Cairns, ed., *Plato*, 1009.

9.   *On Interpretation* 16a1-20, McKeon, *Basic Works*, 40.

10.   Aristotle's clearest statement of what it is for a natural-language sentence to be true is found not in the *On Interpretation* but in the *Metaphysics*: "For it is false to say of that which is that it is not or of that which is not that it is, and it is true to say of that which is that it is, or of that which is not that it is not." *Metaphysics* 1011b26-27, McKeon, *Basic Works*, 749.

11.   Prior, after surveying the history of the doctrine of propositions, says: "There is the tradition. It has a consistency and a faithfulness to its origins which speak for themselves. All its spokesmen agree that a proposition is a form of speech, a sentence, though not any sort of sentence—it must be in the indicative mood, capable of truth or falsehood." Prior, *Doctrine of Propositions and Terms*, 17.

12.   So Abelard in the *Dialectica*, cited in Kneale and Kneale, *Development of Logic*, 205.

13.   This sentence is taken from the *Mahāyānasūtrālaṅkāra*, Lévi, ed., *Mahāyāna-Sūtrālaṃkāra*, 33.

14.   On all this see, classically, Ryle, "Are There Propositions?" Ryle concluded that there are not, but the details of his argument are beyond the scope of this paper.

15.   So, for example, Alvin Plantinga, one of the two or three most important philosophers of religion to write in English in the last three decades, has said: "Necessity, truth, and allied properties are at bottom (as I see it) properties of propositions, not sentences. A sentence is true, on any given occasion of its use, if on that occasion it expresses a true proposition." Plantinga, *The Nature of Necessity*, 1.

16.   Frege, "My Basic Logical Insights," 251. These remarks were probably written in 1915.

17   ". . . eine der arithmetischen nachgebildete Formelsprache des reinen Denkens." This is the subtitle of the *Begriffschrift*. See Geach and Black, eds., *Translations from the Philosophical Writings of Gottlob Frege*, 1. For Frege's own views on the theoretical importance of developing such a discourse, see: "Über den Zweck der Begriffschrift."

18.   Frege's terminology is complex and perhaps not entirely consistent. There are changes as his ideas developed, and this is not the place to explore exactly what he meant by *Satz* and *Gedanke*, and what relations he envisaged obtaining between them.

19.   See, for example, Schiffer, "The Real Trouble with Propositions."

20.   See Geiger and Geiger, *Pali Dhamma*; Stcherbatsky, *The Central Conception of Buddhism*; Carter, *Dhamma: Western Academic and Sinhalese Buddhist Interpretations*: Warder, "Dharmas and Data"; Watanabe, *Philosophy and Its Development*; Hirakawa, "The Meaning of 'Dharma' and 'Abhidharma'."

21.   "Dharma spécial" is used by Lamotte in *Histoire du bouddhisme indien*, 197 & passim; "Super-Doctrine" is used by Rahula in *Le compendium de la Super-Doctrine* "profonde loi" is used by Van Velthem in *Le traité de la descente dans la profonde loi*; and "Further-Dhamma" is used by Horner in "Abhidhamma, Abhivinaya."

22.   For "über den Dhamma" see Geiger and Geiger, *Pali Dhamma*, 118-19; for "concerning the doctrine" see Warder, *Indian Buddhism*, 10 and passim.

23.   The standard, and still the most comprehensive study of the term *abhidhamma* (the Pali form of the Sanskrit *abhidharma*) in the canonical Pali texts is that of I. B. Horner ("Abhidhamma, Abhivinaya"); its findings may be supplemented by those of Watanabe (*Philosophy and Its Development*, 1-45) and Yoshimoto (*Abidaruma Shisō*, 9-19). In what follows I draw heavily upon the work of these scholars, though I do not always agree with them.

24.   MN, 1:472.

25.   In saying this I differ from both Horner (*Middle Length Sayings*, 2:145) and Watanabe (*Philosophy and Its Development*, 25-26), who differ also from each other. I differ also from Buddhaghosa, who glosses *abhidhamma* in the extract cited with *abhidhammapiṭaka* and *abhivinaya* with *vinayapiṭaka* (*Papañcasūdanī*, 3:187). I don't find this persuasive because it seems very unlikely that the term *abhivinaya* ever referred to the *Vinayapiṭaka*: there is certainly no clear instance of it doing so, and in fact it effectively drops out of use as a technical term at a rather early period. If this is correct then it's equally unlikely that *abhidhamma*—at least in those contexts where it occurs in tandem with *abhivinaya*—was intended to have a more specific meaning than its companion. Both terms can appropriately be understood as based upon the extremely ancient division between doctrine (*dhamma*) and monas-

tic discipline (*vinaya*). Buddhaghosa, in giving the terms a more precise (and anachronistic) reading, is forced to break the parallelism of the construction: since there's no *abhivinayapiṭaka* he can't gloss *abhivinaya* with any such term.

26.   See, inter alia, DN, 3:267; AN, 1:289; 5:24; 5:90; 5:201; 5:339; *Vinayapiṭaka* 1:64.

27.   MN, 2:238-243; compare *Mahāgosiṅgasutta*, MN, 1:212-219.

28.   Buddhaghosa glosses *abhidhamma* here simply with *bodhipakkhiyadhamma* (*Papañcasūdanī*, 4:129).

29.   See also AN, 3:392.

30.   This is especially evident in the lengthy discussions of *abhidharma* found in the scholastic compendia called *Vibhāṣā* dating from the very beginning of the common era. These texts survive only in Chinese (Taishō **1545-1547); convenient summaries of their contents, for those (like myself) without access to classical Buddhist Chinese, may be found in Watanabe, *Philosophy and Its Development*, 23ff.; and Takakusu, "On the Abhidharma Literature," 67-146. As far as can be judged, it appears that the two most common Sanskrit verbs used to relate *abhidharma* to *dharma* in this corpus were *saṅgrah-* ('to collect, gather together') and *pravic-* ('to analyze').

31.   The AK itself is a verse text comprising 613 *kārikā* divided into nine chapters. Three major Indic prose commentaries on it survive: a *bhāṣya* attributed to Vasubandhu; a *vyākhyā* attributed to Yaśomitra; and a ṭīkā attributed to Sthiramati.

32.   The italicized section is a translation of the verse under discussion. The AKBh follows the classical form of a *bhāṣya* , which means that it cites in full all of the verses of the AKK on which it comments and (usually) expounds each and every word in the verses.

33.   AKBh on AKK 1: 2a (Pradhan, ed., *Abhidharmakośabhāṣyam*, 2).

34.   See AKBh on AKK 2:24 (Pradhan, ed., *Abhidharmakośabhāṣyam*, 54-55).

35.   AKV on AKK 1:2a (Śāstrī ed., *Abhidharmakośa*, 11); AKT on AKK 1:2a (PT ngo-mtshar TO 21b8-22b2).

37.   AKBh on AKK 1: 2b (Pradhan, ed., *Abhidharmakośabhāṣyam*, 2).

38.   See the lengthy discussions in both AKV (Śāstrī, ed., *Abhidharmakośa*, 12), and AKT (PT ngo-mtshar TO 22b6-23a1).

39.   AKT on AKK 1: 2b2 (PT ngo-mtshar TO 23a1-4).

40.   AKV on AKK 1: 2b2 (Śāstrī, ed., *Abhidharmakośa*, 12).

41.   AKT on AKK 1: 2b2 (especially PT ngo-mtshar TO 23a7-24a6).

42.   AKBh on AKK 1: 2b (Pradhan, ed., *Abhidharmakośabhāṣyam*, 2).

43.   Both Yaśomitra (AKV on AKK 1: 2 [Śāstrī, ed., *Abhidharmakośa* 12]) and Sthiramati (AKT on AKK 1: 2 [PT ngo-mtshar TO 24b1ff.]) provide examples.

44.   See, very clearly, AKBh on AKK 1: 3, discussed, in a very different context, in my "On The Possible Future of the Buddhist-Christian Interaction," 149. A

substantially similar analysis of the meaning of *abhidharma* as a technical term may be found in the *Mahāyānasūtrālaṅkāra* 11: 2 and its commentaries. See Lévi, *Mahāyāna-Sūtrālaṃkāra*, 55-56.

45.   On this complicated process see Bareau, "Les sectes bouddhiques du petit véhicule"; "Trois traités sur les sectes bouddhiques"; *Les sectes bouddhiques du petit véhicule; Les premières conciles bouddhique*; Bechert, "Notes on the Formation of Buddhist Sects"; Frauwallner, "Abhidharma-Studien"; Sakurabe, *Kusharon*, 1-48.

46.   For the Theravada we have: *Dhammasaṅgaṇi, Vibhaṅga, Kathāvatthu, Puggalapaññati, Dhātukathā, Yamaka,* and *Paṭṭhāna.* For the Sarvāstivāda we have: *Jñānaprasthāna, Saṅgītiparyāya, Dhātukāya, Vijñānakāya, Prakaraṇapāda, Dharmaskandha,* and *Prajñaptiśāstra.*

47.   See Nyanatiloka, *Guide*, 4-11.

48.   See DN, 2:125; MN, 1:221; AN, 1:117; 3:179; 3:361.

49.   Extant only in Chinese. See Rockhill, *Life of the Buddha*, 160; Bronkhorst, "Dharma and Abhidharma."

50.   See Pryzluski, *Le concile de Rājagṛha*, 45. The *vinaya* of the Mūasārvastivāda seems to have had great influence upon the *Aśokāvadāna*. See Strong, *Legend of King Aśoka*, 28. Interestingly, the definition of *mātṛkā* that concerns me is not present in the Sanskrit text of the *Aśokāvadāna.*

51.   I should be noted, though, that the term *mātikā* could be, and was, applied to lists other than this one. Norman has noted (*Pali Literature*, 96, 126) that it was also sometimes applied to the list of *vinaya* rules known as *prātimokṣa.*

52.   The most detailed work is to be found in Frauwallner's series of "Abhidharma-Studien" (especially part three), and in Bronkhorst's "Dharma and Abhidharma," and *Two Traditions of Meditation in Ancient India.*

53.   Thittila, *Book of Analysis*, 1ff.

54.   Louis Renou's comments on classical *bhāṣya* style are very relevant here (and I had them in mind when constructing my formal and functional analysis of denaturalized discourse): "Les commentaires classiques dérivent, pour la forme, de la prose des Brāhmana, qui par son contenu était déjà une sorte de commentaire appliqué tantôt au rituel aux hymnes. Mais l'aspect extérieur en a été durci par le long entraînement au genre «sūtra», par l'accentuation progressive du «style nominal». Ce qui, à l'époque védique, était libre jeu de formes analytiques, en dépit de la rigidité, du schématisme du contenu, a abouti maintenant à être un instrument monotone mais puissant de raisonnement, d'interpretation, de dialectique, approprié à servir d'expression doctrinale à tous les types de problèmes et de disciplines. Les caractéres linguistiques 'abstraits' se sont intensifiés: alternance des noms d'agent en -aka- et des noms d'action en -ana-, dérivés abstraits en -ta- ou en -tva-, composés longs, raréfaction des formes personelles du verbe." Renou, *Histoire de la langue Sanskrite*, 133. See also Renou, "Sur le genre du sūtra." Canonical abhidharma is not the same, in genre terms, as the *kārikā*-plus-*bhāṣya* style of classical *śāstra*; but both are types of denaturalized discourse. Both are used by religious élites to universalize their ontological and cosmological claims.

55.   See Reynolds and Lovin, eds., *Cosmogony and Ethical Order.*

References

Bareau, André.
1947 "Les sectes bouddhiques du petit véhicule et leurs Abhidharma-Pitaka." *Bulletin de l'École Française d'Extrême-Orient* 44: 1-11.

1954-1956 "Trois traités sur les sectes bouddhiques attribués à Vasumitra, Byavya, et Vinitadeva." *Journal Asiatique* (1954): 229-266; (1956): 167-299.

1955 *Les sectes bouddhiques du petit véhicule.* Saigon: École Française d'Extrême-Orient.

1955 *Les premières conciles bouddhique.* Paris: Presses Universitaires de France.

Bechert, Heinz.
1973 "Notes on the Formation of Buddhist Sects and the Origins of Mahayana." In *German Scholars on India I,* 6-18. Varanasi: Chowkhamba Sanskrit Series.

Bronkhorst, Johannes.
1985 "Dharma and Abhidharma." *Bulletin of the School of Oriental and African Studies* 48: 305-20.

1986 *Two Traditions of Meditation in Ancient India.* Dordrecht: Reidel.

Carter, John Ross.
1978 *Dhamma: Western Academic and Sinhalese Buddhist Interpretations.* Tokyo: The Hokuseido Press.

Frauwallner, Erich.
1963-1973 "Abhidharma-Studien." *Wiener Zeitschrift für die Kunde Südasiens* 7 (1963): 20-36; 8 (1964): 59-99; 15 (1971): 69-121; 16 (1972): 92-152; 17 (1973): 97-121.

Frege, Gottlob.
1979 "My Basic Logical Insights." In *Gottlob Frege: Posthumous Writings,* edited by Hans Hermes et al., 251-252. Chicago: University of Chicago Press.

1881 "Über den Zweck der Begriffschrift." *Sitzungsberichte der Jenaischen Gesellschaft für Medicin und Naturwissenschaft,* 1-10.

Geach Peter, and Max Black, eds.
1952 *Translations from the Philosophical Writings of Gottlob Frege.*
Oxford: Blackwell.

Geiger, Wilhelm, and Magdalene Geiger.
1920 *Pali Dhamma: Vornehmlich in der kanonischen Literatur.* Munich:
Bavarian Academy of Sciences.

Griffiths, Paul J.
1987 "On The Possible Future of the Buddhist-Christian Interaction."
In *Japanese Buddhism: Its Tradition, New Religions, and Interaction with
Christianity*, edited by Minoru Kiyota et al., 145-161. Los Angeles:
Buddhist Books International.

Hamilton, Edith, and Huntington Cairns, eds.
1961 *The Collected Dialogues of Plato.* Princeton: Princeton University
Press.

Hirakawa Akira.
1980 "The Meaning of 'Dharma' and 'Abhidharma'." In *Indianisme
et bouddhisme: mélanges offerts à Mgr. Étienne Lamotte*, 159-175.
Louvain-la-neuve: Institut Orientaliste.

Horner, I. B., trans.
1941 "Abhidhamma, Abhivinaya in the First Two Piṭakas of the Pāli
Canon." *Indian Historical Quarterly* 18: 219-310.

1954-1959 *The Collection of the Middle Length Sayings.* 3 vols.
London: Pali Text Society.

Kneale, William, and Martha Kneale.
1984 *The Development of Logic.* Oxford: Clarendon Press.

Lamotte, Étienne.
1958 *Histoire du bouddhisme indien, des origines à l'ère Śaka.* Louvain-
la-Neuve: Institut Orientaliste.

Lévi, Sylvain, ed.
1907 *Mahāyāna-Sūtrālamkāra: Expos'de la doctrine du Grand Véhicule
selon la système Yogācāra.* Tome 1 (texte). Paris: Librairie Acienne
Honoré Champion.

McKeon, Richard, ed.
1961 *The Basic Works of Aristotle*. New York: Random House.

Norman, K. R.
1983 *Pāli Literature, Including the Canonical Literature in Prakrit and Sanskrit of all the Hīnayāna Schools of Buddhism*. Vol. 7 fasc. 2 of *A History of Indian Literature*, edited by Jan Gonda. Wiesbaden: Harrassowitz.

Nyanatiloka [Mahāthera].
1971 *Guide Through the Abhidhamma-Piṭaka*. Kandy: Buddhist Publication Society.

Plantinga, Alvin.
1974 *The Nature of Necessity*. Oxford: Clarendon Press.

Pradhan, Pralhad, ed.
1975 *Abhidharmakośabhāṣyam of Vausbandhu*. 2d ed. Patna: K. P. Jayaswal Research Institute.

Prior, A. N.
1976 *The Doctrine of Propositions and Terms*. London: Duckworth.

Pryzluski, Jean.
1926 *Le concile de Rājagṛha*. Paris: Geuthner.

Putnam, Hilary.
1983 *Realism and Reason*. Cambridge: Cambridge University Press.

Quine, W. V. O.
1981 "What Price Bivalence?" *Journal of Philosophy* 78, 90-95.

1974 *The Roots of Reference*. La Salle, Illinois: Open Court.

1973 "Epistemology Naturalized." In *Empirical Knowledge*, edited by Roderick M. Chisholm and Robert J. Swartz, 59-74. Englewood Cliffs, New Jersey: Prentice-Hall.

Rahula, Walpola, trans.
1971 *Le compendium de la Super-Doctrine (philosophie) (Abhidharmasamuccaya) of Asaṅga*. Paris: École Française d'Extrême-Orient.

Renou, Louis.
1956 *Histoire de la langue Sanskrite*. Lyon: ICA.

1963 "Sur le genre du sūtra dans la littérature Sanskrite." *Journal Asiatique* 251, 165-216.

Reynolds, Frank, and Robin Lovin, eds.
1985 *Cosmogony and Ethical Order*. Chicago: University of Chicago Press.

Rockhill, William W.
1907 *The Life of the Buddha and the Early History of His Order*. London: Kegan Paul, Trench, Trübner.

Ryle, Gilbert.
1929-1930 "Are There Propositions?" *Proceedings of the Aristotelian Society*, 91-126.

Sakurabe Hajime.
1981 *Kusharon*. Tokyo: Okura Shuppan.

Śāstrī, Dwārikādās, ed.
1981 *Abhidharmakośa and Bhāṣya of Acārya Vasubandhu with Sphuṭārthā Commentary of Acārya Yaśomitra*. 2d ed. Varanasi: Bauddha Bharati.

Schiffer, Stephen.
1986 "The Real Trouble with Propositions." In *Belief: Form, Content and Function*, edited by Radu J. Bogdan, 82-117. Oxford: Clarendon Press.

Shope, Robert K.
1983 *The Analysis of Knowing: A Decade of Research*. Princeton: Princeton University Press.

Shweder, Richard A.
1989 "Cultural Psychology: What Is It?" Forthcoming in *Cultural Psychology: The Chicago Symposium on Culture and Human Development*, edited by James W. Stigler, Richard A. Shweder, and Gilbert Herdt. New York: Cambridge University Press.

Stcherbatsky, Th.
1923 *The Central Conception of Buddhism and the Meaning of the Word 'Dharma'*. London: Royal Asiatic Society.

Strong, John S.
1983 *The Legend of King Aśoka: A Study and Translation of the Aśokā-vadāna*. Princeton: Princeton University Press.

Takakusu Junjiro.
1904-1905 "On the Abhidharma Literature of the Sarvāstivādins." *Journal of the Pali Text Society*, 67-146.

Thittila [Pathamakyaw].
1969 *The Book of Analysis*. London: Pali Text Society.

Van Velthem, Marcel, trans.
1977 *Le traité de la descente dans la profonde loi (Abhidharmāvatāra-śāstra) de l'arhat Skandhila*. Louvain-la-Nevue: Institut Orientaliste.

Warder, A. K.
1971 "Dharmas and Data." *Journal of Indian Philosophy* 1: 272-295.

1980 *Indian Buddhism*. 2d ed. Delhi: Motilal Banarsidass.

Watanabe Fumimaro.
1983 *Philosophy and Its Development in the Nikāyas and Abhidhamma*. Delhi: Motilal Banarsidass.

Weber, Max.
1946 "Religious Rejections of the World and Their Directions." In *From Max Weber: Essays in Sociology*, edited by H. H. Gerth and C. Wright Mills, 323-339. New York: Oxford University Press.

Yoshimoto Shingyō.
1982 *Abidaruma Shisō*. Kyoto: Hozokan.

Part II

Myth and Philosophy: Similarities and Differences

Chapter 4

Myth, Philosophy, and Religion in Ancient Greece

Arthur W. H. Adkins

A. Introduction: Greek Religion

My task in this volume of essays on the relationship of myth, philosophy, and religion is to discuss the ancient Greek evidence. As frequently happens, it is difficult to carry out this kind of program with the ancient Greek material. 'But the Greeks had a word for it.' Indeed they had, in fact, two of the three words, for both *muthos* and *philosophia* are common Greek words in the classical period. *Muthos* in fact, as Marcel Detienne has recently reminded us,[1] is already current in Homer, though its meaning is not 'myth'.[2] Therein lies a problem for anyone who wishes to study myth and philosophy in the ancient Greek world. 'Myth' and 'philosophy' are both transliterations of ancient Greek words, whose developing meanings we can trace in extant documents. It is tempting to assume that, at least by the time we reach Plato and Aristotle, the transliterations have the same meanings as their Greek ancestors; but this is not the case. For 'religion' we must turn to the Latin *religio*, for there is, significantly—no suitable word in Greek.[3] Myth and philosophy are not related in what is usually thought of as the Greek religious tradition, since that tradition—if

95

indeed we may call it such—had little intellectual content and no body of doctrine.[4] There were no sacred books in ancient Greece. There were culturally authoritative books, notably the Homeric poems.[5] Virtually all of them mention deity, as indeed do most works by ancient Greek authors; and much of our knowledge of one aspect of Greek religion comes from them. But a belief is not more mandatory because it occurs in Homer, merely more likely to gain currency because of the popularity of Homer. (Few would now claim, as Jane Harrison once did, that the Olympians were mere literary toys and playthings of the archaic Greek and that all myth grew out of ritual. The situation is far more complicated than that.)[6] Provided one expressed belief *in* a deity, or even went through the motions of sacrificing when appropriate, it mattered little what one believed *about* him.[7] That is to say, one would not—usually—be punished by one's fellow-citizens for one's beliefs, which could indeed not ascribe worse behavior to the gods than was ascribed to them in the most revered myths,[8] and there was no organized priesthood. One should never forget that in the Greek polis there were no 'priests of the gods,' or even 'priests of a god.' One was 'priest of god *x* at temple *y*' and shared no interests even with other priests of the same deity. The task of the priest was to keep the temple in good repair or to draw to the attention of others that it needed repair, to keep the temple clean, and to perform sacrifices if called upon to do so. What has philosophy to do here? Myth seems likely to be present; but it will be a local myth, different from others concerned with the same deity elsewhere in Greece, and, like most aspects of Greek cult, in most cases unknown to us. Down to the last third of the fifth century BC in Athens, the poets were the 'theologians' in the etymological sense that is the only one that fits the situation: they made mention of the gods in their works, endeavoring to support a religious ethic by the sanctions of deities singularly ill fitted to the task. After the increasing secularization of Athenian values displayed by most of the articulate Athenians[9] of whom we know anything, it was Greek philosophy, not local Greek cult, that came to advise the more articulate Greek on the way life should be lived.[10] For this reason, Greek ethics was always more concerned with moral action than with moral theory.[11] Philosophy supplied much more life-guidance to the articulate and thoughtful Greek from Socrates onward than could the morally unsatisfactory Greek gods.[12]

    In the circumstances, it seems best to consider *muthos* and *philosophia* as well as 'myth' and 'philosophy' to enable us to see how the Greeks used their own language to express their views of the sub-

ject. In addition we should acknowledge that there is little or nothing
to be said about the role of either *philosophia* or philosophy in Greek
religion, before the Hellenistic period at all events, except that philosophers were often critical of Greek religious beliefs and sometimes of
religious practices.[13] As we shall see, the more illuminating approach is
to accept that *philosophia* is the important term and that the tension is
not between *muthos* and *philosophia* in Greek religion but between
muthos and *logos* in Greek *philosophia*.[14] In addition to this, it is necessary
to discuss whether the Greeks distinguished, as the modern scholar
does, between philosophy and myths with a high intellectual content; and
whether an interest in building an explanatory system out of myths affects
the situation. I shall argue this point later with reference to Hesiod and
Empedocles, and also to Plato.

In the present essay I shall attempt to discuss all the foregoing
questions within the context of Greek culture from Homer to Plato
and—very briefly—Aristotle. I shall make as clear as I can the characteristics of both Greek myth and Greek *muthos*, to facilitate comparison
with other cultures and leave it to others to be overtly cross-cultural. I
shall use myth for what I believe modern interpreters would term 'myth'
whether they are studying Hesiod or the Hopi,[15] *muthos* for what the
ancient Greeks term *muthos*. I shall discuss a number of Greek texts in
some detail in the hope of bringing some questions into sharper focus.

B. Muthos *and* Myth, Philosophia *and* Philosophy

(i) Muthos, *Myth, and Rationality*

Let me turn, then, to *muthos* and *philosophia* first. The term
philosophia (love of *sophia*, wisdom) is said to have been used first by
Pythagoras.[16] Other early thinkers were referred to as *sophoi*, wise, without
qualification. Let me emphasize that there are no transcendental overtones in most of the earlier usages of *sophos* in extant Greek literature. The
Seven Sages (*sophoi*) of archaic Greece for the most part gave shrewd practical advice for daily life.[17] For those who do not read ancient Greek, and
even some who do, *sophia* tends to be colored by the role of *sophia* in
Plato's *Republic*, which is atypical, virtually unknown before the *Republic*,
and by no means the only usage of the term even after that dialogue.

Should we distinguish between 'muthic', or 'mythic', and other
modes of thought? That is to say, in either case, is there a clear dis-

tinction, whether within Greece or generally, between the rational and
the nonrational or irrational modes of discourse. And should we also
distinguish between the 'muthic' and the 'mythic'? A mere feeling that
myths, and perhaps *muthoi*, are in some ways an odd way of conveying
information or explanation—if that indeed is the purpose of
myths—does not suffice to prove the point. Rationality is not necessarily demonstrated by the beliefs one holds about the world. The
everyday beliefs which one shares with one's contemporaries may be
rational but incorrect. Until the discovery of Australia it was rational
to believe that there were no black swans.

My next point is so simple that I blush to make it,[18] and should not
make it had I not noticed so frequently in reading learned works on a
variety of subjects that the author was ignoring it: one should always
distinguish between true and false premises (and conclusions) on the
one hand and and valid and invalid arguments on the other, and also
between true and false beliefs and intelligent and foolish behavior in the
light of those beliefs. From the (true) premises 'dogs are mammals' and
'cats are mammals' one might invalidly deduce the (false) conclusion
'dogs are cats', and from the (false) premise 'all cats are marsupials' and
the (true) premise 'no marsupials are capable of true flight' one might
validly derive the (true) conclusion 'no cats are capable of true flight.'
Put in terms of beliefs and behavior, if one believed that Apollo is the
cause of headaches it would be intelligent behavior, on perceiving a
headache developing, to pray to Apollo, unintelligent to take an aspirin.

(ii) Myth and Rationality in Hesiod and Empedocles

(a) Neikos *and* Philia

Let us consider some passages of Hesiod and Empedocles. I select
these writers because they share some important terms. Each of them uses
the terms *philotes* ('friendship')[19] and *neikos* ('strife') to denote what might
be termed principles of organization in general accounts of the cosmos.
Here is Hesiod in *Theogony* (224-29): "And afterwards destructive Night
bore Deceit and *Philotes* and baneful Old Age and strong-hearted Strife.
And hateful Strife bore grievous Toil and Forgetfulness . . . and Killings of
Men, and *Neikea* and Lies and *Logoi* and *Amphillogiai* . . ."

(b) The Rationality of Empedocles

Empedocles used *Philotes* and *Neikos* in his cosmology.[20] There is some dispute about the details of Empedocles' cosmology, but it seems clear that the explanatory tools were primarily earth, air, fire, and water, together with *Neikos* and *Philotes*, which in some way brought about the succession of continuously varying conditions in his cosmos. The two extremes of the endless cycle occur when earth, air, fire, and water are all completely intermingled (*Philotes* in the ascendant) and when all four are separated and arranged in concentric spheres with the heaviest—earth—at the center, and the lightest—fire—at the circumference (*Neikos* in the ascendant). The importance of *Philotes* and *Neikos* is evidently much greater in Empedocles than in Hesiod. One might compare the importance of Eros in the *Theogony*.

I have commented on *philotes* and *neikos* merely because both occur in both writers. My concerns are more general: how do the personalized abstracts of Hesiod and other early writers differ from the abstracts treated as moving causes by Empedocles? Why is Empedocles treated as a philosopher and Hesiod as a writer of myths?[21] Maybe it will be illuminating to ask whether there is an essential difference between them.[22] I shall say only a few words here, since I have analyzed the thought of Hesiod elsewhere.[23]

(c) The Rationality of Hesiod

Hesiod and his contemporaries believed that most of what we regard as the regularities of nature—spring, summer, autumn, winter—and natural catastrophes—earthquake, drought, famine, pestilence[24]—are in fact signs of the approval or disapproval of deities. These deities are treated as the most powerful persons in the cosmos, the superaristocrats. None is omnipotent; indeed, none ought to be omnipotent.[25] Zeus, like the supreme deities before him, Uranus and Cronus, maintains his position by a network of alliances based on kinship, marriage, or reciprocal advantages. Zeus is in power now because he proved the better politician; a mistake might prove his downfall.[26] His worshipers look on Zeus and the other gods as superaristocrats, and not surprisingly endow them with the same kind of values as human aristocrats and the same kinds of motive as actuate human aristocrats in their familial and extrafamilial relationships and in their relations with mortals. Since the Greeks of this period see the hand of the gods everywhere, the stage is set for a *reasoned* explanation of everything that happens in these terms. I have argued elsewhere that

Hesiod's two surviving works constituted a heroic and largely successful intellectual effort to bring order and explanation out of chaos.
Empedocles too is concerned with explaining the world as it is. (Is his
work treated as more philosophical because it is printed in Diels-
Kranz?)[27] I suspect that the real reason is that we tend to classify with
hindsight. We know what turned out to be the fruitful way of thinking
in the long run. In the history of thought, the Empedocles have
proved more successful than the Hesiods.

(iii) Muthos, *Myth, and Rationality*

   (a) Apollo, Agamemnon, and Achilles

So is there no characteristic 'muthic' or mythic mode of thought
in Greece? Does the Greek myth or *muthos* not make moves in logic
which would shock Aristotle? Not many, so far as mortals' transactions
with the gods are concerned. Consider this example: (a) 'Plagues are
signs of the anger of Apollo; there is a plague in our army; Apollo
must be angry.' (b) 'I do not know why Apollo is angry; seers can find
out why gods are angry, and Apollo is a god; therefore we should consult a seer.' (c) 'We should consult a seer; Calchas is a seer, and the
most available seer; therefore we should consult Calchas.' (d) 'Calchas
has told us that Apollo is angry because his priest Chryses has complained to him that Agamemnon has refused to ransom back Chryses'
daughter to him and demands that Agamemnon return her to her
father without recompense, and make an expensive animal sacrifice in
addition; therefore we should return Chryseis to her father on these
conditions.' Any of these logical moves could be expressed rigorously
in a logic of terms or propositions; indeed, as a sequence, they strongly resemble part of Aristotle's account of deliberation (*bouleusis*) in the
Nicomachean Ethics (1112a18-1113a2). It may well be argued that these
examples of reasoning are not relevant, since *Iliad* 1 is neither a myth
nor a *muthos*. It is, however, at least a transaction concerning a god
and several mortals. When—or if—we find a satisfactory cross-cultural definition of myth, we shall be able to decide whether *Iliad* 1 is or is
not one. At all events, the examples show that rational argument was
possible in about 700 BC in Greece. It was not left to Aristotle to
make men rational. However, we may ask whether there is a sense of
'myth' (or indeed *muthos*) in which this kind of rationality is not found.

I am not inquiring whether or not there are invalid arguments in Homer or Hesiod. There are invalid arguments in Plato—and in Aristotle. Nor am I inquiring whether characters in the works of Hesiod or Homer ever *behave* irrationally, whether after careful deliberation or in the heat of emotion. My question is rather whether any fundamental logical principle is consistently ignored in the poems.

(b) The Mythic, the Muthic, and the Logical

Let us consider, then, whether myths or *muthoi* found in extant Greek documents regularly transgress any of the traditional 'laws of thought': the law of identity ('if anything is P it is P'), the law of contradiction ('nothing can be both P and not -P') and the law of excluded middle ('anything must be either P or not -P'). A thing is what it is and not another thing.' 'If this is a donkey it is not a horse.' But this principle does not exclude the existence of mules, each of which is what it is and not another thing. 'If this is a mule it is not a donkey' is true, as is 'If this is a mule it is neither a donkey nor a horse.' Compare 'If this is a mule it is both a donkey and a horse'; but this is simply untrue. It is notorious that in myth—and this at least is certainly found in early Greek myth—natural phenomena are treated simultaneously as features of the landscape and as deities with personalities.[28] So, in a myth similar to one found in many other cultures, Uranus (Heaven), having covered Gaia (Earth), his mother, impregnated her, the result being Oceanus with his deep eddies, Coeus, Creius, Hyperion, Iapetus, Theia, Rhea, Custom-Right, Memory, gold-crowned Phoebe, and lovely Tethys (Hesiod, *Theogony* 126-36). This is a hodgepodge of natural and cultural phenomena, treated also as persons, and deities which were apparently always persons. Hesiod seems to treat them very similarly. Small wonder that Eros has such a prominent place in the *Theogony*.[29]

(c) Nature-Deities, Logic, and Mules

It cannot be denied that the early Greeks, like participants in many other cultures, personalized and ascribed motives to phenomena of this kind. The modern reader may well be prepared to stretch a point in favor of Hesiod, since theogonies are a rather specialized genre. However, a century or so later the Athenian lawgiver Solon, in one of his most prosaic poems, the function of which is to justify his political program, writes in contiguous lines of 'Earth, the mother of the

Olympian gods' and of the black earth of Attica from which he had removed the markers which were everywhere planted in it. My 'Earth' and 'earth' are translating not merely the same Greek word but the same instance of the same word. What can we infer from this? Should we conclude that in the minds of Hesiod and Solon, and other early Greeks, there is nothing to encourage them to assent to the following inferences rather than to reject them? (a) 'if this is a natural feature of the landscape it is not at the same time an anthropomorphic deity' or (b) 'if this is an anthropomorphic deity it is not at the same time a natural feature of the landscape'? We need not demand such abstract expressions. It will suffice if it can be said or thought by archaic Greeks 'if gods look like us (pointing to each other) they do not look like that' (pointing to a river) or 'if gods look like that (pointing to river) they do not look like us.' To achieve a situation similar to 'horse, donkey, mule' we need (1) some anthropomorphic deities who are not at the same time natural features of the landscape, (2) some natural features of the landscape which are not at the same time anthropomorphic deities, and (3) some entities which are neither anthropomorphic deities nor natural features of the landscape, but recognizable as having modified characteristics of each in the way that mules have modified characteristics of each of their parents without belonging to the species of either. The problem is (2): this set seems to be empty. Among the Greek gods there are horses and mules but no donkeys. One might reply that if one lived in a land which bred its own horses but imported its mules it would be possible to distinguish between horses and mules without knowing anything about donkeys. To be sure it would; but if we now turn back to the text of Hesiod, we shall, I think, find little to suggest that Hesiod is making any distinction between (1) and (3). I have already mentioned Uranus (type 3). He also begat the Titans (type 1, apparently) (Hesiod, *Theogony*, 207-8); and while Night's giving birth to Sleep and Dreams might be a trope, readily expressed in less figurative language, her giving birth to black Fate, Death, Blame, and Woeful Lamentation seems much less likely to be figurative. (If these examples are not persuasive, the *Theogony* contains many more.) If extenuation is needed, Solon might today point out that he and his contemporaries and their forbears ascribed such dual nature to only a limited number of entities, i.e. gods, and not to all of those, whereas we have a similar, generally accepted view applicable to all the contents of the cosmos, at a certain level.[30]

   I grant that these deities are peculiar.[31] (Many gods in Hesiod are not of this kind.) But I do not discern any separate form of reasoning, merely a different set of premises and presuppositions. Homer, Hesiod, and their contemporaries also treat certain features of the cosmos as divine beings which may have purposes of their own. But having done so, they use the concept 'nature-deity' in what seems to me to be a rational manner. At all events Hesiod, treating all these deities as intelligent and anthropomorphic,[32] and linked by bonds formed by blood, marriage, and political alliance, constructs in the *Theogony*, when combined with the *Works and Days*, a framework within which the whole of the visible world, and anything which happens to anyone in that world, can be explained. I do not seek to persuade my readers that Hesiod is an unappreciated philosopher, simply that sustained intellectual effort in the interest of synthesis and comprehensible order may be expended by those who are not philosophers.

(d) Rationality and Empedocles

But if we grant this point, where does it leave Empedocles? Are his *Neikos* and *Philotes* efficient causes, general laws, or something else? Is it clear that they are not (a) personalized? (b) deities? (c) anthropomorphic? We can, I think, rule out (c).[33] But can we be certain that they are not still in some sense deities of the Hesiodic kind? Did Empedocles have any vocabulary in which to draw the distinction? It has frequently been observed that at least the earlier pre-Socratics had no problem with accounting for movement in the cosmos. Apparently they were tacitly denying the existence not of deities who would serve as moving causes, but of anthropomorphic deities.

(e) Muthos *and Thucydides*

Let me now turn to the evidence of Thucydides, an avowed foe of *muthos*. Thucydides is frequently treated as a more philosophical writer than seems warranted. Certainly he was an outstandingly perceptive and intelligent thinker, given to thinking about the principles and problems of historical method, but not a philosopher either in the modern or the wider sense. Thucydides claimed to have banished *to muthodes*, the 'muthical', or '*muthos*-like' from his writings. He is evidently sniping at Herodotus, with whom Thucydides, as 'the first modern historian', is often contrasted. It is frequently taken for granted that Thucydides accepts as historical only what a modern historian would accept. In fact, he seems to accept Minos, and all of the events of the Trojan War, as historical. He also accepts the existence of Pelops, and other eponymous ancestors, to whom the names of noble families and geographical areas were traced ('Peloponnese', interpreted as 'the island of Pelops'), presumably including Heracles, son of the god Zeus and the mortal Alcmene,[34] since he uses the term *Heraclidae*, 'descendants of Heracles', for the most aristocratic of the Spartans as freely as he speaks of the Pelopidae, 'descendants of Pelops'. He seems to treat Homer as a historian, but not a very good one. It is true—indeed, notorious—that Thucydides banished the gods[35] as causes from his history, and presumably this is what he meant when he claimed to have excluded *to muthodes*. There is no 'muthical' period, no *illud tempus*, no 'dreamtime', only a period for which the evidence is quite good, and an earlier period for which the evidence has become contaminated by the 'muthical'. It is worthwhile to compare Hesiod, whose mode of thought is *prima facie* very different. Hesiod employs the myth of the four metal *gene*, best rendered by 'races' (*Works and Days* 109-201), a variety of myth found elsewhere. Hesiod's version takes it for granted that each race—Golden, Silver, Bronze, and Iron—is a distinct creation of the gods. Thus far he is within the category of myth.[36] But, as has frequently been observed, Hesiod and his contemporaries knew that an age of prosperity and achievement had immediately preceded their own, which Hesiod represents as one of misery, though not the worst that will happen. In consequence, he introduces the Race of the Heroes between the Bronze and the Iron, and disrupts the schematic myth in the interests of what looks very like history. This seems to be a Greek characteristic. In professing to have excluded *to muthodes*, Thucydides is making a strong truth-claim: in his eyes, the *muthodes* is to be equated with the false.[37]

C. *Myth*, Muthos *and* Logos *in* Plato

(i) *Protagoras*

(a) *Explanation by* Muthos *and Explanation by* Logos

I now turn to Plato, and first to the myth of Protagoras in Plato's *Protagoras*, which is probably the earliest *muthos* in Plato's works. There it is Protagoras, not Socrates, who claims to be the author. That Plato has 'borrowed' a genuine Protagorean work seems improbable, though there was nothing to prevent him from so doing since all published work was in the public domain.[38] It is also improbable that the motive for its inclusion is *merely* unfriendly parody. The speech as a whole contains not only much that is admirable but also much that Plato presumably thought was admirable, since it is endorsed by Plato's Socrates, e.g. the reformative and exemplary interpretation of punishment. Responding to Socrates' statement that he had not previously supposed that *arete* was teachable/taught, and his wily request for enlightenment from Protagoras who claims to teach it, Protagoras inquires of the assembled company whether, 'as an older man to younger men,' he should show them by telling a *muthos*, or by going through (the matter) 'by means of a *logos*.' Those present urge him to do whichever he wishes, and in fact he does both. The implication is that one can convey (the same?) truth in either mode; and in fact Protagoras does both, having suggested that a *muthos qua muthos* is more suited to those who are either relatively or absolutely old when communicating with the young. He also says that it will be more *charien*, charming, elegant, to tell a *muthos*. The emphasis on the difference in ages may represent an appeal to authority where the truth of *muthoi* is in question.

What in Protagoras' long speech (320c8–328c2) is the difference between the *logos* and the *muthos*? We have already observed that Protagoras regards both as being legitimate ways of making his point. (Those who read the *Protagoras* in isolation from other Platonic dialogues may draw the immediate—and false—conclusion that Plato thus portrays Protagoras as a mere 'sophist' and no philosopher.[39] As we shall see, Plato uses both methods himself. I shall inquire below whether he does it in the same way.) Protagoras' *muthos* treats the present situation of mankind as the result of divine (or at all events superhuman)[40] activity in the past, and as being partly due to skills and other qualities which the gods were originally unwilling to share with mankind, an attitude to gods which is not confined to Greece. In early times, Prometheus (Forethought) and Epimetheus (Afterthought) were assigned the task of furnishing the species of animals with appropriate means to protect themselves against other species. Here the *muthos* is evidently in the realm of myth. But these 'mythic' elements are interwoven with very acute observations on the means by which the survival of the nonhuman species is assured. They are naturally furnished with protection against the weather, the predators reproduce in smaller numbers than their prey, and so on. There is no thought of the evolution of species by the survival of the fittest, but we cannot regard either Plato or Protagoras as stupid in not reaching Darwinism at a single bound. Protagoras relates

that the gods wanted mankind to have some means of protection comparable with those of the other animals. Epimetheus persuaded
Prometheus to let him apportion the different means of self-protection.
In his folly, Epimetheus used up all his supplies of hooves, hides, and so
on before reaching the human race. (The names of Epimetheus and
Prometheus suggest a moral fable.) Since the day for completing the
task was at hand, Prometheus first stole fire and the arts and crafts of
Athena and Hephaestus. This solved some, but not all, of mankind's
problems. They had the ability to protect themselves against the weather, but not the art of politics, of which the art of war is a part.
Consequently, being too weak to defend themselves individually against
wild beasts, they attempted to gather together and form poleis, but
behaved unjustly to one another—inasmuch as they did not possess the
political art, *techne*—with the result that they scattered again and continued to be destroyed by wild beasts. Not wishing the human race to be
destroyed, Zeus sent the messenger-god Hermes to bring to them *aidos
kai dike*, mutual respect and justice. All must have these, unlike the arts;
anyone incapable of *aidos kai dike* must be killed, as a disease of the polis.

What makes this story a myth, or at all events a *muthos*? It certainly includes gods as moving causes,[41] whose past actions are used to
explain the present state of society in general and the present practices
of the Athenians in particular. In a sense, the rest of the *muthos* is there
simply to answer the questions Socrates asked (in 319a8-320c1): (a) why,
on matters involving arts or crafts, do the Athenians in assembly accept
the advice only of experts, whereas all are permitted to speak on general
Athenian policy? and (b) why are politicians frequently less 'good' than
their fathers?[42] Note that, strictly speaking, Protagoras has answered
only (a) in his myth. To explain (b) he might have added that *aidos* and
dike are unlike the arts in being essential for anyone who is to live as a
human being; but they are like the arts in that one person differs from
another in his aptitudes for *aidos* and *dike*. Protagoras offers this explanation, or one quite like it (but not till 326e5), in the course of his *logos*,
which offers a very shrewd and perceptive account of the socialization of
the young, and the not-so-young, into the values of society.[43]

(b) Muthos *and* Logos *in the* Protagoras

I shall inquire below whether anything can be learnt about the
truth-claims of *muthos* and *logos*, in general or in Plato—or
Protagoras—from Protagoras' long speech. First let me inquire more

generally how the *muthos* differs from the *logos*. The *muthos* is evidently narrative in form; but the *logos* of the *Protagoras* too is not essentially a close argument but an exposition. The *muthos* is certainly a *muthos* in the sense of 'story', and also in the sense of 'story involving the actions of nonhuman agents'. Since it also explains why the Athenians behave as they do, it may also be categorized in addition as aetiological. It uses a somewhat heightened style. For example, *dikaiosune*, not *dike*, is the word for 'justice' in Attic prose at this time. It also treats *aidos* and *dike* as reified entities rather then capacities or dispositions leading to behavior of certain kinds.

But there is no real conflict between the message of the *muthos* and the message of the *logos*. Protagoras is reported to have said 'Concerning the gods I am not able to have knowledge, neither that they exist nor that they do not exist, nor what they are like in appearance. Many are the factors which prevent knowledge: the lack of clarity in the subject and the shortness of human life.'[44] ·

Modern scholars have interpreted Protagoras' words variously as (a) atheistic, (b) agnostic, and (c) devout.[45] It has been argued, or merely assumed, that if either (a) or (b) is true, Protagoras must regard his *muthos* as expressing no significant truth. But the observations on the survival of species are well observed; and other thinkers of this period combine 'philosophical' theories about nature with writings that the modern reader inevitably regards as less than philosophical or scientific.

Empedocles wrote not only an *On Nature* but also a *Purifications*, using an important term in Greek religion (*katharmos*, related to *katharsis*); Parmenides wrote not merely a *Way of Truth* but also a *Way of Opinion*. Presumably they believed that the non-'scientific' poems conveyed something that it was worthwhile to convey to their readers, even if the modern reader may well suppose that the 'scientific' poem had already ruled out what is maintained in the non-'scientific' poem.[46] In offering both a *muthos* and a *logos* concerned with the same or similar subject matter, Protagoras is in good company.

If we make allowance for the fact that *aidos* and *dike* are treated as things rather than capacities, as is natural to the style, the *muthos* (322d1-5) seems to have the same theory of punishment as the *logos*. Protagoras closes by showing how his *muthos* explains human evaluations. It is democratic in its implications. The *logos* explores Athenian attitudes to the crafts and to *politike arete*. (The phrase is equivocal in the manner mentioned in note 39 above. It possesses connotations both of moral excellence and political skill.) Not to claim 'political excellence' would be absurd, whether one had it or not. But to claim to have skill in carpentry when one had not would be equally absurd.

As is already clear, the *logos* offers the 'reformative/exemplary' theory of punishment, maintains that everyone socializes the young, and claims that the reason why the sons of the politicians are sometimes inferior to their fathers is the same as the reason why craftsmen's sons are. As a professional teacher, Protagoras has painted himself into a corner for he must now acknowledge that he can claim no more than that he is a little better than everyone else at this instruction which all give. 328c3 seems to make the claim that both the *muthos* and the *logos* have performed the same task, or have each contributed to the whole. The *aition* of the behavior about which Socrates asked is given in the *muthos* (322c5ff). The *logos explains* and demonstrates (e.g. 324c8).

Protagoras ends his long speech thus (328c3): "Socrates, I have uttered both a *muthos* and a *logos* of this kind for you, to show that *arete* is something *didakton* ('taught, teachable'),[47] and that the Athenians think so, and that it is in no way surprising that inferior sons come from good parents and good sons from inferior parents." Since Protagoras offers both a *muthos* and a *logos*, presumably he believed that a *muthos*—or perhaps 'even a *muthos*'—might be the carrier of truth. He is making a truth-claim for the *muthos*, but we might well ask about the truth-value of individual sentences in the *muthos*. The question of the relationship between the truth-values of the individual statements in a *muthos* or myth and the acceptability of the myth as in some sense true is an interesting and complex one, to which doubtless different cultures give different answers. I shall discuss Plato's answer later.

(c) Muthos *and* Logos *in Early Greece*

What is the difference between a *muthos* and a *logos*? The answer is not constant. In Xenophanes, a philosopher and (mediocre) poet whose long and productive life spanned the later sixth century and early fifth century, there occurs the line "with pious *muthoi* and pure *logoi*."[48] There is no agreement among scholars over the meaning of either word here, except that it seems to be different from the usage of the later fifth and earlier fourth centuries. Bowra very plausibly suggested 'stories' for *muthoi* and 'themes' for *logoi*, pointing out that Pindar twice uses *muthos* for false stories and that in each case other words in the context establish that 'false story' is meant.[49]

Traditionally, then, in the Greek usage of the archaic period, not all *muthoi* are myths. Nor are all myths *muthoi*. Hesiod introduces the

'Myth of the Five Races' thus (*Works and Days* 106-07): "Or, if you wish, I will tell you another *logos*."

(ii) Gorgias

(a) Muthos *or* Logos?

I now turn to the *Gorgias* myth, narrated by Socrates. Socrates—and presumably he speaks for Plato—denies that the following words constitute a *muthos* (522e3): "For to go to the house of Hades with one's *psuche* swollen with injustice is the worst of all. And if you like, I am willing to deliver a *logos* to explain how this is so. . . . Hear, then, a very beautiful *logos*, which you, I suppose, will think of as a *muthos*, whereas I think of it as a *logos*. For it is on the assumption that they are true that I shall say the things I am going to say."

This claim is to be found at the end of the dialogue in which Socrates has defeated Gorgias, Polus, and Callicles in argument concerning the questions (a) whether the teacher of rhetoric should teach his pupils to be just as well as to be skillful with words, and (b) whether the practice of justice or the practice of rhetoric will better secure one's *eudaimonia*, 'human flourishing'.[50]

Despite his complete inability to find fault with Socrates' (frequently invalid) arguments, Callicles keeps reiterating 'common sense' views, maintaining that Socrates would never win a case in court and that *eudaimonia* interpreted as "material well-being and the means to defend it" should be one's goal at all times, not *eudaimonia* interpreted as "the well-being of one's *psuche*" as Socrates has contended throughout.

Since Callicles is unmoved by Socrates' arguments, Socrates tries another method, the myth/*muthos*, or as Socrates claims, the *logos*, of the *Gorgias*. The question whether Socrates would be successful in an Athenian popular court is swept aside as irrelevant. The important court is elsewhere. In the early years of the rule of Zeus, and previously, the intent was that mortals should be judged at the end of their lives in respect of their justice, the just going to the Isles of the Blest, and the unjust to Tartarus; but since they were judged in life, while still in their bodies, by judges similarly in their bodies, many mistakes occurred, since the judges were misled if the person under scrutiny had a handsome body or fine clothing. So early in his rule Zeus decided to change the practice.

Since that time, *psuchai* have been judged after death—when the *psuche* leaves the body—by a panel of famous judges from the past

(Minos, Rhadamanthus, and Aeacus, themselves dead) with the result that *psuchai* in themselves are judged by other well-qualified *psuchai*, who cannot be misled by the earthly status of the *psuche* in its recent embodied life since they do not know the identity of any *psuche* that comes before them but merely the condition of the *psuche*, on which the scars and malformations caused by an unjust and generally immoral life are plain for all to see.

As the corpse retains characteristics—the scars from wounds, etc., suffered by the living person—so does the *psuche* (524e): Rhadamanthus looks at the *psuche* of each, not knowing whose it is. He may well grasp the *psuche* of the Great King or some other king; but he sees nothing really healthy in the *psuche*, rather that it bears the mark of lashes and is covered with scars from perjured oaths and injustice, and everything crippled by falsehood and nothing straightforward on account of an upbringing without truth (fulness).

In response to the admiration expressed for tyrants earlier in the dialogue, Socrates says that Archelaus, tyrant of Macedon, will be there and that the majority of those who are incurable are kings, tyrants, *dunastai*, and prominent politicians. They, because of their greater ability to do so, commit the greatest and most unholy 'errors'. He cites Homer's Tantalus, Sisyphus, and Tityus as kings, but does not explain what they did to merit such eternal punishment.[51]

How much more *eudaimon* was Thersites,[52] who did not have the opportunity to commit such things. Those most likely to go to the Isles of the Blest are private citizens, most likely a philosopher who 'did his own thing' and did not 'do many things' in his life.[53] Socrates assures Callicles that Callicles will be in the same condition before the Last Tribunal as Socrates before an earthly tribunal (526d2) and adds (527a5): "Perhaps all of this seems to you to be a *muthos* that an old woman might tell, and you despise it, and there would be nothing surprising in your doing so, if by searching we were able to find something better and truer." But the wisest of the Greeks—by whom he means not himself but Gorgias, Polus, and Callicles, the three interlocutors of the *Gorgias*—have been unable to do so.[54]

Injustice is its own punishment, and the *psuche* of an unjust person shows its scars when disembodied at the Last Judgment; but in the next world there is also tenfold punishment for the misdeeds of this life. Those whose *psuche* is incurable—if alive—should be put to death; if dead, they will serve as exempla forevermore. The purpose of punishment is the same as in Protagoras' long speech—*muthos* and *logos*—discussed above, reformative for the majority, exemplary for those who are incurably unjust. Earlier in the dialogue Socrates used a favorite parallelism between body and *psuche*. He claims to have proved that injustice mars the *psuche* in the same way as illness or accident harms the body and reasonably assumes that those with unhealthy bodies would wish to avail themselves of the medical art to restore them to health. Since the harm suffered by those with unhealthy *psuchai* is suffered in the most important part of themselves,[55] and punishment is the counterpart of the medical art, it follows that the best thing one can do for an unjust friend is to hale him into court, while taking every opportunity to prevent one's enemies from ever coming into court at all. The conclusion is bizarre, but it follows from the premises.

(b) A Myth but not a Muthos

We may now ask ourselves what difference it makes whether Socrates' speech is a *muthos* or a *logos*. If one accepts his premise of the immortality of the *psuche*[56] and his arguments that injustice (*adikia*) is or causes 'psuchic' ill health and inferiority, then one should in one's own interest shun injustice. This premise is fundamental to both the arguments of the *Gorgias* and to its myth/*logos*. Indeed, during the arguments Socrates draws a new distinction between *techne* ('art, craft, technical skill') and *empeiria* ('mere knack'). The distinction is based on the ability of the possessor of a *techne* to give a *logos* (account) of what he is doing; and there may be a hint, when Socrates calls his myth a *logos*, that he is claiming possession of a *techne* in such matters.

(iv) Phaedo

(a) Muthos but Not Logos

I now turn to the myth of the *Phaedo*, which Plato portrays as narrated by the imprisoned Socrates to his friends at the end of the last day of his life. It follows an argument on the immortality of the *psuche*. Socrates draws the consequence that immortality renders death more important. Were death the end, the unjust man would be rid of the *kaka*, harm, done to his *psuche* by the way he has lived. But as it is, since the *psuche* is immortal it would have no escape from the harm that its injustice had inflicted on it, and no safety, other than by becoming as excellent and *phronimos*, practically wise, as possible. The soul takes no baggage with it to Hades other than its education and nurture. These are said to benefit or harm the *psuche* immediately on departing on its journey thither. "It is said thus, that[57] on the death of each human being the *daimon*[58] who was allotted to him when he was yet alive tries to get him to 'a certain place.'"[59]

Socrates insists, against Aeschylus, that the road to Hades is complex.[60] Otherwise, why should a guide be necessary? The *kosmia kai phronimos* ('orderly and practically wise') *psuche* follows its guide. The *psuche* that still desires its body flutters near the earth as a ghost, but in the end the allotted *daimon* leads it there against its will.

Those *psuchai* that have committed grave crimes[61] are shunned by the other *psuchai*, and those *psuchai* that are reluctant to leave the body wander about in the utmost distress until, after a certain time has elapsed, they are taken to their fitting abode. The *psuche* that has lived with purity and moderation, however, with gods as its fellow-travelers and leaders, dwells in its appropriate place.

Plato next moves to a mythic account of the world and compares the living to frogs living round a pond—the Mediterranean, one of many such ponds. Water and mist and air have flowed into the hollows of these ponds. The living do not live in the real air, which we call the *aither*. We are in the same situation as would be someone who lived in the depth of the sea and, seeing the stars through the water, believed the sea to be the heavens. If anyone of us could reach the real surface of the earth, he would be amazed by the clarity of the *aither*.

From this beginning, Socrates gradually develops an account of the abode of the dead, linking it with the geography. Socrates makes clear his views on the truth of his geography and eschatology in this *muthos*, at all events (in 108 d1-e2 and 114d-115a): the geography is what Socrates himself believes.[62] I shall discuss his account of the eschatology later.

The method of punishment differs strikingly from that in the *Gorgias*. It seems to be modeled on a state of society when the household was much more the locus of reward and punishment than was the polis.[63] The incurable wrongdoers are not led away by officials appointed for the purpose (114a) but swept by their appropriate *moira*[64] into Tartarus, from which they never return. Those less bad necessarily fall into Tartarus but a year later are swept back to the Acheronian Swamp, the homicides down the River of Lamentation and the parent-beaters down the River of Blazing Fire. The only way to get out is by persuading those whom the *psuche* wronged in life to forgive. Otherwise, it is swept back to Tartarus. Socrates adds "for this was the dicasts' sentence."[65] Minos, Aeacus, and Radamanthus seem to have vanished and to have been replaced by a jury. One possibility is that Plato is drawing on a democratic myth, but in the circumstances, on the last day of Socrates' life, it seems more likely that Socrates is implicitly alluding to the fact that though he is to be executed unjustly on the sentence of an earthly jury, the jury that votes the sentence after death does not make mistakes. (The *Gorgias* must surely be earlier.)

The reward in this myth of those who have lived *hosiôs*, 'in a holy manner,' is to escape from the 'pooliverse'[66] and live on the surface of the earth. Philosophers are the most likely to qualify. Those who do qualify live without their bodies forevermore.[67] Socrates now offers some practical advice. He does not vouch for his account as being correct in detail: it befits no one with any *nous* to do so. "But that this or something like it is the case with respect to our *psuchai* and their dwelling-places, since the *psuche* has proved to be something immortal, it seems fitting to me and worthy to hazard believing that it is the case—for the hazard is a noble one—and one ought to chant such things to oneself.[68] This is the reason why I have been prolonging my *muthos* for some time." Socrates continues by advising all to shun the body's pleasures and its adornments on the grounds that they are alien to the *psuche*[69] and give weight to those pleasures concerned with learning, having adorned his *psuche* not with alien adornments but with its own—that is to say, with temperance, justice, courage, freedom, and truth. A man who has lived in such a manner should be of good cheer as he awaits his journey to the House of Hades.

(b) Muthos *and Myth*

This narrative, which is both *muthos* and myth, is clearly more cautious than the myth of the *Gorgias*, which Socrates treats as a *logos*. Socrates treats the confidence of the *Gorgias* as something that no intelligent person could appropriately have in these matters. So what he narrates here is a *muthos*. It is worth considering what ground is being conceded. In the evaluation of the *Gorgias*, *muthos* is 'mere myth', not to be accepted where *logos* is available, for anything accepted as a *logos* makes a very strong truth-claim. The *muthos* of the *Phaedo* is evidently not regarded as merely fiction, as perhaps a *muthos* in explicit opposition to a *logos* might have been; but, as we have seen, all is on the level of 'it must be something like that, though I won't vouch for the details. The hazard is a noble one.'

(v) Republic

(a) Er and the Eye-Witnessed Muthos

Like the *Gorgias*-myth, the Myth of Er in the *Republic* is set at the end of its dialogue. In the *Gorgias*, after narrating the myth/*logos*, Plato's Socrates says that Callicles may think what is said is merely a *muthos* such as an old woman might tell, but that the three wisest (*sophôtatoi*) men in Greece have not been able to find anything better or truer (*Gorgias* 527a-b). He is evidently referring to the whole dialogue in which Gorgias, Polus, and Callicles have been successively routed by Socrates' often-invalid arguments, not merely to the myth/*logos*. Now, immediately before the Myth of Er, Socrates claims that he has done what he was asked to do by Glaucon and Adimantus at the beginning of Book 2. He has demonstrated the choiceworthiness of justice no matter how dire the consequences of pursuing a just course of life might be. He has shown that justice is an intrinsic good which outweighs any conceivable harm that anyone might suffer in consequence of leading a just life, and that injustice is an intrinsic ill so serious that no amount of success gained by means of unjust behavior could possibly outweigh it. Having carried out this task to his apparent satisfaction, the Platonic Socrates asks that his interlocutors now permit him to restore to the just man the additional rewards that will in fact come to him from being just, not merely status and honor in this life, but beyond it.

The myth he relates is once again concerned with the Last Judgment, and a very strong truth-claim is made. (Socrates calls it a *muthos* in 621b8, nevertheless.) Socrates claims to be reporting an eye-witness—more properly, *psuche*-witness—account of what Er saw when out of his body, which was lying "dead" on the battlefield. Er had been selected to return to the land of the living and warn them of the Last Judgment. Er describes, or rather is reported as describing, the topography of the place of judgment for the newly arrived *psuchai*; the judgment—by unnamed 'dicasts' here, as in the *Phaedo*—and the labeling of the *psuchai* as bound for the place of reward or punishment. They departed to their appointed place. Those who had already been rewarded or punished arrived at *the* meadow (616b2) for the choice of a new life. They encamped "as for a festival," acquaintances recognizing acquaintances and all inquiring about the journeys that the others had taken. Those asked replied in appropriate terms and with emotions appropriate to the tenfold reward or punishment that they had received.

Note that all the immediately specified wrongdoing is political rather than concerned with private life.[70] Socrates' words in 615c2 suggest a belief in limbo and also that Socrates is narrating an account written by someone else.[71] The greatest punishment, with no end, is reserved for tyrants and, of private individuals, those who have committed the greatest crimes.[72] The less power an unjust person has the better for his own sake.

Next (616b4-617d5) the *psuchai* go on a four-day journey to a place where one can see a mythologized account of what was held to be literally the case by the astronomers of the day. A place is found in this cosmos for the traditional *Moirai* (Sharers): Clotho, Lachesis, and Atropos, the 'Daughters of Necessity'.[73] This leads up to the speech of Lachesis:[74]

> The logos[75] of Lachesis, the maiden daughter of Necessity. Ephemeral psuchai, the beginning of another circuit of mortal birth that brings death.[76] No daimon shall cast lots for you, rather shall you choose a daimon. Let him who draws the first lot choose a life that shall be his from necessity. Arete has no master. The more each person honors or dishonors her, the more or less of her shall that person have. Responsibility of the chooser; god without responsibility.

There followed the distribution of the lots, and each *psuche*—except Er, who was prevented since he was to return to continue his own life—picked up the nearest and so established its order in the choice. Then patterns of all kinds of lives, human and animal, far more than there were choosers, were scattered before the *psuchai*. In some cases the choice had evident moral consequences, in others apparently not. The first choice was made by a *psuche* from a well-governed polis (619d6), a person who in the last life had partaken of *arete*, but as a result of good training, not philosophy. His *arete* had been duly rewarded for a thousand years. Despite his training, he still chose the biggest tyranny and only then realized that it included great crimes and misfortunes. The good character acquired in one life is not carried over into the disembodied *psuche*. The point is explicitly made. Before the choice, there is no *taxis* (order, arrangement) of the psuche, since the *taxis* will be a consequence of the choice made. It is justice, not philosophy, that is rewarded in Hades, and injustice punished. Again, the *psuchai* choose their next lives before they reach Carefree River in Forgetfulness Plain, and so might be expected to draw appropriate conclusions from their experiences and contrast them with the experiences of those coming up from punishment, of which they have been told.

Plato's point seems to be that only philosophy can *guarantee* the right choice in general and this choice in particular. Observation or narration of the punishments of others may not suffice. Socrates here turns to address Glaucon, and says that the whole danger for any human being[77] resides in this choice, so that one should take great care to find, if one can, someone who will make one capable and skilled at distinguishing between the good and bad choices of life, and always and everywhere choose the better of what is possible; 'better' meaning 'more likely to lead to the justice of the *psuche*.'

(b) Philosophy, Muthos, *and Salvation*

In the Myth of Er, only philosophy will ensure that one makes the best choice available. But not all can choose to be philosophers. There are many more schemes of lives than *psuchai* to choose them, and enough to furnish even the last chooser with a life that is *agapetos*, as the *prophetes* says (619b2-6). The precise sense of *agapetos* is perhaps unclear but it is certainly not strong enough to enable one to infer that all can become philosophers and so guarantee that the crucial choices will be correctly made.[78] Indeed, Socrates' direct address to Glaucon (618b6-619b8) indicates that in most cases the luck of the draw will mean that a careful balance of pros and cons will have to be made, the pro being any aspect of the life that renders one more just, the con the reverse.

After the choices were complete, the *psuchai* approached Lachesis in the order that the lot had assigned to them. She sent the *daimon* that each had chosen forth with the *psuche* to watch over the soon-to-be-embodied *psuche* and to bring to pass what had been chosen (620d6-e1). After Clotho, Lachesis, and Atropos had each taken a part in ensuring the inevitability of what had been chosen, the *psuchai* passed under the Throne of Necessity and thence to Forgetfulness Plain, across a hot and waterless desert. They then came to Careless River, "whose water no container can hold." Everyone except Er was forced to drink a measure of this water; some, parched by the heat of the desert, drank more than a measure. Since those who drank a measure forgot everything, presumably those who drank more than a measure acquired some additional disability not made clear. Er was prevented from drinking any of the water and so returned to the world of the living, to find his body lying on the funeral pyre.

Socrates himself terms this myth a *muthos*: "and in this manner the *muthos* was saved and did not perish" (621b8). In this account,

Socrates can make the strong truth-claim implied by an account told by someone who had 'been there', and nevertheless term the account a *muthos*. How are we to understand this myth/*muthos* and the sequence of myths—some of which are *muthoi*—in which it occurs? And what are the relationships between the myths, and any links there may be with the other uses of *muthos* that I have discussed?

D. *Myth*, Muthos, *Aristotle, and Greek Tragedy*

Now a few—inadequately few—words on Greek tragedy. When Aristotle used *muthos* for the plot both of tragedy and comedy in his *Poetics* (1449b5, 1450a4, 1451a16), he almost certainly meant to convey simply 'plot' or 'story' for few Greek comedies contain either myths or *muthoi*; and presumably the word has the same connotations in each kind of drama.[79] No extant writer followed him in this usage; and Aeschylus, Sophocles, and Euripides had not had the good fortune of having read Aristotle. But, whatever word the tragic poets used for the plots of their plays, the plots would presumably be regarded as containing the *muthodes* by Thucydides, and as myth by many people; so that Greek tragedy is worth discussing here. Myth or *muthos*, the tragic plot is flexible in some ways: for example, Aeschylus' *Oresteia* is a version of the story, myth, or *muthos* of the House of Atreus which ends on a resolution which required much ingenuity and hard thought. Sophocles and Euripides produce different versions of the death of Aegisthus and Clytemnestra at the hands of Orestes, and the consequences, which evaluate the roles of Orestes and Electra quite differently. The oracle given to Laius is subtly different in Aeschylus' *Seven against Thebes* and in Sophocles' *Oedipus Rex*, and indeed varies within the plays.[80] Some of the changes are made on ethical or dramatic grounds. In Greek tragedy, then, evaluations and motives may be changed but not the events. For a moment in Euripides' *Phoenissae* it looks as though Eteocles and Polyneices are going to settle the dispute amicably. The audience must have been startled; but a happy ending to that story would have been beyond the possible.

E. Some Conclusions

(i) Muthos *and History in Ancient Greece*

Can we learn anything from the myths and *muthoi* that I have discussed here that might be useful in cross-cultural discussion, or are the
Greeks completely atypical? For example, should we in discussion distinguish *muthos* (a) from *logos*? (b) from 'myth'? Is the tendency towards
history and the restriction of the sphere of 'dreamtime' (or *illud tempus*)
uniquely Greek? Hesiod's 'Five Races' myth breaks the mythological
mould and extends in time down to his own day and beyond, and Plato's
myths, whether called *muthoi* or *logoi*, are concerned with what is continually the case. (The exception is the change in the method of holding
the Court of Last Judgment, and that is placed in the Reign of Zeus,
and so—perhaps we may say—in history, since if anything belongs to
illud tempus it is presumably the Reigns of Uranus and Cronus.) Hesiod
places the Golden Race in the Reign of Cronus but tells us little about
it; and few other Greek writers mention the Reign of Cronus explicitly
at all. Thucydides seems willing to believe that if one subtracts the presence of deities as moving causes of the actions of early times, whatever
remains is history.[81] Is this peculiarly Greek? Or is it merely a consequence of the fact that we have only written versions of Greek myths?
We have to grant that we have only polished versions of Greek
myths/*muthoi*, which are likely to have been changed when recorded.
We should, however, distinguish sharply between the recording and use
of myths by a Hesiod and the recording of myths by an Apollodorus,
who assembles from any available source any variant of the myth related
of X, produces a myth about X which no one ever believed, or indeed
knew, and embalms the result. Even Hesiod's method is in some ways a
disadvantage when we compare the Greeks with cultures in which fresh
oral myths are still there for the gathering, since we are presumably
comparing apples with pears. But the Greek material allows us to study
the development and change of myths and *muthoi* and to inquire when
and why the changes were made, over a period in which there was belief
in myths. There are different reasons at different times. Pindar, for
example, rejects myths which he finds morally objectionable.

In general, then, the Greek myth/*muthos* is taken by the Greeks
discussed here to say what it means and to be subject to rational criticism on moral or other grounds. Gods appear in epic and tragedy, and

even Old Comedy; and their appearance, being part of the plot, is part of the *muthos* in at least that sense.[82] But even in the *Prometheus Bound*, all of whose characters are deities of some kind, I can discern no sign that Aeschylus thinks of his play as set in 'dream time', possibly because the play takes place in the Reign of Zeus. (Protagoras' *muthos* begins "there was once a time when gods existed but not mortal species"; but it immediately turns to the question of the creation of animals and man.)

(ii) The Greek Muthos *Open to Criticism*

The view that a *muthos* was not exempt from criticism on moral or rational grounds is, then, established among the more articulate Greeks by the early fifth century BC. (Xenophanes, Pindar, and, in a different way, Aeschylus). On the other hand, pre-Socratic philosophers such as Parmenides and Empedocles produced not only works of *philosophia* in the broader, Greek, sense, but also works which might be placed in the category of *muthos*. The *muthoi* of Plato should be read against this background. The Platonic *muthos* is not the product of Plato's wish to relieve the strain of a hard-fought dialogue with a little fine writing, though the writing is very fine. Plato's myths, whether termed *muthoi* or *logoi*, are intended to reinforce the lesson of the argument and sometimes, as in the *Phaedrus* myth, to provide a solid footing for the arguments in the widest possible sense.[83] Consequently, Plato must be prepared to adapt his *muthos* in detail if effective points are made against its rationality or morality. Socrates' "you may think it's a *muthos* but I think it's a *logos*" in the *Gorgias* makes a strong truth-claim, particularly in a dialogue in which, possibly for the first time, a clear distinction is drawn between *techne* and mere knack on the basis that a *techne* can give a *logos* about its subject-matter and concerns. The retreat in the *Phaedo* is presumably a response to the criticism of Plato's contemporaries, who must have themselves expected a high standard of rationality in such *muthoi*. Plato's final position, in the Myth of Er, offers good credentials for the story but treats it as a *muthos* nonetheless, possibly because in the earlier books of the *Republic* the criteria of knowledge had been made so stringent as to render any empirical statement incapable of fulfilling them. On the other hand, Er had been seeing with the eye of his *psuche*, which in the *Phaedo* is made the criterion for seeing the Forms, which are not, however, mentioned in the Myth of Er and not one of the things about which Er was to report back to the living.

Possibly the *Phaedrus* myth, in which having seen the Forms when out of the body is given crucial importance, is a response to a question raised about this; but I see no indication that Plato wished to produce one mega-myth (or mega-*muthos*) to cover everything, merely to eliminate from the myth or *muthos* contradictions or unwanted effects found in his earlier myths or *muthoi*. Presumably someone complained that the *daimon* of *Phaedo* (107d5-8) "which was allotted to the *psuche* while the person was still alive" had unwanted overtones of determinism. At all events, the words of Lachesis, "No *daimon* shall be allotted to you; rather shall you choose your *daimon*," must surely owe their vigor to their being intended as a rebuttal of something.

However, no simple 'be just and/or philosophical in your (one) life and eternal bliss shall be your reward' eschatology could suffice for anyone who believed in the transmigration of *psuchai*, was a moral philosopher, and took seriously the characteristics of the human beings among whom he lived. If we pass through a series of lives which most of us cannot remember,[84] there must be some means whereby Socrates was born as Socrates, Thrasymachus as Thrasymachus, and Ardiaeus the tyrant as Ardiaeus. In the Myth of Er Plato maintains that the *psuche* is rewarded or punished for its immediately preceding life, is allotted a position in a choice of lives in which the morally foolish will choose foolishly, whatever their position in the draw, while the very best type of life—that of the philosopher—will not be available in sufficient numbers, so that careful balancing of pros and cons will be of crucial importance. Even then, after the *daimon* appropriate to their (in a limited sense) free choice of life-pattern has been assigned to them, Er/Plato maintains that all the *psuchai* are compelled to drink the Water of Forgetfulness, which has characteristics which seem intended to render a mistake in drinking the right quantity very easy. He thus, it seems, gives an explanation why many admirably just and self-controlled persons are not philosophers, or even fortunate in their lives, why persons differ in intelligence,[85] why it is so difficult for the moralist to influence whether by suasion or argument the persons who seem hell-bent for ruin from their earliest years, or to have much influence on the larger number of persons who seem to be capable of limited improvement only. He has not, I think, merely placed the one (moderately) free choice that the *psuche* makes beyond the reach of the living moralist, since the traditional belief in *moira*, here represented by the three *Moirai*,[86] applied only to the most important actions and events in life, not to the fine detail. The moralist has a certain area in which to manoeuvre in his attempts to improve his contemporaries. Plato may well have believed that his experience had demonstrated that this was the actual situation.[87] Plato, like Bernard Williams, has a role for 'moral luck'.

At all events, the Myth of Er is a work of even greater complexity than the other Platonic myths. All are held both by Plato and his contemporaries to make claims to which rational criticism is relevant, and Plato responds to such criticism. The parts of the dialogues which are said to consist of *logos* have the same goal as those which are said to consist of *muthos*. Both contribute in an important manner to Plato's *philosophia*. Plato may be the last philosopher of whom this can be said, or at all events the last philosopher who would be willing to admit it. Why he is willing to do so becomes clearer against the background of Plato's predecessors from Hesiod onwards, in whose writings *muthos* and *logos* are slowly disentangling themselves from each other in a process not completed in the time of Plato, and probably impossible of completion.

Notes

1.   Detienne 1987.

2.   This may prove to be important, since the connotations of the use of *muthos* in Homer and other early writers may persist into the works of later writers where we translate it by 'myth' without a second thought. Alternatively, when Aristotle in the *Poetics* uses *muthos* to denote the plot, the notion of 'story' may have been most in his mind, but the overtones of *muthos* as opposed to *logos*, and the other usages discussed below, are likely to have been present too.

3.   *Religio* has different connotations from 'religion', but I do not propose to discuss the term here, since my concern is with the Greeks.

4.   I am referring to religious practice. Religion as it appears in literature sometimes bears the signs of much hard thought, as in Hesiod and Aeschylus. Aeschylus attempted to solve from within some of the problems posed by the traditional myths, but most thinkers from Xenophanes onwards (6-5 cent.) are iconoclasts in religion and simply reject what they find distasteful. The Athena of literature, even of Athenian literature, is not the Athena who presided over some Athenian cults. As Jane Harrison pointed out long ago (1927), the festivals of the Athenian sacred calendar do not bear the names of the deities under whose auspices they occur in historical times. As Harrison says, the cults presumably antedated the gods. To judge from the first part of the *Seven against Thebes*, the gods of a polis did not have compartmentalized spheres of activity: any god worshiped in cult in the year-round cycle of festivals might be prayed to for any kind of help that was needed.

5.   The Stoics, like most other Greeks, admired the Homeric poems and found them culturally authoritative; but they also found the Homeric deities' values and behavior shocking morally. As a result, they allegorized the deities, reducing them for the most part to oblique descriptions of the weather. See Heraclitus, *Homeric Allegories*, passim.

6.   See e.g. Grant 1962, in whose index are to be found twenty-one subheadings under the entry "Methods, theories and interpretations of mythology," from 'aetiological' to 'year-god', and eight under the entry "Myth, divisions of," from 'allegory' to 'riddle'. Most myths can be brought under more than one of these categories; none of them fall under all of them.

7.   Plato always portrays Socrates as scrupulous about the practice of his religion. See e.g. the words of Alcibiades, *Symposium* 220d4, where Socrates greets the rising sun as a god, and *Phaedo* 118c7-8. One explanation of Socrates' last words with respect to Asclepius is that Socrates is scrupulously concerned to repay a debt to a god who was concerned with the living, even when Socrates was at the point of death and translation to the jurisdiction of a different group of deities. Among the charges against Socrates was that he did not acknowledge the gods that the polis acknowledged, but other new *daimonia* (Plato, *Apology*, 26b4-5). Had he merely added objects of his worship to those worshiped by Athens, and could prove it, it seems likely that he would not have been put on trial or, if put on trial, condemned to death on this charge. (The real *gravamen* of the case against Socrates was founded on political guilt by association, expressed as "corrupting the youth"; but since a political amnesty had been declared, the political aspects of the case could not be openly introduced into court, and without the support of the other charge, Socrates' accusers might not have been able to persuade the necessary 251 of the 501 dicasts present.)

8.   On which see especially Plato, *Republic 2*.

9.   It would be incorrect to write "Greeks." Virtually all our evidence is from Athens.

10.   Adkins 1970.

11.   With *praxis* rather than with *gnosis*, as Aristotle expressed it, *Nicomachean Ethics* 1095a6. Plato's dialogues are full of arguments concerned with the way in which one should live. The Stoics held the same view: e.g. Epictetus, *Enchiridion* 52, though he complains that even philosophers do not practice what they preach. The whole Epicurean philosophy is devoted to delineating the kind of life one should lead. In both Stoics and Epicureans, physics and the principles of reasoning are valued for their contributions to the good life, in the sense of living with a quiet mind.

12.   Plato's *Euthyphro* throws light on this.

13.   For example, Heraclitus and Xenophanes in D-K 1951, Plato, *Euthyphro* and *Republic 2*.

14.   In ancient Greek, *philosophia* lays claim to an omnicompetence in matters intellectual—still reflected in the titles of chairs of e.g. 'natural philosophy' in some older universities—which 'philosophy' does not now suggest. Plato did not explicitly draw boundaries between the fields of *philosophia*. That task was left to

Aristotle, whose taxonomy remained useful at least until the late nineteenth century. In the later fifth and earlier fourth centuries BC in Greece, *sophistes*, 'sophist', was used to denote any 'intellectual.' Protagoras, Gorgias, Socrates, Isocrates, and Plato were all sophists in the language of the day. The use of the term to denote and decry an itinerant and usually bogus professional teacher of subjects that are rather disreputable on intellectual or ethical grounds is almost entirely the result of Plato's efforts.

15.   My belief may of course be false, and I freely admit that I cannot offer a cross-culturally valid definition of 'myth' that satisfies me. This volume of essays may show 'myth' to be an essentially contested term, which needs much more discussion.

16.   See Cicero, *Tusculan Disputations* 5.3.9, Diogenes Laertius, *Prooemium* 12, Apuleius, *Apology* 4.

17.   Where it is possible to give a more 'enlightened' interpretation, as in the case of "know thyself" (ascribed to Chilon the Lacedaemonian) or "nothing in excess" (ascribed to Solon), later commentators have usually given it; but "go bail and destruction is near" (ascribed to Thales) and most other gnomic utterances of the 'Seven Sages' reflect hardheaded prudence.

18.   Simple in the later years of the twentieth century AD, that is. The clear distinction, first made by Aristotle in his *Analytics* in the fourth century BC, is one of that philosopher's many claims to greatness.

19.   Or rather 'co-operative activity.' See Adkins 1963.

20.   Neither Hesiod nor Empedocles was faced with deciding whether he should write the initial letter of these words in upper or lower case. The Greek scripts of this period did not distinguish between them.

21.   The fragments of Empedocles are printed in full in D-K 1951, whereas only three pages of ancient references to Hesiod, containing rather less than seven lines of Hesiodic text, appear there. No one, so far as I am aware, has ever complained of his exclusion.

22.   The reason may be that the *Theogony* and *Works and Days* are not fragmentary enough; but the exclusion suggests a different kind of judgment.

23.   Adkins 1985b.

24.   Some of which are still termed "Acts of God," at all events by insurance companies.

25.   See my discussions in Adkins 1960a; 1960b; 1972b.

26.   Had Zeus himself had a child by Thetis, whose lot was to bear a child mightier than his father, he would have fallen from power. Instead Thetis was married off to Peleus, the result being Achilles.

27.   Hesiod certainly explains more than does Thales, the 'first philosopher'. Whatever he may have meant by claiming that 'water is the first principle,' as Aristotle informs us that he did, the claim cannot have taken him very far on the road from cosmogony to cosmology. At the time, it would have been rational in a familiar sense of the word to accept Hesiod's cosmogony as the better explanatory hypothesis.

28.   This behavior should not be equated with personification, which is a literary device of later date.

29.   For further discussion, see Adkins 1985b, 39-66.

30.   He might note that the particle and wave theories of atomic physics each represent the basic building blocks of the cosmos in terms of phenomena observable in the sensible world, and that in that world the phenomena are incompatible. "The world is not merely stranger than we suppose, it is stranger than we *can* suppose."

31.   For a vividly narrated illustration, see Achilles' fight with the River, Homer, *Iliad* 21.200-323. Homer has set himself a problem. How can Achilles fight with a river if that river has only fluvial characteristics? He calls the River "deep-eddying," but also says that he "gave himself the appearance of a man." Many Greek deities change their shape, e.g. Athena in *Odyssey* 3. But here the River, in trying to subdue Achilles, has some human and some riverine characteristics. Since Hesiod, in a very different genre from Homer, rarely needs to portray the gods' behavior in detail, he throws little light on this. Homer ascribes to the River only such forms of attack and defense as would be possessed by an articulate but otherwise normal river. The problems begin when graphic artists or dramatists try to represent the situation in visual terms, as Aeschylus does in the *Prometheus Bound*.

32.   A deity whose values are shared with his worshipers need not be anthropomorphic. It is not clear what the original shape of 'ox-eyed Hera' or 'grey-eyed' ('owl-faced'?) Athena may have been. But when Zeus pursues Io in the form of a bull, or Leda in the form of a swan, there seems to be no suggestion in the sources we possess—whatever may originally have been the case—that Zeus is 'really' a bull or a swan.

33.   See e.g. D-K 1951, 7B, 62B. Note that Empedocles, writing in hexameter verse, uses *muthoi* of his own words in the *On Nature*, 17B- 14-15, and to indicate what his doctrine is not, says "it is no erring and ignorant *muthos*." The addition of the pejorative adjectives suggests that, as in Pindar, a *muthos* not thus qualified is simply a story.

34.   True, he does not say that Heracles was the son of Zeus; but since few of his contemporaries would have denied it, they would have been unlikely to suppose that Thucydides disagreed unless he said so explicitly.

35.   He did not, of course, fail to take into account the religious beliefs of his characters when these significantly affected their behavior.

36.   The difference between the level of the material culture of Hesiod's Greece and that of the Myceneans whose remains were everywhere still to be seen might have encouraged a belief in other cultural discontinuities, and therefore—the gods being ultimately responsible for everything—new creations. But it seems better to ascribe the belief to the mythical mode of thought.

37.   At all events it should be excluded from history. Thucydides might have used a scale of credibility for judging events beyond a certain point on which, though an event could occur, it was not appropriate for inclusion in a work of the kind Thucydides was writing. Herodotus took a much more cautious—and in the case of empirical universal propositions, surely more 'scientific'—position: "anything could happen in the whole of time."

38.   Though a book-trade existed, 'published' in ancient Greece need mean little more than 'written out in full and read by, or to, one's friends.'

39.   In the Greek of the day, 'sophist' was a term with a broad range that included Protagoras, rhetoricians like Gorgias and Isocrates, and philosophers like Socrates and Plato.

40.   The judgment depends on the status of Prometheus and Epimetheus, who might be regarded either as gods or as 'culture-heroes'.

41.   As did at least the earlier pre-Socratics, who may be distinguished by having nonanthropomorphic deities, rather than as having no deities at all. Thales is reputed to have said "All things are full of *daimones*" (D-K 1951, 1A); and his successors for the most part found little reason to explain the existence of movement in the cosmos. Anaxagoras' Nous notoriously was employed as an initial efficient cause of movement. Apparently the movement then continued without further need of Nous. Democritus seems to have regarded movement in all directions by the atoms as requiring no explanation. If so, he differed from Epicurus who, writing after Plato and Aristotle, was compelled to explain how movement is produced.

42.   There is throughout Protagoras' long speech, and indeed throughout the dialogue, and equivocation between *arete*= justice and *arete*= political skill. See Adkins 1973.

43.   The account is not merely perceptive, but so 'democratic' as almost to leave no function for the sophist as teacher of values. (Plato had the same perception of the effectiveness of such socialization, was appalled by it when carried on in an unorganized kind of way, and attempted in both the *Republic* and *Laws* to ensure that the inhabitants of at least the poleis of those dialogues were socialized into 'right opinion'.)

44.   D-K 1951, Protagoras B4.

45.   It was dangerous to be a professed atheist—that is to say, to deny the existence of the gods worshiped in one's polis and elsewhere under the same names—in ancient Greece. Since the majority of the pre-Socratics hold views which seem to entail the nonexistence of that kind of deity, presumably the pre-Socratics were in general very circumspect. The short list—it tends to be the same short list, handed on from writer to writer—includes Protagoras, but we do not know enough of the context of his notorious utterance to know in which way it was to be understood. Probably Protagoras' words were so cautious as to leave the matter unclear at the time.

46.   Sir Isaac Newton spent much time and working out a chronology of the Bible, from the Creation onwards, and gave the highest importance to this aspect of his life's work. One must consider such matters in the light of the knowledge, and frequently also the values, of the society in which a thinker lived.

47.   A word with such a range of usage readily lends itself to equivocation. The opportunity is not missed in the *Protagoras* (Adkins 1973).

48.   West, line 14; D-K 1951

49.   See Bowra 1938, 357, discussed in Adkins 1985, vol. 1, 181.

50.   This translation of *eudaimonia* was introduced by Cooper (1975). No English word or phrase gives an entirely satisfactory rendering; but 'human flourishing' is much better than the traditional 'happiness'.

51.   See below, p. 115. n. 72.

52.   For whom, see Homer, *Iliad* 2. His behavior is rather insubordinate than unjust. To characterize him as in any way *eudaimon* would have startled Plato's contemporaries.

53.   *Ta hautou praxantos kai ou polupragmonesantos en toi bioi.* My translations are literal. The historical Socrates took a minimal part in politics, preferring to 'do his own thing'; a fact held to be discreditable at his trial, since some who behaved in this manner and 'did their own things' were hostile to the democracy. See Adkins 1976 for more evidence.

54.   Note that this example of rather shaky logic is not in the myth or *muthos*, but in Socrates' comments.

55.   Since the fundamental sense of *psuche* is 'life-principle', no one would be likely to dispute this.

56.   It should not be forgotten that the premise seems necessary to Plato to ground his views on language-using and all the purposes for which he uses the theory of Forms in the *Meno, Phaedo, Symposium, Republic,* and *Phaedrus.*

57.   In the Greek, the words that I have rendered 'it is said thus, that . . .' are followed by *ara*, a particle often used in indirect speech to convey skepticism for the words reported, or at least that one is not endorsing them oneself. Socrates (Plato) seems more cautious here than in the *Gorgias.*

58.   *Daimon* is a vague term in Greek religion, frequently used when, as is usually the case, one does not know which of the gods is the cause of one's good or ill fortune. There can be no allusion to Socrates' own *daimonion*, which both Socrates and his contemporaries clearly regarded as very unusual.

59.   Note the contrast with the specificity of Er's 'the meadow' in *Republic* 10. The *Gorgias* too is much more detailed.

60.   Similar beliefs are found in actual cult (e.g., on the gold plates, once termed 'Orphic', in D-K 1951).

61.   Once again Plato is less specific than in the Myth of Er.

62.   Socrates would have been ill advised to make claim for expert status as a geographer. There were explorers by this time who had eye-witness evidence that the world was not as he maintained.

63.   This should not be overstated. Much more 'self-help' was needed in life in the ancient polis than in modern democratic societies.

64.   For *moira*, see Adkins 1960a, 1972a.

65.   A 'dicast' (*dikastes*) was a member of the large Athenian juries which, in the absence of professional judges, enjoyed great freedom in deciding cases. A jury of

501 Athenians condemned Socrates. There may be a hint that even a large jury, out of the body, would decide justly.

66.   Maurice Dodd, a British cartoonist, regularly portrays the metaphysical and theological debates of crabs in a seaside pool—which they term the 'pooliverse'—provoked by the persons or animals which can occasionally be seen from their point of observation. Not being able to improve on it, I commend Mr. Dodd's term of art to my readers.

67.   Contrast Plato's views elsewhere. More than one 'philosophic' life is usually required.

68.   Of the closing words of Plato's *Crito*, after the speech of the Laws.

69.   In this, the most puritanical and ascetic of Plato's dialogues, the body is treated as not part of the human being. The *psuche* is the real person.

70.   Thersites and Archelaus are singled out. See also Ardiaeus, 615c6-616a4. What *crime* Thersites had committed is unclear. He certainly had ideas 'above his station'.

71.   I doubt whether this is true: there are characteristically Platonic features in all of Plato's myths, and each myth has characteristics that make it suitable for the dialogue in which it occurs. Socrates attributes at least part of his description of the earth in the *Phaedo* to others: 'it is said' 110b5.

72.   We may inquire why Socrates glosses over the 'greater' punishments for impiety (615c2-4), and leaves unmentioned the traditional eternal torture of Tantalus, Sisyphus, and Ixion? Possibly because these three had been admitted into companionship with the gods and were being punished for 'person to person' offences against the gods which no mere mortal in the fourth century BC could hope to emulate. Tityus had attempted to rape Artemis (or her mother Leto). Of Tantalus several different versions are given: he had either failed to keep secrets entrusted to him by Zeus, or offered the gods a 'Thyestean' banquet, or committed similar direct offenses to deity. Sisyphus had offended the gods in a similar manner. These offenses are not acts of injustice but direct threats to the *time* of the gods on a scale which no one who had not enjoyed their privileges could possibly commit, and they evoke an unparalleled response. (These stories might be taken as examples of 'dreamtime', but the Greeks seem to view them in the same manner as other stories involving both gods and men; and modern scholars—wrongly, in my opinion—frequently extrapolate from these few favored individuals who are punished for having betrayed the trust of the gods to all the dead; a belief of which there is no sign in Homer or in the Olympian religion.) For further discussion and references to ancient authors see Adkins 1960a, 67, 81n14, 146, 1960b. It remains surprising that the punishments for the impious behavior of the kind that an ordinary mortal might commit are similarly passed over.

73.   *Moira* denotes personalized shares of life, in terms both of its length and of its quality, which was viewed in terms of one's share of *time* (status-conferring goods and the status and position with which the goods are virtually identified). For discussion, see Adkins 1960b, 1972a.

74.   I have tried to give the 'feel' of the Greek of this speech, which is very laconic, more like Aristotle than Plato in some respects, especially in the memorable last two phrases: "*aitia helomenou; theos anaitios.*"

75.   In the light of the foregoing discussion, presumably *logos* is to be contrasted with *muthos* here. Socrates is making a strong truth-claim.

76.   The Greek translated 'of . . . death' is in a very elevated style.

77.   It is not clear why Socrates restricts the danger to human beings, since a *psuche* previously in a human body can choose to become embodied as a swan, a lion, or any other living creature instead of a human being. Consequently, an indefinitely large number of *psuchai* on any occasion of choice of the next life will have been in nonhuman bodies in their last lives. Note that in the *Phaedrus* myth only those who have seen the Forms before being embodied can be embodied as human beings.

78.   LSJ suggests "that with which one must be content."

79.   Indeed, Aristotle uses the same *occurrence* of *muthos* with reference to both comedy and tragedy.

80.   Aeschylus for the most part works within the myth, justifying it rather than rejecting it.

81.   Thucydides presumably also excluded flying horses, centaurs, hydras, three-headed dogs, and similar fauna. But it is hazardous to suppose that the relationship between what actually happened and what is said to have happened in the traditional myths, legends, and folk-tales of a culture is such as to warrant using Thucydides's methods.

82.   At the moment, at all events, I see no ground for treating any usage of *muthos* as being quite independent of the others.

83.   See above, n. 77.

84.   Pythagoras and Empedocles both claimed to be able to remember their former lives.

85.   The myth of the Golden, Silver, Bronze, and Iron *psuchai, Republic* 415aff., has a part to play here.

86.   Once personalized 'shares', in the archaic/Hesiodic manner. If this is at the forefront of Plato's mind, this is a survival of deities at once personalized and treated as aspects of the culture. But this is such a frequent personalization, and the use of *moira* in the sense of share now so unusual, that Plato may well have perceived them as simply anthropomorphic deities with a specialized role.

87.   For *moira*, see above, nn. 64, 73.

References

Unless otherwise indicated, all classical authors are cited or quoted from the Oxford Classical Texts series. All translations are my own.

Adkins, A. W. H.
1960a *Merit and Responsibility: A Study in Greek Values.* Oxford: Clarendon Press.

1960b "Honour" and "Punishment" in the Homeric Poems. *Bulletin of the Institute for Classical Studies* 7:23-32.

1963 "Friendship" and "Self-Sufficiency" in the Homeric Poems, *Classical Quarterly* 13:30-45.

1970 *From the Many to the One.* London: Constable and Ithaca: Cornell University Press.

1972a *Moral Values and Political Behaviour in Ancient Greece.* London: Chatto and Windus, and Toronto: Clarke, Irwin.

1972b "Homeric Gods and the Values of Homeric Society," *Journal of Hellenic Studies* 92:1-19.

1973 "*Arete, Techne*, Democracy and Sophists." *Journal of Hellenic Studies* 93:3-12.

1976 "*Polupragmosune* and 'Minding One's Own Business': A Study in Greek Social and Political Values." *Classical Philology* 71:301-37.

1985a *Poetic Craft in the Early Greek Elegists.* Chicago: University of Chicago Press.

1985b "Cosmogony and Order in Ancient Greece." In *Cosmogony and Ethical Order,* edited by Robin W. Lovin and Frank E. Reynolds. Chicago: University of Chicago Press.

Barnes, Jonathan.
1979 *The Presocratic Philosophers.* 2 vols. London: Routledge and Kegan Paul.

Bowra, C. M.
1938 Xenophanes, fragment 1. *Classical Philology* 33:363-67.

Cooper, J. M.
1975 *Reason and Human Good in Aristotle*. Cambridge: Harvard University Press.

Detienne, Marcel.
1981 *L'invention de la mythologie*. Paris: Editions Gallimard.

Diels, H., and W. Kranz [D-K].
1951-1952 *Die Fragmente der Vorsokratiker*. 6th ed., 3 vols. Berlin-Grunewald: Weidmann.

Grant, Michael.
1962 *Myths of the Greeks and Romans*. London: Weidenfeld and Nicolson.

Harrison, Jane Ellen.
1903 *Prolegomena to the Study of Greek Religion*. Cambridge: Cambridge University Press.

1907 *Themis*. Cambridge: Cambridge University Press.

Liddell, H. G., R. Scott, and H. S. Jones [LSJ].
1968 *A Greek-English Lexicon*. Revised by Sir Henry Stuart Jones, with a Supplement by E. A. Barber and others. Oxford: Clarendon Press.

Ross, Sir David.
1924 *Aristotle's Metaphysics*. 2 vols. Oxford: Clarendon Press.

West, M. L.
1972 *Iambi et Elegi Graeci ante Alexandrum Cantati*. 2 vols. Oxford: Clarendon Press.

Chapter 5

Kūkai (774-835): Philosophizing in the Archaic

Thomas P. Kasulis

In discussing the relation between the mythic and philosophic in the archaic Japanese world view, I have trouble deciding whether to tell a story or make an argument. So, I will do a little of both. My story will be about Kūkai (774-835), the case of an extraordinary figure who merged high philosophy with the most archaic of religious elements. As for my argument, I will limit myself to one point, namely, that two common ways of understanding the myth/philosophy relation do not adequately explain the early development of Japanese thought, at least as represented by Kūkai.

Let us begin with a few comments about the argument, or more specifically, about the two attitudes toward the archaic that do not fit well our case study. We should remember that the history of philosophy and the history of religion themselves have histories. As we know them today, they have roots in the nineteenth century, an age in which theories of development and progress framed the intellectual context. It was the era of Hegel's and Marx's dialectic, Darwin's theory of evolution, and Comte's theory of stages. The nineteenth century assumed what did not evolve was primitive: archaic religions were primitive religions.

The twentieth century did not bring us to Hegel's universal spirit, or Marx's classless society, or Comte's scientific utopia. On many fronts, we grew skeptical of the thesis that change entails improvement.

Disillusioned, some of us began to look back at the archaic with nostalgia and longing, feeding yet another nineteenth-century tendency—romanticism. Led by European philosopher anthropologists like Levy-Bruhl, we went back into the jungle and found not the primitive, but the pristine, a wisdom of nature we had lost long ago. Paul Radin found there not only wisdom, but even the love of wisdom, in such books as *Primitive Man as Philosopher*.

Given this intellectual context, we often think of the relation between myth and philosophy in one of two ways. One alternative is that the archaic and mythic evolved into, and were superseded by, the philosophic: philosophy is what primitive cultures do after they grow up and face reality. The other alternative is that the mythic discourse of the archaic world is itself philosophy, that myths and philosophical categories are merely variant forms of speculation about cosmic matters. I believe neither theory is adequate and this paper will at least demonstrate that neither can adequately account for what happened in Kūkai's case. For Kūkai, as we shall soon see, the archaic was not equated with the philosophic, but neither did the philosophic replace the archaic. Instead, we will find that Kūkai developed a philosophical system to support the archaic.

So, on with our story. . . .

Let us go back to the early ninth century in Japan, when the Emperor Kammu had recently moved the capital to Heian (Kyōto). In the mountains of Yoshino adjacent to the old capital areas of Nara and Nagaoka, we find a young college dropout sitting in meditation, chanting one million times a *darani* [Skt: *dhāraṇī*], or sacred phrase, to the bodhisattva Kokūzō [Ākāshagarbha]. The man's given name is Mao, although he will call himself by the religious name of Kūkai, "the sky and sea" or "the ocean of emptiness." By imperial edict, future generations would also call him Kōbō Daishi, "the great teacher who promulgated the Dharma."

Why would this man abandon his academic studies in the urban university to undergo austerities in the mountains? Why would he reject the promise of a comfortable bureaucratic career to be an ascetic in the cold of Yoshino? What in this incantation practice could supersede the study of the Chinese classics he enjoys so much and at which he so excels?

Although even establishment religious figures from the Buddhist temples in Nara would periodically retreat into the hills for spiritual rejuvenation, they seldom stayed there for any extended period. The more typical religious denizens of the mountains were the thaumaturgists—wizards and shamans of various ilk—who used the isolation and austerity of mountain life to hone their parapsychological powers either for mystical purposes or practical gain. Just a few decades earlier, one wizard, a maverick Buddhist monk called Dōkyō, had so enchanted the Empress Shōtoku that he acquired a Rasputin-like influence on the court, almost getting himself named emperor until the opposition thwarted his ambitions and sent him into exile. The dark mountain forests undoubtedly also harbored assorted social misfits, those who could not or would not live in society as either farmer or city-dweller: criminals on the lam, the indigent, the sociopaths.

In short, this was an odd place to find a man whom later generations of Japanese would consider the greatest intellectual force in their history. Still, that is where Kūkai was, and to understand his role in the development of Japanese spirituality we must have some idea of why he was there. This involves knowing the relevant social and intellectual context as well as some of Kūkai's own personality traits and biographical background.

The Nara period (710-794) in which Kūkai was born lacked cultural and intellectual coherence. There was no single approved world view or shared value system, but only a fragile detente among conflicting traditions: the indigenous, the Confucian, and the Buddhist. Let us briefly examine each.

The indigenous (that is, the preliterate or proto-Shinto) view believed in a world of awe-inspiring spiritual presences, both malevolent and benevolent, called *kami*. *Kami* could be in the form of deities, mountains, trees, rocks, animals, ghosts, and sometimes even living persons. Prehistoric Japan was inhabited by isolated clans or tribes (*uji*), each with its own ruling priest or priestess and special protective *kami*. As suggested in this ancient poem, a man's elegy to a dead wife, there was no sharp separation between the human and natural:

> Now I know not what to do or say,
>
> Vainly I seek soothing words
>
> From trees and stones.
>
> . . .
>
> Over Mount Ōnu the fog is rising;
>
> Driven by my sighs of grief,
>
> The fog is rising.
>
> (*Man'yōshū* V:794-9)[1]

As in many other ancient Japanese poems, the human emotion (the grief) and the natural phenomenon (the rising fog) are in intimate relation. From archeological and literary evidence, it is clear that the connection was not seen as metaphorical, but causal or magical.[2] In fact, the poet even seems surprised that the trees and stones have no soothing words to offer. The *Kojiki*, for example, claimed that trees and stones once did have the power of speech but a *kami* silenced them for their argumentative boisterousness.

With the introduction of the Chinese writing system in the late fifth century, Japan became a literate culture. Since Chinese and Japanese syntax are radically different (Japanese verbs are highly inflected, for example), the Chinese writing system and Japanese language were not compatible. So educated Japanese aristocrats simply learned to write in Chinese.

In learning Chinese, the Japanese imitated the mainland system of studying and memorizing the Chinese Confucian classics of history, poetry, and philosophy. In so doing, they learned not only the Chinese language but also the Confucian political and ethical values, resulting in the establishment of a Japanese hierarchical bureaucratic system modeled on Tang China. The Confucian vocabulary of social harmony—loyalty, sincerity, filial piety, propriety, humaneness, and so on—became an integral part of public policy statements. The more ritualistic aspects of Chinese Confucianism, such as reverence for the person of Confucius and emphasis on the ideal emperor as ruling with the power of virtue (*de*), did not deeply penetrate ancient Japan, however. In that era, Japanese Confucianism was a social and moral theory, not a religious practice.

Chinese Buddhism, also introduced via Korea, functioned on two levels. On one hand, like Confucianism, it was a mainland intellectual tradition with a huge corpus of texts and more than a millennium of philosophical development. This intellectual aspect of Buddhism was centered in the scholastic temples of the so-called Six Nara Schools. On the other hand, Buddhism was initially most influential because of its aesthetic and ritualistic contributions. The indigenous religion had been markedly austere: *kami* were depicted in neither painting nor sculpture; music and ritual forms were minimalistic. Mainland Buddhists brought sculpture, painting, elaborate rituals, and detailed meditation manuals, along with its large store of sūtras and commentaries. The court was interested in staging elegant rituals for the protection and prosperity of the state. Seeing this predilection as a practical route to imperial patronage, the Buddhists emphasized those thaumaturgical and aesthetic dimensions.

Buddhist theory and Buddhist practice had almost nothing to do with each other, however. The Nara Schools had no explanation of why Buddhist thaumaturgical rituals should work and Buddhist practice was completely unsystematized and unrelated to the formal teachings of the Six Nara Schools. As suggested earlier, the separation of theory and practice took on a geographical distance as well: people studied Buddhist doctrines and texts in the urban scholastic centers but performed their spiritual cultivation practices in the mountains.

By the mid-eighth century, an official cosmology and mythology had already been developed to show that all the *kami* of the clans were actually related in a hierarchy, with the Sun Goddess, the *kami* of the imperial family, at the top. Thus, the official mythology, probably at least in part a self-conscious creation synthesized from various local myths and imported Chinese stories, presented Japan as a single family. Whereas Confucianism supplied a political rationale, the new Shintō mythology supplied a national spiritual identity. This national mythology was not, however, strongly tied to the folk religious level of the indigenous world view. Nature worship, ritual purification, and ascetic practices continued as their own traditions in the rural and mountain regions, where they mixed with Buddhist ascetic practices. There was no developed theory relating the grand Shintō myth to the practical worship of the local *kami*.

The result was a cultural bifurcation between the city and mountains, the Chinese and the indigenous, the scholarly and the ascetic, the intellectual and the emotive, the systematic and the natural, the rational and the awe-inspiring. This tension gives us the cultural context for the significance of young Kūkai's *darani* practice in the mountains. According to the ritualistic handbook called the *Kokūzōgumonjihō*, if one chanted the *darani* to Kokūzō one million times with the appropriate gestures, postures, and visualizations, one would be able to memorize and understand all the key passages from every Buddhist text.[3] It is significant that, unlike Dōkyō for example, Kūkai was interested in powers not of healing or magic, but of the intellect and understanding. He did not want so much to control his world, but to make sense of it. It seems Kūkai wanted to integrate the two worlds of the city and the mountains. Details of his personal life add credence to such an interpretation.

Even to the modern Japanese, Kūkai is something of a riddle, a peculiar blend of two radically different images. A way for us to express the paradox is that Kūkai, even in his own day, was understood to be someone like a Merlin and Thomas Aquinas combined, a mixture of magic and logic.

Let us begin with the Merlin side. In the popular Japanese consciousness, Kūkai is closely associated with miraculous and heroic deeds.
Artifacts throughout Japan attest to his supernormal powers: wooden
buddha images he carved that would not burn, sacred characters he
inscribed in stone using only his fingernails, the site of the great
Daimon-ji bonfires where Kūkai performed a ritual to stop a plague in
Kyōto. Most striking of all is the belief that Kūkai never died in the
ordinary sense of the word, but rather entered a state of permanent
meditation in which his hair and fingernails continue to grow.[4]

These stories account for some of the fascination the Japanese have
for Kūkai's temple establishment on Mount Kōya, one of the more popular religious sites of pilgrimage and tourism in Japan today. Our first
reaction may be to consider Mount Kōya a quaint example of the archaic
and superstitious. There we find the marks of a mystic nature cult: the
musty incense, the dusky interiors, the earth's mossy reclamation of the
gravestones and buildings. From this perspective, Kūkai is a Japanese
Merlin and Mount Kōya a museum for the Druidic relics of Japan's
ancient past, a place where Japanese pilgrims can temporarily divest
themselves of modernity's cloak and once again imagine life among the
naked magic of rocks, trees, and streams.

But there is another side to the story. Merlin wrote no books,
and if he had, he would probably have limited himself to a listing of
spells and charms. Kūkai's writings, on the other hand, reveal an ency-
clopedic knowledge and acute critical skills. Rather than recipes of
incantations, rituals, and magical formulae, they more resemble the
systematic philosophical scope of, say, the *Summae* of Thomas
Aquinas. His critique of all known philosophical schools, *The Ten
Mind-sets* (*Jūjūshinron*), is probably the most comprehensive treatment
of Buddhist thought written in Japan before the modern era.[5] Shaman
he may be been, but Kūkai was also an intellectual giant in the development of the emergent Japanese culture. To understand better how
the thaumaturgical and intellectual elements converged in Kūkai's life
we need only consider a few biographical details.

Kūkai grew up on the island of Shikoku, in what is even today rural
Japan. We can assume, then, that Kūkai's childhood was spent in an area
where the indigenous religious forms were still strong. As a child, Kūkai
knew a world of *kami*, a place where the human and the natural were intimately related. Throughout his life, as we can see from poems he wrote in
later years, Kūkai maintained an intimate connection with the natural world.[6]

At the same time, however, as a member of the Saeki clan (a branch of the Ōtomo), Kūkai was given all the educational benefits of a bright aristocrat. Ōtomo Yokamochi was said to be, after all, the compiler of *Man'yōshū*. On the maternal side of Kūkai's family was Atō Ōtari, a prominent Confucian scholar and tutor to the imperial family. Atō saw promise in the lad and brought him to the capital (then Nagaoka) to be trained in the Chinese classics when he was fifteen. The special tutoring paid off when, at eighteen, Kūkai was accepted into the national college (*daigaku*), the institute for educating future bureaucrats in service to the emperor.

By all secular criteria, it looked as if Kūkai was assured a successful career in government. Something went wrong, however, and he eventually dropped out of the college to undertake a life of religious asceticism in the Yoshino mountains. Kūkai himself is not explicit in his writings about the precise reason for this change. From various hints, however, we can surmise that it was a combination of factors. Negatively, he was disillusioned with the politics and superficial lifestyle of the cities. His writings from this early period have a strongly escapist theme. In his *Aims of the Three Teachings (Sangōshiiki)*, for example, Buddhism is preferred to either Confucianism or Taoism because it is the most otherworldly, the only true escape from the pains of craving in this secular world of ephemeral pleasures. Positively, Kūkai felt most at home when away from the city and, like so many others of his time, he believed religious practice could only be pursued seriously in the mountains. Given his temperament, his upbringing in Shikoku, his sensitivity to the animistic world of pre-Sinicized Japan, Kūkai was not to abandon all that he learned while growing up, whatever the virtues offered by high urban culture.

This returns us to Kūkai's experience in Yoshino. Modern scholars believe the *darani* practice was associated with the so-called Natural Wisdom School (Jinenchi-shū), a quasi-Buddhist Japanese mountain tradition outside the orthodoxy of the Six Nara Schools. It was part of the tradition commonly called today "mixed esotericism" (*zōmitsu*) or "ancient esotericism" (*komitsu*). Lacking any conceptual system, the Natural Wisdom school was, more or less, a collection of ascetics interested in developing thaumaturgical powers and escaping the scholastic environment of the city. The practices were a blend of ancient rituals and new forms of meditation discovered in Buddhist texts. In terms of commitment to personal cultivation, the followers of this school were probably at the pinnacle of their culture, yet they could not possibly compete philosophically with Confucianism and the Nara Buddhist schools. For an individual of Kūkai's intellectual capacity and training, this must have been distressing. Perhaps he hoped the textual omniscience promised by the *Kokūzōgumonjihō* practice would help him connect the practical and theoretical.

In short, what we know of Kūkai's motives in his younger years points to a need for assimilation and intellectual integration. More than anything else, he wanted to get a grasp on the diverse texts of Buddhism and to understand their connections. He also wanted to make sense of the indigenous tradition into which he was born, but which no one in Japan seemed to be able to articulate philosophically. This gives us a key to the personality and the purpose behind his own later thought.

For several years Kūkai seems to have lived the life of an ascetic, but probably also commuting into the city to utilize his increasingly sophisticated textual skills. When about thirty years old, he came across another important esoteric text, the *Dainichi Sūtra (Dainichi kyō*; Skt: *Mahāvairocana Sūtra*), a text translated from Sanskrit into Chinese by the same Shubhākarasiṃha (637–735) who had translated the *Kokūzōgumonjihō*. Kūkai sensed that this text held the key to a systemization of the esoteric tradition, a way of integrating esoteric practice and philosophical doctrine. It was no ritualistic recipe like *Kokūzōgumonjihō*, but a comprehensive view of reality centering on the imagery of the Womb Mandala. That is, it contained not only magic, but also philosophy.

Yet, reading the *Dainichi Sūtra* presented technical difficulties that even Kūkai's already highly developed spiritual powers and scholarly proficiency could not penetrate. One problem was that the text referred to practices unknown in Japan; another, that some knowledge of Sanskrit seemed necessary. In the *Dainichi Sūtra* Kūkai had found a Buddhist text he could not understand despite the textual omniscience supposedly acquired through the *Kokūzōgumonjihō* practice. His conviction about its importance was so strong he left the mountains to study again in the capital. But this time the Japanese capital would not do. He would have to go to Chang-an, the capital of Tang China and one of the great cosmopolitan cities of the ancient world. There he met Hui-guo (746–805), the seventh patriarch of Zhen-yan (Jp: Shingon): "Truth-word" or "Mantra" Buddhism.

According to Kūkai's own account, Hui-guo had been expecting a student from across the sea, was overjoyed to see him, and immediately set to work training the young Japanese monk, knowing that his own days were numbered. Within about seven months, Hui-guo was dead, but not before Kūkai had been officially designated his successor and been charged with spreading the teaching in his homeland. The speed of Kūkai's assimilation of the teachings was undoubtedly a reflection of the spiritual insight developed during his years in the Yoshino mountains. In effect, as a follower of the esoteric traditions in Yoshino, he had already undergone much Shingon training; all he needed to learn in China was how to organize and articulate what he already intuitively sensed.

This is not to say that Shingon teachings were simply handed over to Kūkai in a fully developed form. Scholars generally agree that some of Kūkai's most central teachings, such as the detailed analysis of the ten mind-sets, are almost certainly products of his own invention. So also is his emphasis on the Womb over the Diamond Mandala. In less than a year with Hui-guo, it is unlikely that Kūkai could have learned the entire Shingon system in all its complexity. Most probably Kūkai mastered the key ritual forms and essential teachings while in China, but did not work out the details until returning to Japan. As an authorized Shingon patriarch and its first master in Japan, Kūkai was given extensive authority to trust his own insights.

We cannot here go into the rich details of the Shingon system as Kūkai learned and developed it. In this paper we are mainly interested in how Kūkai integrated the archaic and mythic with the philosophic. To pursue this topic, we need to consider briefly what Shingon esotericism meant for Kūkai and how its cosmological vision could go beyond the mere thaumaturgy of the Natural Wisdom School by generating a philosophical defense of the archaic as Kūkai knew it in Japan.

The key to Kūkai's synthesis of the philosophic and archaic is his formulation of Buddhist esotericism.

> Whereas the Buddha has three bodies, there are two kinds of teachings. Those delivered by the celestial (*ō*) and historical (*ke*) embodiments are called exoteric teachings (*kengyō*). Being publicly expressed and abridged, those words are suited to the [audience's] circumstances. The speeches of the reality-embodiment (*hosshin*), on the other hand, are called esoteric teachings (*mikkyō*). Recondite and profound, those words are the authentic exposition. (KDKZ 2:149)

There are two points to notice in this brief statement. First, the buddha-embodiment most central to his esotericism is not a historical buddha like Shakyamuni or a celestial one like Amida or Kannon. Rather, Shingon's buddha is the *hosshin* (*dharmakāya*) or reality-embodiment itself. In exoteric forms of Buddhism, we should note, the reality embodiment is typically an abstract, usually nonpersonal principle of universal buddhahood that interacts with us humans only through celestial or historical manifestations. For Shingon, however, the reality-embodiment is personal—its name is Dainichi (Mahāvairocana)—and it preaches the dharma as itself.

Secondly, the passage points out that Dainichi, unlike other buddhas, does not adapt his message to the audience. Dainichi's expounding the Dharma is "just between the Buddha and the Buddha: Dainichi deigns to let it be known to us" (KDKZ 3:538). So, Dainichi's teaching is an intimation into which we must be initiated if we are to grasp it. But where do we find this intimation? In the very objects we experience every day through our senses.[7] The entire cosmos is the reality-embodiment's teaching. Each item in the universe's inventory is only a sacred letter in Dainichi's self-expression. The world is literally telling us something.

The mechanics of how Dainichi intimates the Dharma through all the dharmas (phenomena) is too complex to analyze here; it would involve an explanation of Kūkai's theory of mantras, the two mandalas (Womb and Diamond), and mudras, as well as his metaphysics of "sound-word-reality" (*shōjijissōgi*) and his metapraxis of "attaining buddhahood in this very body" (*sokushinjōbutsu*). One point is necessary for us to discuss briefly in our present discussion, however: his idea of "resonance" (*kyō*).

On the cosmic level, the universe and everything in it is nothing other than Dainichi's enlightened activity or function (*yū*). Only from the standpoint of our enlightened activity, however, can we experience the universe itself as Dainichi's activity. Ordinarily, we experience only the macrocosmic world of our senses: the world of individual elements and compounds. On this level, our delusions prevent us from encountering Dainichi's presence. The connection between the cosmic and macrocosmic is the microcosmic. This is the level of resonance, the resonance which is at once the vibration of Dainichi's act and the constituent matter-energy constituting the elements of the macrophysical reality. The purpose of Shingon practice is to attune the practitioners to that subperceptible resonance so that they can intuit the cosmic force behind the empirical world.

As we have already noted, this special sense of "expounding the dharmas" is not intended for us or any other audience. It is only the natural function of Dainichi's enlightened activity to which, if initiated, we can be attuned. Dainichi does, however, "deign to let it be know to us" through *kaji* or "empowerment." Dainichi's resonance is added (*ka*) and we embrace it (*ji*). Insofar as the word *kaji* in Japanese has come to mean any miraculous, magical, or spiritual empowerment, we are brought to Kūkai's philosophizing of the archaic.

As we have seen, the Japanese archaic world view assumed natural events are open to magical intervention. Is such a claim justified? Kūkai and his contemporaries found experiential verification of this claim in extraordinary events under special circumstances involving supernormal individuals. But experience itself can be mistrusted unless it survives the test of explanation. We see a stick bend, for example, when we place it part way into a pool of clear water, but that apparently miraculous phenomenon can be explained away: it is an illusion created by the refraction of light. At this critical point in Japanese history, philosophy had to decide whether thaumaturgical events were illusions or reality. Philosophy had to either explain how they were possible or explain them away. Unlike the other theories available in Japan at the time, Kūkai's Shingon theories gave the archaic world view a philosophical underpinning. Kūkai's own explanations are too technical for us here, but given what we have said so far, we can grasp the direction of his thought by recourse to an analogy: the function and power of music, an analogy suggested by his theory of resonance.

Imagine that as I am going about a daily task there is choral music in the background, perhaps Christmas carolers on the street outside my window. Hearing "Jingle Bells," I tend to nod my head to the rhythm, humming along, or even joining in. Like Dainichi's expounding of the Dharma, the music may not be directly sung for me, but its very nature, like *kaji*, draws me into it as a participant. The more distracted I am, the more caught up in my individual turmoils and problems, the more I may try to shut out the music. But it is still there. So also is the resonance of Dainichi's act.

Now suppose I decide to join the chorus and be part of it. Participation in Dainichi's resonance, like joining in on the music, has its creative aspect. For example, should I sing the melody or the harmony? The song may be already chosen, but how I participate can subtly affect the way the song sounds. Here we have our analogy for thaumaturgy.

The wonder-worker does not change the laws of nature. That would be comparable to changing the song which is being sung. No one has that power; it is always Dainichi's song. Similarly, no note sung by an opera singer can shatter a two-by-four like a crystal goblet: The resonance of the lumber does not lend itself to such influence. Yet, like the individual in the choir, the wonder-worker can subtly influence the overall sound, particularly to the extent the wonder-worker is operating in accord with the natural. Like a strong singer standing next to a singer in the choir who tends to be off-key, the wonder-worker can bring the resonance of the universe into better harmony. The true wonder-worker performs miracles simply by better expressing Dainichi's style as one's own. Wonder-workers do not act on their own; rather, Dainichi's enlightened function (*yū*) resonates powerfully through them, drawing other beings into the harmony. On the macrophysical level, this can seem miraculous. Such is the working of *kaji*.

The Shingon doctrine as developed by Kūkai is more complex than this, but we have already said enough to understand how Kūkai's system managed to integrate the archaic and the philosophic. As our final concern in this paper, we can briefly note how Kūkai's case does not support either of the theories about myth and philosophy described in our introductory paragraphs.

In contrast to the first theory about myth and philosophy we initially outlined, Kūkai did not use philosophy to replace the archaic. Rather, the philosophical metaphysics was used to support many of the presuppositions held by mountain ascetics. First, Kūkai was able to explain in Buddhist terms how thaumaturgical power may be a natural expression of spiritual development. A person attuned to the resonance of Dainichi's *kaji* can bring greater harmony to natural events.

Second, Shingon theory allowed him to confirm that the various *kami*, buddhas, and bodhisattvas are imaginative (but not imaginary) manifestations of a single spiritual principle. In fact, Kūkai encouraged the identification of traditional Japanese *kami* with buddhas and bodhisattvas, the so-called principle of *honjisuijaku*. This supported the inchoate idea of the Yoshino ascetics that somehow Buddhism and Shintō are fundamentally the same. Kūkai showed they were—at least if one accepted the Shingon world view. Furthermore, the Shingon school undoubtedly found it fitting that the central *kami* in the official imperial mythology was the Sun Goddess and that the reality-embodiment was Dainichi, the "Great Sun" Buddha.

Third, that each phenomenon in the world was in itself the Buddha's teaching affirmed the ascetics' emphasis on the spiritual power of nature: the rocks and trees are telling us something. Of course, so too are all the items of city life—the court music, the noise in the streets, the dust from carriage wheels. But with all the macrocosmic distractions, it is hard to focus on the microcosmic resonance. So, in the poem quoted in footnote 6, Kūkai advises us to leave the turmoils of the city: "taking up the secluded religious life, one quickly enters the realm of the Buddha's reality-embodiment." The reality-embodiment's resonance is equally everywhere, but it is easier to be attuned to it when alone in the mountains.

On the other hand, in opposition to the second theory initially discussed in this paper, Kūkai himself obviously did not identify the archaic, mythological view with philosophy. He knew the Buddhist and Confucian philosophical tradition and he must have seen the inadequacy of philosophical explanation in the Natural Wisdom School. He was also acutely aware of the difference between the archaicism of "miscellaneous esotericism" of the *Kokūzōgumonjihō* and the philosophical integrity of the "pure esotericism" of the *Dainichi Sūtra*. So important was the difference to him that he traveled to China to be instructed in the *sūtra*. In his later writings, such as the previously mentioned *Ten Mind-sets*, Kūkai evaluated the strength and weaknesses of the various East Asian philosophies, trying to demonstrate the superiority of the Shingon position. Throughout his life, therefore, Kūkai sought to give the archaic a philosophical expression and justification.

As a final remark on this topic, let us make a comparative observation. If our analysis has been basically correct, Japanese philosophy arose in the context of justifying rather than overpowering the archaic world view. I have argued elsewhere[8] that the opposite tendency can be found in the birth of Western philosophy in Plato and Aristotle. By comparing the two earliest philosophical texts on language in each tradition, Plato's *Cratylus* and Kūkai's *Shōjijissōgi*, we find that Plato's text consciously moved away from the archaic Greek understanding of language as oracular, setting new groundrules for philosophical discourse, whereas Kūkai brought Buddhist philosophy in to support the archaic sense of language as *kotodama* or *mantra*.

Why the difference? Although some "theories of Japaneseness" (*Nihonjinron*) might want to find some profound cultural, psychological, or even genetic reason, the more pedestrian view is that it was mainly the result of external social, political, and historical forces. Greek philosophy was born at the end of the Peloponnesian War, when (from the Athenian view) civilized society was in dissolution. In the cosmopolitan context of ancient Greece, they knew the danger of cultural relativism as a solvent for all general claims to knowledge or value. Indeed, some sophists had already argued in favor of such relativism. What was needed, Plato and Aristotle believed, was a universally valid philosophy based in the individual so that one could carry wisdom and virtue within oneself regardless of whether one lived under the cultural system of the Spartans, Macedonians, or Persians. To accomplish this, one had to move away from the cultural determinateness of the archaic into the realm of logic, rationality, and empiricism.

Kūkai, on the other hand, lived in an era when his own country was struggling for unification, fearful against foreign invasion. The highly articulate philosophies of Confucianism and exoteric Buddhism seemed to cut against the tribal participation in the sacred that had formerly held the ancient Japanese in loosely organized societies. Consequently, Kūkai introduced and developed a universal philosophy, one as rational as any previous Chinese import, but one which would underpin rather than undermine the indigenous Japanese archaicism. This, in the end, was the parting of the ways between ancient Japanese and ancient Western philosophy and, until very recently, the two have shown little sign of convergence.

An alternative, and philosophically more provocative, way of viewing the situation, is to think of Kūkai as not merely using philosophy to justify the archaic, but rather, as contributing a new form of systematic thinking to the repertoire of world philosophies. Kūkai did not merely follow established forms of philosophizing, adapting them to support an argument for the archaic. Rather, he did philosophy in a different way; he philosophized, to develop an image borrowed from Susanne Langer, in a new—in this case, archaic—key.[9] Kūkai presents us not so much with a philosophy about the archaic, as with a model for philosophizing in the archaic.

We should note, first of all, that this differs from most structuralist interpretations of the archaic world view. Such interpretations typically amount to being reconstructions of the "primitive mind" to help the outsider achieve a *Verstehen* of primitive rationality. The *savant* interprets for us the *sauvage*. In Kūkai's case, however, his mind is simultaneously *savant* and *sauvage*. In effect, the very existence of his system explodes the distinction which posits the archaic as a category in the first place. Kūkai's goal is not to explain how it is that strange people called "Shingon Buddhists" are, despite superficial appearances, truly rational. Rather, he argues for a position that only we outsiders happen to call "archaic." For Kūkai, it is simply a description of reality as it is and, given his philosophical arguments, must be.

What is significant in Kūkai's analysis is that he recognizes the other possibility, the kind of thinking that happens to be dominant in the West. He calls it "exoteric" philosophy (*kengyō*) and he attempts to show its philosophical limitations. Kūkai's philosophical challenge to us as philosophers is for us to justify our world view to him, not for us to develop a hermeneutic such that we can have a *Verstehen* of his rational, albeit "wrong" (the implicit assumption in the words "archaic" or "primitive"), world view.

Let us conclude, then, with a few comments on the structure of Kūkai's special form of philosophizing. This is no place to enter into a systematic formulation of a mode of thinking that intends to shake, if not shatter, the assumptions behind the mode dominant in the modern West. But we should not leave our topic without some clearer sense of at least two disharmonies in "exoteric thinking" that are the target of Kūkai's philosophical thaumaturgy.

(1) In Kūkai's thought we find a clear shift away from what we can consider to be the visual metaphor for philosophical discernment. Even our Western preference for balance, for example, is visual in the sense of quantitative symmetry. Philosophy for us is like playing with blocks: to make our structure stand, we must balance opposing forces (two blocks on this side must be matched by either two blocks or by one double-sized block on the other side). Aesthetically, our ideas try to have the balance of a bouquet, not the asymmetry of an *ikebana* arrangement.

As a Shingon or mantric philosopher, Kūkai gives more prominence to the auditory. One implication of this preference is that harmony supersedes balance as the model. For Kūkai, the resolution of the philosophical problem is not like an image's coming into clearer focus, but like the resolution in a musical chord. Rather than standing in an opposing balance, the different elements merge into each other. Harmony is a resonance in sound (a process) rather than the balance of opposition (a stasis).

If Kūkai's analysis stopped there, we would end up with one of those now trite contrasts between East Asian and Western philosophy. But Kūkai's system deals with the visual as well as the auditory. He does this through his theory of the mandalas, the geometric mapping of world views. Significantly, in Kūkai's system the mandala appeals to the mental, just as the auditory appeals to the verbal, dimension of human being. And the two are not opposed or balanced, but rather serve as interrelated tones in the harmony of chords.

To complete the harmonization between the human and cosmic, we must have the third note in that chord, the somatic. For Kūkai this is the dimension of the mudra, the gestures of bodily movement. We fathom reality only through the mutual and simultaneous participation of the corporeal, the mental, and the verbal, what are technically called the "three intimacies" (*sanmitsu*). This observation about how reality is known brings us to the second philosophical challenge presented by Kūkai's philosophizing in the archaic.

(2) Kūkai's philosophical system presents an alternative model for understanding the relation between theory and praxis. For Kūkai, as for the mainline Western tradition, metaphysics is necessary as that disci-

pline which answers the question: what is the structure of reality such that things and events (*physis*) are related as they are? In the modern Western tradition, the companion to metaphysics has become episte-mology, the discipline which asks: what is the rational basis for our knowledge (*episteme*) of reality? We may note that our metaphysics and epistemology must be compatible. We cannot satisfactorily maintain, for example, a metaphysical monism (reality is a single being without differentiation) alongside an epistemological empiricism (we know reali-ty primarily through the data received via the senses). Since the senses give us an experience of diversity rather than oneness, how we know a monistic reality cannot be through the senses.

Kūkai's contribution to this philosophical investigation is his belief that the true companion to metaphysics is not epistemology, but what can be called "metapraxis." Metapraxis asks the question: why does the traditional practice (*praxis*) work as a means to knowing reality? That is, in contrast to epistemology, metapraxis inquires into the experiential rather than the logical basis of knowledge, into how we get to the posi-tion from which knowing is possible rather than into how knowledge works. In fact, epistemologies, insofar as they are practiced, generally make various metapractical assumptions. For example, an empiricist epis-temology requires in practice a process of training whereby one learns to detach oneself from affective preferences about how things should be: since reality is known only through the senses and not the emotions, we must learn how to become "objective observers," for example. Kūkai would point out that the scientific method is not, therefore, just a theo-retical stance, but a way of experiencing and a way of interpreting that experience. It is, in his terms, a "mind-set" (*jūshin*) developed within a certain mode of thought and behavior.

From Kūkai's perspective the weakness in replacing metapraxis by epis-temology is that epistemology is disembodied. It assumes that knowledge can somehow be discussed independently of the special training and disci-pline out of which it evolves. Yet, in theory we all know that knowledge is always achieved through—notice how our language reveals the irony—the insights of the academic "disciplines." Whereas epistemology asks, for exam-ple, "what kind of knowledge is sociology and what metaphysical assump-tions does that mode of knowing necessarily make?", the metapractical ques-tion is "how does one become a sociologist and what metaphysical assumptions lie behind that self-imposed praxis as a mode of knowing/liv-ing?" Much of the postmodern interest in the sociology and power of knowl-edge, we may note, arises from bringing metapractical questions to epistemological theories. The postmodernist typically asks not for the rational basis of the purported knowledge, but rather inquires into the social forces influencing what the thinker is trained to think about and know.

The implication of this emphasis on metapraxis over epistemology for the study of religion is startling. Much of the philosophy of religion in the West for the last half-century has focused on the epistemology of religious truth claims: What kind of knowledge is religious knowledge? From what we have learned from Kūkai, however, the question should be: How does one become religious and what metaphysical assumptions lie behind the self-imposed praxis as a mode of knowing/living?" Too often, we Western scholars of religion have separated out the liturgical (the symbolic, the mythic, the participatory) from the doctrinal (the metaphysical, the epistemological, the reflective). In effect, we have sharply bifurcated what we think of as the archaic from the modern aspects of religious life. To the extent our case study of Kūkai shatters this bifurcation, it opens the door to new vistas on the relations between myth and philosophy.

Notes

1.   This translation is by The Nippon Gakujutsu Shinkokai in their *The Manyōshū* (NY: Columbia University Press, 1965).

2.   A classic study of the religious world view found in *Man'yōshū* is Hirano Shinkei's *Kodai Nihonjin no seishin kōzō* [The structure of the spirit in the ancient Japanese] (Tokyo: Miraisha, 1966). The overall interpretation of ancient Japanese spirituality most influential in the development of this paper is that of Yuasa Yasuo, especially in his *Kodaijin no seishin sekai* [The spiritual world of the ancients] (Tokyo: Mineruva shobō, 1980). On the value system portrayed in the ancient myths recorded in this era, see John C. Pelzel's essay "Human Nature in the Japanese Myths," in *Japanese Culture and Behavior: Selected Readings*, ed. Takie Sugiyama Lebra and William P. Lebra (Honolulu: University Press of Hawaii, revised edition, 1974).

3.   For a carefully researched, yet pithy, account of the spirituality Kūkai encountered in the Yoshino mountains see Sonoda Koyu, *"Kodai bukkyō ni okeru sanrinshugyō to sono igi"* [Mountain practices and their significance in ancient Buddhism], in Kūkai, ed. Wada Shūjō and Takagi Shingen (Tokyo: Yoshikawa Kobunkan, 1982).

4.   The technical term used for Kūkai's present status is *nyūjō* (entrance into meditation). In his *Kōbō Daishi no nyūjōkan* (A perspective on Kōbō Daishi's *nyūjō* [1929]), Morita Ryūsen was the first scholar to bring the techniques of modern scholarship to bear on the history and doctrinal significance of this phenomenon.

5.   There is no translation of *Jūjūshinron* into a European language. *Hizōbōyaku*, an abridged version of this work, is translated in part by Yoshito S. Hakeda in his *Kūkai: Basic Works* (NY: Columbia University Press, 1972) as "The Precious Key to the Secret Treasury."

6.   The following poem expresses well his thoughts on the matter.

Why I Go Into The Mountains

You ask, "Teacher, why do you go into that deep cold—

That unsafe place among the deep, steep peaks

Where the climb is painful and the descent difficult,

That place where the mountain *kami* and tree spirits make their home?"

* * *

"Oh, don't you know? don't you know?

Human life being what it is, how long can you go on?

Thinking, thinking of this day and night, gnawing at your guts;

Like the sun setting in the western mountains, your life is half-gone.

Like a walking corpse, your years are half-spent.

There's no point in staying on and on [in the city].

I must go. I must. I cannot stay.

So, this teacher of the great emptiness (*kū*) does not stay, does not.

This child of [Shingon Buddhism's] milky sea (*kai*)

Does not weary of seeing Mount Kōya's rocks and pines,

And is continually moved by its clear-flowing streams.

Do not take pride in the poison of fame and gain.

Do not be consumed in the fiery world of delusion.

Taking up the secluded religious life, one quickly enters the realm of the Buddha's reality-embodiment (*hosshin*; Skt: *dharmakāya*)."

                                                           (KDKZ 6:732)

In this and future references KDKZ refers to *Kōbō Daishi Kūkai Zenshū* [Complete works of Kōbō Daishi Kūkai] (Tokyo: Chikuma shobō, 1983-1985).

7.   See, for example, the following typical passage:

[Dainichi] Buddha's expounding (*seppō*) necessarily uses expressive characters (*monji*). These characters are located right in the world of our senses, the six realms [of sight, sound, smell, taste, touch, and introspection]. Their ground is the reality embodiment's three intimacies (*sanmitsu*). These three intimacies even pervade at all times the entire world of dharmas. All five kinds of wisdom and all four manifestations of the reality embodiment are inherent, without exception, in each and every realm of the universe.(KDKZ 2:265)

8.   T. P. Kasulis, "Reference and Symbol in Plato's *Cratylus* and Kūkai's *Shōjijissōgi*" in *Philosophy East and West* 32:4 (Oct. 1982), 393-405.

9.   Susanne K. Langer, *Philosophy in a New Key: A Study in the Symbolism of Reason, Rite and Art* (Cambridge: Harvard University Press, 3rd edition, 1957)

References

Hakeda, Yoshito S.
   1972 *Kūkai: Basic Works*. New York: Columbia University Press.

Hirano Shinkei.
   1966 *Kodai Nihonjin no seishin kōzō*. Tokyo: Miraisha.

Kanaoka Shūyū.
   1979 *Kūkai jiten*. Tokyo: Tōkyōdō shukkan.

Kasulis, T. P.
   1982 "Reference and Symbol in Plato's *Cratylus* and Kūkai's *Shōjijissōgi*." *Philosophy East and West* 32:4, 393-405.

Katsumata Shunkyo.
   1970 *Mikkyō no Nihonteki tenkai*. Tokyo: Shunjūsha.

Kitagawa, Joseph M.
   1987 "Master and Savior." In *On Understanding Japanese Religion*, 182-202. Princeton: Princeton University Press.

Kiyota, Minoru.
   1978 *Shingon Buddhism: Theory and Practice*. Los Angeles: Buddhist Books International.

Kūkai.
1965 *Kōbō Daishi Zenshū*. 3rd ed. Edited by Yoshitake Inaba, *et al.* Kōya-san: Mikkyō bunka kenkyū-sho.

1983-1985 *Kōbō Daishi Kūkai Zenshū*. 8 vols. Tokyo: Chikuma shobō.

Langer, Susanne K.
1957 *Philosophy in a New Key: A Study in the Symbolism of Reason, Rite and Art*. 3rd ed. Cambridge: Harvard University Press.

Mikkyō jiten hensan kai.
1987 *Mikkyō dai jiten*. Reissue. Kyoto: Hōzōkan.

Morita Ryūsen.
1929 *Kōbō Daishi no nyūjōkan*. Tokyo: Yamashiroya.

Nippon Gakujutsu Shinkokai.
1965 The Manyōshū. New York: Columbia University Press.

Pelzel, John C.
1974 "Human Nature in the Japanese Myths." In *Japanese Culture and Behavior: Selected Readings*, edited by Takie Sugiyama Lebra and William P. Lebra, 7-28. Rev. ed. Honolulu: University of Hawaii Press.

Sonoda Kōyū.
1982 "Kodai bukkyō ni okeru sanrinshugyō to sono igi." In *Kūkai*, edited by Wada Shūjō and Takagi Shingen, 40-65. Tokyo:Yoshikawa Kōbunkan.

Tamaki Kōshirō.
1974 "Kūkai no bukkyō." In *Nihon bukkyō shisō ron*, 231-265. Kyoto: Heiraku-ji shoten.

Yamasaki Taiko.
1988 *Shingon: Japanese Esoteric Buddhism*. Boston: Shambhala.

Yuasa Yasuo.
1972 *Kamigami no tanjō*. Tokyo: Ibunsha.

1980 *Kodaijin no seishin sekai*. Tokyo: Mineruva shobō.

1981 *Nihonjin no shūkyō ishiki*. Tokyo: Meicho kankōkai.

Chapter 6

Antinomy and Cosmology: Kant Among the Maori

Gregory Schrempp

There has always existed in the world, and there will always continue to exist, some kind of metaphysics, and with it the dialectic that is natural to pure reason.

—Immanuel Kant, *Critique of Pure Reason*

The cosmogonic recital of the Maori, as of many other Polynesian peoples, takes two distinct forms, one that of a prose narrative depicting the decisions and feats of various founding heroes, and the other that of a cosmic genealogy that terminates in all of the beings that

While the project of relating Maori cosmology to Kantian philosophy is my own, I have taken on some of the other main foci of this paper from my teachers, whose influence I gratefully acknowledge. My concern with the two contrastive forms of cosmology is one that I inherited from Valerio Valeri, while my interest in the relationship between cosmology and political process has been influenced particularly by Marshall Sahlins. Earlier versions of this paper were presented to the Departments of Anthropology at the University of Chicago and the University of California Santa Cruz, and to the colloquium on "Religions(s) in Culture and History" at the University of Chicago. I am particularly grateful for the critical commentaries provided by Frank Reynolds, Thomas Kasulis, Jonathan Smith, and Jenifer Curnow.

presently make up the universe.[1] In this paper I will explore this particular dualism in light of the doctrine of "the antinomy of pure reason," a set of arguments formulated by Immanuel Kant to show that reason engaged in cosmology necessarily ends up "divided against itself," that is, compelled by both members of a number of pairs of contradictory propositions. Many of the contrasts that emerge in the two Maori cosmogonic forms align, at least roughly, with those that Kant has encompassed in the antinomies.

There are several motives for this exploration. First, there is the obvious one: to see whether Kant's analysis might be useful in attempting to understand this characteristic of Maori cosmological thought. Secondly, every study of one society by a member of another society involves, at least implicitly, a process of comparison. The dualism of Maori cosmology is the kind of cultural phenomenon that a Western observer could easily highlight as a sort of exotic species of thought—and I admit to being so inclined at times. The value of Kant here lies in the perspective it presents for thinking about the Maori practice in relation to the Western cosmological tradition. In the Kantian view the dualism of Maori cosmology might not be very interesting in itself, since a dualistic tendency is seen as of the essence of reason so engaged. What might be interesting, and worth pursuing, are, rather, the differences in the ways in which a dualistic tendency is developed and deployed in various cultural traditions.

Thirdly, this exploration takes us directly to some crucial issues in the development of Western academic anthropology, specifically, the relationship of anthropological theory, in its formative phase, to Kantian and Neo-Kantian epistemology. Emile Durkheim in particular absorbed much of Kant in constructing his sociological perspective. But it is as if Durkheim decided to restrict his interests to the first half of the *Critique of Pure Reason* only, the Transcendental Analytic, or the section that sets out the "a priori categories of the understanding." The "antinomy of pure reason" is set out as part of the Transcendental Dialectic, the second of the two main divisions of the *Critique*. Durkheim's failure to deal with this second part raises a number of questions and also invites speculations concerning what Durkheim might have had to say regarding the sociological character of cosmology had he pursued the Dialectic. Though these are concerns that cannot be systematically followed up in this presentation, they are well kept in mind as a general background condition of the present situation of academic anthropology.

Finally, there is a proximate stimulus to the Kantian perspective in the comment with which J. Prytz Johansen, one of the greatest European scholars of Maori society, opens his discussion of "The Kinship Group":

> If one could picture to oneself a person like KANT among the old Maoris—which indeed is difficult—one should not be surprised if to the fundamental categories of knowledge, time and space, he had added: kinship.[2]

The statement appears to be intended as a kind of metaphorical assertion of the centrality of "kinship" in Maori thought; indeed Johansen goes on:

> The whole cosmos of the Maori unfolds itself as a gigantic "kin", in which heaven and earth are first parents of all beings and things, such as the sea, the sand on the beach, the wood, the birds, and man. Apparently he does not feel quite comfortable if he cannot—preferably in much detail—give an account of his kinship whether to the fish of the sea or to a traveller who is invited to enter as a guest.[3]

But I find this statement, when considered literally, to be even more intriguing than when read metaphorically—though in need of a rearrangement of priorities. Kant would not have altered his categories in recognition of kinship, but perhaps would have attempted to alter prevailing notions about "kinship" in light of his categories—thus producing a sociological version of his so-called Copernican revolution. There is a point in his analysis of cosmology at which Kant, who in fact is extremely deft at concrete imagery, invokes genealogy in the midst of a rumination on the problem of the infinite regresses into which certain categories, such as "cause," might lead:

> Can we say that the regress is *in infinitum*, or only that it is indeterminately far extended (*in indefinitum*)? Can we, for instance, ascend from the men now living, through the series of their ancestors, *in infinitum*; or can we only say that, so far as we have gone back, we have never met with an empirical ground for regarding the series as limited at any point . . . [4]

One can surmise that the Maori strategy of formulating cosmogony as genealogy is a practice that would not go unappreciated by Kant.

Before proceeding, it is necessary to comment on the nature of my use of Kantian theory, which in some respects is rather selective.

There is, first of all, the issue of what is meant by the "antinomies," for Kant presents this doctrine in several different forms. The *Prolegomena to Any Future Metaphysics* contains a particularly terse, summarizing statement:[5]

1

Thesis

The world has, as to time and space, a beginning (limit).

Antithesis

The world is, as to time and space, infinite.

2

Thesis

Everything in the world is constituted out of the simple.

Antithesis

There is nothing simple, but everything is composite.

3

Thesis

There are in the world causes through freedom.

Antithesis

There is no freedom, but all is nature.

4

Thesis

In the series of world-causes there is some necessary being.

Antithesis

There is nothing necessary in the world, but in this series
all is contingent.

This summary is accompanied by the comment:

Here is the most singular phenomenon of human reason, no other instance of which can be shown in its any other use. If we, as is commonly done, represent to ourselves the appearances of the sensible world as things in themselves, if we assume the principles of their combination as principles universally valid of things in themselves and not merely of experience, as is usually, nay, without our *Critique*, unavoidably done, there arises an unexpected conflict which never can be removed in the common dogmatic way; because the thesis, as well as the antithesis, can be shown by equally clear, evident, and irresistible proofs—for I pledge myself as to the correctness of all these proofs—and reason therefore sees that it is divided against itself, a state at which the sceptic rejoices, but which must make the critical philosopher pause and feel ill at ease.[6]

Thus, the antinomies as presented in the *Prolegomena*, are four pairs of contradictory propositions, accompanied by a promise that there are forceful arguments supporting each thesis and antithesis.

The full arguments themselves are found in the *Critique of Pure Reason*, where the antinomies are set out within a more elaborated architectonic. The fact that there are four antinomies follows from the general plan of the *Critique*, in which the "categories" are organized under four headings: quantity, quality, relation, and modality. The four antitheses each present a potentially infinite series or regress, and the four theses each present an idea that terminates that particular series or regress (the idea of a border in time and space terminates the seriation belonging to space and time; the idea of an indivisible substance terminates the idea of qualitative decomposability; the idea of a first cause terminates the regress of causes). And Kant presents, arranged in columns directly adjacent to one-another, pairs of detailed arguments that purport to prove both the thesis and antithesis of each antinomy.[7] It is to these sets of arguments that critical discussions of "the antinomies" most frequently gravitate.

But at yet other points in the *Critique*, Kant develops something like a *generic* characterization of cosmological antinomy, a characterization that suggests a common structure to the four antinomies that are specifically developed into full arguments.[8] In this generic characterization, cosmological antinomy emerges as a conflict between the fact that certain categories lead by their nature into infinite series or regresses of "conditions," on one hand, and, on the other, a "principle of reason" amounting to the fact that, presented with such series, reason attempts to bring them to completion—attempts to ascend the series of conditions to an "unconditioned." While there would seem already to be a tug-of-war merely in the conflict between seriation and completeness, Kant tends to picture the conflict, rather, as lying in the fact that the "unconditioned" can be thought in two equally compelling ways. It can be envisioned either in the form a terminating condition, or in the idea of an infinite series itself thought of, precisely because infinite, as unconditioned by any further term. Because it is the most abstract, this generic characterization of cosmological antinomy would seem to hold out the most cross-cultural potential, and the discussion that follows takes its main inspiration from it.

Closely related to the issue of what one draws out as comprising "the antinomies" is a basic methodological issue: What kind and degree of intellectual similarity or universality must be presupposed to exist interculturally in order to make this particular, admittedly far-flung, comparison? It is clear that Kant envisioned the antinomies within an architectonic that included all other aspects of his epistemology. Therefore, one might reasonably ask whether, in order to make a valid comparison, one must not also show that the Maori espouse, for example, a conceptualization of time and space similar to Kant's own.[9] There are three main points to be made regarding the requirements of cross-cultural comparison, all of them important in clarifying the attitude toward Kantian epistemology that is adopted here.

The first point is that the parameters of what one could compare would be relative to what one takes as constituting the antinomies, as discussed above. If one takes as "the antinomies" the sets of detailed arguments themselves, one is led to ask whether the more technical concepts, "substance" or "necessary being" and so on, have analogues in non-Western cultures. This would be a legitimate investigation, and, to some extent I will explore such possibilities, even as far as setting up my analysis in terms of the particular categories which Kant invokes to present his doctrine. But, since I am particularly focusing on the more generic characterization of cosmological antinomy, the "bottom line" of what I am suggesting as common to Maori cosmogony and Kantian philosophy is just the kind of structural conflict suggested above. This kind of conflict could be induced by any category of the type that, in carrying the subject from one object to another, carries itself over as a category (as, for example, "cause" carries one over from an object to an anterior object, and in the process carries itself over as a category applicable to the anterior object as well). Kant's Transcendental Dialectic is strongly imbued with a concern that is too easily lost sight of in the study of categorial systems, namely that categories, or at least some of them, lead us beyond, and have consequences for the nature of consciousness that are larger than, any specific empirical application of them—or even of the sum of their empirical applications.

The second point is that Kant seems to have considered a conscious knowledge of the principles of "transcendental idealism" as a prerequisite for a theoretical resolution of the antinomies, but *not* as a prerequisite for what one might refer to as their basic manifestation. For accompanying Kant's formulations of the antinomies are recurrent allusions to the tradition of Western metaphysics as a kind of *locus classicus* of the antinomy of pure reason concretely manifesting itself. Specifically, for two millenia metaphysics has haggled over such issues and failed to settle them. Thus, to the several forms, noted above, that the "antinomies" take as a philosophical doctrine, it is quite clear that the antinomies are yet one thing more to Kant, namely, a historical generalization aimed at a set of tangible data.[10] Kant clearly saw "the antinomy of pure reason" as a generalization abstract enough to hold for metaphysics in general despite the variety of distinct doctrines about the nature of time and space that are contained in this tradition, and despite the fact that such doctrines were, in Kant's view, based upon fundamental misunderstandings of the nature of time and space. There is every indication that Kant thought of antinomy as a universal characteristic of pure reason, though the universality that is implied is potential only. The claim is less that the antinomies will be manifested everywhere than that anyone who should attempt to settle cosmological questions will find the resources of reason such that it can generate equally compelling proofs in opposed directions. And therefore, any claim to have solved such issues will amount to arbitrary dogmatism.

Now, the Maori appear to have had maximally invested themselves in cosmology: they have adopted cosmology as the privileged idiom of their self-definition, sense of values, and political/social theory. If any society can be expected to have exhausted the possibilities of this concern, it would be this one. Given the Maori predilection for cosmology; given the universalist inclinations of Kantian epistemology; and given finally the fact that Kant himself clearly was willing to use the "antinomy of pure reason" not merely as a disembodied philosophical doctrine, but as a historical generalization about the basic character of attempts to do cosmology, the project of considering Kant's theory in relation to Maori society does not strike me as radically un-Kantian.

But this brings us to the third issue: To what extent must one be a Kantian, in the sense of accepting the central tenets of "transcendental idealism," in order to espouse the antinomies as an analytical tool? In the overall scheme of the *Critique of Pure Reason*, one of the purposes of the antinomies is to show that there are conflicts that cannot be laid to rest *unless* one adopts the central tenets of "transcendental idealism," especially the famed phenomenon/noumenon distinction. But I would argue that one can separate the antinomies as a more or less descriptive statement about certain properties of cosmological thought, from Kant's use of them as a support for "transcendental idealism." Indeed some such distinction would seem necessary to Kant's strategy itself, since transcendental idealism is posed as a means of resolving an old and perennial problem of metaphysics. In various other ways Kant provides the basis for distinguishing between antinomies as problem and transcendental idealism as solution. For example, he finds in Zeno of Elea an early recognition of the divided nature of cosmological thought.[11] It is true that Kant in a rhetorical flourish attempts to retrospectively imbue Zeno's formulations with the spirit of transcendental idealism. Yet Kant is clearly adding his own twist to Zeno. There is no evidence that Zeno independently enunciated "transcendental idealism"; and to the extent that Zeno is taken as having adumbrated the "antinomy of pure reason," the tradition of Zeno can only be taken as an articulation of the problem as distinct from Kant's specific attempt at solution.

Kant's attempt to lay the antinomies to rest takes the form not of a decision in favor of either of the poles of any of the antinomies, but rather of a general claim that the problem itself turns out, in light of "transcendental idealism," as wrongly conceived. His notions of the proper way of conceiving of the antinomies ramify through his entire philosophical system. My concern in this analysis, however, is not with Kant's preferred resolution, but rather with his characterization of the problem. For the "antinomies" display in a sophisticated and wide-ranging way certain problems faced in the cosmological endeavor, and perhaps intrinsic to it. Kant's formulation might be examined ethnographically—here, as a first step, in terms of its adequacy as an abstract descriptive characterization of the dualism of Maori cosmology. But the question of whether "transcendental idealism" provides a resolution, or the only possible resolution, of the antinomies—let alone whether it makes any sense as a philosophical system at all—is not the issue here. I take as my purpose merely an initial exploration of what seems to be a parallel insight, occurring within two cultural/intellectual traditions, about the basic nature of cosmology.

Finally, it should be noted that, in anthropology at least, the term *cosmology* has the character of being, on one hand, one of the most frequently invoked analytical terms, and, on the other hand, one of the least critically examined. What do we mean by this concept? In the context of this exploration, we might ask whether our tacit use of "cosmology" does not itself involve antithetical tendencies: on the one hand, the recognition that there are categories that pull the subject beyond the bounds of sensible experience, and, on the other, some blind disposition to seek completion, either in the form of ultimate boundaries, or some *final* statement of their impossibility.

The Third Antinomy

For the following discussion I will focus upon the prose and genealogical accounts written by Te Rangikaheke, a chief of the Arawa tribe of the north island of what is now New Zealand. With respect to the issues involved in the third antinomy, this formulation can be taken as fairly typical of Maori cosmogony in general. Te Rangikaheke's prose account is already widely known to scholars, since it is the source for the prose cosmogony that was published by the colonial Governor George Grey in his *Polynesian Mythology*.[12]

In Kant's *Prolegomena*, the thesis of the third antinomy is "There are in the world causes through freedom." The antithesis is "There is no freedom, but all is nature." In the more complex statement of the *Critique*, this antinomy is posed as:[13]

Thesis	*Antithesis*
Causality in accordance with laws of nature is not the only causality from which the appearances of the world can one and all be derived. To explain these appearances it is necessary to assume that there is also another causality, that of freedom.	There is no freedom; everything in the world takes place solely in accordance with laws of nature.

It is this antinomy which gave rise to my project and which is the main focus of my argument. For the most immediately noticeable difference in the two Maori cosmogonic forms lies in the respective ways in which they portray the motive force of cosmogenesis. Earlier I called attention to Kant's own figurative use of the principle of one of the two forms of Maori cosmology, namely genealogy. By happy coincidence it turns out that Kant would also have appreciated the idiom of the other, that is, the prose form of Maori cosmogony. For as part of the "freedom" pole of the third antinomy, Kant presents the following argument:

> If, for instance, I at this moment arise from my chair, in complete freedom, without being necessarily determined thereto by the influence of natural causes, a new series, with all its natural conse-

quences *in infinitum*, has its absolute beginning in this event, although as regards time this event is only the continuation of a preceding series. For this resolution and act of mine do not form part of the succession of purely natural effects, and are not a mere continuation of them.[14]

It so happens that the cosmos-creating decision of the Maori prose cosmogony is also a decision to stand up. Te Rangikaheke's story can be summarized as follows:

Rangi (Sky) and Papa (Earth) at first cling together, enclosing their children in darkness. The children multiply and seek for a way that they might grow. Some argue that the parents should be killed, while others argue that, rather, they should be separated, so that only one, the earth, might remain a parent to them, while the other, the sky, would become distant to them. They agree to separate the parents, with Tāwhiri (Wind) dissenting. Each of the children, in turn, attempts to separate the parents: Rongo (Sweet Potato), Tangaroa (Fish), Haumia (Fernroot), and Tū (Man). Finally, Tāne (Trees), by putting his head down and feet up, is able to push up the sky.

When the parents are indeed separated, then for the first time can be seen the myriad of beings hiding inside the hollows of the bosoms of Rangi and Papa. Tāwhiri, because he had not agreed to the separation, decides that he will fight against all of the others; and so, when the sky is pushed up, rather than remaining on the earth mother with the rest, he stays within the hollows of the sky as it is pushed upwards. There, in consultation with the Sky, he raises up a brood of descendants to send in attack against his brothers—these descendants being various types of clouds and meteorological phenomena.

When the children of Tāwhiri have become numerous, they are sent out against the other sons of Sky and Earth. They attack Tāne (trees), and snap them apart so that they fall to the ground to rot. They strike out against Tangaroa, who runs off to the sea. The descendants of Tangaroa, however, diverge, one group, the descendants of Ika-tere, going to the sea and becoming fish, the other, the descendants of Tū-te-wehiwehi (lizards), heading to the land. In parting they exchange insults, the former telling the latter that they will be caught by fires in the fern, the latter telling the former that they will be served in baskets of cooked food. The one group cries "Us to the land," the other "Us to the sea"; and hence there is a saying to that effect.

Tāwhiri and his brood turn to attack Rongo and Haumia, but the Earth Mother protects these by hiding them in the folds of her body.

Then Tāwhiri turns against Tū, who is vexed as a result of the fact that, in the gnawing of Tāwhiri and his brood, he alone has stood to fight. Tāne was broken up; Tangaroa ran to the sea; Rongo and Haumia ran to the land. Tū alone was brave in the face of Tāwhiri; they were equal to one another in fighting.

When the anger of Tāwhiri is assuaged, Tū himself turns against his brothers to seek vengeance against them for their failure to help him fight Tāwhiri. He makes nets to catch the children of Tangaroa, and throws them ashore. He goes after Rongo and Haumia; and even though the Earth Mother has hidden them in the folds of her body, he sees their topknots sticking up and spears them with a digging stick, throwing them on the land to be dried by the sun. He fears that Tāne will be able to raise up a brood to send against him; and so he attacks the children of Tāne (the birds) with snares. So Tū's brothers are all eaten by him, and are thus made *noa* (ordinary, no longer sacred) as a retribution for their sending him alone to fight Tāwhiri; all of them are killed and eaten, because Tū alone was brave enough to fight. When Tū has eaten and thus made *noa* his brothers, the *karakia* (traditional incantations) are separated from one another, and also Tū's various names.

The prose account is permeated by a sense of contingency: what happened might not have, and in two different ways. First, what actually happened reflects a decision that was made regarding two alternatives that were considered (the debate, and attempt to establish consensus, over whether to kill or separate the parents). And secondly, the course that was decided upon might have failed, and almost did fail, in the execution. The contingency is highlighted by the fact that only the final possible effort succeeds. The very terminology of the prose account is a terminology of "will," involving concepts such as "thinking," "having an idea," "deciding," "making plans," "agreeing/disagreeing," "standing firm," and so on.[15]

One could go on at great length concerning the implications of the idea of "standing" for the Maori. Tū ("Stand") is the Maori god of war, and in this capacity the term connotes steadfastness and bravery.

Tū is also one of the original group of cosmological beings, and in some accounts, including the present one, he is the progenitor of humanity, his particular resoluteness eventuating in human superordinacy over the rest of nature. There are certain variations in different tribal accounts, but one of the invariants is a concern with posture and specifically with the ability to extend legs straightly, in order to push sky and earth apart and create the space of human existence. In some cases the failures are portrayed as a sickly family whose names bear epithets suggesting difficulties in standing and walking. As Lévi-Strauss has repeatedly pointed out, walking posture and its defects (e.g., limping) constitute a recurrent cosmogonic theme, one often intricately connected with a theory of man's place in nature (a notion that scientific evolutionism has also found to be of some merit).[16] One can of course make too much of Kant's invocation of a decision to stand up as an epitomizing example of "freedom"; crumpled up over his manuscript and looking forward to his famous daily walk, it is understandable that this particular example of "freedom" should leap to mind. But in the Maori case one cannot overestimate its significance. It carries the weight of the decisiveness and resolution that shape the cosmos and engender the particular species-character of humans.

The same general emphasis on willfulness as the necessary motive force of cosmogenesis continues throughout the subsequent phases of the prose cosmogony. The various children of Sky and Earth are, in their initial condition, pictured as nondescript, as being no particular kind of thing. But once Sky and Earth are separated, there is a scramble to develop life-strategies, and the development of the myriad forms of the natural world takes the form of a series of debates concerning such strategies, the various beings ultimately insulting oneanother on their respective views, and going off to live in divergent ways. The parting of ways between land animals and fish is a particularly famous event, but there are many others. One account tells of the parting of mosquitos and sandflies—for the mosquitos want to attack man by night, and the sandflies by day.[17] The coming into being of the entire biosphere is constituted in a spirit in which species character follows species commitment and act. Yet it must be noted that there is a paradoxical character to the "spontaneity" of will, specifically, in that the exercise of will produces its own, though only very general, kind of regularity. That is, differentiation of forms of life through spontaneously emerging choices of ways of life, forms a general paradigm of cosmogenesis within the prose cosmogony.[18]

Following this initial diversification in ways of life, there is a phase of cosmogenesis dominated by a sort of demigod-trickster figure, Māui, who carries out such deeds as fishing up the land, snaring and slowing the sun so that its course is appropriate for human life, and stealing fire for human use. Māui is perhaps the quintessentially willful being, and his famous deeds are once again presented as self-assertions against the parent (his mother, in a recapitulation of the original cosmic situation, keeps Māui in a dark, stopped-up room from which he must initially extricate himself before going to work on the specific details of the world). Following Māui, the next great era is the human era, specifically migrations to New Zealand and the establishing of land claims. The heroes in this era are navigators of great prowess and cleverness. In both of these phases there is a recurrent theme of success through craft and deception. This theme of deceitfulness among founders is in fact found in many mythologies, and has brought forth a number of interpretations, psychoanalytic and otherwise. What is of interest here is not any immorality of theft, but the amorality of it—placing the processes of cosmogenesis outside of what can be accounted for through the regularity of law, whether natural or social.

Now, on the other side of the third antinomy, Kant has in mind processes that work by virtue of regular and consistent laws of nature and devoid of "spontaneity of will." In the other Maori portrayal, the "genealogical" account, cosmogenesis takes the form of a regular and overarching process, expressed in two main ways: through consistent allusions, in the elements used to construct the genealogy, to organic processes of growth or gestation; and through repeating mathematical patterns. Particularly common in the first kind are terms designating types of roots and root fibres.[19] The mathematical pattern is the more dominant in the account considered here. The first cosmic sequence is:

> The night, the night, the first night, the second night, the third night, the fourth night, fifth, sixth, seventh, eighth, ninth, tenth, hundredth, thousandth, indefinitely manyeth.[20]

Night is followed by Nothing, then Searching, Seeking, Pursuing, Sky, Earth, and Cloud.[21] Each of these elements, up to and including Sky, is presented with essentially the same series of numerical epithets as Night. For Sky there is also a "qualitative" series of epithets connoting spatial extent and degrees of lightness and darkness,

Big Sky, Long Sky, Short Sky, Dark Sky, Very Dark Sky,
Lowering Sky, Dark Colored Sky, Glowing Sky, Gloomy Sky,
Intensely Dark Sky, Gleaming Sky.[22]

Earth appears with the numerical epithets, Cloud with a qualitative series
(similar to that attached to Sky). Then there is the statement: "The coming
out into the bright light, into the day light," and the genealogy continues,
eventually leading to the human ancestors of the Maori tribes.

It is important to note, then, that the genealogy does not merely
list in order of procreation the beings who appear in the prose account;
rather it casts these in a distinctive model of cosmogenesis, one based on
a regular and patterned unfolding. The sequence of epithets in the
above example contains a series of four models of increase, each more
powerful than the last. First, there is mere repetition (The night, the
night); then an arithmetic sequence (one through ten), then an expo-
nential sequence (ten, hundred, thousand), and then finally the use of a
term (*tini*) that connotes the "innumerable." The Maori genealogical
portrayals of cosmogenesis have often elicited the discourse of natural
sciences from Western scholars, especially in the characterization of the
essential process as one of "evolution."

However, while it does seem to be the case that the genealogical
cosmogonies locate the motive force of cosmogenesis in the continuity
of an overall process, it is not quite accurate to claim that there is no
reference to the vocabulary of "will." This particular genealogy, and
many others, contain terms such as "searching," "seeking," "pursuing"; these terms appear to be allusions to the dissatisfaction of the
children with the original state of affairs as recounted in the prose
account. What is noteworthy in the genealogical accounts, however, is
that, rather than emphasizing major disruption, such terms are taken
up within the patterned regularity and repetitiveness that constitute
the overall process. Terms such as "the searching" here take a grammatical form roughly analogous to a gerund, or a nominalized
verb—that is, an action thought of as a thing.

These last observations present the occasion for posing a broader
and at this point rather impressionistic comment: if something like the
valences of the Kantian third antinomy are manifest in the Maori dual
(i.e., prose vs. genealogical) representation of cosmogenesis, they are
manifested not so much in the genealogical account as "natural process"
and the prose account as "will," but rather in the form of the genealogical account as the recasting of will as natural process, and the prose

account as the recasting of natural process as will. As an example in this latter direction, i.e., the recasting of natural process as will, I call attention to the fact that some of the very rhythms that underlie the regularity of the genealogical account—that is, seasonal cycles of plant and fish life—become, in the course of the prose account, subject to human will. This happens when Tū, ancestor of humanity, conquers and eats his brothers (who are ancestors of the other natural species) and thereby renders them *noa* (no longer sacred). Tū as a result receives a *karakia* (incantation, spell) that permits control of each of the other beings.

> So his older brothers were made *noa*, and thence his *karakia* were separated, a *karakia* for Tāne-mahuta, for Tangaroa, for Rongo-matane, for Haumia, for Tū-matauenga. The reason he sought for these *karakia*, was in order to be able to cause his older brothers to return as food for him . . .[23]

Unlike the situation that Kant thought he saw in Western metaphysics, here we seem to have a self-aware dialectic, in which each formulation is responsive to the other, subordinating the same elements under a different framing attitude regarding the "cause" of the cosmos. This self-awareness is evident most obviously in the fact that the prose and genealogical accounts focus on the same "people" (especially Sky and Earth and their brood), but in many other minor ways as well.[24]

Many of the best sources on traditional cosmogonic recital, including the one considered here, are manuscripts written by Maori people in the mid-nineteenth century. While it is more difficult to infer whether there were contexts which favored one form or the other, one can at least infer from these sources that a knowledge of and alternation between the forms was a widespread practice.

The First and Second Antinomies

As noted at the outset, a contrast in modes of motive force of cosmogenesis distinguishes the two main Maori formulations of cosmogenesis, and the contrast seems to be similar to that depicted by Kant in the third antinomy; this has been the main focus of my presentation. Kant calls the third and fourth antinomies "dynamical" since they have to do with the propulsive force of origination and therefore of "dependency of existence" within the cosmos. I will not here deal specifically with the fourth antinomy—which opposes the idea of a "necessary being" to the idea of the contingency of all things—because it is some-what redundant with the third. This seeming redundancy of the third and fourth—i.e., the "dynamical"—antinomies is not, however, the case with respect to the first and second antinomies, which deal with exten-sion and divisibility, and are termed "mathematical." The first antino-my can be divided into the spatial and temporal dimensions; and then the first and second, or "mathematical," antinomies can be displayed in their main features through the following arrangement:

— that the universe is limited:
    — as to extent in space
    — as to extent in time
    — as to the extent of qualitative divisibility

vs.

— that the universe is infinite:
    — as to extent in space
    — as to extent in time
    — as to extent of qualitative divisibility

These various mathematical axes are useful in characterizing the differ-ences between the Maori prose and genealogical cosmogonies, for along each axis the two forms do seem to pose an antinomy. The antinomies posed are not always rigorously characterizable as between the "finite" and the "infinite," as in the Kantian formulation; in some instances the contrast would seem to be more properly characterized as between the finite and the indefinite.[25] Nonetheless, I will briefly consider the Maori material in relation to the various mathematical axes—partly because there would seem to be at least some limited analogies with the con-cerns of the Kantian antinomies, and partly because the mathematical axes form, in any case, a useful grid through which to explore the phe-nomenon of cosmological antinomy more broadly.

If the motive force of the Maori prose cosmogenesis is "will," the cosmic problem to which it is applied is the finitude of space; the cos-mos-initiating act is that of wresting some space by propping Sky and Earth apart. The product of this effort seems to be a "closed" uni-verse, with earth as lower and sky as upper barrier. In some accounts the celestial bodies are said to be attached to the front of Sky's body facing downward to earth; and most of the accounts suggest that the space of being must be in an ongoing way held open, i.e., that Sky and Earth must be propped apart against their own desire to unite.

Space in the genealogical account is more difficult to comment upon; the most notable characteristic vis-à-vis the prose account is the less focused concern on spatial finitude. As noted earlier there are some terms ("searching," "seeking") that would seem to be allusions to the original enclosed condition. Yet this spatial concern certainly is not the crux of the account. This theme is, rather, absorbed as one set of elements in a larger configuration of patterned expansiveness. And within that longer stream there is a set of epithets that seem to engage the idea of space in the form of a free adducing of varying spatial characteristics ("Big Sky, Long Sky, Short Sky"). One can say minimally that there is a contrast between a universe that is spatially finite—in which spatial finitude is indeed its single most salient characteristic—and one that does not appear to be so defined.

But there is another approach to the spatial character of the two accounts, an approach that is both simpler and more attentive to the *modus operandi* of the two accounts. For there are certain images that spatially define the cosmos in the two accounts. In the prose account, the image is of male and female seeking to sexually unite, and the space of the cosmos is the distance between them. In the genealogical account, the dominant images are that of an open numerical series and that of organic growth, such as a spreading plant.[26] The different spatial images belonging to the two accounts suggest a contrast of the finitely extensible to the indefinitely extensible. As noted earlier, the prose and genealogical accounts mutually incorporate and subordinate one-another's claims. Both the principle of expansion and the principle of containment are present in both the prose and genealogical accounts. In the prose account expansion is subordinated to containment: the supreme achievement is a mere contingent holding-open of the cosmos against its implosive tendency. In the genealogical account, containment is subordinated to expansion—the original containment being recast as merely one set of elements in a pattern of ongoing expansion, modeled on organic growth, or, in some cases, on an open, compounding numerical series.

The two accounts also differ in the way that they construct the cosmos temporally. While there may be in the prose cosmogony a vague sense of the timeless existence of Sky and Earth, the cosmos itself has a definite beginning point in their separation. The prose cosmogonies tend to single this pair out as the starting point of the cosmos; the composer of the account under consideration here, who had been introduced to Christianity, in fact specifically draws an analogy between the cosmological position of this pair and that of the being that Christian metaphysics regarded as the "first cause" of the universe:

> According to Pakeha [European] tradition, God alone made man, Sky and Earth, and all things. To Maori people, Sky and Earth were the sources.[27]

In the genealogical accounts, on the other hand, the essential processes of cosmogenesis goes back further; the basic patterns are already clearly and fully laid down in elements that precede Sky and Earth, i.e., in such prior elements as "night" and "nothing." The motive force that is characteristic of genealogical cosmogenesis (i.e., a set of regular and patterned progressions) thus goes back at least relatively deeper in time than does the motive force that is characteristic of the prose cosmogony (i.e., the actions of willful beings). The first things of the prose account are temporally secondary things in the genealogical account; this seems to hold as a general rule in Maori cosmogony even though many other genealogical accounts do not proliferate terms as profusely as Te Rangikaheke's.

Te Rangikaheke's sense of the genealogical regress could almost be said to be infinitist. As noted before, the genealogical account makes recurrent use of mathematical epithets that culminate in the term *tini*, which might be translated as "innumerable." Jenifer Curnow, who has extensively studied the writings of Te Rangikaheke, comments on these particular mathematical series:

> Each sequence is numbered, and yet beyond number; its length can be counted to a thousand, but beyond that the period of time is so great it is myriad (*tuatini*).[28]

Elsewhere she refers to these series as suggesting a "vastness of time" or even an "infinite sequence."[29] Thus this genealogical account is punctuated by a term which suggests if not an infinite regress, then one that is at least beyond enumeration.

The antinomy belonging to quality is, finally, the most complex and potentially interesting antinomy, though it also must be admitted that what is to be sought in the Maori formulations is most clearly by way of analogy only. At issue for Kant is the question of the qualitative decomposability of the "real" of the universe, and specifically the issue of whether this proceeds infinitely or ends in ultimate, indivisible substances. In the Maori formulations, all qualities are personified, and I do not see anything exactly equivalent to the venerable metaphysical concept of "substance." Yet one of the intellectual issues pervading Maori cosmogony, and many other traditional cosmogonies, is a concern with the number of kinds of things in the universe, coupled with an assumption that the qualities of some things arise as combinations of the qualities of others.

The intellectual operation that I will consider in the Maori case is that of epithetization, i.e., the practice of adding qualifying epithets to main nominal terms in either the prose or the genealogical accounts. The analysis will thus consist not so much of introducing new material as of reexamining those we have already considered, but with an eye toward the ways in which "qualitative distinctions" are envisioned —and also towards a process that in these accounts is closely connected with such distinctions, i.e., hierarchicalization. The underlying rules of genealogy and prose seem to differ fundamentally on this process of epithetization. In the genealogical account, the qualifying epithets are rather freely adduced, while in the prose cosmogony, there is a definite principle of limitation. The ostensible difference can be seen by recalling and comparing the appearance of some of the specific "people." In the prose account, Sky for example occurs as:

Sky

Sky in the genealogical account occurs as:

> . . . first Sky, second . . . indefinitely manyeth. Big Sky, Long Sky, Short Sky, Dark Sky, Very Dark Sky, Lowering Sky, Dark Colored Sky, Glowing Sky, Gloomy Sky, Intensely Dark Sky, Gleaming Sky.

In the genealogical account of the ultimate origins of the universe, each primordial term in the genealogy is subjected to a series of qualifying epithets (numerical, spatial, or of a third type connoting shades of lightness and darkness). In the prose account, the process of epithetization occurs only once, specifically in relation to the ancestor of humanity, Tū, in consequence of his conquering in battle and eating of his brothers (in the event summarized above). The narrator follows the recounting of this event with the comment:

> When his brothers were defeated by him, then his [Tū's] names were separated: Tū-ka-riri, Tū-ka-nguha, Tū-kai-taua, Tū-whakaheke-tangata, Tū-mata-whāiti, Tū-matauenga. His names were made equal in number to his brothers.[30]

It might initially seem a bit presumptuous to infer any significance from this one prose occurrence of the process of epithetization. However, considering the use that is made of epithetization in the prose account, *there can be only one occurrence*—only one being with a highly "composite" character. For here the epithetization—which also might be called, in Dumont's term, "encompassment"[31]—is reserved for the expression of hierarchy, and very directly so in the sense that each epithet qualification must be specifically justified by the subordination of some specific cosmic entity (so that Tū's epithets are said to be equal to the number of beings he has subordinated).

Ultimately, both prose and genealogy in fact function to create a relation of superordination for one being to others in a set; but with respect to the compositeness of particular beings they work in opposite ways. The prose account creates hierarchy precisely through an economy of composition—the fact that one of the beings in the story, through the events that transpire, ends up more composite, or more encompassing, than the others. Genealogies, on the other hand, create hierarchy not among the beings within the same genealogy, but for the one being at the end of the genealogy in relation to other beings with their own genealogies.[32] And in the latter strategy hierarchy is created more effectively precisely to the extent that the elements in the genealogy are subdivided (or should one say multiplied?) through epithetization, since the final being in any genealogy encompasses all that is contained in it. Thus, in sum, with respect to qualitative divisibility of main terms, the prose cosmogony seems once again to work by virtue of a principle of necessary limitation, and the genealogical by virtue of an attitude of (perhaps theoretically limitless) proliferation. And, once again, the different representations characteristic of the two cosmogonic formulations are representations of the same original "people."

The fact that the Maori cosmogony (in either form), and the cosmogonies of many other cultural traditions as well, are personified, i.e., invoke "persons" as the idiom for dealing with the problem of the amount and kinds of things in the universe, may stem from a human capacity for grasping individual persons as ensembles of qualities. Lévi-Strauss proposed at one point that "proper names"

> form the fringe of a general system of classification: they are both its extension and its limit. When they come on to the stage the curtain rises for the last act of the logical performance.[33]

This statement is true, but only in certain contexts. Particularly in the case of exemplary and cosmically founding persons, there is another kind of process—not one that ends with an individual, but rather one that starts with an individual and decomposes the unity implied in this construct (infinitely?). The myriad characteristics and alternative appelations drawn in Christian litanies (for example, the litany of the Blessed Virgin) might be a process analogous in this respect to the epithetization of the various first elements of Maori cosmogony. Marcel Mauss once commented that

> we have at our disposal, especially in mythology, cases of what I call 'mental reverberation', in which the image is endlessly multiplied, so to speak. Thus Vishnu's arms, each the support of an attribute. Thus the feather head-dresses of the Aztecs' priest-god, each feather of which is a different fragment of the soul of the god. For here is one of the fundamental points both of social life and of the life of the individual consciousness: the symbol—an invoked genie—has a life of its own; it acts and reproduces itself indefinitely.[34]

The only problem with Mauss' comment is that, in so tightly binding this process to religious symbolism, it threatens over-mystification, dismissing in advance the possibility of analogies that might be drawn between this kind of operation and those through which formal metaphysics has approached the problem of the qualitative divisibility of the universe. For this is clearly a problem common to, and in relation to which, it is sometimes difficult to draw a precise line of demarcation between, "mythology" and "philosophy."

Antinomy and Cosmology

The above considerations sketch some possible points of contact between the Maori dual representation of cosmogony and the Kantian characterization of the antinomy of pure reason. It should be noted that there are complex issues posed by the fact that Maori cosmogony is actually recited. Put simply, while it may be possible to state, by way of ontological argument, that the universe has no beginning, it is difficult to imagine how one would recite or "perform" an account of such a universe. Seemingly intrinsic to performance is the act of beginning. The basic logic of the Maori genealogical account seems to be that of a regress of causes even though, perhaps as necessitated by the constraints of recital, the regress lapses into a vague fade-out (or, in the directionality of the recital, a fade-in)—in some cases with an enigmatic first term ("the nothing"), in some cases with an unpursued cyclicality ("night"). Some such strategy might represent the best possible compromise between an attitude of ontological infinitude and the pragmatic finitude of performance. There is an even more significant sense in which Maori cosmology is "performed." For in the Maori case one is confronting in cosmology an entire form of life: lived reality is, at any moment, the present terminus of the ongoing world-genealogy and world-historical tale. One finds in cosmology, for example, many paradigms of ongoing political strategy and practice, which, in turn, grounded in cosmology, embody the dual character thereof.[35] Starting from social/political life, one could even envision in the antinomies a yet unexplored dimension to the classical Durkheimian project—that of sociologically grounding the Kantian topography of reason.[36] But that would be another project; here it is enough to call attention to the several possible levels on which Maori cosmology appears to be under a constraint of performance that is more marked—or perhaps merely of a different character—than that of Western metaphysics. And there are no doubt many other ways in which the two traditions differ.

But such differences do not mean that one tradition cannot shed light on the other, for the differences might be conceived as various deployments of certain possibilities and limitations inherent in cosmology as a project. The foregoing exercise suggests, among other things, certain possibilities of internal structure within cosmological/cosmogonic formulations. It does seem that the complete set of "theses," or alternatively the complete set of "antitheses," can be taken as forming a general strategy of internal cosmological structure, for on many levels the members of each set "go together." For example, a motive force of "spontaneity" would not presuppose an extended temporal duration, while a force of natural causation would seem ipso facto to induce a temporal regress of causes. There would seem to be a natural tendency toward proportionality between the degree of qualitative diversity attributed to the cosmos and the extent of the temporal/spatial continuum in which this is thought to develop. *On all of these dimensions simultaneously*, the one Maori account, the prose account, seems committed to upholding finite domains, while the other account, the genealogical, allows cosmological speculation to proceed at least relatively farther —and as though oblivious to any need to posit ultimate limits.

There are further ways in which Kant's formulations might be of use in attempting to construct a cross-cultural perspective on cosmology. To the extent that antinomy is a recurrent characteristic of cosmology, one might extrapolate possible strategies of resolving antinomies. Three in particular suggest themselves:

1. To make noncontradiction the preeminent value, thus requiring individual cosmologists to dogmatically choose one side or the other. This seems to be, in Kant's view, the history of Western metaphysics: a permanent wavering, in the debates among different practitioners, between equally defensible positions.

2. To make completeness the preeminent value, or in other words, to make the first imperative that of thinking out all the possibilities of cosmology, and then, secondarily, to devise strategies to cope with the necessary consequences of that mandate, one of which is contradictory accounts. Maori cosmology might lie somewhere in here. But it must immediately be cautioned that such a suggestion should not be taken as lending support to the idea, associated most closely with Lévy-Bruhl, of the existence of a form of non-Western rationality that is indifferent to contradiction. In Kant's characterization of the antinomies, two imperatives of reason, consistency and completeness, end up opposed to one another. The choice of one imperative, in an endeavor that precludes attainment of both, cannot count as implying an "indifference" toward the other. As alluded to at several points in this paper, it is clear that, given the two Maori accounts, efforts are made to harmonize them insofar as possible—to the extent that the general impression created by the two accounts is often more of complementarity than of contradiction. If the Maori allow, or indeed insist upon, opposed accounts both being given a place, this would seem to be less a matter of indifference to contradiction than of a positive valuation of rational exhaustiveness. Finally, it should be noted that a part of Kant's resolution of the third and fourth antinomies consists in his assertion that the contradiction in these antinomies is merely an apparent contradiction. Both of the opposed pairs of propositions can be true, because there is a shift in reference between them.[37] While it is not obvious from the texts themselves that there is some such shift in reference, or in the "sense" in which the two accounts are respectively held to be true, such a possibility certainly cannot be ruled out.

3. To forswear thinking about such issues, or at least to forswear thinking about them in the ways that give rise to the antinomies

in the first place. This would seem to form the main thrust of Kant's solution: "transcendental idealism" is, among other things, an attempt to transcend some (in Kant's view, very natural) assumptions that are brought to the cosmological endeavor in its usual, precritical formulation, and which are, Kant argues, the source of the "illusion" that is demonstrable in the antinomies. Kant's resolution thus involves a rejecting of the problem itself in its usual definition. There is of course much to be pursued, and which has been pursued by many scholars, in the particulars of Kant's reconceptualization of the concerns of traditional metaphysics. But it should be noted as well that this general kind of resolution—one that rejects or in some way attempts to transcend the usual statement of the endeavor—may not be unique to Kant. Both in the Western cosmological tradition, and in some non-Western traditions, can be found instances of cosmological formulations whose essential move seems to be a positing of cosmological problems, and then a rejection (in the form of either total dismissal or radical reformulation) of the very problems that have been posed.[38]

Maori cosmology is dualistic, and Kant presents a sophisticated characterization of the nature of cosmological thought that argues that this pursuit is in its nature dualistic; in this sense Kant's perspective may be of use in attempting to probe the inner logic of Maori and other similar cosmologies. But of even more direct importance is the suggestiveness of the Kantian perspective in relation to the issue of intercultural comparison—an issue that is at least implicitly present in any study of one culture by a member of another. There is perhaps a natural thrill in discovering exotic phenomena; and there is, in particular, a long-standing European tradition of viewing the South Pacific as a rich source of cultural exotica, a tradition which could be subtly or not-so-subtly invoked in portraying Maori dualistic cosmology. Here, however, Kant might give the enthnologist reason to pause, for he presents a perspective from which Maori cosmological dualism needs no special or "esoteric" explanation. In Kant's view, the dialectical character of cosmological thought is no less a fact in the Western cosmological tradition, though the history of metaphysics is the history of the attempt to deny it.

It is of course interesting to speculate about what Kant would have had to say regarding Maori cosmology. To be sure, "transcendental idealism" for Kant formed the only acceptable resolution of the antinomies; yet the recognition of the dogmatic irresolvability of the antinomies was the first step towards this resolution. Kant might have seen the Maori cosmological achievement as having something in common with that of Zeno, as embodied in the latter's famous series of cosmological paradoxes. For even if they did not invent "transcendental idealism," the Maori seem to have at least recognized and thus escaped the futility inherent in attempting a dogmatic solution to such issues—an attempt which, suggests Kant, "under the name of metaphysics has for centuries spoiled many a sound mind . . ."[39]

Notes

1.   Cf. Valeri, "Constitutive."

2.   Johansen, *Maori*, 9.

3.   Ibid., 9.

4.   Kant, *Critique*, 452.

5.   Kant, *Prolegomena*, 80.

6.   Ibid., 80-81.

7.   Kant, *Critique*, 396ff.

8.   Ibid., 300ff.

9.   The clarifications that follow are motivated in part by criticisms raised in Jonathan Smith's response to my presentation in the conference on "Religion(s) in Culture and History."

10.   There would be a worthy project in the investigation of the "antinomy of pure reason" specifically as a historical generalization. Such an approach would provide a refreshing alternative to the usual way in which the antinomies are subjected to critique—that is, in terms of the internal coherence and logical force of the specific arguments that Kant lines up against one-another.

11.   Kant, *Critique*, 446ff.

12.   The original sources for the account that Grey published (*Polynesian Mythology*) are now found in three folders (43, 44, 81) of the Grey New Zealand Maori Manuscripts (GNZMMSS) of the Auckland Public Library. I have written about these elsewhere in more detail (Schrempp, "Tū Alone"), and the summary of the prose account that follows is taken largely from my earlier analysis. Curnow has also written about these accounts (Curnow, "Wiremu"). The present translations are mine, though I have consulted Grey's and Curnow's. The Maori story of the separation of Sky and Earth is of course a variation on a widespread Old World cosmogony, having numerous similarities, for example, to Hesiod's *Theogony*.

13.   Kant, *Critique*, 409.

14.   Ibid., 414.

15.   As embodied in such passages as:

Then Tū sought for some plan by which to turn and subdue his brothers on account of their weakness in the face of Tāwhiri's revenge over the parents, such that it had been he alone who had been brave enough to fight. (Te Rangikaheke, "Ngā Tama," 894).

16.   Examples of the sickly family theme can be found in White (*Ancient History*). Lévi-Strauss discusses the mythological significance of ambulation at several points (e.g., *Structural*, 212; *From Honey*, 464).

17.   For example, see Best, *Tuhoe*, 991ff.

18.   See Valeri, "Constitutive," 11ff.

19.   Numerous examples can be found in Best, *Maori*, 55ff.

20.   Te Rangikaheke, "Tūpuna," 915.

21.   The term here translated as "Cloud" might alternatively be translated as "Day."

22.   Te Rangikaheke, "Tūpuna," 915.

23.   Te Rangikaheke, "Ngā Tama," 895-96.

24.   See also Schrempp, "Tū Alone," 22-24, 35[n.10].

25.   "Indefinite," as a privative term, is potentially very ambiguous; here I utilize it to call attention to the absence of any indication that limits should exist. This usage of course is not equivalent to "infinite." Yet "indefinite" in this sense contrasts less strongly with "infinite" than does "indefinite" in the other sense in which it is sometimes invoked, i.e., as implying an assumption of limits, but which have not yet been defined.

26.   Even though Te Rangikaheke does not invoke the spreading plant image in his genealogy of primordial origins, it is interesting to note that he does invoke this image in his genealogy of his more recent ancestors, specifically those who migrated and settled New Zealand (see Schrempp, "Tū Alone," 27-28).

27.   Te Rangikaheke, "Ngā Tama," 893.

28.   Curnow, "Wiremu," 124.

29.   Ibid., 123-24.

30.   Te Rangikaheke, "Maori," 55.

31.   Dumont, *Homo*.

32.   See Valeri, "Constitutive," 37, 40.

33.   Lévi-Strauss, *Savage*, 215.

34.   Mauss, *Sociology*, 21-22.

35.   Cosmology is, among other things, the backdrop and idiom of Polynesian political theory, which seems to consistently recognize two forms of political legiti-

mation, that of ordered genealogical succession and that of "usurpation." The former process involves a kind of necessity, succession being determined as a predictable consequence of genealogical rank (including seniority of birth). The other
involves an interruption of this rule, in favor of legitimation by the willful and decisive actions of a given individual. Each of these processes abrogates the unity of
process espoused in the other. The two forms of political legitimation are both
thoroughly cosmologically grounded—the one in the regular, inevitable patterns of
the original genealogy, the other in the tale of the decisive actions of the first
beings, in which usurpers are typically genealogically junior members of lineages.

36.   Durkheim restricted his interest in Kant to the Transcendental Analytic, the
part of the *Critique of Pure Reason* that sets out the categories, and neglected the
Transcendental Dialectic, or the section that deals with the antinomies that develop when these categories are applied beyond the bounds of experience.
Durkheim's main ambition with regard to the Analytic amounted to an attempt to
ground the categories in society, for example:

> the category of class was at first indistinct from the concept of the
> human group; it is the rhythm of social life which is at the basis of the
> category of time; the territory occupied by the society furnished the
> material for the category of space; it is the collective force which was
> the prototype of the concept of efficient force, an essential element in
> the category of causality. (Durkheim, *Elementary*, 488)

While I am satisfied at this point merely to make the observation that to
describe cosmology in the Maori case is at the same time to characterize
social/political process, Durkheim, had he consulted the Transcendental Dialectic,
might have pursued the interrelationship much further, and in a specifically "socio-
logical-reductionist" fashion. He might have claimed to have found, in the equal
necessity of "regularity" and "spontaneity" to social/political life, the ground of the
ultimate equal compellingness of these forms of causality. And he might have found
the social grounds for the other antinomies too—for example, in regard to space, in
the fact that the social ethos of a given tribe demands, on the one hand, the conviction that its space, coterminus with all human value, is firmly circumscribed; and
on the other hand, an opposed "other" (which demands its own other, etc.).

It is probably fair to say that many anthropologists of the present day have an
ambivalent attitude towards the Durkheimian project: unable to go along completely, but glad that Durkheim made the arguments he did, for they present, if
overzealously, the case for a sociological component of epistemology. It seems
likely that Kant would have rejected the social-functionalist teleology that underlies Durkheimian epistemology. But it is also worth noting that in abandoning
metaphysics insofar as the interests of substantive knowledge were concerned,
Kant nevertheless pronounced a belief that the metaphysical impulse, like everything in nature, must be "intended for some useful purpose," and bequeathed this
impulse to a study that was more broadly conceived than formal epistemology; for

> the question does not concern the objective validity of metaphysical
> judgments but our natural predisposition to them, and therefore does
> not belong to the system of metaphysics but to anthropology. (Kant,
> *Prolegomena*, 102)

37.   Kant's own attempt at resolution of the third antinomy should not be neglected in considering the Maori material. In an argument that figures centrally in his critique of "practical reason," Kant concludes that both poles of the dynamic antinomies can be true. Insofar as humans are phenomenal, their actions cannot be represented other than according to the causality of nature; but insofar as humans are noumenal, another principle—"freedom"—is possible. Since they have different referents, the (seemingly) opposed propositions are not contradictory.

38.   On the basis of data from Ojibwa, Bororo, and Tikopian society, Lévi-Strauss has called attention to a recurrent cosmogonic pattern, in which the first cosmogonic move consists of some reduction in the total amount of things that comprise the cosmos, often in such a way as to move from a theoretically limitless amount to an amount that is humanly manageable and significant. Lévi-Strauss has suggested that

> discontinuity is achieved by the radical elimination of certain fractions of the continuum. Once the latter has been reduced, a smaller number of elements are free to spread out in the same space, while the distance between them is now sufficient to prevent them overlapping or merging into one another. (*Raw*, 52)

In terms of a broad spectrum of general types of solutions to cosmological issues, this pattern may have something in common with Kant's attitude towards cosmology. In both cases, a part of the solution to cosmological questions lies precisely in abandoning such questions—at least for certain purposes. For Kant, this meant the abandonment of cosmology insofar as "science" was at issue. In the specific examples that Lévi-Strauss treats, it is as if the first cosmogonic move is precisely the abandoning of cosmology (or a concern with all possible things) in favor of sociology (or a concern with those things that are of special human significance, such as the objects that will serve as clan-emblems).

39.   Kant, *Prolegomena*, 66.

References

Best, Elsdon.
    1925 *Tuhoe*. Wellington: The Polynesian Society.

    1976 *Maori Religion and Mythology*, vol. 1. Wellington: Government Printer.

Curnow, Jenifer.
    1985 "Wiremu Maihi Te Rangikaheke: His Life and Work." *Journal of the Polynesian Society* 94:97-147.

Dumont, Louis.
1970 *Homo Hierarchicus*. Chicago: University of Chicago Press.

Durkheim, Emile.
1965 *The Elementary Forms of the Religious Life*. New York: Free Press.

Grey, George.
1855 *Polynesian Mythology*. London: John Murray.

Johansen, J. Prytz.
1954 *The Maori and His Religion*. Copenhagen: Ejnar Munksgaard.

Kant, Immanuel.
1965 *Critique of Pure Reason*. Translated by N. K. Smith. New York: St. Martin's Press.

1983 *Prolegomena to Any Future Metaphysics*. Indianapolis: Hackett.

Lévi-Strauss, Claude.
1967 *Structural Anthropology*. Garden City: Anchor Books.

1970 *The Savage Mind*. Chicago: University of Chicago Press.

1970b *The Raw and the Cooked*. New York: Harper and Row.

1974 *From Honey to Ashes*. New York: Harper and Row.

Mauss, Marcel.
1979 *Sociology and Psychology*. London: Routledge and Kegan Paul.

Schrempp, Gregory.
1985 "Tū Alone Was Brave: Notes on Maori Cosmogony." In *Transformations of Polynesian Culture*, edited by A. Hooper and J. Huntsman, 17-37. Auckland: The Polynesian Society.

Te Rangikaheke.
"Ngā Tama a Rangi." Ms. (GNZMMSS 43) at Auckland Public Library.

"Tūpuna." Ms. (GNZMMSS 44) at Auckland Public Library.

"Maori Religious Ideas and Observances." Ms. (GNZMMSS 81) at Auckland Public Library.

Valeri, Valerio.
n.d. "Constitutive History: Genealogy and Narrative in Hawaiian Kingship." Ms. in preparation.

White, John.
    1887 *The Ancient History of the Maori*, vol. 1. Wellington:
    Government Printer.

Myth, Philosophy, and Poetics

Chapter 7

Hymn to Vāc:
Myth or Philosophy?

Laurie L. Patton

Ṛg Veda 10:71, the hymn to Vāc, or speech, is one of the shorter hymns of the *Ṛg Veda*, yet many scholars of Indian thought and practice have postulated it as a "key" to a right understanding of the Vedic world as a whole. Jan Gonda, in his *Vision of the Vedic Poets* (1963) has written:

> All that which the poets left as understood in the form of half-veiled elements, words with double meanings, throughout the hymns, is codified so to say in this poem. It is in this light that one must read the *Ṛg Veda* if one wants to grasp fully the understood intentions.[1]

Two most recent treatments of the hymn—by Frits Staal (1977), and Willard Johnson (1980)—continue in this tradition, yet they portray that key in very different ways. Staal's reading is a linguistic one concerned with the philosophical category of Vāc, meaning language, and Johnson's reading is a devotional one concerned with the relationship of the individual seers in the sacrifice to the mythological Vāc, meaning "goddess of speech."[2]

The fact that there are two divergent translations and interpretations of a Vedic text is not, in and of itself, such a remarkable thing. What is interesting, however, is the nature and scope of their differences. Johnson and Staal disagree profoundly about who and what Vāc actually is. The difference underscores a significant issue in the interpretation of Vedic and other texts, for it raises the question whether those ways of thinking we habitually call "abstract," such as philosophy, are somehow distinct from those ways of thinking we habitually call "imagistic," such as mythology or poetry. I would like to argue that Vāc may well be both a mythological image and the philosophical concept to be abstracted from that image; it can evoke in our minds the picture as well as the notion.

Several methodological points are in order here before we turn to our two interpreters. First, in our using the *Ṛg Veda* to challenge the boundaries between myth and philosophy, we are primarily concerned with rehabilitation of the poetic and symbolic character of its hymns. For the purposes of this paper, I would distinguish poetic from nonpoetic discourse as Schlegel does: "the non-poetic view of things is the one that sees them as controlled by sense perceptions and by the determinations of reason; the poetic view is the one that interprets them continuously and finds in them an inexhaustible figurative character."[3] Moreover, I would also argue that the Vedas confront us with what Ricoeur[4] has called "the inseparability of symbolism and interpretation": A symbolic discourse *invites* us to any number of interpretations. The Vedic hymns issue any number of such invitations: They conspicuously show paradox ("From the man Virāj was born, and from Virāj came the man" RV 10:90), ambiguity (Yama's dogs of death in RV 10:14, 10-12 may kill you, but they also give back the life they endanger), and multivalency (When is Agni a god and when simply fire?). One could greatly multiply such examples.

My critique of Staal and Johnson is that their approaches do not give Vāc room to be a poetic image, flexible enough to incorporate several meanings at once—both abstract and concrete. The operative notions of "language" and "speech" in both Staal and Johnson fail to incorporate all of these possibilities. Thus their interpretations are limited by their assumptions that paradox, ambiguity, and multivalency are not Vedic intentions.[5]

Second, our reading must also include an understanding of the hymn as it exists in a ritual context. Here, our purpose is not to analyze the functions of the *hotar* priest, the officiant responsible for recitation during the *yajña*, (the sacrifice), but simply to construct an interpretive framework which includes ritual meanings as well as poetic and philosophical ones.[6]

The above discussions of poetic and ritual meanings brings us to our third methodological point. We will read this poem with a concern for both external and internal structure, as a singular work as well as a work continuous with other Vedic hymns. The Vedic hymns must be read and interpreted relative to each other, as they have been by scholars such as Renou, Brown, Staal, O'Flaherty, Johnson, etc. Yet we must not ignore the fact that they hymns were also handed down as discreet entities, and therefore must have structural considerations of their own. Although Staal is more attentive to internal patterns than Johnson, both interpreters seem to make the assumption that the structural considerations of a single hymn must be determined primarily by its context—the "verbal symposium" for Johnson and the generic "ritual arena" for Staal. Thus, our reading of the hymn, both in relation to other hymns and with respect to its own internal structure, might be seen as a critique in and of itself—as a plea for a more balanced approach.[7]

Finally, the result of these considerations should be a better translation. In this paper, however, we are primarily concerned with the interpretive complications entailed in the process of translation itself, and will leave the translation to another occasion.

The task of this paper, then, is threefold: first, we will juxtapose the two treatments of Johnson and Staal, briefly outlining the ways that their theoretical perspectives affect both their translation and their interpretation of the hymn. Second, we will show how these two treatments, although sensitive and illuminating, are limited by their inability to allow a multifaceted reading of the hymn. Finally, using philosopher Suzanne Langer and historian of religion Wade Wheelock, we will develop some rudimentary interpretive categories that would better allow the hymn's dimensions to come to light. Let us turn, then, to our interpreters.

Johnson and Staal: The Enigmatizing Image and the Philosophy of Language

Johnson (*Poetry and Speculation of the Ṛg Veda*, 1980) bases his analysis on the somewhat problematic notion of the "enigmatizing image."[8] This concept is crucial to his understanding of both textual and ritual language—the language that is used in the Vedas and in the sacrificial symposium which the Vedas describe. He reconstructs a scenario in which the essential function of language is to communicate enlightenment to the unecstatic and to "mediate between the penetration of the undersurfaces of reality and the speculative formulation of what is thereby understood."

Johnson goes on to show how enigmatizing images functioned in a ritual context:

> The enigmatizing images of Ṛg Vedic speculation functioned . . . to awaken consciousness to the noumenal implications of experienced phenomenal forms. Sanskrit speculation began in part with the serious contemplation of these shock-producing images that enigmatized Ultimate reality, with the institution of the Ṛg Vedic symposium.[9]

The rest of his reconstruction, is, in fact, dependent upon this idea of enigmatizing image. The sacrificial symposium, for Johnson, is the forum in which these images were actually produced; he sees several hymns in the Ṛg Veda as describing the ritual process by which these images were composed and responded to by other participants, with or before or during the sacrifice. To quote him again:

> In the symposium contest, priests were prepared for the sacrifice by mentally grappling with verbal formulations evocative of *brahman*. The peculiar enigmatic formulations deliberately attempted to force them to leave ordinary consciousness to reach other, enhanced, paranormal modes that would permit full, visionary participation in the sacrifice, thus guaranteeing its total effectiveness.[10]

Johnson sees the enigmatizing images as being used in an agonistic sense, the priestly oratorical contests. The form of the contest is a verbal disputation, a response by the contestants to the questions posed by the *brāhmaṇa* priests who are described in the Vedas as "overseeing" the ritual and being in charge of its "meaning."

Despite the contestual atmosphere, however, the production of enigmatizing imagery takes place in a ritual context which "encourages mystical participation in the cosmic reality":

> 10:71 addresses itself to the feminine form of brahman (vāc, holy word) evoking a bhakti-like eulogy to brahman personified as a female goddess . . . exhibit[ing] the particular devotion of each contestant for his patron deity in the contest.[11]

Johnson is approaching the hymn with a concern for what makes the most devotional and ritual sense; he is asking how Vāc can be incorporated into the actual procedure and community of a sacrificial symposium.

Frits Staal, on the other hand, is concerned with the notion of the permanence of language as it has been expressed by Indian philosophical systems such as Vedānta, Mīmāṁsā, Sāṁkhya Yoga, and Kasmir Śaivism. Staal is searching for a root for their common belief that language is of divine or transcendent origin, and thus is drawn to the Vedas, and especially to 10:71 as a philosophical precursor of this notion.

Thus, Staal is primarily concerned with the way Vāc makes linguistic and philosophical sense. He uses such concepts from the outset. "Metalanguage," or "language about language" is his overarching category. Vāc is a metalinguistic concept incorporated into a metaphysical musing upon the origins of language in the universe. For him, Vāc functions as a grammatical category in the mind of the Vedic poet, and his task is to explore what its components, development, syntactical functions, and ritual use might have been.

As we shall see later on, he sees ritual as a kind of subset, albeit a crucial one, to these larger notions about language, and not, as Johnson would, as a spatial configuration containing a group of participants. With these notes in mind, let us turn to our translations:

Johnson	*Staal*
1. Oh Bṛhaspati, the first beginning of Vāc was when they came forth giving names. What (before) was their best, what was spotless, placed hidden in mystery was manifested because of love right before the eyes!	1. Bṛhaspati, when they came forth to establish the first beginning of language, setting up names, what had been hidden in them as their best and purest good became manifest through love.
2. It has been like (farmers) winnowing grain with a basket, when they with mind have made Vāc. Then the companions recognize (others of the) brotherhood, for they place their auspicious mark in Vāc.	2. When the sages fashioned language with their thought, filtering it like parched grain through a sieve, Friends recognized their friendship. Their beauty is marked on the language.
3. Through sacrifice they followed the tracks of Vāc. They discovered her inhabiting the ancient seers. Having brought her back they placed her in many places. (Now) seven laudators praise her in unison.	3. They traced the course of language through ritual. They found it embodied in the seers. They gained access to it and distributed it widely. The seven chanters cheered them.

4. Many a one seeing Vāc does not (really) see Vāc. And many a one hearing does not (really) hear her. But also to many does she reveal her body, like a beautifully clothed bride desiring her husband.

4. Many who look do not see language. Many who listen do not hear it. It reveals itself like a loving and well-adorned wife to her husband.

5. Indeed, they say, many in the brotherhood are intoxicated into immobility. These they do not urge into oratorical contests. Such a person competes with a milkless māyā. Hearing Vāc (for him) is without fruit and without flower.

5. Many have grown rigid in this friendship. They are not sent to the contests. Such a one goes with the power of a milkless cow, for he has heard language which is without fruit and without flower.

6. He who abandons a comrade, his fellow in knowledge, shares not even a portion of Vāc. If he hears her, in vain he hears; surely he does not fathom the way of the well done.

6. He who abandons a friend who knows with him has no share in language. If indeed he hears, he hears in vain, for he does not know the path of good action.

7. Though each possesses eyes and ears, companions are unequal in swiftness of mind. . . . [Johnson does not translate the rest of this verse. See below.]

7. Though all the friends have eyes and ears, their mental intuitions are uneven. Some are like shallow ponds, which reach up to the mouth or armpit, others are like ponds which are fit for bathing.

8. When brāhmaṇa companions sacrifice together, fashioning with the heart mental flashes, then surely many a one is left behind because of lack of insight; while many others far beyond go, having solved the brahman enigma.

8. When minds's intuitions are shaped in the heart, when brahmins perform rites together as friends, some are wittingly eliminated, others emerge on account of the manifest excellence of the power of language.

9. Those who do not take prior and later (contest positions) are not brāhmaṇas, nor do they participate in the (accompanying) Soma rites. They evilly approach Vāc, and unenlightened they weave on the loom (of sacrifice) with gossamer.

9. Those who do not improve or progress are not real [brahmins], who do not take part in the Soma libations. They use language in the wrong fashion; they weave flowing waters without understanding.

10. All the compatriots rejoice with the companion returned with glory, victorious in the assembly contest. For he removes their faults and bestows nourishment (on them), and he is well prepared for (future) contest.

11. [Johnson does not translate this verse.]

10. All rejoice about the friend who emerges famous and victorious in the assembly. He dismisses harm, he bestows food. He is fit for the contest.

11. One sits down multiplying the wealth of verse. One chants a chant in the Śakvarī meter. One sets forth the newly born knowledge. One lays out the measure of the rites.

Interpretation

We obviously cannot attempt a complete analysis of all the words used in the hymn. Significant differences will be touched on as they draw out the underlying assumption of each translator. Johnson's approach I have termed "ritual/devotional," (the use of mythological content in the symposium is implied here) and Staal's "linguistic/philosophical."

As may be surmised from the preceding analysis, Johnson is more concerned with the physical details of Vāc as she appears in the symposium than with any philosophical coherence. As he puts it, "the Vedic image appropriates meaning through its mode of concreteness." For him, Vāc herself acts as such an image within the hymn, concretizing in the form of a deity the ineffable qualities of the power of speech. It is not surprising, then, that in verse 1, Johnson chooses the nominal Vāc and adds "right before the eyes," presumably to portray the idea of a kind of theophany. And, as we have noted, Johnson believes that the ritual context of Vāc is what gives her reality: So, in verse 2, Vāc creates an elite brotherhood (*atrā sakhāyaḥ sakhyāni*) revealing the members of the secret society to one another. In verse 3, moreover, Johnson stays with the Sanskrit word *yajña*. In addition, in Johnson's mind Vāc must be anthropomorphized; she is even hypothesized to have iconographic representations. In his scheme, there can be no meaning to Vāc without imagining or seeing her. Vāc makes "tracks" (*padavīyam*) and "inhabits the ancient seers" (*ṛṣiṣu praviṣṭām*). His phrase, "Having brought her here and distributed her widely" (*tām ābhṛtyā vy adadhuḥ purutrā*) describes the solicitous care lavished on Vāc whereby her

images are set up in various places for cultic worship. The seven lauda-
tors thus "praise" her (*abhi sam navante*) in these places. In verse 5,
Johnson again illustrates his ritual concerns, translating *sthirpītam* as
"intoxicated into immobility"—a state which renders the contestant
useless for the contest in an almost comical personal portrait of the
drunken Vedic poet. In verse 6, we see further how Vāc must be seen
as an image in order to be understood. Johnson comments on this
verse, "not all men truly understand what they hear of the sacred word,
and consequently what they see." In verse 8, Johnson chooses the
phrase "brahman enigma" in keeping with his theme of the enigmatizing image in the Vedic symposium. In verse 9, he notes that some men
are excluded because they do not take up a disputing position and
remain unenlightened, "not visionary," and thus unable to participate
in *yajña*. Surprisingly, for one who is so concerned with ritual context,
Johnson does not translate the last verse of the hymn, since he claims it
is not germane to his discussion of enigmatizing image.

For Staal, on the other hand, Vāc's qualities are not enfleshed or
imagined. In verse 1, he chooses the more generic "language" over
any nominal form such as Vāc or Speech. Staal comments that in
choosing "language," he intends to distinguish it from mere sound, a
component part of language. In verse 2, Staal also chooses the more
generic "friendship," which does not have the ritual connotations in
English that Johnson's "brotherhood" does. In verse 3, Staal, not surprisingly, also translates *yajña* with the more general word "ritual,"
rather than sacrifice. He also sees the "praise and cheering of the
seven chanters" not as an expression of devotion to Vāc, but as meaningless sound that existed as a component part before the whole of
meaningful language became manifest. In verse 5, Staal sees *sthīrapi-
tam* as swelling which has been checked, or arrested. "Grown rigid" is
thus his translation, for he wants to portray a process of linguistic stul-
tification. In verse 8, Staal's "manifest excellence of the power of language" stands in stark contrast to Johnson's rendering "brahman enigma" mentioned above. Finally, Staal does not omit the last verse, but
sees it as referring to the central meaning of the hymn: that sound and
structure preceded language, but it is through the marriage of the two
that language comes into being. This marriage is brought about by
ritual, as described in the last verse. The priests correspond to philosophical and linguistic categories. The *hotar*, reciting mantras, multi-
plies the verse. The *udgātar* chants the *sāmans* of the *Sāmaveda*, multiplying the sound. The *brāhmaṇa* priest is the guardian of the meaning,

as mentioned above. The *adhvaryu* is the measuring priest, who consummates the marriage by achieving the unity of sound and meaning through the syntax of ritual. For Staal, the sages thus related sound and meaning to each other through the structured domain of syntax, which was ritual in origin and so remains in character.[12]

Overall, Staal sees Vāc as a collection of abstract qualities, which take the form of contrasting pairs. He outlines the following series of distinctions to illustrate his point:[13]

Language is hidden.	Language is manifest.
It is hidden in the sages and embodied in the seers.	It is widely distributed by the sages.
It is looked at and listened to (without understanding).	It is seen and heard, with understanding.
It is fruitless and flowerless.	It reveals itself.
It is used in the wrong fashion without understanding.	It is reached by deep intuitions.

The main point of the hymn for Staal is that language originated when hidden knowledge became manifest, i.e., when meaning was attached to sound. As we have seen, it is ritual, in verse 11, that effects the marriage of sound and meaning—it acts as the ordering catalyst. "Sounds were ritually brought to life," as he writes,

> just as in later times a yantra, a bronze image or a piece of clay is animated by *prāṇaprastiṣṭhā* rites—rites of consecrating and enlivening. When the rites were ignored language ceased to develop and became rigid. When they were performed, brahman was found and language flourished.[14]

For Staal, then, the Vedic poet did not have the intimate knowledge of a goddess in a mystical vision: he had an intuitive sense of the components of language—the phonetic, the semantic, and syntactical.

Critique of Johnson and Staal: Vāc in the Ṛg Veda

We turn now to a consideration of the limitations of these two theories. In order to do this, we must first ask what we can know of Vāc from reading her other hymns. Although there are several occur-

rences of the word Vāc in the *Ṛg Veda*, the main sources for the symbol Vāc are hymns 1:164, 10:71, and 10:125.[15] A consideration of the
hymns reveals several basic aspects: First, Vāc (from 10:168, 1:164, 4-
5, and 10:125:3) is something mysterious, that which must be brought
to light. Hymn 1:164, for instance, recalls Vāc's division into segments, three parts hidden in secret which humans do not stir into
action, although the fourth part is indeed what men speak. Inspired
priests alone have access to the other "hidden" three parts, thus Vāc is
revealed in fullness to only a select few.

Second, from the bulk of 1:125 and 1:164, we see that Vāc figures centrally in the formation of the cosmos. In 10:125, 7, in self-
praise, Vāc takes on more, explicit aspects of a creator deity: "I gave
birth to the father on the head of this world. My womb is in the
waters, within the ocean. From there I spread out over all creatures
and touch the very sky with the crown of my head." In this same
hymn, Vāc also dwells in many places and in many forms, as many
creator deities are wont to do, "pervading sky and earth" in verse 6,
and in verse 8, "like the wind, embracing all creatures."

Third, Vāc is also the nourisher and enabler of the sacrifice, and
the inspiration of those officiating at it. Hymn 1:164, verse 35, cites the
brāhmaṇa priest as being "the final abode of speech." And, in a less dramatic passage, hymn 10:125, verses 2 and 3, Vāc expresses benevolence
to those who sacrifice, and in an Agni-like fashion, claims preeminence
among those to whom the sacrifice is given. Vāc's discriminatory powers in the sacrifice are also alluded to, as they are in RV 10:71. In hymn
10:125, verse 4, Vāc proclaims, "the one who eats food, who truly sees,
who breathes, who hears what is said, does so through me."

Fourth, in both hymns, Vāc is identified with the other gods in
some way. In 1:164, 45-46, Vāc is called Indra, Mitra, Varuna, Agni,
Yama, and Matarisvan. Vāc is also the One Real (*ekam sat.*). In 10:125,
however, Vāc is not given the names of these gods, but moves with them.

Although both Johnson and Staal's view of Vāc would agree with
the generalized notion that Vāc figures centrally in the formation of the
world and the performance of the sacrifice, the hymns present us with
several ambiguities which are not resolved by their analyses. It is not
clear from the verses above what the nature of Vāc's relationship to the
sacrifice really is. We cannot tell whether Vāc acts as a deity and inspira-
tional force, an intellectual force, an iconic or aniconic force. To be sure,
Vāc as a symbolic problem is not unique, given the many Vedic symbols
which vacillate between iconicity and aniconicity. Yet unlike Agni, Soma,

and others, Vāc does occupy the peculiar position of being a nonelemen-
tal, nonmaterial, and indeed, self-reflexive force in the sacrifice. As a
Vedic entity apart from RV 10:71, then, Vāc still vacillates between two
Western intellectual arenas—a concept or category and a substantive
deity with attributes that require iconographic representation.

In light of these verses, several problems arise from Johnson and
Staal's interpretations as we have sketched them. Let us enumerate the
problems confronting Johnson when he interprets the hymn with an
exclusive concern for its "concrete" meaning. As mentioned above,
Johnson's scheme turns entirely upon the problematic notion of enigmatizing image uttered by the symposium participant. We must first
ask, "Exactly how are Vedic images enigmatizing in this situation?"[16]
Even if they are strange or out of context, as he describes it, they remain
images, with connotations and associations like any other. Images cannot be solely "enigmatizing"; as Johnson himself admits, they also have
referents, which serve to indicate, and in some cases, clarify.

Second, in his scenario, Johnson sets up an interlocking dependency between deity and devotion. He thereby insists that language
gains meaning through ritual only when language is presented externally in the form of a deity: he entertains no other possibility. In this
way, his interpretation renders all of the images within a hymn as
wholly dependent upon something which is going on outside the
hymn—the ritual worship of a deity. Images become reduced to mere
"expressions of" and "referents to" this larger reality. As he puts it,
"ritual is a means of participating in a cosmic process of which the
enigmatizing image is the expression."[17] In this way, Johnson does not
treat these images as if they played a structural role within the poem
itself, and thus impoverishes their richness as poetic images.

Johnson also makes the related assumption that Vāc, or language, is essentially discursive in nature. In her status as enigmatizing
image, her main role is to *inform* the ritual participants about the ineffable. He does not fully explore the other abstract possibilities of Vāc,
her other linguistic functions. As we shall see below, language used in
the context of ritual does not merely communicate; on the contrary, it
has a number of other functions—to create a situation, to express an
attitude or intention, and may, in some cases, be devoid of any informational content whatsoever. But because in Johnson's view, Vāc only
communicates transcendent vision, we are forced to assume that the
distinction between those who fail and those who succeed in the sacrifice is based solely upon their ability to effectively "express themselves" through an enigmatizing image.

Finally, because of this equation of visionary consciousness and potency of ritual, Johnson commits himself to the concept of a "sacred" speech which effects such power. For him, "ordinary language" when married with vision, creates "sacred"[18] language in a ritual contest. Words are endowed with creative power only insofar as they are given it by the goddess, *Vāc*. Moreover, only the goddess Vāc has the power to distinguish sacred speech from ordinary speech. In this scenario, we are forced to assume profane language, but we have no idea how it works, or whether there is any relationship between Vāc as sacred word and words which are not sacred.[19]

Staal's analysis is far more complex. On the one hand, it is far more insightful in paying attention to the internal structure of the hymn and discerning a rhythm to the imagery. On the other hand, since for Staal the poem's composers were speculative philosophers concerned with the origins of language,[20] those images only serve to tell a philosophical story: First there were chants, and meaning, and they were separate. Then ritual arrived to unite them into language.[21]

There are problems in this conceptual story, however, just as there are in Johnson's concretized scenario. A brief discussion of his earlier work might be helpful here. In his study of Vedic ritual, (1970, 1979, 1980, 1986), Staal has asserted the importance of linguistic categories in the anthropological analysis of ritual.[22] He refutes the idea that ritual is a language, or even a "system of meaning and symbols," but that it is, like a language, a "rule governed activity." In another study (1980), he attempts to show that an exclusively syntactic analysis of ritual is not only possible but fruitful. Syntax, in his mind, can completely account for the ritual facts.[23]

Moreover, Staal does not stop in defining ritual as entirely "rule governed activity"; he then makes the leap that ritual rules need not have any significance—they can remain ordered arbitrarily, but not "meaningfully." If ritual has no "rhyme nor reason" and expresses things in a "roundabout" fashion, it follows for Staal that any explanation of ritual *in terms of meaning* is not helpful. He uses Isadora Duncan's famous statement to illustrate: "If I could tell you what it meant, there would be no point in dancing it."[24]

Thus, ritual is a kind of ordering, but meaningless, syntactical agent in hymn 10:71. It is the ordered domain which gives sound, or chanting, depth and life, making coherent "language" or Vāc. For Staal the hymn is a kind of musing about ritual itself, as it was originally connected to language. it is a "hymn of knowledge" because it reflects upon these origins.[25]

Moreover, Staal uses 10:71 to assert that because ritual simply organizes language, it does not refer to anything outside of itself. Sweeping aside Durkheim, Eliade, et al., he writes:

> Ritual . . . does not place great emphasis on celebrating or re-enacting myths, prehistory, or the creation of man or of the universe. Nor does it have to reflect social structure. . . . Its primary function is to contribute to the origin and development of language.[26]

To him, RV 10:71 affirms that, since the Vedic poets were speculative linguists concerned with the origins of language, then even in a ritual context, participants are not concerned with "meaning" as it might signify something "other" or "transcendent" outside the ritual. They are concerned only with joining linguistic categories to one another to create and develop language.

Our critique of Staal will begin, then, with several points on his notion of "meaning" and ritual.[27] With his view of ritual, what are we to make of verse 10? It states that the one who emerges victorious from the assembly (which we must assume to be some kind of "rule governed activity") bestows food and dismisses harm, and is "fit for the contest." How can we assume that these are simply side effects of the assembly, as Staal might have it, and not the motivations and "meanings" of the assembly itself? And if ritual is not in some way correlated with the social order, but is primarily concerned with the origin and development of language, what are we to make of the "friendship creating" capacity of Vāc in verse 2?

Second, even if for Staal it is not helpful to assume that rituals express meaning,[28] his only criterion for meaning and meaninglessness in ritual still remains the expression of a referent. Must that be our only criterion for meaning? One might posit instead that while rituals may not refer, they are "motivated"; they have a sense which is accessible in various ways to all participants. The language of verse 10, cited above, seems to support this idea.

Third, for Staal, illogicality is an important feature of ritual's meaninglessness.[29] In his analysis of verse 2, he writes:

> various things are referred to as preceding the origin of language. One of these is presupposed in the phrase, 'the seven chanters cheered them.' This cheering could not have been in language without circularity.[30]

Why is circularity all of a sudden a hindrance to making sense of a Vedic hymn? Why is logic and directness so determinative in ascertaining the meaning (or lack thereof) in the development of Vedic ritual? If anything, circularity is one of the very techniques which the Vedic poets delighted in the most; reversal of space and time, and a disregard for a chronological order is the stuff of the *Ṛg Veda*. Staal himself emphasized this view of Vedic hymns elsewhere.[31]

Fourth, in spite of his metalinguistic emphasis, there remains a nonlinguistic "event" in Staal's thinking. He does not tell us *how* or *why* ritual is the sudden catalyst that attracts meaning and sound to one another to make language. We are left with a kind of "big-bang" theory of language which assigns ritual a quasi-mystical role.[32] The mysterious metamorphosis of linguistic elements into language through ritual remains a mythical and not a philosophical event.[33]

Thus, the two most recent translations of hymns 10:71 leave us with many assertions about Vāc, but they do not, as Todorov[34] would have, it lead us back to the question posed by the symbolic nature of the text itself. On both a poetic and a ritual level, these scholars' views of language sell us short. Language, viewed primarily as an informative device which has the magical power to produce enigmatizing images makes Vāc in Johnson's view a kind of Vedic muse, and the hymn primarily a description of her power. This interpretation binds Vāc to the context of a ritual and a panegyric, without giving it the breadth or depth that Vāc might have had in situations other than the poetic contest. Language, viewed as a philosophical category risks rendering the hymn as an isolated liturgical tract which bears no relation to other hymns in the *Ṛg Veda* and reduces ritual to a "language-producing" function.

Vāc as a Portrait of a Problem in the Study of Myth, Philosophy, and Religion

The interpretive problem that a juxtaposition of Staal and Johnson presents is not simply a problem of linguistic disagreement. It is a problem of insufficient models with which to view the abstract notion of "language" in a mythical and ritual context. The problem thus lays bare our ideas of what it means to think mythically and philosophically, for the "notion" and the "myth" cannot be neatly separated in the hymn. The problem is complex: First there is the possibility of both abstract and concrete renderings of Vāc. Moreover, these renderings must be considered from both a compositional and a ritual level. The poem's internal structure as well as its integration into the structure of *yajña* must be considered.

Language as Sacred Object: An Overview

In the plethora of early material written in the field of history of religions on the relationship between words for deities and words for objects, there is little said about the ways in which Western culture thinks about words as religious objects in themselves. Since then, the study of cultural, philosophical, and even religious ideas about language has been left to linguists such as Chomsky, anthropologists such as Leach, philosophers such as Wittgenstein, and literary critics such as Barthes, while the historians of religion buried themselves with the rich imagery of cosmogonic myths, high gods, and the like. "Language" as a mythical category doesn't have the imagerial flavor of an Agni, a Soma, or a Zeus. Nor does it lend itself easily to comprehension as a venerated object, such as the trident of Śiva or the toe of a saint. Nor does it seem very "other," since it remains very much human bound and not very numinous in everyday discourse.

Langer's Poetic Formulation

How can we give "language" back its imagerial flavor? Philosopher Suzanne Langer's theory helps us along this path. Although she precedes much of contemporary literary theory, her notion of poetic creation remains the most useful for our purposes. First, she implicitly allows room for any number of characterizations of Vāc, since all have equal status as poetic elements. Second, she enables us to respect the internal structure of the hymn as a single composition, according it the independent status which Johnson and Staal deem less significant in their search for a definitive meaning. Moreover, as mentioned in the above section on naming, she helps us to delineate further how Johnson and Staal fall into the trap of assuming that poetry and ritual are discursive and communicative.

According to Langer, under the modern aegis of the scientific method, we have missed a trick in the philosophy of language. Communication by words is the key concept in our studies of language, and thus poetry as "emotive discourse" takes its place beside regular language as a vehicle for communication of information. As Langer points out, however, poetry is not a kind of discourse at all. We are wrong to assume that if a writer writes declarative sentences he or she must be making statements, or "taking us into his confidence."[35]

Modern theory dismisses what Langer calls the "formulative function" of poetic language. Poetry uses language as its material and discursive speech as its motif, but does not create a series of signals. It creates what Cecil Day Lewis has called "the poetic image," and what Langer herself prefers to call "semblance." A semblance is a creation in words, or, as she writes, "the creation of a perceptible human experience which, from the standpoint of science and practical life, is entirely illusory."[36] Considering poetry as a self-contained entity, then, we are freed from having to consider, under different rubrics, the sense and truth value of what the poet is saying, the context in which he says it, and the skill with which he executes his message. We ask, first and foremost, not "what is the poet trying to communicate?" but "what has the poet created, and how did he do it?"[37] For, no matter how faithful the image, it is a pure image, "unmixed with bits of actuality."

Viewed as poetry, then, we do not have to conclude that 10:71 holds two irreconcilable notions of language within its verses. With images as poetic elements, each an intrinsic and necessary part of the poem, we may then consider how the concrete and the abstract interact, instead of opting for one above the other. Before doing so, however, let us examine how Langer aids us in further delineating the problem of Johnson and Staal. Langer enables us to see that Johnson reads the hymn with a more communicative notion of language, as we have shown. Moreover, his view of the Vedic poet is also influenced by the same idea: Johnson renders what Langer would call a "purely psychological reading" where the poet's mystical experience is communicated and expressed. His failed contestant, for example, has undergone the personal experience of intoxication into immobility. Langer would criticize Johnson for treating the poem as a psychological document, "forcibly making statements out of its lines, and expanding their meaning far beyond anything that serves the poetic figment."[38]

Johnson's mistake is in assuming the enigma is an end in itself, that mysteries are to be communicated and solved through speech. Johnson can only cope with the transformative power of the hymn by insisting on the highly problematic "protobhakti" hypothesis; He does not see how Vāc or speech itself might be the agent of transformation.[39] An obscurely rendered mystical inspiration remains the sole basis for his analysis; he operates from the rather tired assumption that what is "obscure" in any religious text must therefore also be "mystical," or "expressive of mystical experience." Langer answers this assumption by asserting that obscurity need not always have a "mystical" referent:

> Even obscurity, which always goads critics into paraphrasing problematical lines, is a poetic element, something is created by the difficulty of diction, the sense of incomprehensibility.[40]

Langer's ideas also give us further insight into Staal's thinking. Staal subjects the poem to a series of verificational analyses, where logic is the driving principle. We see this most clearly in his analysis of verse 3, cited above, where "circularity" of logic determines his translation. Staal wants the hymn to narrate linguistic events, yet he misses the point that Vāc as an image in a hymn is a semblance, entirely created, and not simply a particularly effective way of "telling things."[41]

As we have mentioned, Staal is not entirely "context-determined"; he does attempt a synchronic approach to the hymn, rendering its internal structure as a series of images whereby Vāc is hidden and manifest. He restricts himself, however, as we noted above, by postulating that these are only ritual ideas and tendencies, ritual "logic" and not poetic elements.

What happens when we actually look at the hymn more boldly, using Langer's assumption that poetic statement, allusion, imagery, grammatical form, word, and rhythm all have essentially and purely creative functions? Although we will not here attempt a thorough analysis of meter, assonance, etc., a strictly internal analysis of imagery as imagery yields a rather useful result, based on, but not entirely consonant with, Staal's two columns (see p. 189, above). We can discern how the poem is made up of a series of contrasting characterizations, along the lines of hidden and manifest. Yet these are not simply contrasts to be extracted as themes from the poem as a whole. Each verse presents an image of what might be called the "emergence" or "externalization" of speech. Each verse takes us from internal to external modes of Vāc, from Vāc's places in people, physical beings, to its place in the outside world, from embodiment to dispersal. In verse 1, a hidden secret is revealed. In verse 2, through the internal process of fashioning Vāc within thought, an external alliance (sākhyā) is recognized. In verse 3, Vāc is taken from its internal place within the sages and portioned "out" to many. In verse 4, we see the selectivity with which Vāc is revealed, or externalized; not all internal places are places where Vāc can dwell. In verse 5, we have an image of a profitless manifestation, where Vāc is transformed by an unworthy interior to a "milkless," or powerless, external effect. In verse 6, we have the same image of internal and external betrayal. In verse 7, interior mental intuitions then emerge as unequal, as shallow or deep ponds. In verse 8, the interior intuitions of mind determine the emergence of those who are skilled in the use of Vāc. In verse 9, "impostors" embodying speech have profitless external activity (weaving on *sirīs*). In verse 10, a friend (embodied) emerges victorious and bestows blessings in the outside world. In verse 11, the movement runs from the priests who embody sound and language, the hymn singer *hotar*, the chanter *udgātar*, and the *brāhmaṇa* caretaker of knowledge, to the priest who arranges the sacrifice in the outside world, *athvaryu*.

This theme of interior and exterior imagery is also traceable in a more general way throughout the larger structure of the hymn. The hymn moves from the first "discovery" of speech in the seers, a very interior image, to a portrayal of the manifold uses and abuses of speech in the outside world, to the very public poetic contest, to the ultimate emergence of a power of speech which affects the whole world.

We might view the hymn, then, not as a statement at all, but as a brilliant patterning, through a series of images of the *activity of speech itself*.[42] Speech is a process whereby what we know internally is somehow made manifest externally, and the hymn is a poetic rendition of this very movement. And the obscure verses, such as the intractable word *brahman* in verse eight, might be viewed as "the poetic element of obscurity" mentioned above, giving the hymn an aura of incomprehensibility, and the power of language an air of mystery which it surely must have had. Seen in this way, the hymn does not describe or inform, it simply portrays, by setting up semblances and creating its own organic rhythm of emergence. It is, in Langer's terms, "living form."

Wheelock's Situational Speech

So much, then, for the formulative function of the hymn. By asking, what did the poet create? we can see that he created a pattern of Vāc, both within each verse and within the hymn as a whole. And this, we might add, is perhaps a more accurate portrayal of the Vedic conception of Vāc: it is an active, dynamic force whose movement the hymn reflects. Yet how do these "patterns of speech" take hold in ritual contexts? As we have mentioned, we know the hymns were recited during the sacrifice. Since we are not postulating an icon, as Johnson does, nor are we postulating a linguistic basis for ritual, as Staal does, how do we fit poetic image into sacrificial model? Two concepts help us think about how language can be formulative in a ritual context; the first, Wade Wheelock's notion of "situational speech" (1978, 1982, 1984) and the second, a consideration of the notion of embodiment.

Like Langer, Wheelock allows for the creative properties of speech within such remote and obscure rituals as those prescribed by the Vedas. Using the New and Full Moon Sacrifice (NFM) as his text, he notes that while the ritual lacks any obvious unity in theme, he also shows that the ritual has an underlying unity, somewhat similar to Tambiah's notion of ritual as a series of meaningful constituents (words, acts, and objects) strung together in a rule-governed sequence.[43]

Wheelock's main concerns are the words of ritual, and he sets out to provide a taxonomy of constituent parts of NFM ritual language. Toward this end he makes use of J. L. Austin's notion (1962) of the "locutionary act" to show that speech has a performative to it; to make any utterance, according to Austin, is to accomplish that act. As is by now well known, language is not only used to communicate a description of reality but actually to bring about affairs by the mere utterance of a statement. John Searle's *Speech Acts* supports his idea that speech is "performing language according to rules."[44] Yet the rules which Searle develops for performative speech are only applicative to ordinary language. Ritual language, like poetic language, has its own set of special rules for performance.[45] Ritual speech, for instance, does not always involve a speaker or hearer, as ordinary speech does. Nor does it always have informational content; ritual may use a fixed text where all the participants know what's coming next. Like Langer, Wheelock rejects the notion that ritual speech is primarily discursive in nature and that declarative statements are only designed to inform and communicate. Moreover, ritual speech is joined by other symbol systems that may use a variety of media.

The intention of ritual speech, on the other hand, is to create and allow for a known and repeatable situation. One of the most important ways that ritual speech "situates" the performance is through "characteristic language," the main category of Wheelock's taxonomy. Characteristic language sets up an identity with the participant and the truth of a situation.[46] For example, when the priest at an NFM sacrifice says, "I pick up this grass with the arms of Indra," his speech is a way of characterizing his relationship to Indra; it both creates his identity with Indra and recognizes that it is already a fact. It both presents and facilitates recognition of a new situation. The "arms of Indra" speech act and others like it are caught in an insoluble dialectic; it alters the status of a subject whose status is in fact already well known.[47]

Moreover, Wheelock's "identity-establishing" function of characteristic speech possesses a certain flexibility. This kind of speech may involve identities with things other than deities, such as abstract entities and material objects. Grass, happiness, prosperity, as well as gods such as Indra and Soma are all entities with which ritual speech is capable of setting up an identity. Wheelock, in his "Taxonomy of Sacrificial Mantras" mentions that the function of the *adhvaryu* priest in the NFM sacrifice, is to enlist the help of potent forces embodied in the sacrificial objects.[48] He goes on to note that

> the goals of the sacrifice are won not only by pleasing the invited gods, but in large measure through the manipulation of the physical components of the ritual, whose true and powerful identity is made effective by the mantras.

He further notes that such characteristic speech is, not surprisingly, usually marked by the present indicative.

A complementary approach to 10:71, then, is simply to ask how the hymn might have been used as situational speech in ritual. Again, we can discern patterns and styles of speech, yet this time not through image, but through tense, or to put it another way, not through noun but through verb. Verses 4-10 all use some form of the present indicative; we might easily construe these verses as the setting up of the parameters of a ritual situation such as the Vedic symposium. In this sense, Johnson and Staal both agree that this is one of the main functions of the hymn. These verses act as rules of the situation, determining who may participate and who may not (verses 5 and 6 are especially good examples of this). More importantly, if the main function of the hymn is to formulate a relationship between participants and Vāc, the hymn can encompass several possibilities at once, including philosophical and devotional. The verses create a ritual situation which includes a variety of media for these relationship—both concrete (seeing and hearing in v.3, and partaking in Soma libations in v.9) and abstract (correct action in v.6, the shaping of mental intuitions in v.8).

When viewed as the structuring image of the poem and not as a "mystical" external referent, Vāc provides a powerful illustration of the context-creating power of language. Her sudden appearance in the beginning creates an expansive contextual past; her continued presence at sacrifice and within each seer creates an equally expansive contextual present. In this light, the structure of the hymn itself does not insist on being either metaphysical musing or the worship of a deity. It simply insists upon the establishment of a relationship of oneness with Vāc in ritual.

Vāc as Embodiment and Abstraction

We have noted that Vāc can be rehabilitated as a more flexible symbol through the models of Langer and Wheelock, but what makes Vāc a powerful symbol? Both Langer and Wheelock admit that there is a "formulative" power of words which allows them to "create" a poetic image or situation. Johnson, as we have seen, attributes a belief in the creative power of speech to the Vedic poet. Yet all these scholars are content with leaving their analyses at that point.[49] But the words *formulative, magical,* and *creative* do not seem to do justice to an entity which has associations with the beginning of sacrifice, the first seers, (verse 2-3) and, even if only in a linguistic way, the beginning of the universe.

Here we must expand our interpretation of the hymn as poetic formulation and as situational speech to take account of the fact that it is *formulation within a cosmological framework*, a framework having to do with the origin of language, the origin of the universe, and the origin of the sacrifice. Vāc has an association with the beginnings of time, an ability to create distinctions between those who can participate in the sacrifice and those who cannot. In short, Vāc connotes a power which manifests itself in the world and interrupts the homogeneity of experience. In this sense, this description of Vāc is consonant with Eliade's notion of "hierophany," although we use "experience" and not "space" here, as Eliade would, because Vāc does not have the spatial or natural connotations that a thunderbolt or tree might have. Moreover, we would not go on to describe Vāc as a "sacred" power, since as mentioned above, the term is not used by Vedic poets and introduces a problematic and unhelpful distinction. However, we *may* usefully construe from the Sanskrit that Vāc *does* interpolate itself, creating division in the world in rather profound cosmological ways.

The notion of "hierophany," however modified, and its attendant morphological considerations do raise an interesting question at this point: Is it even possible to include the experiential aspect of Vāc in our analysis without positing the problematic "enigma of protobhakti" of Johnson? How might the Vedic poet himself experience Vāc as power-

ful? The answer, I believe, is given by the poem itself. More specifically, the poem portrays Vāc as embodied in physical human beings. The
poet uses the language of hierophany to discuss this embodiment: Vāc
is "discovered" or "found" inhabiting or "embodied" in the seers (v.3).
In 1:164,35, moreover, we remember that "this [brahman] priest is the
final abode of speech." Embodiment in humans, then, can be seen as
the ultimate expression of the power of Vāc. If the thunderstorm manifests its power partly through its flash and majesty, so language manifests its power through embodiment in humans. Viewed in this way, it
is the embodiment of language, not necessarily the "body" of Vāc as a
goddess, which makes it powerful. Its capacity to describe, apprehend,
and interrupt experience shows up not only spatially, in nature, but ver-
bally, through the flesh of the Vedic seers.

This idea is hinted at but not elaborated in both Johnson and
Staal. We have remarked that the only "mysterious" thing in Staal's
philosophical analysis is ritual, the way that it marries sound and meaning. Ritual is also the only physical, bodily category in Staal's analysis.
Certainly, when language is viewed so abstractly, its bodily aspect might
be a mystery, left unexplained or relegated to "compulsive" behavior. As
we have seen above, Johnson hints at this idea more directly when he
writes, in a footnote, that the creative power of words is "generally
attributable to divine beings in the *Rg Veda*, so that here its attribution
to a human being, albeit a divinely inspired seer, is remarkable."[50] What
remains "surprising" and "mysterious" in their analyses has to do with
Vāc's manifestation in the bodily world of human beings performing the
sacrifice. This need not be entirely surprising. In fact, if one analyzes
the hymn directly, as we have attempted, the only verifiable element in
it is that *human beings speak*. Assuming Todorov's insistence that the text
itself bring us back to its symbolic nature, we might assume that this fact
is not only intelligible to us, but that it is significant as a symbolic element of the hymn as well.

On Semblance and Situation

We are now in a position to view the relationship between formulative and characteristic speech, between semblance and situation
in a Vedic context. The working material, or clay, of the *hotar* priest, is
the hymn. As we have seen, Vāc as the subject of the hymn is given a
distinct character and movement through the formulative function of
poetic language. It is not, though, an a priori assumption of a deity or

a concept, but through the properties of poetic image, that Vāc assumes effective status in the sacrifice. Nouns and verbs work together to create independent, self-contained images of emergence, as noted above, involving both abstract and concrete possibilities, as does speech itself. Neither Staal nor Johnson move with Langer and Wheelock in asserting the associative and creative power of language—not as a means of communicating psychological or philosophical information, but as a means of fashioning something new. We might say: Vāc is portrayed, thus Vāc is created and becomes creative. Thus the poetic image must be the primary category in our analysis.

The function of the *hotar* priest—his potter's wheel—is recitation. From our text (verse 11) he is "multiplying the wealth of verse" or in O'Flaherty's more aesthetic translation, "bringing to blossom the flower of verse." Yet if we are to take the creative power of language seriously, his activity is not just a matter of invoking the gods. It is a matter of giving ontological status to an image, which in turn, allows ritual speech to establish identification with that image. Although Wheelock does not address the issue of imagination directly, it is important to note here that situational speech is impossible without the power of imagination; something has to be imagined, and imagined powerfully, in order for there to be an identification set up, say, between the reciter's arms and the arms of Indra, the *hotar's* words and the powers of Vāc. The image then acts not just as a transmitter of cosmic knowledge, but as a mediator between what is recited and what is acted, semblance and situation.

Last, as we have seen, this power of imagination does not necessarily take static form. As a matter of Vedic principle, in fact, it takes a fluid form, a form of movement. Vāc is in this way no different from Agni who emerges from the waters and ascends to the heavens, or Soma who descends from above and also inhabits the seers and sacrificers. Their power lies in the fluidity of form. Hymn 10:71 creates this fluidity on two levels—by portraying Vāc as emerging in the various individual situations of each verse, and more generally by portraying Vāc as emerging from the body of the seer into the poetic contest and the world.

In interpreting, then, we are setting up heuristic devices which describe a process of the imagination. When we describe this process for Vāc, as for other Vedic symbols, we engage in the implicit proposal of several levels of meaning. Vāc suggests a tension, say, between "language" and "ritual" as self-conscious notions; this would require the reflexivity of what we call "philosophy" to elaborate. Vāc also suggests a tension between speech as performed by humans and speech as performed upon humans; these are experiential properties requiring the immediacy and concreteness of what we call "mythology" to elaborate. Neither of these tensions is elaborated in the hymn itself, but hymn 10:71 contains the seeds of both. Moreover, hymn 10:71 as part of the larger Vedic symposium tells us that the contestual process of emergence involves both tangible, physical realities and disembodied ideas—the abstract mulling over of possibilities within an embodied context. Vāc's power lies in the ability to emerge both embodied in humans and disembodied as an abstraction.

One might go further to suggest that this tension in fact is the tension between "explanation" and "further mythmaking" we experience in any commentarial tradition which follows a symbolic discourse; the implicit proposal of several levels of meaning in symbols require *both responses*. The juxtaposition of storytelling ("He was conceived by the power of the Holy Spirit, and born of the Virgin Mary. He suffered under Pontius Pilate, was crucified, died and was buried . . .") and abstract notions ("I believe in the Holy Spirit, the Holy Catholic Church, the communion of saints . . .") in the Apostle's Creed might be a more familiar example of this double response to symbolic discourse.

Finally, our attempt to gain a more balanced view of *Ṛg Veda* 10:71 returns us to the question that Jean Rudhart and Marcel Detienne[51] asked of the Greeks: Is not the nature of the mythic image to resist codification and to attend instead to "the lived experience, sufficiently basic to be repeated, to be reproduced, and thus to resist intellectual analysis attempting to break up its unity?" We can understand Vāc because we speak ourselves and know something of speech's nature. The myth of Vāc, like other myths, is a "rationalism other and wider than conceptual intelligence, capable of rediscovering religious meaning in worldly experience through symbolic images." We rightly risk the title "symbolist" in this conclusion. In acknowledging the power of symbolic discourse, we may reify it. Yet if we have returned some honor to lived experience as a perceptual tool, relevant to both myth and philosophy, the risk is worth taking.

Notes

1.   Gonda, *Vision*, 23.

2.   Johnson and Staal do, of course, have grammatical differences as well as interpretive ones. The present and past translations of verse 3, *abhi saṃ navante*, is one among several examples.

3.   Todorov, *Symbolism*, 19.

4.   Ricoeur, *Rule of Metaphor*.

5.   A word of caution is in order here, however. In our attempt to restore a poetic value to Vāc as a mythic image and to distinguish poetic from nonpoetic discourse, we must also avoid subsuming all the various aspects of Ṛg Vedic discourse under the term poetic. For our purpose, we must necessarily emphasize and give primacy to the image, and claim that, for the Ṛg Veda at least, the substance of both its myth and its poetry are images. Yet it would be misleading to claim that mythic and poetic discourses are always synonymous. Several distinctions between myth and poetry can and should be made. Myth, for example, also involves the presence of narrative elements, and the Vedas may be (and indeed have been) analyzed solely with respect to cosmological and mythological narratives. Ṛg Veda 10:71 is no exception.

6.   We might note in this regard that many Vedic scholars argue against the permanent marriage of myth and ritual in the Vedic case, emphasizing instead their separate developments. We might also mention that Ṛg Vedic verses must undergo various modifications in pitch and accentuation to be incorporated into the *Sāmaveda*, and be fit fur ritual use. Yet the hymn itself (see verse 11) seems to assume that the hymn and the ritual are inextricably related in some level, and we shall take it at its word.

7.   Obviously, for a thoroughly balanced approach, one would need to take into account the work of Indian interpreters who view the hymn from within the Hindu tradition. Modern interpreters include Kunhan Raja (1963) and Manilal Patel (1938); earlier interpreters include Patañjali in his *Mahābhāṣya*, the author of the *Bṛhaddevatā*, (attributed to Śaunaka), and Sāyana, among others. One might also mention the potential usefulness of poeticians such as Abhinavagupta, Mammaṭa *(Kāvyaprakāśa)*, and his predecessor Ānandavardhana, who develop and describe various aspects and phases of the symbolic process.

8.   Johnson, *Speculation*, 11.

9.   Ibid., xxiv.

10.   Ibid., 10.

11.   Ibid., 12.

12.   Staal, "*Ṛg Veda* 10.71," 12.

13.   Ibid., 8-9.

14.   Ibid., 12.

15.   W. Norman Brown (1968) provides an exhaustive analysis of Vāc's role in the much-exegeted hymn 1:164, and touches upon parallels in the other two hymns as well.

16.   I am grateful to Prof. David Gitomer, University of Chicago, for this insight.

17.   Johnson's use of I. A. Richards' terms *vehicle* and *tenor* to describe the enigmatic image should also be scrutinized here. As Todorov suggests, I. A. Richards maintains a hierarchy in asserting that direct meaning is nothing but an instrument for the indirect and does not have tenor in itself. This criticism would fit nicely with the rest of our critique of Johnson; as we show, he subordinates all other meanings of Vāc to be the "instruments" of the "indirect" meaning of Vāc as an enigmatizing image.

18.   This use of the word *sacred* introduces us to its usual definitional problems. Proudfoot, Baird, J. Z. Smith, Staal, and others have analyzed these exhaustively. As one scholar rather appropriately states, "Perhaps even defining myth as the doings of sacred beings and sacred places is defining one enigma with another, because the sacred is as difficult to put a handle on as myth" (Paul Griffiths, Myth and Philosophy Colloquium, Spring, 1987).

19.   Johnson takes the classic view that the magical power of names is the primary property of language; names themselves hold cosmological meaning. He writes in a footnote "the setting up of names (v. 1 *nāmadheya*) is the divine power of creation through the holy word" (p. 148). And, as mentioned above, the use of *māyā* in verse 5 does not imply illusion, but creative power, "the ability to manifest, as in the beginning, through verbal means alone."

20.   Because Vāc does not imply an obviously agentive force such as a deity, Staal sees no reason to give creative, magical power to the act of naming as Johnson does. Instead, Staal makes an explicit distinction between *nāmadheya*, the setting up of names, and *vācārambhana*, the beginning of language. Following later texts, such as the *Chandogya Upaniṣad*, he claims that naming does not possess magical power; it only differentiates the multitude of things. Language, on the other hand, expresses the self of man.

21.   Staal also tells the same story in his 1979 article, "The Meaninglessness of Ritual" and in his 1980 article, "Ritual Syntax."

22.   Staal mentions Jakobson's phonological influence on Lévi-Strauss, Pierce's semantic influence upon Singer, and Austin's pragmatic influence on Tambiah. Staal himself has referred to Austin's "performatives" as important to the study of Vedic ritual (1970)—a concept we will return to below.

23.   Two important concepts resulting from syntactical analysis of ritual are "embeddedness" and "modification." Embeddedness is the principle by which certain rituals are encased within one another in a system of syntactical relations. Modification is the principle whereby those rituals which occur within other rituals (as well as on their own) are modified according to the ritual in which they are embedded.

24.   Staal, "Ritual Syntax," 120. His use of this quote is telling here. Isadora Duncan herself was pointing to the mere *inadequacy* of words to portray a meaning—not to the "obsessiveness," "compulsiveness," or "meaninglessness" of her activity, as Staal might have it.

25.   This knowledge of origins thereby attributes to the Vedic seers a privileged epistemological position. Staal writes:

It is tempting to . . . assume that the seers had knowledge of events, to which we do not ordinarily have access. It is not wise to subscribe to the facile assumption that the people we study know at most what we know ourselves. (Staal, "Metalanguage," 321)

26.   Staal, "*Ṛg Veda*" 10:71," 13.

27.   As Penner notes, it is important not to ignore the Fregean distinction between "sense" and "reference"—that meaning should not be based only on referential capacity. In 1986, Staal modifies his stance in answering Penner. He states that it would be absurd to say that rituals are ·meaningless because they do not refer. Staal nonetheless asserts that his analysis demonstrates that the assumption that rituals express meanings, in the way that language does, is not only unnecessary, but inaccurate and misleading.

28.   It is interesting to note there that in an earlier essay (1980), Staal asserts the opposite: activity—ritual being ideal activity—expressed man's awareness of himself and paved the way to the construction of theory and language. Staal himself comes close to a notion of "creating meaning" elsewhere in his speculations upon the development of man's consciousness of himself as an agent. Staal asserts that although ritual did not refer to anything, it did create (and even express!) a sense of self-consciousness. (Staal, "Meaninglessness of Ritual," 14) This development might strike one as an immensely "meaningful" event!

29.   See Staal's "Ritual Syntax" for further discussion of logic and syntax in ritual. There, he comments:

Had there been no ritual, meaning could have been attached to sound in a more direct fashion. In particular, composite meanings could have been represented by composite sounds in a straightforward manner, as is indeed the case in some systems of logic, and as is significantly absent from natural language. (Staal, "Ritual Syntax," 139)

30.   Staal, "*Ṛg Veda* 10.71," 10.

31.   See Staal, "Ritual Syntax."

32.   He states that the syntax of ritual, often made up of meaningless, but highly structured sounds, is the "state immediately preceding language" that survives in religion as mantras and magic spells. This absence of language is also a quality of mystical states, he goes on, "which can be induced by ritual, recitation, or silent meditation on mantras"—in short by syntactical, and not meaningful, entities (1979). He further asserts that the importance of ritual in human development is evidenced by these generally archaic features of ritual and mysticism. Moreover, we have seen that Staal attributes to the Vedic seers some kind of mystical knowledge of primordial events, as cited above in his 1975 essay. In "Ritual Syntax," (138) he cites RV 1:164 to show that seers were aware of a golden age when ritual practices and mystical insight were common. However, Staal's statement does not explain ritual's magical quality.

33.   Here we might also add that the term *mystical insight* itself implies a referential meaning of some sort—unless Staal is thinking here of a pure state of emotional excitation.

34.   Todorov, op. cit., 19.

35.   Langer, *Problems*, 145-47.

36.   Ibid., 149.

37.   Ibid., 155.

38.   Ibid., 153.

39.   This hypothesis is also posited by many anthropologists of poetic discourse. For these scholars, myth, or more specifically, the mythic image expressed in language, is the medium through which something new is made known, communicated. Indeed, there need not necessarily be an *actual* physical image present while such discourse is happening: public conversation itself, such as a poetic contest, may be a way of accomplishing and bringing into being a new situation, a new deity, a new time. Michael Silverstein's notion of "maximally creative language"—that which is not context-dependent but context-creating—is relevant here. Although we will address this issue in more detail later on, Silverstein notes that in poetic and ritual language, diagrammatic images can be analyzed as part of the structural layering of the poem itself, and need not necessarily "refer" to any actual image outside of the text (in Janowitz, "Language of Ascent," 217).

40.   Langer, op. cit., 159.

41.   Ibid., 153.

42.   This sense of portrayal is echoed in part by Eliot Deutch's discussion of the aesthetic concerns in the study of myth. As he sees it, meaning might exist only in and through an articulation of myth. Meaning does not exist separately, only later to be given some expression in the myth; it simply doesn't exist apart from the myth. Similarly, the content of a work of art does not exist apart from the content as it is formed in that particular work of art (Myth and Philosophy Colloquium, 1986).

43.   Wheelock, *Ritual Language*, 7ff.

44.   Although a detailed description of the rules of speech performance would bog us down at this point, it is important to note that the development of this kind of rule system is important to any analysis of the spoken word. Silverstein's analysis of the use of parallelism in ritual speech is one such example.

45.   Ibid., 27ff.

46.   Ibid., 32.

47.   Although Michael Silverstein does not mention Wheelock's work, he develops an analysis that comes very close to (and extends) Wheelock's idea of the transformative power of ritual language. For him, utterances which occur in relatively similar places in the ritual have some special metaphorical, pseudodefinitional relationship, which at a higher structural level of the ritual in effect suggest categorical identity (p. 5). The higher level provides the "diagrammatic images" —icons which are both "of the context of the rite and invoke the context of the

rite." For Silverstein, the transformative power of a rite is the transformation of the diagrams and thus of the context—such images are reshaped and moved as the discourse moves from beginning to end. Thus these diagrams create and recreate the contexts of use. Ritual language can thus both index the transformation that is occurring and at the same time provide an icon of that transformation (in Janowitz, "Language of Ascent," 217).

48.   Wheelock, "Taxonomy," 365.

49.   Even Silverstein's rather dramatic "metaforces of power" only addresses the linguistic aspects of the situation.

50.   Johnson, *Speculation*, 148.

51.   Detienne, *Creation*, 122-23.

References

Arapura, J. G.
    1977 "Some Perspectives on Indian Philosophy of Language." In *Revelation in Indian Thought: A Festschrift in Honor of Professor of T. R. V. Murti*, edited by Harold Coward and Krishan Sivarma, 15-44. Emeryville, California: Dharma Publishing.

Brown, W. Norman.
    1968 "The Creative Role of the Goddess Vāc in the Ṛg Veda." In *Pratidanam: Indian, Iranian, and Indo-European Studies Presented to F. B. J. Kuiper*, 393-97. The Hague: Paris.

Cassirer, Ernst.
    Language and Myth. New York: Dover Publications, Inc.

Commaraswamy, A. K.
    1981 *Figures of Speech and Thought*. New Delhi: Munishiram Mancharlal Publishers Pvt., Ltd.

Detienne, Marcel.
    1986 *The Creation of Mythology*. Translated by Margaret Cook. Chicago: University of Chicago Press.

Gonda, Jan.
    1963 *The Vision of the Vedic Poets*. The Hague: Mouton and Co.

    1950 *Notes on Brahman*. Utrecht: J. L. K. Beyers.

Gopal, Ram.
1983 *The History and Principals of Vedic Interpretation.* New Delhi: Concept Publishing.

Langer, Suzanne K.
1957 *Problems of Art: Ten Philosophical Lectures.* New York: Charles Scribners Sons.

Janowitz, Naomi.
1984 "The Language of Ascent: Lévi-Strauss, Silverstein and Maaseh Merkabah." *In Anthropology and the Study of Religion,* edited by Moore and Reynolds, 213-28. Chicago: Center for the Scientific Study of Religion.

Johnson, Willard.
1980 *Poetry and Speculation in the Ṛg Veda.* Berkeley: University of California Press.

O'Flaherty, Wendy.
1981 *The Rig Veda.* New York: Penguin Books.

Patel, Manilel.
1938 "A Study of *Ṛg Veda* 10:71." In Visvabharati Quarterly 4:143-151.

Raja, C. Kunhan.
1964 *The Quintessence of the Rig Veda.* Bombay: D. B. Taraporevala Sons Pvt., Ltd.

Renou, Louis.
1955 "Les Pouvoirs de la Parole dans le Ṛg Veda." In *Etudes Vediques et Panineennes* 1:1-27. Paris: E. De Boccard.

Ricoeur, Paul.
1977 *The Rule of Metaphor.* Translated by Robert Czerny with Kathleen McLaughlin and John Costello, SJ. Toronto: University of Toronto Press.

Silverstein, Michael.
1979 "Language Structure and Linguistic Ideology." In *The Elements,* 193-247. Chicago Linguistics Society, Paris Section.

Staal, Frits.
1975 "The Concept of Metalanguage and Its Indian Background." *Journal of Indian Philosophy* 3:315-54.

1977 "Ṛg Veda 10:71 on the Origin of Language." *In Revelation in Indian Thought: A Feschrift in Honour of Professor T. R. V. Murti,* edited by Harold Coward and Krishna Sivaram, 3-14. Emeryville, California: Dharma Publishing Company.

1979 "The Meaninglessness of Ritual." In *Numen* 26, Fasc 1:2-22.

1980 "Ritual Syntax.: In *Sanskrit and Indian Studies, Essays in Honour of Daniel H. H. Ingalls,* edited by M. Nagatomi, et al, 119-143. Dordrecht, Holland; Boston: D. Reidel.

1986. "The Sound of Religion." In *Numen* 33, Fasc 1:33-64.

Tambiah, S.
1968 "The Magical Power of Words." In *Man* n.s., 3:175-208.

Todorov, Tzvetan.
1982 *Symbolism and Interpretation.* Translated by Catherine Porter. Ithaca: Cornell University Press.

Wheelock, Wade.
1978 *The Ritual Language of a Vedic Sacrifice.* University of Chicago Dissertation.

1980 "A Taxonomy of Mantras in the New and Full Moon Sacrifice." In *History of Religions* 19:4.

1982 "The Problem of Ritual Language." In *Journal of the American Academy of Religion* 50:1: 49-69.

Chapter 8

Beyond Philosophy: Suhrawardī's Illuminationist Path to Wisdom

Hossein Ziai

i

Is there a dimension in the religious tradition of Islam related to "Myth, Philosophy, and Practice" confined neither to the prevalent juridical nor to the historians' interpretation?* As a participant in the Colloquium I began to probe this question in earnest. I looked beyond the Muslim jurists' and theologians' views of religious life, including thought and practice, shaped purely on the basis of God's revelation to Muhammad codified as a complete set of laws— *the sharī'a*.[1] In examining the intellectual traditions of Islam I concentrated on a school of philosophy known as the philosophy of illumination, *ḥikmat al-ishrāq*. This philosophical way, while including the impact of Hellenic philosophy on Islamic intellectual traditions, as does the Islamic Peripateticism, attempts further to incorporate a special initial and

---

* I wish to thank professors Amin Banani, Herbert Davidson, and Thomas Penchoen for having read versions of this paper and for their helpful comments.

intuitive grasp of the whole of reality. In its attempt at a total formulation of reality the philosophy of illumination aims to construct a consistent system based on a prior innate knowledge. This prior knowledge is claimed to be based on an *experience* of reality not confined to
cogitation and simple sense perception. The language of the philosophy of illumination in its attempt to combine philosophical construction and poetic perceptions is beyond ordinary language and ultimately mytho-poetic. As I examined, with a comparative eye, the varied
texts in this tradition of philosophy in Islam, comparing its discursive
language to its metalanguage of the experienced and the imagined, a
set of issues presented themselves. These comprise questions relating
to a type of experienced knowledge which in practice continues to
inform and shape the world view not only of individual philosophers
and thinkers, but also of a larger group of poets as it relates to their
conception of God, man, and nature. Through a conscious use of
poetic language employing metaphor and using symbols of widely
known myths and legends, the illuminationist, *ishrāqī*, tradition was
able to go beyond the formal Peripatetic philosophical teachings and
in so doing influence a much wider audience. This is evidenced in the
widespread use of illuminationist terminology, symbols, and
metaphors in mystical poetry and in allegorical mystical and philosophical tales. In this tradition, poetic wisdom came to be considered
the final means by which man was to learn his position in the world.
The illuminationist dimension in the civilization of Islam may be
thought of as mystical indeed, but should not be identified purely with
Sufism and with the history of Sufi orders. Here the language of myth,
legend, and allegory is used to narrate stories that convey an experience of life not confined to the recitation of a singular revelation.
Ordinary language is replaced by metaphor, and poetic wisdom comes
to be the recognized end of philosophy.

In order to show the interconnection among myth, philosophy,
and poetic wisdom I shall concentrate on the allegorical formulation of
the philosophy of illumination, whose main proponent is the twelfth-
century Persian sage Shihāb al-Dīn Suhrawardī—the Divine Master as
he is referred to in the texts—who in the year 1191 was executed by
order of the Ayyubid Sultan Saladin in Aleppo, on charges of proclaiming prophethood.[2] His major writings have been published by the late
Henry Corbin whose contribution to our understanding of Suhrawardī's
thought and its impact on the development of "Iranian Islam" cannot be
overestimated.[3] The philosophy of illumination is heir to an ancient

Iranian religious world view that posits the material and the spiritual as necessary attributes of a single undivided reality. In systematically reformulating the principles of this world view on a mystical plane related to, but not restricted by Islam, Suhrawardī ensured its continuity in Iranian culture in a vastly more profound and dynamic way.

To fully appreciate the poetic, metaphorical, and ultimately experiential character of illuminationist wisdom, it may be useful to deal briefly with the significant analytical and systematically philosophical part of the philosophy of illumination that serves as the discursive grounds on which it is founded.[4] As with the systematic Peripatetic Islamic philosophy (predominantly the Avicennan doctrine) before him, Suhrawardī's philosophical works begin with the study of logic, continue with physics, and culminate with metaphysics. Suhrawardī makes major methodological, structural, and conceptual changes to the traditional systematic philosophy of his time. The most significant distinguishing character of these changes is in Suhrawardī's departure from Peripatetic epistemology. At the very outset of constructing an epistemology Suhrawardī rejects the Aristotelian theory of definition. The illuminationist theory does not accept the value of a unitary formula of an essentialist definition as a step in constructing philosophy. The Aristotelian *horos*, the Avicennan *al-ḥadd al-tāmm*, is rejected by Suhrawardī on the grounds that the *summum genus* plus the *differentiæ* of a thing to be defined cannot be exhaustively enumerated in any definition. Thus an essentialist definition is considered to be only a turn of phrase, *tabdīl al-lafẓ*—a tautology—that does not convey knowledge of essence. In the language of current analytical philosophy Suhrawardī's views can be summed up by stating that the illuminationist view does not accept the validity of any definition by extension, and that a definition by acquaintance may be considered a valid type in certain cases.[5] A thing's essence may be known not through a constructed definition of it, but through an "experience" which, in the illuminationist terminology, is stated to be a vision, *mushāhada*, of the thing as-it-is.[6] The same principle of vision is explained to apply to the corporeal as well as to the noncorporeal realms. In the activity of external sight, "vision" takes place at the moment when a sound eye meets an illuminated object—potentially knowable—when no obstacles exist between the two, and when a medium for the vision, i.e. light, is present. In internal or illuminationist vision, *mushāhada*, *ishrāqiyya*, "vision" takes place based on a similar principle. Here the subject is the philosopher-sage who has prepared himself to "see" through praxis. The object is the illuminated and potentially knowable object of the realm of experience, known as the *mundus imaginalis*, and light is a noncorporeal light that emanates from the source referred to as the "Light of Lights," *Nūr al-anwār*. Illuminationist epistemology is thus based on direct vision, and knowledge is nonpredicative but depends on a relation, *iḍāfa*, between the subject and the object. The laws that govern illuminationist vision, such as its time and place, apply only to the separate realm of the *imaginal* and not to the corporeal. For example the time involved in a vision is a time without duration and thus measureless, called *ān*, and *where* it takes place is not *in* extended space. Illuminationist vision takes place in a durationless instant in a place that is not here or there nor above nor below. The realm of experience, the *mundus imaginalis*, is real yet separate from the subject, who, however, when having a vision actually comes to "reside" there.[7] In his theory of vision Suhrawardī does incorporate an Avicennan doctrine of intuition, *ḥads*, yet by giving it a fundamental role in the way knowledge of essence is obtained he moves further than Avicenna towards a philosophical position that I propose to call "primacy of experience and vision." In this paper I will omit discussing the philosophical side of the theory of illumination and vision and concentrate rather on the metaphorical and allegorical works by Suhrawardī. For this is the domain wherein a final poetic language is employed to create new myths that combine symbols and metaphors that continue to inform man of the experience of the whole of reality.

ii

The goal of the Philosophy of Illumination is to gain an unqualified knowledge of that which cannot be qualified: beyond a knowledge of God in His oneness, and of the identity of oneself with His being, its goal is the cognitive *experience* of a state of consciousness where all identities are obliterated, and with it all expressions and references.[8] Those who possess it are invariably referred to as the People of Truth, of Reality, or of Love. This knowledge is argued as being superior to all other types of knowledge, including knowledge based on observation and argumentation. For while the latter rests on, and is limited by, the Active Intellect,[9] the proof of the former lies in the direct experience of its validity. The following story is cited by Suhrawardī by way of illustrating this contention:

One of the sufis was asked, 'What is the proof of the creator's existence?' He replied, 'The morning renders the lamp unnecessary.' Another of them says, 'One who seeks God through logical proof is like someone searching for the sun with a lamp.'[10]

In illuminationist terminology, this knowledge is nonpredicative and forms a "science based on 'presence,' and vision'," *al-ʿilm al-ḥudūrī al-shuhūdī*, which serves as the basis for that which is subsequently acquired and explained through philosophical construction.[11] In its methodology, therefore, the philosophy of illumination employs discursive reasoning only in order to systematically depict the results of visions. In other words, it only makes use of the method of Peripatetic philosophy but does not consider it to be an end in and by itself. In sum, its definition and praxis are based on a primary intuition of time-and-space, and on a perception of reality that is extrasensorial.

From a philosophical point of view, *ḥikmat al-ishrāq* is, or intends to be, a perfect synthesis between the Peripatetic and the Platonic schools of thought. Suhrawardī incorporates a reconstructed theory of knowledge in which intuitive reasoning, *al-aḥkām al-ḥads*, comparable to the Aristotelian notion of "quick wit,"[12] together with the coupled process of vision-illumination, *al-mushāhada wa'l-ishrāq*, serves as the foundation for the construction of philosophy. In this respect he has, while employing the Avicennan term *al-ḥads*, given intuition a general epistemological priority confined by Avicenna only to certain ranks of individuals such as prophets.[13] Thus in the Avicennan view intuition is used to explain specific phenomena[14] and does not receive the same position in the foundation of a theory of knowledge as it does in illuminationist epistemology. Using a modified Peripatetic terminology, Suhrawardī identifies intuition, first, as an activity of the intellect *in habitu*, *ʿaql bi'l-malaka*,[15] and secondly, as the activity of the holy intellect, *al-ʿaql al-qudsī*;[16] but the most important activity of intuition is the subject's ability to perceive the intelligibles and the essence of things instantaneously and without guidance.[17] "Judgments of intuition," *aḥkām al-ḥads*, *ḥukm al-ḥads*, are thus valid forms of inference[18] and are of the rank of demonstration.[19]

Given the nature of its praxis, however, the philosophy of illumination has to be further qualified as a mystico-philosophical tradition which, rooted in Zoroastrianism and further influenced by Islam, provides a personal, spiritual, and always ecstatic way for contemplating, discerning, influencing, creatively shaping, and finally living, reality.

The structure as well as the individual components of the techniques by which this wisdom is attained are analogous to other highly evolved traditions such as Buddhism and classical yoga and, like them, find many points of correspondence with primitive and archaic rites of passage that transform a neophyte into a person of a qualitatively altered status and sensibility. Within the latter category, the closest analogy in terms of the ordeals and the initiatory pattern of the journey of the soul, the spatio-temporal concepts and the symbols used to depict them, and in the value given to magical prowess, is to be found in shamanic rites. For the esoteric knowledge gained by the initiated—usually though not necessarily through a master of initiation—may manifest itself in such occult powers as clairvoyance, the ability to heal, foretell the future, conjure up images, walk on water, and change his form at will.[20] In sum, the Philosophy of Illumination is a unique synthesis of concepts and traditions as old and primal as those of the hunting societies of the paleolithic age and as late and refined as those of medieval Islamic culture.

The outstanding mode of presentation and instruction of this philosophy—both textual and oral—while didactic in style, is mythological in form and poetic in essence, myth and poetry being the most suitable media for eliciting an experience of an object and for expressing the transcendental and often paradoxical measures of reality. Suhrawardī's use of myth and metaphor—both ancient Iranian and Judaeo-Islamic—is personal, creative, and synthetic and departs from the mainstream tradition in Islam where myth is neither the source of inspiration or the stuff of revelation. The Koran recognizes a selection of Biblical legends as testimonials of prophethood, *nubuwwa*, in the Abrahamic traditions, but it creates no myths of its own. Logos is the *kalima*, word of God, and the practice of religion is inspired and directed by what is derived from revelation, *waḥy*, and the personal way, *sīra*, of the Prophet Muhammad—the seal of the prophets, *khātam al-anbiyā'*, with whom revelation ends. In contradiction to this official notion, illuminationist philosophy holds that revelation is a continuous process manifest through personal revelation, *ilhām*, and vision-illumination, *mushāhada-ishrāq*: "God is not miserly that He close the doors of revelation and vision," insists Suhrawardī.[21] Revelation is not confined to the rank of prophets but is, in fact, accessible to all seekers, although more so if they have a special "aptitude," or are more "worthy," or "wise,"[22] words well descriptive of Suhrawardī himself. One of his most poetic compositions entitled *On the Reality of Love, or the Solace of Lovers*, for instance, which is an interpretation of a Koranic revelation based on the Old Testament legend of Joseph—here in allegorical form—begins *as* a cosmogonic myth thus:

> Know that the first thing God created was a glowing pearl He named Intellect, *'aql*. . . . This pearl He endowed with three qualities, the ability to know God, the ability to know itself, and the ability to know that which had not existed and then did exist. From the ability to know God there appeared *ḥusn*, who is called Beauty; and from the ability to know itself there appeared *'ishq*, who is called Love. From the ability to know that which did not exist and then did exist there appeared *ḥusn*, who is called Sorrow. Of these three, who sprang from one source and are brothers one to the other, Beauty the eldest gazed upon himself and saw that he was extremely good. A luminosity appeared in him, and he smiled. From that smile thousands of cherubim appeared. Love, the middle brother, was so intimate with Beauty that he could not take his eyes from him and was constantly at his side. When Beauty's smile appeared, a consternation befell Love, who was so agitated that he wanted to move. Sorrow, the youngest, clung to him, and from his clinging the heaven and earth appeared.[23]

The tale goes on to relate how the brothers separated after the creation of Adam and how Beauty came to reside in Joseph and increased thereby; that Jacob grew intimate with Sorrow and Love became Zuleikha's companion. And so on through twelve chapters Suhrawardī uses his own version and interpretation of this Biblical legend to expound on the nature and attributes of the human soul and the divine source of his condition. In interpreting the word of God, the claim to truth rests with the man who is at once a mystic, a philosopher, and a poet. "The worst era," adds Suhrawardī, is when the world is devoid of the wisdom of such a sage, when "the mind soars no more, the doors of revelation are shut and the paths of visions are blocked."[24]

It should come as no surprise that over and above the appeal of its theoretical propositions, it is the practical end of the philosophy of illumination as a way of life and gnosis that came to dominate the Iranian mystical experience in the post-Islamic era. And heirs to the same traditions, it was the mystic poets of Persia—those farthest-reaching messengers of the Iranian world view—who went on to act as the main communicators of this ideology to a receptive audience that cuts across the Persian speaking world to this day.

The study of an illuminationist path of knowledge that reaches beyond philosophy should invite general interest among humanists, particularly in the fields of semiotics, the history of religions, and comparative mythology. I shall attempt to present the principles of this subject in terms that may serve such a purpose and will, therefore, focus on examining the nature of the illuminationist experience and the symbolic system in which it is expressed, and omit discussion of the theoretical foundations of the Philosophy of Illumination and its place in the history of Islamic philosophy.

Some remarks on the nature of the illuminationist universe and the type of people—real or fictitious—that reside in it are required. The cosmos in which the illuminationist experience unfolds is four-fold:[25] 1) the world of controlling lights, *'ālam al-anwār al-qāhira*; 2) of managing lights, *'ālam al-anwār al-mudabbira*; 3) of intermediaries, *'ālam al-barāzikh*, also of bodies; and 4) of dark-and-light-seeking suspended forms, *'ālam al-ṣuwar al-muʿallaqa al-ẓulmāniyya waʾl-mustanīra*. The first world, that of controlling lights, is similar to the rank of the Plotinean universal intellect; it is noncorporeal and should be considered as the first station from where light is propagated from what is called the "Light of Lights." The second world, also called the "Isfahbad lights," manages the celestial domain, the movements of the spheres, and the affairs of men. In this last capacity the Isfahbad lights, especially the light called "Isfahbad al-Nasut," serves the same functions as the peripatetic Active Intellect. The third world, called Barzakh, is the world of corporeal entities, simple elements, and material compounded bodies. The fourth world, the *'ālam al-mithāl*, also referred to as the "Heavenly Earth Hūrqalyā," or to use Corbin's rendition, the *Mundus Imaginalis*, is the most amazing and awe inspiring of all. The spiritual substances of this world that include the luminous (the good) as well as the dark (evil) beings may appear as Epiphanies, and although they are not situated in Euclidean space, are real, *mutaḥḥaqaq fī 'ālam al-mithāl*, and can be experienced, and "seen," in the sense that they are accessible to a vision-illumination, *mushāhada wa ishrāq*.[26]

The champions who populate this realm, Imagemakers, *Aṣḥāb al-Barāyā* (lit., *those who possess the ability to create images*), Wayfarers, *sālikūn*, or the Brethren of Abstraction, *Ikhwān al-Tajrīd*, as they are variably called, constitute a category of prophets, sages, "divine" philosophers, kings, warriors, and mystics that include the Prophet Muḥammad, Pythagoras, Plato, the ideal king of the Avesta—Kaikhusrow—the greatest hero of the Iranian national epic—

Rustam—and a long list of mystics that includes the martyred al-Ḥallāj, Ḥasan al-Baṣrī, Dhu'n-Nūn al-Miṣrī, Sahl al-Tustarī, Abū Yazīd al-Bastāmī, Ibrāhīm ibn Adham, and even Junayd and Shiblī.[27] Of particular interest is the exclusion of philosophers such as Alfarabi or Avicenna in favor of Hermes, Asclepius, Empedocles, Socrates, Plato, and others. Indeed the visionaries, *arbāb al-mushāhada*, are said to be in opposition to the Peripatetics[28] and are distinguished from them by their ability to gain knowledge of all intelligibles without recourse to teachers or texts,[29] their inner vision allowing them to dispense with cogitation, *fikr*, altogether.[30]

The individual who has obtained illumination through intuition has undergone a transition from a simple subject, *al-mawḍūʿ*, to a knowing subject, *al-mawḍūʿ al-mudrik*, to a knowing, creating subject, *al-mawḍūʿ al-mudrik al-khallāq*. This means a transformation from the natural state, *nāsūt*, where man has to follow the ordinances of religious law, *Sharīʿa*, to the first excited state where he seeks the object of quest beyond the confines of religion and reason, and finally to the state of unity, when as a knowing subject he enters the realms of power and divinity, *jabarūt* and *lāhūt*, and obtains knowledge of the invisible world, *al-ʿālam al-ghayb*, and of the reality, *ḥaqīqa*, of things and, thus, the power of creation, *kun*, (be!). This state of creation known as *maqām kun*, is derived from the Koran XVI:42, *naqūl lahu kun fayakūn*, "[God] said to it, 'Be!' and it was."[31] It is in this final phase of creation where the individual soul obtains a vision of the Isfahbad lights—an imagery taken from Zoroastrian cosmology—and joins the exalted company of the Brethren of Abstraction,[32] so called because they are free from the bondage of corporeality. "The divine Plato," says Suhrawardī in his *Intimations*, "has related a story concerning [the experience] of his soul. . . . 'It so happened that I had retreated to my soul, and I had removed my body from extended space, *jānib*, and I had become as though abstracted, without body, stripped of natural clothings, absolved from Prime Matter, *hayūlā*. So I realized that I [had become] a part of the elevated noble world, *al-ʿālam al-aʿlā al-sharīf*.'"[33]

Another class of intuitively illuminated persons who act as God's vicegerents on earth[34] and are named as members of this noble world are historical rulers such as the first four Caliphs: Abū Bakr, ʿUmar, ʿUthmān, and ʿAlī. In fact, the Brethren of Abstraction are individuals who often serve political functions, the term *political* being taken in its broadest sense as referring to actions and relations that affect social units beyond the person's immediate circle of associates. This attitude also reflects on Suhrawardī's list of the luminaries taken from Persian mythology, epic, and legendary history, so that the magician-medicine man-king Afrīdūn of the Avesta who can change his shape at will, as well as the legendary Sasanian sage and king's counselor, Buzurgmihr, who is credited with—among other things—discovering the rules of chess, are also counted among the illuminati. From Avestan mythology he also borrows the concept of the Farrah-i Īzadī, Divine Glory, which signifies a sometimes personified celestial quality that resides in and identifies the most exalted among men.[35] In Suhrawardī, this Divine Glory is depicted as light and, as in the earlier tradition, is retained so long as the person is deserving of it; or in Suhrawardī's usage, continues to recognize its existence in himself. The illuminationist experience may in fact be summed up by saying that it is an experience of one's own being as a substantial light.

As the "Epiphanies of the Cosmos," *Mazāhir al-'ālam*, members of this spiritual fraternity are responsible for channeling wisdom, or Sacred Knowledge, *al-khamīra al-muqaddasa*, in history, the wisdom that is synthesized in Islam, the quintessence of which is captured by Suhrawardī himself. The source of this wisdom is fourfold, the exemplar in each case being Hermes, the father of philosophy; Plato, the divine philosopher; Kayumarth, the progenitor of mankind [Gayo-maretan, the first man/mortal in Avestan mythology]; and the Brahmins who are collectively referred to as the "sources of Indian wisdom."

The process by which this wisdom is attained is nowhere methodically delineated by Suhrawardī himself. However, it is possible to extrapolate from his writings a paradigm that describes it in terms of an ecstatic-like rite of passage in to Hūrqalyā that is marked by four stages of preparation, visionary experience, illumination, and definition. No one is barred from walking this path for it is submitted that every man possesses its two fundamental requirements: intuition, and a portion of the light of God.

The first stage consists of a rite of separation and is properly marked by ascetic practices and mental exercises that prepare the candidate for initiation. A forth-day fast "with a little agreeable food" that is ritually clean and legitimately acquired is prescribed, to be followed by a purgative consisting of 'whatever is dear to the person,' "possessions, property, material things, psychological and carnal pleasures."[36] This is to be repeated until the person "can see things not with the physical eye but through the eye of logic" which is how "the people of reality" see things. The mental exercises should be directed toward gaining self-knowledge which is said to form the basis for the attainment of unqualified knowledge. When in a personal vision induced after a night of ascetic practices Suhrawardī confronts Aristotle with the problem of knowledge, *mas'alat al-'ilm*,[37] the "Master of Philosophy" as the latter is called replies: "Revert to your self (or soul)."[38]

The search for "perception" and "discovery," *mushāhada wa mukāshafa*, undertaken in a state of self-contemplation will bring the candidate to "see" his own essence and to recognize the "I" as that which knows his own self, *dhāt*. Indeed, according to a fundamental component of the illuminationist epistemology, knowledge of the soul is self-constituted, for every individual is cognizant of his essence by means of that essence itself.[39] In this preparatory stage, then, the successful candidate will come to accept the reality of his own existence and admit the truth of his personal intuition.[40] "So I entered my soul," declares Plato in the *Intimations*, "and went outside of everything else. I thus saw in my soul things of beauty and worth, and things that glisten and radiate, and [I saw] amazing beautiful primordial things."[41] In a treatise entitled *The Shrill Cry of the Simurgh*, it is suggested that even without ascetic practices it is possible at times to experience this heightened sensibility spontaneously and without warning as when one is present in an open prayer-field amidst a sonorous festive crowd, or in the pitch of a clamorous battle, or on a galloping horse that takes the breath away.[42]

The second stage of this journey is said to occur in a state between sleep and wakefulness where "one hears horrible voices and strange cries." It unfolds by virtue of the "polar" mechanism of vision-illumination, *mushāhada-ishrāq*, while the person is still in the same "unconscious state."[43] For the process to succeed, one has to eventually cease using the five external senses, replacing them by the internal ones: "When the inner eye is opened, the outer eye should be sealed to everything."[44] Elsewhere in a dialogue between Love and Zuleikha, the process is described in different terms as 'scaling the nine barriers' that lead to the City of the Soul.[45] In Suhrawardī's personal experience, the process is achieved not through cogitation nor speculation but "through something else."[46] This "something else," as we are told by the author himself and by the commentators Shahrazūrī (13th c.), Quṭb al-Dīn al-Shīrāzī (14th c.), and later by Hirawi (17th c.), is that special experiential mode of knowledge called "illuminationist vision," *al-mushāhada al-ishrāqiyya*.[47] The epistemology of this vision is worked out in great detail by Suhrawardī and is the subject of much discussion by all later com-

mentators, reformulated and reexamined by one of the leading twentieth-century Muslim *ishrāqī* philosophers, Seyyed Kāzim 'Assār.

Vision-illumination is accompanied by sensations of ecstasy,
khalsa, euphoric pleasure, *ladhdha*, and eventually, by a total numbness
of the body.[48] In the beginning it induces visionary experiences of
flashes of light, or lightning bolts of different degrees of duration and
intensity, which are at times accompanied by thunderous sounds such
as are not heard in the world. This veritable son-et-lumière constitutes fifteen stages and culminates in a spectacular vision of a "glitter-
ing divine light," *al-nūr al-ilāhī*, so violent that it tears the body limb
from limb.[49] This light then penetrates the seeker in the form of a
series of "apocalyptic lights," *al-anwār al-sāniha*; that illuminate him in
such a way that he may go on to obtain a knowledge that will then
serve as the foundation of real sciences, *al-'ulūm al-haqīqiyya*.[50]

Vision-illumination acts on all levels of reality. On the human
level it acts sense-perceptibly as the sight, *ibsār*, of an object, *al-mubsar*,
that is illuminated, *mustanīr*, by the sun, which in Suhrawardī's
Zoroastrianizing nomenclature is called the "Great Hūrakhsh," (Av.
Hvar Khšaeta, "the radiant sun"[51]). The process of self-realization which
began in the first stage induces in him a vibrant eagerness, *shawq*, to
"see" the being just above it in perfection, and it is this act of "seeing"
that will effect the process of illumination.[52] On the cosmic level, every
"abstract light" is directly illuminated by the Light of Lights, and sees
the "lights" that are above it, a gradational upward movement which is
possible because each "light" instantaneously, at the moment of vision,
illuminates the one lower in rank to itself.

The propogation of light from its highest celestial origin to the
lowest terrestrial elements[53] is achieved by means of intermediary
principles called the "controlling/managing lights" *al-anwār al-ghāhi-
ra/mudabbira*,[54] a class of which—called the "Isfahbad lights"—directly
illuminate the human soul, and as already stated, enable it to receive
knowledge.[55] In other words, the power of the eye to "see" derives
from a hierarchical structure that reaches up to a single source.[56] Also,
according to the same paradigm, it is ultimately possible to "see" the
emanating-by-essence, *fayyāḍ bi al-dhāt*, Light of Lights,[57] everything
else being a degree of its intensity and thus "connected" to it without
any disjunction, *infiṣāl*.[58] The Light of Lights is the most apparent to
itself, and therefore the most self-conscious being in the universe,[59]
and its luminosity, *nūriyya*, essence, *dhāt*, and power, are the same.[60]

The relevance of the imagery of light to a philosophy of illumination is self-evident and ultimately springs from the sun's unremit-

ting, brilliant, warm, and fructifying presence in the heavens. In particular though, it is rooted in a universal association of light with lucidity and knowledge, a symbolism that from a phenomenological point of view derives from the sun's transparent luminosity. Again, and in light of the context and collection of symbols that appear in Suhrawardī's works, it can be explained as a vestige of the Zoroastrian heritage where it is the symbol par excellence of Ahura Mazdā's eternal creation and stands for the highest moral principal. Also light imagery is a common Platonic, Aristotelean, and Plotinean metaphor, but the view that where light is no longer therein does exist real dark beings is specifically Zoroastrian. In the philosophy of illumination as in the Zoroastrian tradition, the "Light of Lights" is at once ideal and real, both an abstraction of the incorporeal quality of celestial existence and a quality of these ideal forms when they are personified on earth. Thus, while the transparent quality of light is used as an abstract symbol by Suhrawardī to signify knowledge, the brilliance and heat generated by it are used in a literal sense as it were to signify the candidate's inner illumination. Their combined effect engenders a new metaphysical condition in such a way that the enlightened man becomes a source of light, i.e. knowledge, himself, while the dark beings, who also dwell in the *mundus imaginalis*, will continue their attempt to prevent the light from emanating from the source.

In this respect, too, Suhrawardī's usage of what may be called the "Iranian" form of this symbolic code resembles Zoroastrian concepts for it duplicates, on a philosophical and mystical plane, the ideological concept earlier referred to as the "Farrah-i Īzadī," the god-given mark of distinction possessed by the glorious few, which though an abstract quality in essence, may at times be personified as well.[61] Compare, for example, Suhrawardī's notion that "incorporeal souls" obtain an "image of the light of God," *mithāl min nūr Allah*, which the faculty of imagination imprints upon the "tablet of the sensus communus," *lawḥ al-ḥiss al-mushtarak*. It is by means of this image that they obtain control over a "creative light," *al-nūr al-khāliq*. Through the instrument of the creative acts of the illuminated subject's imagination, vision takes place, that is, knowledge is obtained.[62] It may be noted that in both Zoroastrian doctrine and in Suhrawardī a person may lose his right to the continued possession of this source of power and glory.[63]

Some general remarks deduced from Suhrawardī's accounts of the cosmographic features of the territory wherein the visionary experience does take place is in order before proceeding further. Hūrqalyā or *ʿālam al-mithāl*, at times *ʿālam al-khayāl*, as it is called by Suhrawardī and *terre céléste* or the *mundus imaginalis* by Corbin, has already been mentioned as the fourth dominion of the illuminationist cosmos. This is a land beyond the corporeal, of the essence of the fabulous, *hūrqalyā dhāt al-'ajā'ib*; it is the eighth clima, *al-iqlīm al-thāmin.*[64] Access to it is gained through the active imagination when it becomes mirrorlike, turning into a zone where an epiphany, *maẓhar*, may occur. One is said to travel in it not by traversing distances but by being witness to "here" or "there" unsituated and without coordinants. Seeing sights in this clime is identified as effects suffered by the soul, or experiences within the self-consciousness of the objective ipseity. The *mundus imaginalis* is an ontological "realm" as it were whose being, though possessing the categorical attributes, i.e. they have attributes of time, place, relation, quality, quantity, etc., are abstracted from matter; which is to say that they are ideal beings with a substance, usually depicted in a metaphorical term as light, which differ from the substances of other beings only in respect to their degree of intensity.[65]

Thus it can be seen that Hūrqalyā is a region suspended between the purely intelligible and the purely sensory, where time is not an Aristotelian measure of distance, nor space a Euclidean extension in time. But for all its *imaginalis* qualities, this is, in the words of Corbin, a "concrete spiritual universe." Like Jacques Duchesne-Guillemin before him,[66] Corbin qualifies the *mundus imaginalis* in terms of what he calls a "neo-Zoroastrian Platonism" where he states: "It is most certainly not a world of concepts, paradigms, and universals," for the archetypes of the species that populate it have "nothing to do with the universals established in logic." Rather, they are an "autonomous world of visionary Figures and Forms" that belong to "the plane of angelology."[67]

A word of caution must be said here against the temptation to identify the *mundus imaginalis* with Plato's Realm of Ideas. Suhrawardī himself is quite specific on this point and distinguishes between his suspended Forms, *al-ṣuwar al-mu'allaqa*—which are the real beings of the eighth clima—and the Platonic Forms. Platonic Forms are discrete and distinct entities, or things, in the realm of intelligible lights, while the real beings of Hūrqalyā are part of the continuum of the *imaginalis.*[68] Later commentators of illuminationist philosophy divide the *mundus imaginalis* into a continuous and a discrete realm, *mutaṣil wa munfaṣil*, defining the discrete one as a self-constituted realm separate from individual particularization, and the continuous one as a realm which may appear as a series of epiphanies, or as creative acts produced by the imagination.

Let us now look at an allegorical and narrative account of a visionary experience related in *The Sound of Gabriel's Wing*, with the young Suhrawardī himself as the neophyte, which interestingly enough has structural correspondences to a rite of initiation proper into manhood. It occurred one dark night, says Suhrawardī, "when I had first emerged from the women's chambers and some of the restrictions of infants had been lifted from me."[69] Our sense of the transitional quality of his state is strengthened by the following combination of imagery: awakened by a dream and overcome by despair, the youth heads for the men's quarters, candle in hand, where he wanders till the break of dawn. Here he ventures into his father's *khānaqāh* (a chamber for sufi gatherings), that is, into a sacred ground closed to women that brings him into the primity of the spiritually eminent. The idea of separation from the profane world is sealed by another image: he shuts tight one of the two doors of the *khānaqāh*, that is, the one that opens to the city. The account of his ecstatic journey into the wonderland begins as he turns the handle of the second door, the one that leads out into the field. It is here that this "untutored," "unworthy," "unenlightened," "naïve child" as he is called by a master, is to receive instruction that will change his status forever.

In our account of Suhrawardī's allegory of a sojourn in this realm, the land Hūrqalyā, we note that as in quest journeys of traditional tales, his first startling, exotic, and unexpected encounter takes place just across the threshold of the world which he is about to leave. One step beyond the door of the *khānaqāh* that opens to the field, he beholds a group of old men of supreme grace and beauty, with white hair and splendid garments, seated on a magnificent tiered throne. Typical of the quality associated with the experience of the *mysterium*, the youth is struck with a dreadful sense of awe and wonder. Again, following a traditional pattern, his initial fear is dispelled after he makes contact with the strangers. "Pray, sir," he asks the one seated on the lowest level, "from which direction have my lords honoured us with their presence?" "We are a group of abstracted ones," replies the old man, "come from the direction of Nākujā-ābād, *lā makān*."[70] "In which clime is that?," asks the mystified youth. "In the clime to which your index finger cannot point" comes the reply, and we know that Nākujā-ābād—literally "No-Wheresville"—being the negation of space itself, may not be located on any earthly map. In the treatise on love cited earlier, Sorrow calls it the Sacred Abode where his home stood in the Region of the Soul, Rūh-ābād, on Beauty Lane.[71]

The fairytale quality of the above image is discernible enough, but the type of elegiac grace and mythic nostalgia stimulated by the internal rhyme of the original Nākujā-ābād cannot be translated. The word evokes an existential yearning to recapture a mythical time and territory of perfect and primordial qualities now lost, except to the imagination. Elsewhere Suhrawardī situates it on the summit of Mount Qāf, a motif borrowed from Islamic tradition which in post-Islamic Iran came to be identified with Harā, the great cosmic mountain of the *Avesta* that rises at the center of the world. In a treatise entitled *The Red Intellect*, the initiation master tells the novice—here depicted as a fettered falcon in search of freedom—that like himself, the novice too "has been brought" from Mount Qāf, and that "eventually everything that exists returns to its initial form." The Red Intellect himself is no less a person than "the first child of creation," elsewhere depicted as a glowing pearl. He is a traveler in constant motion who has seen the Seven Wonders of the world which are enumerated as Mount Qāf itself, the Pearl-that-glows-by night, the Ṭūbā tree, the Twelve Workshops, David's chainmail, the sword Balārak, and the Spring of Life. In the description of each entity that follows, Mount Qāf stands as a symbol for the perilous barrier (of eleven stages) that has to be crossed before one may reach the inner dominion beyond the sensible world. Other than using the linguistic terminology of a mystical philosophy, Suhrawardī resorts to myth as metalanguage in order to communicate the extrasensory dimension of this imaginary land.

The rest of the text of *The Sound of Gabriel's Wing* is in the form of a dialogue between the old man and the youth. Acting as an initiation master, this tailor-traveler, as he calls himself, who knows God's Word by heart, guides the youth through a cosmic tour, or "an arrangement of the existential order, the angelic realm, and the occult mysteries of heaven and earth,"[72] to use a description for the object of knowledge from a treatise entitled *The Shrill Cries of the Simurgh*. As elsewhere in the teachings of Suhrawardī, verses of the Koran and on occasion of the Torah are cited in the text and invested with an illuminationist interpretation. By the time the session ends the apprentice has learned "enough of the science of tailoring" to be able to patch up a garment when needed. And although it is unlikely that he should learn much of God's Word in his condition, he is taught "a strange alphabet" by means of which he may "learn any chapter," i.e., any science, that he should wish to in the future.[73]

On the source of, and the interconnection between, the Word and the Spirit, for instance, we learn that God has several Great, luminous, Words of hierarchical value, the first of which stands to the rest as the sun does to the stars. From it issue an intermediate series of Governing Words called the "Incoherents," and these are the angels. The last is Gabriel, the Word that engenders the innumerable, inexhaustible category of Lesser Words that include human spirits and are themselves a prerequisite for ascending to the presence of God. From here it is argued that Jesus is both Word and Spirit, which two we are told exist in every man as well, and "being so closely interconnected," "stand for one reality."

The text goes on to warn that the ignorant may misinterpret this miraculous constitution when it manifests itself outwardly in a man, an example being the predicament of Sulaymān Tamīmī who was accused of sorcery; the man defended himself by explaining that he was, rather, "one of God's words." Suhrawardī himself is known as a *khāliq al-barāyā*, creator of images,[74] and said to have engaged in magic, *nayranj*.[75] Likewise, the words of another sufi master, Abū-ʿAlī Fārmadī are ridiculed by a fanatic who calls them "the ravings of a madman." Elsewhere in a treatise called *A Day with a Group of Sufis* he says "the mad call such a one mad" who isolates himself from mankind for he cannot find words to describe his "delight in the unseen things."[76] The inner dialectics of the Word/Spirit in this treatise are better appreciated when we note that the passage begins with the novice asking the master whether he and the other nine men over "worship" God, i.e., address him in words, and the answer is, "No. . . . If we were to worship, it would not be by the tongue but with a limb that knows no movement," which is to say, with the spirit.

The one word to use in order to describe the structure of reality as it is thus far revealed is *hierarchical*, and in so far as the essence of the foremost entity is eternal and unchanging, it may be further qualified as absolutist. As evidenced by the grade-system of lights earlier discussed, this structure is at once a conceptual frame within which the dynamics of reality are described and a functional means by which it comes to be known. The source of all light is one, and gnosis is achieved by ascending the scale of lights which are illuminated by it in a descending order. In this treatise other than the classes of Words noted above, the ten-tiered throne itself is arranged in an ascending order of rank, ending at the topmost level with a "master teacher" who instructs the one below him, and so on back down. Of these only the lowest in rank may converse with the uninitiated who occupies a similar position in the human structure. Another example is an allegory of an astrological map in the form of a translucent sphere of eleven inner layers that the master points out to Suhrawardī in the courtyard of the *khānaqāh*. Animals, water, sand, and luminous discs are found within particular areas of its layers, which are themselves the handiwork of the ten masters. Again, it is only the lowest two layers that may be penetrated. Elsewhere Mount Qāf which surrounds the world, i.e., the external senses to be overcome by the seeker, is said to consist of eleven other mountains, the first two of which are highlighted as being extremely hot and extremely cold. It must be underlined that this insistence on overreaching the sensible world does not amount to a denial of its reality as for instance in Indian thought where salvation is viewed as an ultimate and unqualified negation of existence. The two are rather posited as concomitant necessities of one another. One may even go so far as to say that this duality is celebrated, as when the newly created Adam is described by Love to be "an amazing thing, both heavenly and earthly, both corporeal and spiritual," who has received "not only the other side, but a portion of our own realm as well."[77]

This latter contention is further supported by the fact that the structure reveals a second, horizontal axis, which in symmetrical, relativist terms qualifies another set of the attributes of reality. No single category defines this set which may relate to physical, metaphysical, moral, intellectual, emotional, spiritual, or other attributes of either the macrocosm or the microcosm. This is represented in our text by the Archangel Gabriel's two wings. As the master explains to the youth, his right wing is of pure light; it is associated with enlightened souls, and its totality "is an abstraction of the relation between his being and God." His left wing is marked with dark spots; it is associated with "the vainglorious world of sound and shadow . . . the Wrath, the Awful Cry and the events [of the Last Day]";[78] it is a "sign that Gabriel's being has one side toward not-being." And so, "if you look at the relation of his being to God's being, it has the attribute of His being." When you look at the realization of his essence, *istiḥqāq-i dhāt*, it is the realization of nonexistence and a concomitant to possible existence, *lāzim-i shāyad-būd*.[79]

The horizontal axis is repeated in the description given of God's angels, the "messengers" who, as the master points out, are said in the Koran (XXXV:1) to be "furnished with two, and three, and four pairs of wings." The relationship between the two axes is revealed in the master's additional comments on the same Koranic verse: "The two are mentioned first because 2 is the closest of all numbers to 1, then 3, then 4. Thus, having two wings is nobler than having three or four." In his totality, then Gabriel signifies the *axis mundi*: on the vertical level he represents eternal order and the one God—albeit on a different scale—from whom he is issued; on the horizontal level he represents a simultaneous spread of possibilities, i.e., infinity, finitude, and potentiality, and mankind who issue from him. By being No. 2 in order of hierarchy and having only two wings in the symmetric order, in his flight upward or down, and in the expansive spread of his wings, Gabriel is the first in whom the total structure of reality is crystalized, this being a direct superimposition of the horizontal axis on the vertical one. Other forms may symbolize the same concept on different planes, such as the Active Intellect, Isfahbad-i Nāsūt, Jesus Christ, or Sraush. This is because their essence reveals the same double axis, by virtue of which they share in the ability to move between two worlds. On the human scale this position is represented by Adam who elsewhere is defined as an "amazing" creature for he is both heavenly and earthly, corporeal and spiritual.[80] The parallelism with Zurvanite interpretations of Zoroastrianism which posit two creative principles of light and dark that issue from a single, eternal source—Time— is plain and needs no further comment. Suffice it to say that in Suhrawardī the system remains on the level of a metaphysical construction and does not strictly speaking translate itself on the moral plane as does its religious antecedent.

One last vision of a different order should be mentioned before ending our account of Suhrawardī's illuminationist journey. Prompted by a question on the part of the youth, the master embarks on a discourse on generation, regeneration, and perpetuity; motion, motivation, and stasis, using the less esoteric imagery of family, food, and progeny, which, combined with the attainment of knowledge, is the object. He explains that each of the ten old men has a mill, and although celibate, a son to manage it as well. The speaker himself has innumerable sons who are periodically born to a slave girl who sits at the center of the mills. When her eyes meet the master's in direct opposition with each revolution of the millstone, she conceives. Each son takes his turn at managing the four-leveled mill, and then joins his "father" for good, never wishing to return to this perilous state again. During all of this, the state of the masters remains constant and unchanged. In other words, once the toil of material existence or existence on the level of the senses is ended, the 'son' may represent the vertical axis along with the 'father'. Until then, like the two-winged Gabriel, he possesses qualities of both axes and symbolizes the point of the cross that is itself symbolic of the totality of reality.

"Then, as day was breaking in my father's khānaqāh," says the narrator of the tale *The Sound of Gabriel's Wing* as he ends his account, "the outer door was closed and the door to the city was opened. As merchants began to pass by, the group of old men disappeared from before my eyes. In my perplexity and regret at the loss of their company I sighed and moaned, but it was of no use." The youth had entered the dark chambers guided by the light of his own candle; he leaves it now as the whole world is illuminated by the light of the sun. Dawn becomes a symbol with two opposing referents: on the material level it announces a new day, a return to the "city"—here, the world of the senses—and on the spiritual level, an altered state of mind, enlightenment, and the world beyond.

The sun-candle alternation, suggesting as it does the relation between the real and the imaginary, or to look at it from another angle, the ethereal factor that separates the two is not an isolated image. In many of his treatises Suhrawardī refers to Sīmurgh, the fabulous bird/medicine-man of Persian mythology and epic poetry, to express the same complex of concepts. Sīmurgh appears in the *Avesta* as a primordial falcon with his nest on the Tree of All Seeds and Healing from which all edible and medicinal plants are produced.[81] According to Middle Persian sources it is the beating of its wings that breaks the twigs and scatters the seeds of the tree, an image that Suhrawardī transforms to Gabriel and all that is engendered from him. Finally, in the *Shāhnāma* his nest is atop Mount Qāf, and endowed with magical powers, he is the protector *par excellence* of his favorite epic heroes. In Suhrawardī he turns into the archetype of the Active Intellect and the life-force of creation: "At every instant a Sīmurgh comes from the Ṭūbā tree to the earth and the one that is on the earth simultaneously ceases to exist."[82] It is the image of this bird who "flies without moving" and "soars without wings,"[83] and whose reflection blinds the beholder,[84] that best captures the essence of the visionary experience: intense, paradoxical, fantastic, primordial, mysterious, ecstatic, awesome, and swift as thought. But "don't you know that all these are symbols?" says the old master when the youth asks him to describe the form of Gabriel's wings. "If taken at face value," they "produce nothing."

This visionary experience in the world of images opens the gates to the third state of illumination during which, equipped with that "strange alphabet" that is the illuminationist methodology, the initiated man may set himself the task of obtaining knowledge of the whole. Lastly, he may broach the fourth state which consists of a philosophical definition and construction of the knowledge gained and of committing it to writing by means of what is called *lisān al-ishrāq*, the "language of illumination." This is a mode of communication that, to judge by Suhrawardī's life and works, includes not only texts such as those just presented, or the linguistic code as such, but also the meta-language of nonverbal codes transmitted by the presence and personality of the sage himself.[85] Textual and historical evidence indicates that a circle of initiates received such communication from Suhrawardī in his lifetime, although it is hard to determine with certainty whether they formed a fraternity, properly speaking.[86] But while his violent end on charges of sacrilege may have inhibited any interest in that direction in the period following his death, his legacy was preserved and propagated through Persian literature.

In conclusion it may be suggested that the illuminationist path to wisdom gained dominance in post-Islamic Iran because its holistic world view and syncretistic approach to reality was able to absorb the new Islamic ideology and reformulate it in a relevant way that retained some of the essential premises of the old tradition. It gained appeal over and above strictly analytical and rational tendencies in Islamic thought in part because it continued to seek the perfect form, though on a mystical plane, and because it employed a philosophical method of investigation and instruction that achieved order through diversity. Likewise its mode of expression recreated a vision of the perfect beginnings, evoking the hope that it can be eternally recovered even amidst the chaos of the present. To sum up, the Philosophy of Illumination never ceases to promise that there is method to this madness.

Notes

1.   For a discussion of the concept of Divine Law, *Sharī'a*, in Islam, see Fazlur Rahman, *Islam*, 100-116.

2.   For a discussion of circumstances leading to Suhrawardī's execution see Thackston, *The Mystical and Visionary Treatises*, pp. 1-4. Detailed accounts of Suhrawardī's biography are to be found in historians of philosophy such as Ibn Abī ʿUṣaybiʿa, Qifṭī, and especially in Shahrazūrī's *Nuzhat al-Arwāḥ*, vol. 2, 119-42. Shahrazūrī's account is of particular interest because he is himself an illuminationist philosopher.

3.   I do not wish to here give an exhaustive list of Corbin's many works on Suhrawardī, but I shall refer the interested reader to Corbin's *En Islam Iranien*, where volume 2 entitled "Sohrawardī et les Platoniciens de Perse" is entirely devoted to the study of illuminationist philosophy; and to his "Prolégomènes II," in Suhrawardī, *Opera II*, 1-102.

4.   The distinction between discursive philosophy, *ḥikma baḥthiyya*, and intuitive philosophy, *ḥikma dhawqiyya*, is a crucial one in the philosophy of illumination. This distinction is discussed in detail by Suhrawardī and is similar to the distinction as applied to the works of Aristotle. (See, for example, Victor Kal, *On Intuition and Discursive Reasoning in Aristotle*, especially 44-53.) Illuminationist wisdom, according to Suhrawardī, may only ensue when the intuitive, *dhawqī, and* the discursive, *baḥthī*, are completely and harmoniously blended together by a rank of divine philosophers known as *al-ḥukamāʾ al-mutaʾallihūn*. See, Suhrawardī, *Opera II*, 11-12. Commentators, especially al-Hirawī, discuss the types and ranks of philosophers who combine *dhawq* and *baḥth*. See al-Hirawī, *Anwāriyya*, 12-14.

5.   See, Mehdi Ha'iri Yazdi, *Knowledge by Presence*, 99-106. Ha'iri Yazdi argues that illuminationist theory of knowledge and Russel's theory of knowledge by acquaintance have two points in common. However, it should be made clear that the idea of intuitive knowledge in illuminationist philosophy is not restricted and that Suhrawardī does claim that intuitive knowledge has the same rank as demonstration and thus not subjective simply.

6.   'Vision of a thing' in illuminationist epistemology is equated with knowledge. This specifically intuitive mode of knowledge is called "knowledge by presence," *al-ʿilm al-ḥuḍūrī*, in the more Platonizing traditions of Islamic philosophy, and is discussed in detail by Ha'iri Yazdi. See, Ha'iri Yazdi, ibid., especially 73-161.

7.   The Brethren of Abstraction, *Ikhwān al-Tajrīd*, have real experience in the separate realm of the *imaginalis*. See Suhrawardī, *Opera II*, 242-43; 253. The commentator al-Hirawi argues that the Brethren of Abstraction are of the same rank as the sage-philosophers who have perfected discursive as well as intuitive knowledge, and he includes among their rank prophets, *anbiyā*, and saints, *awliyā*. See al-Hirawī, *Anwāriyya*, 223-24.

8.   In a section in one of his allegorical visionary treatises, *The Simurgh's Shrill Cry*, Suhrawardī discusses the idea of self-annihilation in the Being of God and focuses on a rank of sages "the most masterly of all" who have "destroyed expressions and eradicated references," and with it any indication to an objective ipseity. See Thackston, *The Mystical and Visionary Treatises*, 95.

9.   Suhrawardī, *Opera I*, 74, 88, 90.

10.   Thackston, *The Mystical and Visionary Treatises*, 90.

11.   See Suhrawardī, *Opera II*, 116. Cf. idem, *Paths and Havens: Physics*, fol. 198r-201v. For a detailed analysis of the distinction between 'knowledge by presence,' *al-'ilm al-ḥuḍūrī*, and 'knowledge by concept formation and confirmation,' *taṣawwur wa taṣdīq*, see Ha'iri Yazdi, *Knowledge by Presence*, 75-80, 121-25.

12.   See Aristotle, *Posterior Analytics*, I.33, 89b10-20. Cf. Suhrawardī, *Intimations: Physics*, fol. 69r; idem, *Paths and Havens: Physics*, fol. 201v.

13.   Avicenna's contributions to a theory of intuition have been extensively studied by Professor Herbert Davidson who generously shared his vast knowledge of the subject with me, for which I am grateful. See, for example, Herbert Davidson, "Alfarabi and Avicenna on the Active Intellect," *Viator, Medieval and Renaissance Studies*, volume 3 (1972), 167ff.

14.   See Rahman, *Prophecy in Islam*, 14-20.

15.   E.g., Suhrawardī, *Intimations: Physics*, fol 69r. See also Rahman, *Prophecy in Islam*, 30-35.

16.   E.g., Suhrawardī, *Intimations: Physics*, fol. 65v, 69r.

17.   Ibid.

18.   Suhrawardī, *Intimations: Physics*, fol. 64v; idem, *Opera I*, 57, 440; idem, *Opera II*, 109.

19.   E.g., Suhrawardī, *Opera I*, 57: "*al-ḥads al-ṣaḥīḥ yaḥkum bi-hādhā dūna ḥāja ilā burhān.*"

20.   Usually in the last section of his theoretical works Suhrawardī discusses the extraordinary capabilities of the most noble sage-philosophers. See for example, Suhrawardī, *Opera II*, 505.

21.   Suhrawardī, *Opera II*, 10. This most significant passage in Suhrawardī's writings is commented on by al-Hirawī: "This is because the Active Intellect is always present on the Clear Horizon (Koran: XXIII: 81) which is the final end of the intelligible world, and there is no stinginess in the principles [of being], thus the gates of emanation, *fayḍ*, . . . and revelation, *mukāshafa*, could not be closed." (*Anwāriyya*, 4-5).

22.   See Suhrawardī's *A Day with a Group of Sufis*, translated by Thackston, *The Mystical and Visionary Treatises*, 37-38; and Suhrawardī's *The Red Intellect*, translated by Thackston, ibid., 43.

23.   Thackston, *The Mystical and Visionary Treatises*, 62-63.

24.   Suhrawardī, , *Opera II*, 10. Cf. al-Hirawi, *Anwāriyya*, 4.

25.   This division is much-contested by Mullā Ṣadrā, who divides the cosmos (*al-'ālam*) into the traditionally accepted triplicate form as follows: 1) the world of sense perception, this world; 2) the unseen world/the world of the hereafter; 3) the intelligible world (*Ta'līqāt*, 147 margin). See, also, Fazlur Rahman, "Dream, Imagination and *'Ālam al-Mithāl*," 169-72.

26.   The visionary experience is such that the person sees "forms most beautiful and artful who speak to them . . . and they will see suspended forms, *muthul mu'alaqa*, ... and they will hear most thunderous sounds." Suhrawardī, *Opera II*, 240.

27.   Suhrawardī, , *Opera III*, 76.

28.   Suhrawardī, , *Opera I*, 496.

29.   Suhrawardī, , *Opera III*, 446.

30.   Ibid.

31.   This amazing state of creation through which the "Brethren of Abstraction can create any subsistent form they wish" (Suhrawardī, *Opera II*, 242), is further associated with the ability to revive the dead (*iḥyā'-i amvāt*) by the commentator al-Hirawī (*Anwāriyya*, 223).

32.   See Suhrawardī, , *Opera I*, 73, 73n., 95, 103, 113; idem, *Opera II*, 242, 252.

33.   Suhrawardī, , *Opera I*, 112.

34.   Suhrawardī, *Opera III*, 447: *ū khalifa-yi khudāy buvad dar zamīn.*

35.   The nineteenth Avestan hymn, the Zāmyād Yašt, is dedicated to the Xvarenah [Xvarr(ah), Farnah].

36.   These are instructions given to Suhrawardī himself by his master; see *A Day with a Group of Sufis*, translated by Thackston, *The Mystical and Visionary Treatises*, 48.

37.   Suhrawardī, *Opera I*, 70-74.

38.   Suhrawardī, *Opera I*, 70: "*irji' ilā nafsika.*"

39.   Ibid.: ". . . *adrakta dhātaka bi-dhatikā.*" The self-conscious, self-constituted subject is to be compared with Avicenna's so-called *l'homme volant* (Peters, *Aristotle and the Arabs*, 173). See Rahman, *Avicenna's Psychology*, 8-20; idem, "Dream, Imagination and *'Ālam al-Mithāl*," 170-71.

40.   Suhrawardī, *Opera II*, 248.

41.   Suhrawardī, *Opera I*, 112. Science of Lights, *al-'ilm al-anwār*, which is the foundation of the philosophy of illumination is said by the commentators (both al-Hirawī and Shīrāzī) to be "in agreement with Plato's beliefs. . . . This is mentioned in his books called the *Timœus* and the *Phœdrus* as well as in his epistles, *rasā'il.*" (*Anwāriyya*, 7.)

42.   Thackston, *The Mystical and Visionary Treatises*, 91-92.

43.   Ibid., 93.

44.   Ibid., 49.

45.   Ibid., 66.

46.   Suhrawardī, *Opera II*, 12: *lam yuḥṣal lī awwalan bi'l-fikr wa al-naẓar bal kāna ḥuṣūluhu bi amrin ākhar thumma ṭalabtu al-ḥujja 'alayhi.*

47.   See al-Hirawī, *Anwāriyya*, 6; Shīrāzī, *Sharḥ*, 16-17.

48. See al-Hirawī, *Anwāriyya*, 222.

49. Suhrawardī, *Opera II*, 252; idem, *Opera I*, 108, 114. The fifteen stages of the visionary experience is discussed in detail by al-Hirawī, *Anwāriyya*, 239-42.

50. See, for example, Suhrawardī, *Opera II*, 4, 13, 40, 257.

51. Originally worshiped in Zoroastrian Iran as both the physical phenomenon and the god that represented it, the sun, Hvar, came eventually to be identified with the god Mithra, and like him, is invoked three times a day in the liturgy; see Mary Boyce, *A History of Zoroastrianism*, vol 1, *Handbuch der Orientalistik*, 8 Bd., 1 Abs., Lf. 2, (Leiden/Köln: E. J. Brill, 1975) 69.

52. Suhrawardī, *Opera II*, 139-41: "*wa kull wāḥid yushāhid Nūr al-Anwār.*"

53. Ibid., 142-43.

54. Ibid., 139-40, 166-75, 185-86. Note that the managing lights function on the human level as *al-anwār al-insiyya* (*Opera II*, 201), as well as on the cosmic level as *al-anwār al-falakiyya* (*Opera II*, 236).

55. Ibid., 201, 213-15.

56. Ibid., 134.

57. Ibid., 150.

58. Ibid., 137, 146.

59. Ibid., 124.

60. Ibid., 121-24.

61. In the *Avesta* it departs from Yima in the form of a bird; in the Middle Persian epic *Kārnāmak ī Artaxšir i Pāpakān*, it unites with the future king in the form of a ram. For a discussion of the concept and sources see Arthur Christensen, *Les Gestes des rois dans les traditions de l'Iran antique*, Paris: Paul Geuthner, 1936, 9-41.

62. This is when the knowing subject, as the self-conscious monad, becomes the creative subject.

63. Thus, for instance, Yima and Kavi Usan among Avestan kings who submit to the moral faults of arrogance and 'falsehood', i.e., commit an act against cosmic order.

64. See Suhrawardī, *Opera II*, 254-55; Cf. al-Hirawī, *Anwāriyya*, 222, where Hūrqalyā is said to be one of the imaginal spheres, *aflāk-i mithālī*, "traveled" to by Pythagoras.

65. Cf. Corbin, *Terre Celeste*, trans. Nancy Pearson. (Princeton: Bollingon Series XCI:2: Princeton University Press, 1977) 82-89. Note also Suhrawardī's own theory of the categories in which he only considers substance, quality, quantity, relation, and motion—all of which are given to degrees of intensity and are processes more than they are ontic distinct entities.

66. Duchesne-Guillemin, *The Western Response to Zoroaster* (Oxford: Oxford University Press, 1958) 132.

67.   Corbin, *Man of Light in Iranian Sufism*, 6.

68.   See, for example, Shīrāzī, *Sharḥ*, 511: *wa al-ṣuwar al-muʿallaqa laysat muthul Aflāṭūn fa-inna muthul Aflāṭūn nūriyya thābita fī ʿālam al-anwār al-ʿaqliyya*, [the suspended forms, *ṣuwar,* are not the Platonic Ideas, *muthul aflāṭūn*, because the latter are luminous and *fixed* in the realm of intelligible lights].

69.   Thackston, *The Mystical and Visionary Treatises*, 27.

70.   Suhrawardī, *Opera II*, 242.

71.   Thackston, *The Mystical and Visionary Treatises*, 66.

72.   Ibid., 95.

73.   Ibid., 30.

74.   Shahrazūrī, *Nuzhat al-Arwāḥ*, vol. 2, 122.

75.   Muḥammad al-Dimashqī, *al-Dāris fī Tārīkh al-Madāris*, 2: 184: *yaʿrifu* [Suhrawardī,] *al-kīmiyā' wa shay'an min al-shuʿwadha wa'l-abwāb al-nārinjiyyāt*.

76.   Thackston, *The Mystical and Visionary Treatises*, 50.

77.   Ibid., 69, 70.

78.   Ibid., 33.

79.   Ibid., 32.

80.   Ibid., 69.

81.   See Boyce, *A History of Zoroastrianism*, vol. 1, *Handbuch der Orientalistik*, 8 Bd., 1 Abs., Lf. 2 (Leiden/Köln: E. J. Brill, 1975) 88-89.

82.   See Thackston, *The Mystical and Visionary Treatises*, p. 39, n. 2, who cites Koran, XIII:29: "They who believe and do that which is right shall enjoy blessedness (*tuba*)" as the source for the name of a tree of Paradise. This motif is found as early as Tabari, XIII, 147ff., attributed to the oldest authorities such as Abū-Hurayra and Ibn ʿAbbās. The identification of Ṭūbā with the Avestan life-giving tree in Suhrawardī is self-evident.

83.   Thackston, *The Mystical and Visionary Treatises*, 89.

84.   Ibid., 40. Note that in Suhrawardī's retelling of the famous tragedy of Rustam and Isfandiyar the invulnerable hero becomes blinded by the reflection of Sīmurgh in the polished iron and mirrors used in fashioning the battle gear of Rustam and his horse. In the *Shāhnāma*, a two-thronged arrow dipped in a magic solution concocted by Simurgh accomplishes the job.

85.   *al-Qā'im bi'l-ishrāq, and al-qā'im bi'l-kitāb*, the person upon whom illumination (the teaching and the text) rests, as used by Suhrawardī and the commentators indicate the oral discourses associated with the teaching illuminationist philosophy. See Suhrawardī, *Opera II*, 244, 256, 260.

86. See Shahrazūrī, *Nuzhat al-Arwāḥ*, vol. 2 126-27.

References

Aristotle.
    1966 *Metaphysics*. Translated with commentaries and glossary by Hippocrates G. Apostle. Bloomington and London: Indiana University Press.

Avicenna.
    1951 *Livre des directives et remarque*. Translated by A. -M. Goichon. Paris: J. Vrin.

    1954 *al-Shifā': al-Burhān* [The Healing: Demonstration]. Edited by A. R. Badawi. Cairo.

    1960 *al-Shifā': al-Ilāhiyyāt* [The Healing: Metaphysics]. Edited by G. C. Anawati and S. Zayid. Cairo.

    1960 *Kitāb al-Ishārāt wa'l-Tanbīhāt* [The Book of Directives and Remarks]. Edited by Mahoud Shahābi. Tehran: Tehran University Press.

    1963 *Livres des Définitions*. Edited and translated by A. -M. Goichon. Cairo: Publications de l'Institut Français d'Archeologie Orientale du Caire.

Boyce, Mary.
    1975 *A History of Zoroastrianism*, vol. 1, *Handbuch der Orientalistik*, 8 Bd., 1 Abs., Lf. 2. Leiden/Cologne: E. J. Brill.

Corbin, Henry.
    1971 *En Islam Iranien*, Paris: Galimard.

    1976 *L'Archange empourpré*. Paris: Fayard.

    1977 *Terre Celeste*. Translated by Nancy Pearson. Princeton: Bollingon Series XCI:2: Princeton University Press.

    1978 *Man of Light in Iranian Sufism*, Translated from the French by Nancy Pearson. Boulder & London: Shambala.

    1985 *Livre de la sagessse orientale*. Paris: Verdier.

Davidson, Herbert.
    1972 "Alfarabi and Avicenna on the Active Intellect." In *Viator, Medieval and Renaissance Studies*, vol. 3, 167ff.

al-Dimashqī, Muhammad.
1951 *al-Dāris fi Tārīkh al-Madāris*. Damascus: n.p.

Duchesne-Guillemin.
1958 *The Western Response to Zoroaster*. Oxford: Oxford University Press.

Fakhry, Majid.
1970 *A History of Islamic Philosophy*. New York: Columbia University Press.

Ha'iri-Yazdi, Mehdi.
1982 *Knowledge by Presence*. Tehran: Cultural Studies and Research Institute.

al-Hirawī Niẓām al-Dīn.
1980 *Anwāriyya* (eleventh-century Persian commentary on the *Philosophy of Illumination*). Edited by H. Ziai. Tehran: Amīr Kabīr.

Ibn Abī Uṣaybiʻa.
1884 *Ṭabaqāt al-Aṭibbā'*. Edited by A. Müller. Köningsberg i Pr.

Kal, Victor.
1988 *On Intuition and Discursive Reasoning in Aristotle*. Leiden: E. J. Brill.

Peters, F. E.
1968 *Aristotle and the Arabs*. New York: New York University Press.

Plato.
1969 *The Collected Dialogues*. Edited by Edith Hamilton and Huntington Cairns. Princeton: Princeton University Press.

Plotinus.
1969 *The Enneads*. Translated by Stephen Mackenna. New York: Pantheon Books.

al-Qifṭī.
1968 *Tārīkh al-Ḥukamā'* [History of the Philosophers]. Eleventh-century Persian trans. Edited by Bahman Dārā'ī. Tehran: Tehran University Press.

Rahman, Fazlur.
1952 *Avicenna's Psychology*. London: Oxford University Press.

1958 *Prophecy in Islam*. London: George Allen & Unwin Ltd.

1959 *Avicenna's De Anima*. London: Oxford University Press.

1964 "Dream Imagination and *'Ālam al-Mithāl.*" *Islamic Studies*, 3: 167-180.

1979 *Islam*, 2nd edition. Chicago: University of Chicago Press.

Ritter, Helmut.
1937-1938 "Philologika IX: Die vier Suhrawardī." *Der Islam*, vol. 24 (1937): 270-86, and vol. 25 (1938): 35-86.

Shahrazūrī, Muḥammad.
1976 *Nuzhat al-Arwāḥ*. Edited by S. Kh. Ahmad. Haydarābād: Dā'irat al-Maʿārif al-ʿUthmāniyya.

Shīrāzī, Quṭb al-Dīn.
1313-1315 A. H. *Sharḥ Ḥikmat al-Ishrāq* [Commentary on the Philosophy of Illumination]. Tehran: n. p.

Shīrāzī, Ṣadr al-Dīn. "Mullā Ṣadrā."
1313-1315 A. H. *Taʿliqat: Sharḥ Ḥikmat al-Ishrāq*. Tehran: n. p.

Suhrawardī Shihāb al-Din Yaḥyā.
Kalimat al-Taṣawwuf [Maxim on Sufism]. MS. Tehran: Majlis, Majmuʿa 3071.

1945 *Opera Metaphysica et Mystica I*. Edited with an Introduction by Henry Corbin. Istanbul: Maarif Matbaasi.

1954 *Oeuvres philosophiques et mystiques: Opera Metaphysica et Mystica II*. Edited with an Introduction by Henry Corbin. Tehran: Institute Franco-Iranien.

1955 *Manṭiq al-Talwīḥāt* [Logic of the Intimations]. Edited by A. A. Fayyāz. Tehran: Tehran University Press, 1334 solar.

1969 *Kitāb al-Lamaḥāt* [The Flashes of Light]. Edited by Emile Maalouf. Beirut: Dar an-Nahar.

1970 *Opera Metaphysica et Mystica III*. Edited by S. H. Nasr. Tehran: Institut Franco-Iranien.

al-Mashāriʿ waʾl-Muṭāraḥāt [The Paths and Havens]. MS Leiden: Or. 365.

al-Talwīḥāt [The Intimations]. MS. Berlin 5062.

Thackston, Wheeler M., Jr.
1982 *The Mystical and Visionary Treatises of Shihabuddin Yahya Suhrawardī*. London: The Octagon Press.

Myth, Philosophy, and Exegesis

Myth, Inference, and the Relativism of Reason: An Argument from the History of Judaism

Howard Eilberg-Schwartz

The use of others to define ourselves is a technique that Hayden White refers to as ostensive self-definition by negation. As he puts it, " . . . when the need for positive self-definition asserts itself but no compelling criterion of self-identification appears, it is always possible to say something like: 'I may not know the precise content of my own felt humanity, but I am most certainly not like that,' and simply point to something in the landscape that is manifestly different from oneself."[1] Myth has frequently been one of the "thats" to which the traditions of Philosophy and Science have pointed in their quest to define themselves. There have been numerous ways in which Philosophy and Science have attempted to

The research and writing of this paper was made possible by a grant from the Lilly Foundation, Indianapolis. I was helped in its preparation by my colleagues Paul Lauritzen (John Carroll) and Richard Kalmin (The Jewish Theological Seminary). The material has undergone substantial revisions in light of comments by colleagues at the colloquium on Religion(s) in Culture and History, The University of Chicago Divinity School. I especially wish to acknowledge the useful criticisms of Jeffrey Stout (Princeton).

differentiate themselves from the object called "Myth." Some of the more popular schemes appeal to a spectrum defined by various rational criteria such as closed/open, critical/noncritical, reflective/nonreflective, systematic/inconsistent, logical/prelogical, and so forth.

By this view, Myth falls closer to the end of the spectrum defined as "irrational": it is a closed system that can never be refuted by outside evidence. It protects itself against any new challenge by elaborating ad hoc hypotheses that do not essentially change the framework. Myth is also situational in that it only meets challenges when they arise. It does not go looking for them and hence does not achieve the internal coherence that we associate with Philosophy or Science. Consequently, although Myth has an implicit logic, it has no formal logic. It does not, in other words, contain second order reflection and hence does not consider what constitutes a valid argument and why. The emergence of Logic, therefore, signals the demise of Myth.

By contrast, the genres of Philosophy or Science are often said to be more self-critical. They search for inconsistencies in their own theory and therefore seek and achieve an internal coherence that is not characteristic of Myth. The origins of Philosophy and Science, therefore, can be traced to the emergence of logic and epistemology, and their achievements depend on a second-order discourse that continually criticizes and revises the framework in which discourse takes place. Continual reflection on thought, therefore, is responsible for change and growth of knowledge. The emergence of critical thinking itself has been attributed to, among other things, literacy, technological development, and social differentiation. In one form or another, these views can be associated with names like Lévy-Bruhl, Tylor, Frankfort, Cassirer, Popper, Douglas, Leach, Horton, and Goody.[2]

The possibility of distinguishing Myth from Philosophy and Science, therefore, has and perhaps always will be entangled in the question of rationality and relativism. Specifically, the attempt to distinguish genres of discourse according to a spectrum of rationality requires that the criteria of rationality in question be universal and not simply specific to some local context. But if, as Winch asserts, "criteria of logic are not a direct gift from God,"[3] but are themselves simply the product of consensus and norms, then it may be inappropriate for an interpreter to evaluate a belief or set of beliefs from an alien culture or alien context according to criteria of rationality cherished by his or her home culture or context. By this view, what counts in one context as a good reason for holding a belief or good ways of reasoning about one's beliefs may not count as such in another context. If so, then distinctions like Myth and Philosophy or Myth and Science are ready for the scrap heap. What appears as lesser and greater quotients of rationality may in the end simply be alternative forms of rationality.

The relativity of Reason is not a very popular doctrine these days. For obvious reasons, rationalists are unwilling to accept the notion that reason or logic is relative to given cultural contexts. As Newton-Smith puts it:

> The difference between them and us is not a difference in what is a reason for something but a difference as to whether the conditions in question obtain. This fact which I will call the *conditionalization of reason* shows the reason is not relative and explains why it can appear to be so. We should not simply assume that different things are reasons for others. We should consider their web of belief. We are likely to find that difference is explicable in terms of difference in beliefs about what conditions actually obtain. *This means that if we shared their beliefs about what conditions obtained we would tend to share their beliefs about which beliefs are reasons for which beliefs.* That is, we are assuming that there is a similarity in how we reason about beliefs. On the relativist alternative we assume diversity at two levels: beliefs about the world and beliefs about the relation between beliefs. And methodologically this is not very promising (second italics supplied).[4]

In other words, all people reason in basically the same way about their own distinctive and idiosyncratic beliefs. Differences between us and them, therefore, boil down to disagreements about substantive issues rather than formal differences in ways of reasoning. This position, however, is not limited to just rationalists. Soft relativists often adopt a very similar perspective. Indeed, this idea has a long standing tradition in twentieth-century anthropology. As Evans-Pritchard puts it, the Zande "reason excellently in the idiom of their beliefs, but they cannot reason outside, or against, their beliefs because they have no other idiom in which to express their thoughts."[5] Similarly, conceptual relativists such as Kuhn take for granted that people reason in similar ways from within their own conceptual schemes. According to Kuhn, historians of science

> confront growing difficulties in distinguishing the scientific component of past observation and belief from what their predecessors had readily labeled 'error' and 'superstition'. The more carefully they study, say Aristotelian dynamics, phlogistic chemistry, or

caloric thermodynamics, the more certain they feel that those once current views of nature were, as a whole, neither less scientific nor more the product of human idiosyncrasy than those current today. If these out of date beliefs are to be called myths, *then myths can be produced by the same sorts of methods and held for the same sort of reasons that now lead to scientific knowledge* (emphasis supplied).[6]

For Kuhn, therefore, scientists have always reasoned in basically the same ways even though they have often arrived at different conclusions.

It is not surprising that a relativist theory of reason is so unpopular. One who entertains that position is automatically associated with Lévy-Bruhl's theory of prelogical mentality. To discredit the strong relativist, therefore, the rationalists and soft relativists need only snicker and say, "You don't really endorse the views of Lévy-Bruhl, do you? (e.g., Newton-Smith, Lukes, and Hollis). Surely we could not understand a group of people if they did not have the same forms of reasoning as we do?" For reasons I will discuss below, I think this argument misrepresents the views of the strong relativist and consequently does not at all damage his or her position.

In what follows, I endorse a strong relativist position. That is, I argue that there are alternative forms of rationality and that these forms of reasoning are as reasonable in their context as any possible competitors. Consequently, one cannot always invoke the same criteria of rationality to evaluate two different discourses. To support this view, I discuss the emergence of a perplexing form of inference that is ubiquitous in the literature of the ancient rabbis (200-600 CE). This form of reasoning has a number of problematic features that would disqualify it as a valid form of inference in most if not all contexts in American culture, including the university, courtrooms, high schools, and most situations in everyday life. Consequently, the question emerges as to why this form of reasoning retained its credibility over such a long period of time within rabbinic culture. I will account for its endurance by showing how it takes its part in a myth—a closed set of discursive practices—which makes it credible and which it in turn helps to validate. As a result of this myth, the problems inherent in this form of reasoning are either invisible to the rabbis or irrelevant. I suggest, therefore, that there is no independent standard of appeal that would enable us to judge this form of inference as inferior to various alternatives without at the same time calling into question the entire rabbinic religious enterprise. If so, then what counts as rational, or in this case what counts as an inference, is itself nothing more than the product of local consensus, that is, a set of practices that constitute a myth.

Inference and Rabbinic Judaism

One of the most frequently used forms of inference in the literature of the rabbis is an argument called *qal va homer* (pronounced "kal va homer"), which literally means "light and heavy."[7] In this context, I am interested in the complex form of the *qal va homer*, which should not be confused with its simpler sibling, also known as a *qal va homer* argument.[8] The simpler form of this argument is a recognizable kind of inference commonly called an *a fortiori* argument (e.g., God regrets the bloodshed of the wicked, all the more so the bloodshed of the righteous, M. San. 9:5). Although the complex form of the *qal va homer* is a sibling of this familiar kind of inference, it is fundamentally different. It is so different in fact that the force of the inference is lost on those who have not already been trained to recognize the complex *qal va homer* as a valid form of inference.[9]

The complex form of the *qal va homer* argument is invoked when the sages want to infer the rules that govern a new situation from information that is given in Scripture (or the oral tradition) about other situations. Essentially the argument rests on comparing two situations and noting the presence or absence of certain variables in each. For example, suppose the sages want to determine whether variable y is present in situation B. To determine an answer, the sages turn to another situation A in which y does obtain but x does not, where x is a variable that is present in B. The information available is presented in the following chart, where + signifies the presence of the variable and - represents its absence.

	Situation A	Situation B
variable x	-	+
variable y	+	? (unknown)

The argument runs as follows:

> If A lacks trait x but possesses trait y (A=-x, y) and B possesses trait x (B=x), then B must possess trait y. The reasoning that legitimates the conclusion is as follows: First, since A lacks x and B possesses it, B is greater or "heavier" than A. Therefore, since A possesses y, B is likely to possess it as well. Second, since y is present where x is not (as in situation A) then y is more likely to be present than x. Therefore if x is present (as in situation B) then one can expect y to be present as well. For both of these reasons, one may conclude that y will be present. in B.[10]

Let me provide a concrete example of how this argument is actually used. In the discussion in question, the sages consider whether a particle severed from a corpse has the power to contaminate when overshadowed by a tent (Mishnah Eduyot 6:2).[11] Two sages believe that a particle from a corpse does have such power and justify their position by appealing to a *qal va homer* argument. Their argument takes as given the following three facts (illustrated in the chart below): 1) a corpse that is overshadowed by a tent contaminates anything that is under that tent, 2) a living body does not have the power to contaminate in a tent, but 3) a severed particle from a living body has such power.[12]

	(A) living being	(B) corpse
(x)		
whole body contaminates in a tent	-	+
(y)		
severed particle contaminates in a tent	+	?

On the basis of this information two sages reason as follows:

> Now if a living being does not contaminate under a tent, but a severed particle from it does (A=-x, y), and a corpse does contaminate under a tent (B=x), then does it not follow that a severed particle from a corpse will contaminate (y)?

To put the argument in somewhat simpler terms, it runs as follows:

> Since a corpse (B) contaminates under a tent (x) and a living body (A) does not (-x), it seems reasonable to conclude that dead things are greater sources of contamination than living beings (B>A). Moreover, since a severed particle from a living being contaminates in a tent and a living being does not, one may conclude that unwhole things contaminate more than whole ones (y>x). Therefore, one may reasonably infer that a severed particle from a corpse contaminates in a tent since it is both dead and unwhole. The argument, therefore, rests on both a horizontal (B>A) and vertical (y>x) relation.

The difficulty in understanding this argument is not simply a consequence of the substantive issues at hand (although that adds to the difficulty). I suggest that it is also a function of the peculiar notion of inference that operates in rabbinic culture. Until one is trained to understand how the rabbis argue, one has trouble following the rabbis' mode of reasoning.

Let me develop this point by using the same form of inference to talk about a more accessible subject. Let us imagine that two new planets are discovered: Hearth, a distant star about which we have little information, and Thearth, a closer star about which we have a great deal of information. We wish to determine whether the shumans, the people on Hearth, need oxygen as humans do here on Earth. According to information available, plants on the planet Hearth require oxygen rather than carbon dioxide.

	A. Earth	B. Hearth
(x) plants need O_2	-	+
(y) people need O_2	+	?

Adopting the sages' line of reasoning, we could argue as follows:

> Since on Earth plants do not need oxygen but people do (A=-x, y), then on Hearth, where plants need oxygen (B=x), is it not logical that people also require oxygen (y)?

Although we are no longer talking about purity and impurity, the argument nonetheless remains difficult to follow. This is because the argument rests on what we would consider problematic assertions. First, on the basis of the vertical relations (A=-x, y), the author of the argument assumes that people need oxygen more than plants. Since plants on Hearth need oxygen, it follow that people on the planet also need oxygen. Second, based on the horizontal relation (A=-x, B=x), the author reasons that life on Hearth requires oxygen more than on Earth (B>A). It follows, then, that since humans need oxygen, shumans also require oxygen.

Immediately, however, one wants to protest that the conclusion is unwarranted. The information given is simply not sufficient to make any reasonable inferences about people on Hearth. To begin with, it is problematic to make any generalizations about the use of oxygen from the requirements of oxygen on Earth. The fact that on Earth people and not plants need oxygen does not mean that the same relationship necessarily obtains on other planets. At the very least it would seem reasonable to inquire about the need of oxygen on Thearth, a planet about which we have more information. One would at least want to rule out the possibility that on that planet plants use oxygen but people require carbon dioxide. If people need carbon dioxide and not oxygen on Thearth that same pattern could obtain on Hearth.

By the same token, it seems risky to assume that since plants need oxygen on Hearth that the need for oxygen is generally greater on Hearth than Earth (B>A). Indeed, the fact that plants need oxygen on Hearth would make one suspicious that Hearth differs so radically from Earth that any generalization derived from the former may be irrelevant to the later. Consequently, one would want to gather as much information as possible about the use of oxygen on Hearth before hazarding an inference. If one learned, for example, that fire on Hearth consumes carbon dioxide rather than oxygen as is the case on Earth that fact would confirm the suspicion that the need of oxygen on Hearth is determined by different factors than on Earth.

The difficulty, then, seems to arise because we are not trained to make an inference in cases where the sages are willing to do so. Specifically, the sages have assumed that by comparing A and B with respect to one variable they have established a fixed hierarchical relationship between A and B [one is weightier than the other with respect to some principle]. The obvious problem with such an assumption is that a single variable (x) is generally not sufficient to make any correct generalizations about the relationship between two situations or objects. Although B > A with respect to x, it is generally the case that A > B with respect to some other variable that is equally relevant to the matter in question.

The same problem arises in trying to hazard an inference about the relationship between two variables when one has only a single situation on the basis of which to generalize. The fact that A possesses y and lacks x does not necessarily mean that y is more likely than x to be present in other situations. Therefore, the generalization "people everywhere need oxygen" does not follow from the fact that on Earth people and not plants require oxygen.[13]

At this point one might object that my imaginary argument is misleading since it deals with questions which in theory are empirically verifiable, whereas the rabbis invoke the *qal va homer* in their discussions of legal and moral matters which are of a different order. To be charitable to the rabbis, therefore, one must seek an analogy that deals with legal and moral questions, not natural phenomena. As the following imaginary argument suggests, the rabbis' form of reasoning is as perplexing in the context of a legal or moral discussion as in the context of a discussion of natural phenomena.

Imagine entering the supreme court of Hearth and hearing the following decision by a leading justice concerning the question of whether Hearth women must care for babies:

> On the basis of our constitution, we know that men are not obligated to care for animals but must care for babies (A=-x, y). The constitution also stipulates that women must care for animals (B=x). Is it not reasonable that women must also care for babies (B=y)?

	A. Adult men	B. Adult women	Potential Objection C. Adolescent girls
caring for animals	-	+	+
caring for babies	+	?	-
Potential Objection caring for house	+	-	

The justice goes on to explain her reasoning as follows:

> Since women must care for animals and men need not do so, we can conclude that women are obligated to be more nuturant than men (B>A). Furthermore, since men must care for babies and not animals, we conclude that it is more important to care for babies than animals (y>x). For both of these reasons, women must care for babies.

Even though we are now dealing with a legal context, this sort of reasoning still appears problematic. Without at least inspecting other relevant categories and variables one cannot know whether the argument is valid. For example, suppose the Hearthen constitution also specified that adolescent girls had to take care of animals but not babies. Such a rule would suggest that the obligation to care for animals may in some cases be present without the obligation to care for babies (x>y). Furthermore, suppose the constitution specified that men must care for the home but women are exempt from this obligation. From this ruling one would conclude that men are in some respects under greater obligation than women to care for things (A>B on variable z). Both the case of adolescent girls and the variable of caring for the home would show that the argument is invalid as it now stands. This kind of inference, therefore, is problematic because it does not take account of other information that may be available and relevant.

It remains unclear, therefore, why the sages are willing to hazard an inference on the basis of the given information. Objections of the sort just described can always be and frequently are brought against the sages' arguments. This is because there almost always is relevant information available that the author of the argument did not bother to consider. Such objections, for example, can be leveled against the rabbinic argument cited earlier. In fact, another sage challenges that argument with precisely the kind of objection that I have just described.

	A. living being	B. corpse
(x) whole body contaminates in tent	-	+
(y) severed particle	+	?
(z) contaminates pile of cushions	+	-

The assumption that corpses are greater contaminators than living beings (B>A) can be rejected by taking into account the power of the human body to contaminate a pile of pillows. A living body that discharges nonseminal discharge (z) can contaminate all the cushions that are beneath it, but a corpse cannot (on variable z, A>B).[14] *The relationship between a living body and a corpse, therefore, depends on the particular variable on which they are compared.* By the same token, although no sage formulated such an objection, one can readily refute the assumption that being unwhole grants an object the power to contaminate. Severed flesh from a living being, for example, does not contaminate in a tent (M. Eduy. 6:3). Thus, the power to contaminate is not necessarily increased by the quality of being unwhole. Given that the sages' form of argument is generally susceptible to these sort of objections, it is difficult to understand why they are willing to risk an inference without first gathering as much information as possible. Why do they never cite more than two situations to support their contention that variable x and y are related in a particular way? Why do they never take account of more than two variables to make plausible their assertation that B>A?

You still may not be convinced that we are dealing here with a form of inference that is peculiar. You may be wondering whether the *qal va homer* is a form of reasoning by analogy or by precedent which, after all, plays a substantial role in science and law.[15] Although the *qal va homer* may resemble an argument by analogy and be subject to similar sorts of criticisms, there is a fundamental difference. Analogical arguments begin from the recognition of *similarities* between two objects. In an argument from analogy, one reasons that since A and B both have variable x, and A also has variable y, then B might have variable y, if x and y are related. For example, an analogical argument about Hearth might take the following form: Since on hearth plants need carbon dioxide as on Earth, we may infer that plants on Hearth produce oxygen as on Earth. We might, of course, be wrong. But here the strength of the argument rests on the similarity between Hearth and Earth and it is the strength of that similarity that gives the argument its force. By contrast, the *qal va homer* argument begins from the recognition that one object has a variable that is *lacking* in another. On Earth, plants do not require oxygen whereas on Hearth they do have that requirement. The difference that the *qal va homer* takes as its initial premise (B has what A lacks) would in many cases be sufficient to make an argument by analogy unacceptable.[16] For all the reasons given above, I consider the *qal va homer* an unfamiliar and hence peculiar sort of inference.

Ironically, the characterization of the *qal va homer* thus far has been exceedingly charitable. As I shall now suggest, there are reasons to think the *qal va homer* is even more unusual than I originally made it out to be. Specifically, in the account offered above I gave the sages the benefit of the doubt by assuming that the posited relationship between x and y is reasonable. Therefore in the imaginary *qal va homer* cited above, I invoked the variables of plant life, human life, and oxygen (humans have a greater need for oxygen than plants, $y > x$ with respect to oxygen). It was, moreover, the relationship between these variables that gave the *qal va homer* a semblance of rationality. Although the argument was flawed, we were at least able to understand why someone might be tempted to infer that people on Hearth require oxygen. We understood, in other words, how the "mistake" came about.

By contrast, when the variables that are invoked in a *qal va homer* are unrelated to one another, the inference appears totally absurd and even incomprehensible. This is evident from the following imaginary argument about Hearth's inhabitants. Subsequent studies have determined that shumans (the occupants of Hearth) in fact breathe carbon dioxide. Based on this additional information, the question arises as to whether they have the ability to speak:

> Since humans do not breathe carbon dioxide but do speak, then is it not reasonable to assume that shumans, who do breathe carbon dioxide, must be able to speak?

	A. Humans	B. Shumans
(x) breathe carbon dioxide	−	+
(y) speaking ability	+	?

This inference seems ridiculous because we have no independent reasons for assuming that breathing carbon dioxide and speaking are related to one another. A *qal va homer*, therefore, makes no sense whatsoever if the variables in question are not related to one another in a fixed way. Given this fact, it would seem necessary for a sage who is constructing a *qal va homer* to inspect other sorts of instances to see whether the relationship between the variables actually holds. But in many cases it is obvious that an inspection of this sort has not taken place. Consequently, the sages often make inferences when the variables in question have no known or demonstrable relationship to one another.

This is the case in the following discussion which concerns the potential of certain fluids to make food susceptible to impurity. According to early rabbinic law, food can only become contaminated if it has first been moistened by certain fluids, including water, milk, blood, and fruit juices. All the sages agree that such liquids can make food susceptible to impurity when the liquids have first been subject to human intention.[17] That is, if a person intends to use them for some purpose or intentionally removes them from their source, the liquids can make any food upon which they fall susceptible to impurity.

In the following discussion, Aqiba wants to prove that animal's milk can make food substances susceptible to impurity even if the milk was never subject to human intention. Aqiba believes, for example, that if the milk falls directly from a cow's udder onto a food substance, that substance can be contaminated. To make his case, he appeals to the paradigm of mother's milk, which all sages acknowledge has the power to make food susceptible to impurity regardless of intention.

> If mother's milk (A), which is used exclusively for the nourishment of children (and not adults -x) makes food susceptible to impurity even if it is not subject to human intention (y), then is it not logical to assume that animal milk which is used by children and adults (x), makes food susceptible to impurity even if it is not subject to human intention (y)? (Mishnah Makshirin 6:8)

	mother's milk	animal milk	oil, juice
children and adults drink it	-	+	+
makes food susceptible to impurity even if not subject to intention	+	?	-

Aqiba takes for granted that the more a fluid is put to human use, the greater its potential to make food susceptible to impurity. Aqiba does not give any reasons for this view. Presumably he bases this assumption on the fact that only fluids that are useful can make food susceptible to impurity. He reasons, therefore, that the more useful something is, the more power it should have to render food susceptible to contamination. Since animal's milk is used as nourishment by more categories of persons than mother's milk (B>A on variable x), then its potential to make food susceptible to impurity should not be less than that of mother's milk. Consequently, intention should be irrelevant in the case of animal milk as it is in the case of mother's milk.

The problem with this argument is that the premise has no instances that support it and several that refute it. As Aqiba's interlocutors point out, olive oil and grape juice are used by adults and children yet they do not make food susceptible to impurity unless they are already objects of intention (see chart on previous page). From these instances it would seem reasonable to infer that there is no relationship between the extent of a fluid's use and its potential to make food susceptible to impurity.[18] This example, therefore, shows that the sages sometimes construct a *qal va homer* argument without knowing or being able to show that the variables in question actually are related to one another. This is the essence of the *qal va homer*: If B has a variable that A does not, the rabbis may conclude that it is "heavier" than A. On that basis, they may expect it to have some other variable that A does have, *whether or not x and y are demonstrably related.*

I suggest, therefore, that the *qal va homer* represents a form of inference that those schooled in Western institutions would not only find difficult to follow but would reject as invalid. One can only imagine ethnographies written by classical rabbis:

> American children and adults show an inability to understand a simple *qal va homer.* Presented with such a problem they say one cannot infer any conclusions whatsoever. They insist that they need more information to make any inference and hence appear unable to focus their attention narrowly on the variables in question. Consequently, they often draw on personal experience to supplement the information given in the problem. By contrast, those Americans who have been trained in rabbinic yeshivas are generally able to solve the *qal va homer* reasoning. We thus conclude that certain features of American culture, most notably the importance of television, makes it difficult for children to learn to concentrate on just the information given.

I am of course parodying the cross-cultural work done on verbal problems of logic. Luria, Bruner, Cole, Scribner, and Hallpike have suggested that people in other cultures have difficulty solving syllogisms and other sorts of verbal problems.[19] When presented with such tasks, they often ignore the logical relations contained in the premises and allow their past experience to dictate the answer. As an example, consider the following conversation taken from Cole's study of the Kpelle.[20]

> Experimenter: "Spider and black deer always eat together. Spider is eating. Is black deer eating?"

Subject: "Were they in the bush?"

Experimenter: "Yes."

Subject: "They were eating together?"

Experimenter repeats problem: "Spider and black deer always eat together. Spider is eating. Is black deer eating?"

Subject: "But I was not there. How can I answer such a question?"

Eventually the subject says that black deer was eating.

Experimenter: "What is your reason for saying that black deer was eating?"

Subject: "The reason is that black deer always walks about all day eating green leaves in the bush. When it rests for a while it gets up again and goes to eat."

Cole, Scribner, and Hallpike have argued that the ability to solve syllogisms and other verbal problems of logic depends on the development of certain cognitive skills such as understanding the nature of inclusion (All people are mortal, Socrates is a person . . .), learning to reason on the basis of premises, and knowing to disregard personal experience. These abilities, they suggest, are ones acquired during schooling, when a person learns to think about situations that are not immediately at hand.

These psychological studies, however, have been greeted with skepticism from some quarters.[21] The failure of people to solve verbal problems of logic has been attributed to the unfamiliarity of their content, or to the artificial nature of the experimental situation. Hutchins, for example, argues that if thinking is observed in its natural setting, such as contexts of litigation, the experimenter would find that so-called traditional people reason in ways with which we are familiar. Based on his study of Trobriander land disputes, Hutchins concludes that

> the clear difference between cultures with respect to reasoning is in the representation of the world which is thought about rather than in the processes employed in doing the thinking. It is clear that Trobrianders cut the world into a different set of categories from those we entertain, and that those categories are linked together in unfamiliar structures. But the same types of logical relations underlie the connections of propositions in our conception and theirs, and the inferences that are apparent in their reasoning appear to be the same as the inferences we make.[22]

According to Hutchins, therefore, the experimental results on cognition are by definition misleading. No matter how hard the experimenter works to make the test a familiar subject, it will always be unnatural since it occurs within an experimental framework. Such tests simply demonstrate that traditional people do not know how to respond to the artificial character of an experimental situation.[23]

The *qal va homer* is relevant to this discussion in two different ways. First, it provides a counterexample to the conclusions that Hutchins derives from his study of Trobriander legal discussions. In this case, we have an unusual form of inference that is not elicited in an experimental situation but that arose spontaneously in the "natural setting" of the rabbis' legal discussions. The presence of the *qal va homer* in rabbinic culture, therefore, shows that what counts as a valid form of inference may vary in different "natural settings."

Second, the *qal va homer* suggests that the ability to draw an inference may not be a matter of cognitive skill as much as logical convention. To put it differently, what we call "cognitive skills" may simply be the ability to recognize and manipulate local conventions of reasoning.[24] The fact that an American student would fail to understand a rabbinic inference would not signify that the American lacked the cognitive skills necessary to carry out that operation. Rather, it would suggest that the American had not yet learned to recognize the norms that validate that form of inference. If forms of reasoning are matters of convention, it follows that other beliefs and practices in the culture will place some constraints on what counts as a valid argument. As I will suggest below, the *qal va homer* counts as a valid form of inference in rabbinic culture because of the role it plays in a larger set of discursive practices.

The presence of a peculiar form of inference in rabbinic culture also raises some interesting questions for the position put forward in a series of articles by Hollis, Lukes, and Newton-Smith.[25] Developing the implications of Quine's ideas about translation, they argue that if translation from one culture to another is possible, it must be the case that there are universal criteria of rationality. Without a "bridgehead," a "massive central core of human thinking which has no history," there can be no possibility of translation. These writers disagree on the content of this core. The stronger version of the argument, put forward by Hollis and Newton Smith, suggests that the bridgehead includes logic in general, or, as Hollis puts it, "rules of coherent judgment which a rational man cannot fail to subscribe to."[26] Lukes seems to be making a somewhat weaker claim. In his view, the core must include inference (if p and if p implies q then q) and the principle of noncontradiction. But other criteria of rationality may vary according to local context.[27] These writers assert, therefore, that the anthropologist is caught in a dilemma. He or she must either renounce relativism or deny the possibility of translating between cultures. As Lukes puts it, "if the members of [group] S really did not have our criteria of truth and logic, we would have no grounds for attributing to them language, thought or beliefs. . . ."[28]

The discussion of the *qal va homer*, I suggest, shows that the strong argument is both misleading and wrong and that the weaker argument is contradictory and trivial. To begin with, the strong version of this argument inaccurately characterizes the position of the strong relativist. The relativist never claimed that the reasoning of other people is totally different. To attribute that position to the relativist is what I call the "Lévy-Bruhl caricature." Lévy-Bruhl suggested that primitive thought almost never recognizes the kinds of contradictions we do. If that were true, translation probably would be impossible. The coherent relativist, by contrast, is suggesting that, although there is some overlap or common ground between cultures, there are also interesting and important moments of divergence. The rationalist argument from translation, therefore, does not at all address the central claim of the relativist position. The rationalist argues that translation is impossible if another group of people consistently reason in completely unfamiliar ways. The relativist, however, does not see how the rationalist moves from that insight to the more general claim that forms of reasoning never vary. Indeed, the discussion of rabbinic inference shows that on this point the rationalists are simply wrong. What counts as logic does vary from context to context both within and between cultures. On the relativist view, therefore, translation remains possible even though people *sometimes* reason in unfamiliar ways.

The relativist also disagrees with the rationalist on the character of the bridgehead that is required for purposes of translation. The relativist does not believe that the common ground between all cultures is the same, that "there is a massive central core of human thinking which has no history." Even if translation requires a bridgehead, that bridgehead may vary depending on who is doing the translation and the particular needs of the translation.[29] Therefore, although the notion of inference that predominates in our culture may not coincide with the rabbis', some other groups (Newton-Smith's imaginary Herns, for example) may find that it matches their own. If so, their ethnography of the rabbis could use the *qal va homer* as part of the bridgehead. In the judgment of the relativist, therefore, the bridgehead is simply an ad hoc affair that varies with circumstance, not a constant unchanging core that contains Logic with a capital "L."

In addition, the relativist is not convinced that the bridgehead must contain criteria of rationality. The relativist believes that shared forms of life are far more important than shared criteria of rationality in allowing for the possibility of translation. We can translate the discourse of another culture because we share similar ways of living (we eat, drink, live, die, gather food, etc.). If it is overlapping forms of life that enable translation to occur, then the bridgehead may not have to include rational criteria at all. There is no contradiction, therefore, in translating rabbinic discourse yet claiming that the rabbis recognize an unusual form of inference.

The relativist also finds problematic the weaker version of the rationalist argument as put forward by Lukes. As noted above, Lukes recognizes that some rational criteria are the product of local consensus. However, he insists that at least two criteria of rationality are universal, namely, the principle of noncontradiction and inference. But Lukes goes on to say that the local criteria of rationality sometimes override the universal ones.[30] The relativist thinks this is a contradictory position. Either we have universal criteria of rationality or we do not. If they are universal, it makes no sense to say that in some contexts other local criteria of rationality supersede them. Admitting that universal criteria are superseded is an admission that criteria of rationality vary with context.

The *qal va homer*, moreover, shows that Lukes's claims about inference are essentially harmless to the relativist position. Presumably Lukes would say that the *qal va homer* actually proves the point he wishes to make, namely, that inference is universal. Although the *qal va homer* is a different kind of inference, it is still an inference because it can be described by the symbolic notion "if p and if p implies q then q." But if that is all the rationalist wants to claim, the relativist is willing to concede this point. The relativist does find it useful to believe that other people exist and that people reason in some fashion or other. However, the relativist does not think this concession undermines his or her position. For even if all people reason in a form that can be described by the formula "if p and if p implies q then q," that does not mean that all people make the same kind of inferences. If p implies q in one context, it may not have that implication in another. The weaker argument, therefore, is trivial because it leaves the relativist position intact.

Logics and Myths

If criteria of rationality vary with context, as I have suggested they do, it is the context that lends them their credibility. What appears as a logical difficulty from the standpoint of one set of beliefs or practices may be invisible or completely irrelevant from the standpoint of another. In the case of rabbinic inference, therefore, we need to understand why the logical problems that seem so apparent in the *qal va homer* did not lead the rabbis to reject it as a valid form of inference. More specifically, why did they not worry about the threat of anarchy that is latent in the *qal va homer* argument?

The *qal va homer* is potentially anarchical in two different respects. First, using such an argument one can justify whatever conclusion one wishes. To prove that B possesses trait y, one simply must find some A that has y but lacks some variable x that is present in B. It is always possible to find an object or situation that satisfies those conditions. At least one sage realized the lack of constraint on the *qal va homer* argument.

> Rab Judah said in Rab's name: No one is to be given a seat on the Sanhedrin [the ancient supreme court of the Jews] without being able to prove on the basis of Scriptural texts that those crawling things that Scripture lists as unclean are actually clean. Rab said: I shall put forward an argument to prove their cleanness. If a snake which causes so much uncleanness through killing is nonetheless clean,[31] then does it not follow that other crawling things are clean since they do not spread uncleanness by killing?

> (Babli Sanhedrin 17a-b)[32]

The author of this passage realizes that one can formulate a *qal va homer* argument that reaches a conclusion that directly contradicts information given in Scripture. This is tantamount to an admission that the *qal va homer* can prove whatever one wishes.

The second anarchical implication of the *qal va homer* is closely related to the first. For every inference that can be formulated, one can always find a refutation. To do so, one simply has to cast doubt on the posited hierarchical relationship between B and A or between x and y. Since the relationship between A and B is based on the comparison of A and B according to one variable only, it is always possible to challenge the alleged relationship. This may be accomplished by appealing to a third variable z that reverses the hierarchical relationship between B and A (schematized in the chart below). Although B>A on variable x, A> B on variable z. Consequently, A may also be greater than B on variable y (eq. M. Eduy. 6:2). One can also undermine the posited relationship between x and y by showing that in a third situation C, variable x is present but y is not. Therefore, C refutes the idea that y is generally more present than x.

	Qal Va Homer		Possible Objection
	A	B	C
x	-	+	+
y	+	?	-
Possible Objection			
z	+	-	
Refutation of Objection from C			
u		-	+

Although every *qal va homer* can be refuted, a refutation does not put an end to the argument. On the contrary, the sage who originally proposed the *qal va homer* now has two options available. If the objection came from another situation (C), he can always argue that the cited situation is irrelevant by citing another variable (u) on which B and C differ. In this way, the relationship that holds between x and y in situation C is declared irrelevant to situation B. Failing that, he can easily formulate a new *qal va homer* that arrives at the desired conclusion. Of course, his opponents can always defeat the new argument as well. He in turn can always offer a new *qal va homer*.

It is never clear, therefore, what brings such a discussion to closure at a given point. Surely another objection or another *qal va homer* could always be found. It is also difficult to understand why in some cases the sages are willing to accept a *qal va homer* argument as a justification for a law (e.g., Mishnah Zebahim 12:3). Certainly that inference can be refuted like all the rest. Nor should we be surprised that in most cases such arguments often end at an impasse with the point of law never clearly decided (M. Ker. 3:10). Those cases in which a *qal va homer* successfully survives refutation seem to be the consequence of the debater's endurance rather than the power of the argument. Without going into any detail, let us look briefly at one of these endless arguments:

1. Said Rabbi Aqiba, "I asked Rabbi Eliezer the following: 'Consider the case of a person who inadvertently violates the prohibition against working on the Sabbath by performing similar kinds of work on successive Sabbaths. Is he or she liable for one sin-offering for all the violations or a separate offering for each?'

2. "He said to me, 'The person is obligated to bring a sin-offering for each and every violation. This conclusion may be derived by qal va homer:

3. "'If the law against having intercourse with a menstruating woman (A) does not distinguish ways in which the violation occurred nor various levels of sin (-x), nonetheless considers a person liable for each and every violation (y), then in the Sabbath law (B) which does discriminate kinds of violations and levels of sin (x), is it not logical that a person who violates that law is liable for each and every violation (y)?'

A=-x, y and B=x. Therefore B>A and B=y

4. "I said to him, 'No, [that inference is unwarranted, for] how can you infer [anything about the Sabbath law from the laws of the menstruant] since the latter involves two warnings (i.e., he is warned against intercourse with her and she is warned against intercourse with him) while the Sabbath law involves only one warning [people are warned not to violate the Sabbath, not vice versa]?'

A>B on variable z

5. "He replied, 'I can prove it from the laws regarding a man who has intercourse with a minor during her menstrual period. In that case, only one warning is involved [i.e. he is warned, but a minor is not warned], yet such a person is liable for each and every violation.'

C=-x, y and B=x therefore B>C and B=y

6. "I said to him, 'No [your conclusion is unwarranted, for] how can you infer [anything about the Sabbath from the case of the menstruating minor]. Even though the latter is not warned now, she will be later in life [when she is old enough to be obligated to the laws], whereas the Sabbath is never warned.'

C>B on variable u

7. "He said, 'I can prove it from the laws regarding a man who has intercourse with an animal. [Here at last Eliezer finds a case that

does not involve two warnings, for an animal is not warned against intercourse, just as no warning is given to the Sabbath].'

D=-x, y and B=x therefore B>D and B=y

8. "I said to him, '[I still do not accept your argument, because] an animal is like the Sabbath, [that is, I have the same question about it as about the Sabbath. You cannot prove one case with another one that is equally dubious].'"

How do you know that D=y?

(Mishnah Ker. 3:10)

Even a cursory glance at the structure of this argument illustrates the problem I am raising: First, a question is raised. Second, an answer is given. Third, a *qal va homer* is offered to support the answer. This *qal va homer* argues that B>A. Fourth, the argument is rejected because on another variable A>B. Fifth, another *qal va homer* is brought to support the answer. Here the argument rests on the claim that B>C. Sixth, this argument is rejected when it is shown that on another variable C>B. Seventh, another *qal va homer* is offered on the basis of situation D. Eighth, it is rejected because the original assumption (D=y) has no support. Buy why did the dispute end here? Why did Eliezer not offer another *qal va homer* to support his view? It is not clear. Indeed, later rabbinic commentaries often suggest alternative forms of the *qal va homer* that earlier sages might have used.

As is now evident, the consequences of accepting the *qal va homer* as a valid form of inference could easily have posed severe theological and sociological difficulties for the sages' larger religious enterprise. Among other things, that enterprise involved the attempt to explicate the divine will for situations that were not specifically mentioned in Scripture or the oral tradition. The sages claimed that they alone had the authority and wisdom to serve as interpreters of God's will. But surely the appeal to the *qal va homer* could have seriously compromised such claims. If all arguments could be refuted, on what basis could they possibly be sure that a particular ruling was correct or, even more importantly, represented what God intended? How could they possibly have avoided arousing the suspicion among themselves and among those outside the rabbinic community that they could prove whatever they wanted and consequently that they were making it up as they went along? Furthermore, even if they were willing to recognize their own constructive role in the unfolding of the law,[33] how could they deal with the potential anarchy that the *qal va homer* seemed to entail? Whose *qal va homer* would be accepted and on what grounds? There were, it seems, good reasons for the sages to have repudiated the *qal va homer* as a form of argumentation. Yet, strangely enough, it remained the most popular form of argument. Why is this so?

I suggested above that what appears to be a logical difficulty in one context may not appear so in another. In other words, behind every reasonable argument there is a myth that makes it so. A myth in this sense is a set of practices and assumptions or just simply a form of life that enables a given form of reasoning to operate. That style of reasoning in turn serves to validate the other practices and assumptions that comprise the myth. Together myth and logic constitute a closed and mutually self-affirming set of practices and assertions. As Feyerabend expresses it, "we do not really understand a myth unless we accept its claim for absoluteness and try to find out how it is realized."[34] I would add that we also do not understand alternative forms of reasoning unless we find the myth that allows them to appear logical.

The notion of myth presented here departs from the more conventional definition of myth as a narrative or story by means of which a people define themselves and locate themselves in their world. The conception of myth as a set of practices and assumptions that constitutes a form of life subsumes and goes beyond the notion of myth as narrative. It includes not only the story people tell to explain who they are, where they came from, and why they do what they do, but the specific practices that get justified by and linked to that narrative framework.

The broader conception of myth offered here has several advantages over the narrower definition. To begin with, it shows how the concept of myth remains relevant to traditions, like that of the rabbis, that generally repudiate the narrative genre. The rabbis say very little about the story that informs and legitimates the rabbinic community, and consequently, it has to be inferred from rabbinic practice. But this means that the story itself cannot be artifically severed from its connection to practice. We cannot speak of the rabbinic myth without at the same time making reference to rabbinic practice. To know the rabbinic myth about the origin and character of Scripture is to understand their practices of interpreting Scripture. Their myth, then, is the way we translate their practices into narrative form. In addition, the notion of myth as form of life has the advantage of making alternative forms of reasoning comprehensible. Narratives by themselves cannot explain the persuasiveness of alternative forms of reasoning. It is the actual implementation of a story in practice that determines what will count as reasonable.

Perhaps the most outstanding ethnographic account of how logic and myth mutually confirm one another is Evans-Pritchard's study of Azande witchcraft. In that work, Evans-Pritchard is concerned with problems similar to the ones raised here. Specifically, he considers why the Azande do not realize the absurdity of using a poison oracle to make various life decisions. The oracle involves asking a question and then administering poison to a fowl. The fowl's death signifies a negative answer to a question, its survival a positive response. Evans-Pritchard spends a good portion of his book considering why the Azande do not see or take very seriously the kinds of objections that we might have to such a practice. What he discovers is that the Azande form of life constitutes a closed set of practices and assertions in which each assertion and practice can be backed up by other assertions and other practices which are themselves supported by the former ones. For example, the fact that the same question receives contradictory answers from the oracle does not raise doubts about the validity of the practice. On the contrary, the Azande offer a number of "secondary elaborations" to explain away the difficulties: the wrong variety of poison was gathered; there was a breach of a taboo, witchcraft or sorcery interfered, the owner of the forest where the poison was gathered was angry and so forth.[35] Rather than undermine the credibility of the oracle practice, a contradiction between oracles actually serves to validate the existence of magic and witchcraft which themselves necessitate the practice of oracles. Evans-Pritchard concludes, therefore, by arguing that

> Azande observe the action of the poison oracle as we observe it, but their observations are always subordinated to their beliefs and are incorporated into their beliefs and made to explain them and justify them. Let the reader consider any argument that would utterly demolish all Zande claims for the power of the oracle. If it were translated into Zande modes of thought it would serve to support their entire structure of belief. For their mystical notions are eminently coherent, being interrelated by a network of logical ties, and are so ordered that they never too crudely contradict sensory experience but instead, experience seems to justify them.[36]

As I shall now suggest, the *qal va homer* endured in rabbinic discourse for similar sorts of reasons. Specifically, its survival is made possible by the existence of a distinctive set of assumptions and discursive practices that had already emerged in the early rabbinic community and which eventually came to dominate the rabbinic enterprise.[37] The *qal va homer* retained its plausibility because of the contribution it made to sustaining these assumptions and practices. In turn, these practices and background assumptions made the sages' form of inference seem entirely credible. The *qal va homer*, then, endured because it took its place in a closed and self-validating set of discursive practices—a myth—that rendered the kinds of logical difficulties that we detect in the *qal va homer* irrelevant and unproblematic. In what follows, I discuss this myth and the role that the *qal va homer* served in its formation and persistence.

There are two basic assumptions that inform the later rabbis', and to a lesser extent the earlier rabbis', legal commentary to Torah (i.e., to the written Scriptures and oral tradition).[38] First, they believe that God is the perfect Author and consequently that there is no redundancy in the Torah. Every paragraph, sentence, word, and even letter was carefully selected by God and hence is laden with significance. Nothing about Scripture's formulation, therefore, is arbitrary or simply a matter of style. Second, according to the sages God expects interpreters of Torah to exercise their critical faculties in understanding the divine text. That is, the interpreter must infer from Scripture what is not explicitly said. Together, these two assumptions generate a third fundamental assumption, namely, that God did not include in Scripture information that a careful interpreter could infer from other parts of Scripture. To have done so would have been redundant on God's part. In other words, the sages assume that in formulating each part of Scripture (or the oral tradition), God anticipated all the logical arguments people might make from other parts of Scripture. When logic could produce the desired conclusion, God did not include that information in the text. But if logic would lead to an improper conclusion or would produce equivocal results, God added information in Scripture (or the oral tradition) that would override the mistaken conclusion or clear up the ambiguity.

As one might expect, these assumptions generate a distinctive type of interpretive practice. Pages and pages of rabbinic legal commentary are devoted to showing that had God not included in the Torah a given word, phrase, or verse, the correct law could not have been known. A given interpretation of Scripture, therefore, is significantly strengthened by proving that logic could not have produced the answer in question. Indeed, if the information in question could have been derived by logic, then the given interpretation must be wrong, for God would not have specified something that was superfluous. The demonstrated failure of logic, therefore, verifies the perfection of the Torah and omniscience of the divine Author. Each time it is shown that the Torah anticipates and rules out a wrong conclusion potentially derived by logic or gives a ruling where logic could only have produced ambiguity, the sages show that God anticipated all possible logical arguments in formulating Scripture.

It is perhaps already obvious that the logical problems inherent in the *qal va homer* make it perfectly suited for this discursive practice. Since one can construct a *qal va homer* to arrive at any conclusion one wishes and since one can always refute such an argument, it is always possible to show that logic would have failed to give the proper conclusion or that logic would have led to equivocal results. Therefore, given any statement in Scripture or in the oral tradition, the sages can always prove that it was necessary for God to have specified that information. By invoking a *qal va homer* argument, they can always show that logic would have led the interpreter astray or failed to provide any conclusive information at all.

The following example illustrates how the *qal va homer* functions in this way. The passage at hand (Babli Qiddushin 4b) discusses whether a verse from Deuteronomy contains superfluous information. This verse (Deut. 24:1) states that "If a man takes a wife and has intercourse with her and she does not please him because he finds something obnoxious about her he writes her a bill of divorce . . . and sends her away from his house." The sages consider whether the phrase "and has intercourse with her" is redundant.

> 1. The Scriptural statement "and has intercourse with her (Deut. 24:1)" indicates that a woman can be acquired through the act of intercourse.

> 2. [Is this statement not superfluous for] could that ruling not be deduced logically [from other information given in the Torah]?

> 3. [The logic is as follows:] If a widowed woman who is obligated to marry her brother-in-law cannot be acquired by an exchange of money but can be acquired through the act of intercourse (A=-x, y), then a single woman who can be acquired by exchange of money (B=x), is it not logical (*ỹnwdyn*) that she can be acquired through the act of intercourse (y)?

> A=-x, y and B=x therefore B>A and must have y.

4. The case of the Hebrew maidservant (C) refutes the previous argument: She is acquired by the exchange of money (x) but not through intercourse (-y).

C=x, -y therefore although B=x it too may lack y.

5. [How can you use the case of the maidservant as an objection?] Since a Hebrew maidservant is not acquired as a wife (C=-z), will you use her case as a refutation of the case of the single woman (B) who is acquired as a wife (z)?

Since B>C on variable z, it is possible B>C on variable y, the variable in question. Consequently, the objection at 4 is rejected and the argument at 3 appears valid.

6. Scripture says "and have intercourse with her." Why need it say that [given that that information can be derived by logic as specified at 3]?

7. It is necessary because it anticipates the objection of Rav Ashi who said that one can refute the argument [at 3] at the very outset from the case of the widowed woman. Since a widowed woman (A) is obligated to marry (u), can one use the case of a widowed woman to derive conclusions about the single woman (B) who is not obligated to marry (-u)? [Surely not].

On variable u, A>B; the same may be true on variable y. Thus, the logic of 3 is refuted.

8. Consequently, Scripture had to specify "and have intercourse with her," [for otherwise one would not know that the act of intercourse established a marriage relationship between a man and woman].

In this passage, the *qal va homer* assumes a function quite different from that which it served in the examples cited earlier. In those examples, the *qal va homer* was invoked in an attempt to decide what the law should be in a new situation. Here, by contrast, the *qal va homer* is used to demonstrate that nothing in the Torah is unnecessary.[39] One might describe this role of the *qal va homer* as *verification by way of failure*. It is the failure of logic that demonstrates the perfection of God's teaching.

The two functions of the *qal va homer* are each tied to different aspects of the rabbis' self-understanding as interpreters of Torah. The sages believed their role was to determine how God intended them to respond to situations not explicitly specified in Scripture. When they were functioning in this role they appealed to the *qal va homer* to unpack what was implicit in Scripture. But the sages also arrogated to themselves another role as well, namely, to display the extraordinary beauty of the Scriptural text and by extension the perfection of its Author. In this capacity, the sages used the *qal va homer* to show that God had only included in the Torah information that could not be derived by logical inquiry.

Although the *qal va homer* is used in both of these ways in the earliest rabbinic writings, its primary function in these sources is to justify a new law.[40] For example, in twenty-three out of twenty-nine cases in the Mishnah the *qal va homer* is invoked to justify a new ruling. In only six of twenty-nine cases is it used to show that Scripture anticipates and rules out a mistaken conclusion potentially derived by logic.[41] In subsequent rabbinic sources, however, the reverse is the case. In these writings, the *qal va homer* almost always serves as a way of demonstrating the aesthetic perfection of Torah by showing that logic would either have led to the wrong conclusions or led to equivocation. The longevity of the *qal va homer* argument within rabbinic tradition is closely tied to the increasing importance within the rabbinic community of demonstrating the perfection of the divine word.

The sages' peculiar form of inference, therefore, made credible their assumption about the aesthetic beauty of God's teaching and the latter in turn made possible the survival of the *qal va homer* form of reasoning. Without the *qal va homer*, or at least a form of argument with analogous properties, the sages' specific set of assumptions about Scripture's perfection would have been undemonstrable and hence untenable. Their understanding of Scripture presupposed a form of reasoning that could be manipulated to justify any answer and that could always be refuted. But if the sages' form of inference validated their assumptions about Scripture, the reverse was also the case: their understanding of Scripture proved that this form of reasoning was valid. By showing how verse after verse of Scripture anticipates and corrects mistaken conclusions derived by the *qal va homer*, the rabbis proved that in writing Scripture God anticipated the use of this particular form of inference. Since God expected interpreters of Scripture to reason in this fashion, the sages' confidence in the *qal va homer* could not have been shaken by pointing to the logical problems intrinsic to this form of inference. To paraphrase Evans-Pritchard, let the reader consider any argument that would totally undermine the validity of the *qal va homer*. It would have done nothing to challenge the rabbis' faith in their form of reasoning, for it was embedded in a set of discursive practices and assumptions that it helped to validate and which in turn made it credible. The sages could not have given up the *qal va homer*, therefore, without at the same time questioning the very religious enterprise in which they were engaged. Their form of inference was part and parcel of their form of life.

At this point, I could conceivably be accused of "vulgar Wiggensteinianism." In claiming that logic and myth fit snugly together I am making it difficult to understand the possibility of criteria of rationality having a history. How could one who holds this sort of position ever make sense of the fact that people sometimes criticize earlier criteria of rationality? This question is in fact one of the central charges leveled by MacIntyre against Winch's *Idea of a Social Science*.[42] But this challenge leaves unscathed the present analysis of the *qal va homer*. The *qal va homer* survived in rabbinic tradition for at least six hundred years. The problem in this case, therefore, is not to explain why criteria of rationality have a history but why they remained stable over so long a period of time.[43]

The above analysis suggests, therefore, that the rationalists are wrong: there are alternative criteria of rationality and what counts as a good argument or valid inference from the standpoint of one myth does not necessarily count from the standpoint of another. Moreover, the existence of other forms of rationality does not rule out the possibility of understanding or "translation." We can understand the rabbis because we are familiar with forms of life that overlap with theirs. We know about life forms that revolve around believing Scripture is from God and that God is a perfect Author. It is the overlapping in forms of life, not universal criteria of logic, that allows translation to occur.

Reason, therefore, is always relative to some myth, that is, to some set of assumptions and to certain discursive practices that have been given by God, the ancestors, or other powers that be. Consequently, attempts to describe differences between genres of discourses in terms of formal criteria of rationality may often be misleading. To say, for example, that the Western philosophical tradition is more concerned with procedural rationality than is rabbinic tradition would, in my judgment, be wrong. it would be wrong because by the standards established by the sages' own practices their form of inference is as valid as ours. The *qal va homer* was as reasonable for the sages as the syllogism was for Aristotle.

Ironically, the above analysis also suggests that the rabbis and the rationalists have a great deal in common. Both groups treat their own criteria of rationality as if they were "a direct gift from God," that is, as the only criteria of rationality that are possible or plausible. But in asserting this, both commit the fallacy of monotheism; they assume that their God is the only God. But as the relativist knows, there are many gods and each has its own idea of what constitutes rational thinking.

Notes

1. White, *Tropics*, 151-52.

2. Lévy-Bruhl, *Natives Think*; Tylor, *Primitive Culture*; Frankfort et al., *Before Philosophy*; Cassirer, *Symbolic Forms*; Popper, *Conjectures*; Douglas, *Purity*; Leach, *Political Systems*; Horton, "African Thought;" Goody, *Savage Mind*. None of these authors holds all of these views but each at one time or another has argued that rational criteria can be used to differentiate Myth from Philosophy or Science. Horton, in particular, has substantially revised his views in a subsequent essay (Horton, "Tradition and Modernity").

3. Winch, *Social Science*, 100.

4. Newton-Smith, "Relativism," 111-12.

5. Evans-Pritchard, *Witchcraft*, 159.

6. Kuhn, *Structure*, 2.

7. For other discussions of this form of reasoning from other perspectives, see Handelman, *Slayers of Moses*, 3-51; Jacobs, *Talmudic Logic*, 3-8; Kunst, *Type of Inference*, 976-91; Lieberman, *Hellenism*, 47-63; Mielziner, *Talmud*, 130-41; Schwarz, *Hermeneutische Syllogismus*.

8. Examples of the complex form of the *qal va homer* in the Mishnah include: Peah 6:6, M.S. 3:10, Pes. 6:2, 6:5, Yeb. 8:3, Ned. 10:6-7, Naz. 7:4, Sotah 6:3, B.Q. 2:5, Sebu. 3:6, Eduy. 6:2, Zeb. 8:12, 12:3, Men. 8:5, Hul. 2:7, 10:1, Ker. 3:7-10, Bek. 9:1, Tem. 6:4, Neg. 10:9, 10:2, 13:10, Nid. 4:6, Mahk. 6:8, Yad. 4:7. Examples in the Mishnah of the simple form of the *qal va homer* argument include: Ber. 9:5, Sheb. 7:2, B.B. 9:7, Qid. 4:14, San. 6:5, Avot. 1:5, Hul. 12:5, Bek. 1:1, Neg. 12:5.

9. I disagree, therefore, with Lieberman, *Hellenism*, 56, and others who assume that the rabbis' *qal va homer* argument is identical with the *a fortiori* arguments accepted in Greek philosophy. Only the simple forms of the *qal va homer* would have been recognizable as an *a fortiori* argument. The complex form of the argument would have been unfamiliar and unintelligible to those outside the rabbinic community.

Specifically, the force of the simple form of the inference (e.g., If God regrets the bloodshed of the wicked all the more so the bloodshed of the righteous [M.

San. 6:5]) rests on an unquestioned background assumption (that God cares more about the righteous than the wicked). This is precisely how the complex *qal va homer* differs from its simpler sibling and thereby becomes problematic. The complex *qal va homer* does not take for granted an unquestioned background assumption but attempts to reach a generalization of this sort as part of the argument. It is the way in which this generalization is reached that makes the complex form of argument strange. As I explain below, the sages rely on only one situation to reach a generalization and then attempt to use that generalization to make inferences about other situations. In most cases, one situation does not provide sufficient information on the basis of which to reach a generalization of this type. Those outside the rabbinic community would refuse to draw an inference on the basis of the information upon which the sages base their argument.

10. Jeffrey Stout convinced me that the relationship between variables x and y are also at issue in some forms of the *qal va homer* argument. In a subsequent study, however, I hope to show that not all *qal va homer* arguments are the same. Some take account only of the relationship between A and B and ignore the relationship between variables x and y. This other form of *qal va homer* is even more perplexing than the form in which both the relations between A and B and x and y are at issue. I provide an example of this type of *qal va homer* below.

11. I have simplified the substance of the discussion by using the word *particle*. At issue in this discussion is the case of a severed appendage from a corpse that lacks an olive's bulk of flesh. Rather than use the cumbersome expression "an appendage that lacks an olive's bulk of flesh" I simply use the shorthand "particle." According to the Mishnah an appendage ['*br*] is any segment of the body that contains a bone. The sages claim that the body has 248 such segments (Mishnah Ohalot 1:8).

12. Everyone agrees that a severed appendage from a corpse or living body contaminates in a tent when it has an olive's bulk of flesh attached to it. In this passage the sages take for granted that a particle (i.e., an appendage without an olive's bulk of flesh) from a living body does contaminate in a tent. Elsewhere, however, the Mishnah denies that such a particle has such power (see Ohalot 2:3).

13. As noted above, it is this problematic feature that distinguishes the complex from the simple form of the *qal va homer* argument.

14. If a man who has discharged nonseminal discharge sits on a pile of ten cushions, all ten of them are contaminated. By contrast, a corpse only contaminates through contact. Hence if a corpse is placed on a pile of ten cushions, it contaminates the first one with corpse uncleanness. The first one then contaminates the second one, which has a reduced level of uncleanness. The second one makes the third unclean, but the third does not have the power to contaminate any other cushions.

15. See, for example, Hesse, *Models*, for an analysis of the role of analogy in science.

16. As Hesse, *Models*, 90-92, shows that would depend on whether the difference ("negative analogy") is essential to the positive area of the analogy. Ironically, the sages often reject a refutation of a *qal va homer* based on precisely the kind of difference that supports the *qal va homer* in the first place. For example, consider a typical *qal va homer* (A=-x, y, and B=x, therefore B=y).

Possible
Objection

	A	B	C
x	-	+	+
y	+	?	-

Refutation of objection:

		B	C
u		-	+

Note that the difference between A and B (A=-x, B=x) enables the argument to proceed. But then imagine that an objection is brought from situation C. Here x is present and y is not which suggests that in B, y also could be absent. Frequently, the sages will refute C by appealing to a third variable u which shows that C and B are disanalogous. Since C has u and B does not, C is irrelevant to B and therefore cannot serve as a refutation of the *qal va homer*. But note that the kind of difference that supports the *qal va homer* initially (A=-x, B=x) is now taken as reason for refuting the objection (B=-u, C=u). So the sages themselves recognize this kind of difference as sufficient grounds for saying two things are disanalogous but they nonetheless use this kind of difference to construct an argument!

17. On the role of intention in making food susceptible to impurity, see Neusner, *Form Analysis*; and Eilberg-Schwartz, *Human Will*, 28-29, 44. On the general relationship between intention and impurity in rabbinic culture, see Eilberg-Schwartz, *Human Will*; "Creation and Classification"; and *Savage in Judaism*.

18. It is true that Aqiba trivializes these contrary instances by claiming that there is a difference between juice and oil, on the one hand, and milk, on the other. Milk, he argues, is a liquid from the outset, but juice and olive oil are originally food substances. It is not clear what Aqiba can mean by this. Surely the oil and juice are in the fruit in the same way that milk is in the breast or udder. Moreover, one could turn Aqiba's refutation of the refutation back against Aqiba's own argument: if juice and oil are not analogous to animal's milk, then animal's milk is not analogous to mother's milk since different categories of people use it.

Therefore, unless Aqiba can offer a positive instance to support his premise, it is difficult to understand why he is willing to dismiss negative instances out of hand. Indeed, by invoking the criterion of the fluid's original state, Aqiba simply proves my point. He shows that it is permissible to argue on the basis of variables that have no demonstrable relationship to one another. In this case, there is no reason at all for thinking that the original state of a fluid should be relevant to its potential to make food susceptible to contamination.

19. Luria, *Cognitive Development*; Bruner, *Cognitive Growth*; Cole, *Cultural Context*; Cole and Scribner, *Culture and Thought*, Hallpike, *Primitive Thought*.

20. Cole, *Cultural Context*, 187.

21. See, for example, Hutchins, *Culture and Inference*. Cole and Scribner, *Culture and Thought*, 166, have also significantly qualified their own conclusions.

22. Hutchins, *Culture and Inference*, 128.

23. Hutchins, *Culture and Inference*, 8-14.

24. Fernandez, *Persuasion*, 172-87, moves towards a similar conclusion.

25. Hollis, "Limits," "Reason and Ritual," "Winchcraft," "Social Destruction;" Lukes, "Problems," "Relativism;" Newton-Smith, "Relativism." Walsh, "Constancy," makes a similar argument about the role of the historian.

26. Hollis, "Social Destruction," 74.

27. Lukes, "Problems," 210. When Hollis, "Reason," 232, and Lukes, "Problems," 210, 207, say that inference is universal, it is not clear whether they are arguing that all people make inferences or whether they are making a stronger claim, namely, that all people make the same kind of inferences. At times, even Lukes seems to be making the stronger sort of claim. For example, Lukes, "Problems," 210, argues that Winch in fact comes close to his own position by implying "that it is the content of the propositions, not the logical relations between them, that is dependent on social relations between men."

28. Lukes, "Problems," 210.

29. Barnes and Bloor, "Relativism;" Hertzberg, "Winch."

30. Lukes, "Problems," 211.

31. When snakes kill humans and animals they increase impurity in the world because a corpse and carcass are sources of contamination. The carcasses of snakes are considered clean because Scripture does not list the snake among those crawling things that defile (Lev. 11:29-32).

32. See also Yerushalmi Berachot 4:1 (22a). According to this passage, Rabbi Yohanan asserted that a man who is not qualified to offer a hundred arguments for declaring a reptile ritually clean or unclean will not know how to open the trial of capital cases with reasons for acquittal.

33. Some sources in rabbinic writings suggest that the rabbis believed God turned over to them the authority to interpret the divine law. By this account, whatever the sages decide by definition constitutes the divine will. As I have argued elsewhere (Eilberg-Schwartz, "Reader in the Write," and "Who's Kidding"), this view does not represent the rabbinic movement as a whole. But even if it did, the rabbis would still have to deal with the fact that two different sages might arrive at contradictory conclusions by employing the same form of argumentation.

34. Feyerabend, *Knowledge*, 38. The conception of a closed system is reminiscent of Horton's original essay, "African Thought." However, I am not committed to several of Horton's assumptions. Horton assumes that a traditional society is unaware of alternative conceptions of the world. It is this lack of awareness that makes them so committed to the view of the world that dominates. Consequently, a challenge to that view cannot overthrow the framework because it is the only framework available. The members of the society respond to challenges, therefore, by elaborating ad hoc assumptions that protect the only view of things that they have.

I am not making this sort of claim. It seems to me that a closed set of practices and assumptions does arise simultaneously with and perhaps in response to competitors. In fact, this is the view that Horton adopts in his most recent article, "Tradition and Modernity." By my view, what protects a world view from being overthrown is the way in which it is embedded in a set of practices, or a form of life.

35. Evans-Pritchard, *Witchcraft*, 155.

36. Evans-Pritchard, *Witchcraft*, 150.

37. In claiming that these assumptions and practices were less prevalent in the early rabbinic community than in the later rabbinic community, I follow Neusner, *Judaism*, who argues that the Mishnah and Tosefta were the earliest rabbinic documents and that the exegetical legal literature such as the Mechilta, Sifres, and Sifra testify to the nature of rabbinic Judaism at a later date. Halivni, *Midrash*, by contrast, holds that the exegetical legal literature contains material that is older than the Mishnah and Tosefta. For a variety of reasons I find Halivni's argument unconvincing. But even if Halivni is right, the basic thrust of my argument retains its validity. If Halivni is right, then the myth that lies behind the *qal va homer* is already securely in place in the earliest rabbinic community.

38. The term *Torah*, as I am using it here, refers to the written Scriptures as well as the independent oral tradition that the sages assume existed. It is not clear whether the sages believe the oral tradition was actually given by God to Moses or was simply divinely inspired. Nonetheless, they do assume that its formulation is as perfect as the written Scriptures.

39. I thus disagree with Neusner's characterization of the *qal va homer* in his study of Sifra (*A History*, 1986, 9: 67-68). Neusner argues on the basis of his study of Sifra that "one polemic fundamental to Sifra's purpose . . . is to demonstrate the inadequacy of reason unaided by revelation. Time and again Sifra asks, "Does this proposition, offered with a proof-text, really require the stated proof of revelation? Will it not stand firmly upon the basis of autonomous reason unaided by Scripture?" Neusner, however, misses the point when he sets up an opposition between revelation and reason. The sages are arguing that reason cannot produce the correct answer *based on the limited information given in other parts of Scripture*. But the point is not to denigrate reason as Neusner suggests. Rather the exercise is to explain why God considered it necessary to include a given statement in Scripture. By my account, God formulated Scripture with the expectation that humans would use their reason. So reason itself is a necessary factor in determining what constitutes a valid exegesis of Scripture.

40. In making this statement, I am again following Neusner, *Judaism*, by assuming that the Mishnah and Tosefta are earlier sources than the Sifra, Sifres, and Mechilta. My argument, however, does not rise or fall on the issue of historical development. If the Mishnah and Tosefta do not represent the earliest sources, then the reason the *qal va homer emerged* and flourished is that from the outset of the rabbinic enterprise the rabbis understood their role as interpreters to include revealing the perfection of Scripture.

41. Instances in which the *qal va homer* serves to support a new ruling include Peah 6:6, M.S. 3:10, Pes. 6:2, 5, Yeb. 8:3, Ned. 10:6-7, Naz. 7:4, B.Q. 2:5, Shebu. 3:6, Eduy. 6:2, Zeb. 8:12, 12:3, Hul. 2:7, Ker. 3:7-10, Neg. 10:9, 13:10, Nid. 4:6, Mahk. 6:8, Yad. 4:7. Those passages in which the *qal va homer* is used to show how Scripture anticipates and rules out a mistaken conclusion are Sotah 6:3, Men. 8:5, Hul. 10:1, Beq. 9:1, Tem. 6:4, Neg. 10:2.

42. MacIntyre, "Understanding Religion," 67-68.

43. Further research is necessary to establish when the *qal va homer* actually disappeared from rabbinic literature. I suspect that it did not remain a valid form of inference in the literature beyond the Talmuds. If so, then the disappearance of the *qal va homer* coincides with the demise of the classical rabbinic myth.

References

Barnes, Barry, and David Bloor.
    1984 "Relativism, Rationalism, and the Sociology of Knowledge." In *Rationality and Relativism*, edited by Martin Hollis and Steven Lukes, 21-47. Cambridge: MIT Press.

Bruner, Jerome, Rose Olver, Patricia M. Greenfield, et al.
    1967 *Studies in Cognitive Growth*. New York: John Wiley & Sons.

Cassirer, Ernst.
    1955 *The Philosophy of Symbolic Forms*. Vol. 2. Translated by Ralph Manheim. New Haven: Yale University Press.

Cole, Michael, John Gay, Joseph Glick, and Donald Sharp.
    1971 *The Cultural Context of Learning and Thinking*. New York: Basic Books.

Cole, Michael, and Sylvia Scribner.
    1974 *Culture and Thought*. New York: John Wiley and Sons.

Douglas, Mary.
    1966 *Purity and Danger*. London: Routledge and Kegan Paul.

Eilberg-Schwartz, Howard.
    1986 *The Human Will in Judaism: The Mishnah's Philosophy of Intention*. Atlanta: Scholars Press.

    1987 "Creation and Classification in Judaism: From Priestly to Rabbinic Conceptions." *History of Religions* 26 (4):357-81.

    1987 "When the Reader is in the Write: A Review Essay of José Faur's Golden Doves with Silver Dots." *Prooftexts* 7 (2):194-208.

    1988 "Who's Kidding Whom?: A Serious Reading of Rabbinic Word-plays." *Journal for the American Academy of Religion* 56 (1):501-23.

1990 *The Savage in Judaism: An Anthropology of Israelite Religion and Ancient Judaism*. Bloomington: Indiana University Press.

Evans-Pritchard, E. E.
1976 *Witchcraft, Oracles and Magic Among the Azande*. Abridged Edition. Oxford: Clarendon Press.

Fernandez, James.
1986 *Persuasions and Performances: The Play of Tropes in Culture*. Bloomington: Indiana University Press.

Feyerabend, Paul K.
1962 *Knowledge Without Foundations*. Oberlin: Oberlin Publishing Company.

Frankfort, Henri, H. A. Frankfort, John Wilson, and Thorkild Jacobsen
1946 *Before Philosophy: The Intellectual Adventure of Ancient Man*. Baltimore: Penguin Books.

Goody, Jack.
1977 *The Domestication of the Savage Mind*. Cambridge: Cambridge University Press.

Halivni, David Weiss.
1986 *Midrash, Mishnah, and Gemara: The Jewish Penchant for Justified Law*. Cambridge: Harvard University Press.

Hallpike, C. R.
1979 *The Foundations of Primitive Thought*. Oxford: Clarendon Press.

Handelman, Susan.
1982 *The Slayers of Moses: The Emergence of Rabbinic Interpretation in Modern Literary Theory*. Albany: State University of New York Press.

Hertzberg, Lars.
1980 "Winch on Social Interpretation." *Philosophy of Social Science* 10:151-71.

Hesse, Mary.
1966 *Models and Analogies in Science*. South Bend: University of Notre Dame Press.

Hollis, Martin.
1970a "The Limits of Irrationality." In *Rationality*, edited by Bryan Wilson, 214-20. Oxford: Basil Blackwell.

1970b "Reason and Ritual." In *Rationality*, edited by Bryan Wilson, 221-39. Oxford: Basil Blackwell.

1972 "Witchcraft and Winchcraft." *Philosophy of Social Science* 2:89-103.

1984 "The Social Destruction of Reality." In *Rationality and Relativism*, edited by Martin Hollis and Steven Lukes, 67-87. Cambridge: MIT Press.

Horton, Robin.
1970 "African Thought and Western Science." In *Rationality*, edited by Bryan Wilson, 131-71. Oxford: Basil Blackwell.

1977 "Traditional Thought and the Emerging African Philosophy Department: A Comment on the Current Debate." *Second Order* 6 (1): 64-79.

1984 "Tradition and Modernity Revisited." In *Rationality and Relativism*, edited by Martin Hollis and Steven Lukes, 201-60. Cambridge: MIT Press.

Hutchins, Edwin.
1980 *Culture and Inference: A Trobriand Case Study*. Cambridge: Harvard University Press.

Jacobs, Louis.
1961 *Studies in Talmudic Logic and Methodology*. London: Vallentine, Mitchell.

Kuhn, Thomas.
1970 *The Structure of Scientific Revolutions* Second Edition. Chicago: The University of Chicago Press.

Kunst, Arnold.
1942 "An Overlooked Type of Inference." *Bulletin of the School of Oriental and African Studies* 10 (4):976-91.

Leach, Edmund.
1979 *Political Systems of Highland Burma*. London: The Atholone Press.

Lévy-Bruhl, Lucien.
1985 [1910] *How Natives Think*. Translated by Lilian A. Clare. Princeton: Princeton University Press.

Lieberman, Saul.
1950 *Hellenism in Jewish Palestine*. New York: The Jewish Theological Seminary of America.

Lukes, Steven.
1970 "Some Problems About Rationality." In *Rationality*, edited by Bryan Wilson, 194-213. Oxford: Basil Blackwell.

1984 "Relativism in Its Place." In *Rationality and Relativism*, edited by Martin Hollis and Steven Lukes, 261-305. Cambridge: MIT Press.

Luria, A. R.
1976 *Cognitive Development: Its Cultural and Social Foundations.* Translated by Martin Lopez-Morillas and Lynn Solotarof. Cambridge: Harvard University Press.

MacIntyre, Alasdair.
1970 "Is Understanding Religion Compatible with Believing?" In *Rationality*, edited by Bryan Wilson, 62-77. Oxford: Basil Blackwell.

Mielziner, Moses.
1968 *Introduction to the Talmud.* New York: Block Publishing Company.

Neusner, Jacob.
1975 *A History of the Mishnaic Law of Purities.* Part 7, *Negaim, Sifra.* Leiden: E. J. Brill.

1980 *Form-Analysis and Exegesis: A Fresh Approach to the Interpretation of the Mishnah.* Minneapolis: University of Minnesota Press.

1981 *Judaism: The Evidence of the Mishnah.* Chicago: The University of Chicago Press.

1986 *The Oral Torah: The Sacred Books of Judaism.* Harper and Row: San Francisco.

Newton-Smith, W.
1984 "Relativism and the Possibility of Interpretation." In *Rationality and Relativism*, edited by Martin Hollis and Steven Lukes, 106-22. Cambridge: MIT Press.

Popper, Karl.
1965 *Conjectures and Refutations.* New York: Basic Books.

Schwarz, Adolf.
1901 *Der hermeneutische syllogismus in der talmudischen litterature.* Karlsruhe.

Tylor, Edward.
    1871 *Primitive Culture: Researches into the Development of Mythology, Philosophy, Religion, Language, Art and Custom*. London: J. Murray.

Walsh, W. H.
    1976 "The Constancy of Human Nature." In *Contemporary British Philosophy*, edited by H. D. Lewis, 274-91. London: George Allen & Unwin.

White, Hayden.
    1978 *Tropics of Discourse*. Baltimore: The Johns Hopkins University Press.

Winch, Peter.
    1958 *The Idea of a Social Science and Its Relation to Philosophy*. London: Routledge and Kegan Paul.

Chapter 10

Vedānta, Commentary, and the Theological Component of Cross-Cultural Study

Francis X. Clooney S. J.

It is difficult enough to study the rituals or myths or philosophy of a culture other than one's own.[1] There are special additional difficulties in studying a system of thought such as India's Vedānta, which includes not only such complex data but also particular, nuanced attitudes about that data. Moreover, the initial problem one has to confront in studying Vedānta is to discover what those attitudes are: whichever text one may pick up, one finds oneself *in media res*, stumbling in on a conversation which began long before one's arrival and in which strong opinions are expressed. Vedānta is like a conversation in which a number of people are speaking at once and often from opposing positions and opposite corners of the room; they come and go, and continue to speak even while out of the room—and occasionally in languages unknown to their conversation partners. As is often the case in such matters, much of what is important is left unsaid. One doesn't hear what one expects to hear, and instead hears what sounds like a lot of noise.

If one chooses, as I have, to begin reading *Uttara Mīmāṃsā Sūtra Bhāṣya* of the early eighth-century thinker, Śaṅkara,[2] and so to listen in on the Advaita, or Non-Dualist, Vedānta's[3] conversation, it is necessary to look not only at that *Bhāṣya*, or commentary, but also to the text Śaṅkara is commenting on, the *Uttara Mīmāṁsā Sūtra* [henceforth *UMS*] of Bādarāyaṇa (from the fourth to fifth centuries). These four hundred-plus aphorisms themselves were composed with the intention of organizing and legitimating the views of the old upaniṣads on cosmology, anthropology, and soteriology; the upaniṣads themselves, of course, were composed in continuity with and distinction from the even older brāhmanas and Vedic hymns and take deliberate stances toward that material.

But the situation is even more complex: as a Vedāntin, Śaṅkara inherits the vastly complex world view of the Mīmāṁsā, that older system of ritual thinking and exegesis which, centuries before Bādarāyaṇa, beginning with the *Pūrva Mīmāṁsā Sūtras* of Jaimini [second century BC], had reorganized and rethought the Vedic hymns and rubrical texts and rites in order to defend as rationally plausible a ritually defined yet dharmic universe. Although not simply a Mīmāṁsaka of the ritual school, Śaṅkara is nevertheless (at least) '75%' one, a true "Later [Uttara] Mīmāṁsaka." One cannot understand his methods or his questions without looking into the Mīmāṁsā, its projects, and his developments of them.

To go further: Śaṅkara's is the first and dominant commentary on Bādarāyaṇa's text, but it is soon surrounded by the texts of competing schools of thought which in varying degrees diverge from his views. Bhāskara (late eighth century), Rāmānuja (eleventh), and Madhva (thirteenth), to name but a few major figures, read and interpret the classic texts differently, arguing the legitimacy of their views in preference to his. Although later than Śaṅkara, they may draw on interpretations older than his; in some cases they may simply read the texts better. Moreover, new extratextual forms of religiosity and non-Sanskritic materials were always important factors affecting the way the older texts were read by the newer schools of Vedānta.[4] Finally, each of these commentators' positions are further elaborated in subcommentaries and sub-subcommentaries which clarify and refine the issues involved while at the same time introducing new issues and concerns. They continually propose refinements of interpretation which we must take into account in attempting to fix the meaning of the texts.

The Centrality of Canon and Commentary in Vedānta

To read Śaṅkara is thus to become intricately involved in the whole, wider context. Just as an anthropologist might seek to understand a native informant's data through understanding the whole village in which he or she lives, a reader of Vedānta must become involved in the texts, taking sides and making judgments, asking questions, respecting silences, and understanding unasked-for answers. While the arduous task of interpretation applies to all kinds of texts, its difficulty is accentuated by the commentatorial agenda, where interpretation is a conscious issue, and handled according to defined rules. For Śaṅkara's Mīmāṁsā-Vedānta tradition is consciously exegetical, engaged primarily in explicating and defending its canon of texts—for the Mīmāṁsakas, the Vedic *mantras* and *brāhmaṇas;* and for the Vedānta , the upaniṣads. As evidenced centuries earlier in the *Sūtras* of Jaimini, the texts are used to identify and arrange the world of ordinary experience—the *loka*—as the religiously significant world of *dharma*, the *vaidika* realm.[5] Although he differs with the Mīmāṁsakas on a number of issues, Śaṅkara agrees that the received texts define the horizon within which the elements of religion and culture are to be understood. With a skill and ease which may at first seem capricious, he is able to use, reuse, introduce, drop, and then reintroduce all kinds of artifacts from religious discourse. There is a "surrender" to the text at the core of all this; his method makes sense in terms of this surrender. Moreover, this encompassment of myth, philosophy, and praxis by Scripture and commentary provides us with the formal key to his intellectual project. Discovering how he thinks from within the texts is also more basic, I believe, than a piecemeal consideration of the individual cases of his philosophical acumen or theory of language or his readings of particular upaniṣadic texts. We may of course select out the various elements and "reconstruct" them, but this is a new project, ours and not Śaṅkara's.

It is my suggestion that while various approaches to the Vedānta are valid, it is best to begin by focusing on its canon-making/commentatorial nature: Vedānta is a system of thought which presupposes and builds on the fact of a *canon*, a consciously limited and defined corpus of inspired texts, and takes a commentatorial attitude toward that limited body of material; it sees the world through that consciously limited textual frame and interprets all other human and religious data—reason, argument and philosophy, symbol, myth and cosmology—as elements encompassed and included by that larger frame of the canon. To see Vedānta as a tradition of text and commentary is to gain a central insight into the whole Vedāntic enterprise. How do we begin to explore it in this way? Help is available from many sources, of which two are particularly pertinent.

Recent work by Jonathan Z. Smith and George Lindbeck can help us in this regard. Smith has recently made pertinent and programmatic comments on the general issue of canon and commentary, particularly in his essay entitled "Sacred Persistence."[6] He urges his colleagues in religious studies to take seriously the theological phenomenon of canon as well as the implied succession of *exegetes or commentators* whose charge is constantly to reexplain the world in terms of that canon of normative texts. He suggests that "the radical and arbitrary reduction represented by the notion of canon and the ingenuity represented by the rule-governed exegetical enterprise of applying the canon to every dimension of human life is that most characteristic, persistent, and obsessive religious activity" (Smith, 1982, 43). In my view, a large part of the Vedānta project is to be characteristically defined as a defense of a "radical and arbitrary reduction" of the world to a Vedic world.

George Lindbeck's *The Nature of Doctrine* contributes to the same line of thinking from another angle. The book is on the whole a relevant and perhaps unexpected ally in consideration of comparative study, presenting as it does a coherent and useful cultural-linguistic model for "post-liberal" theology, a model that could also have significant ramifications for a comparative study of texts. Lindbeck develops what he terms the "cultural-linguistic model," in which theology learns from disciplines involved in the study of religion: "It has become customary in a considerable body of anthropological, sociological, and philosophical literature . . . to emphasize neither the cognitive nor the experiential-expressive aspects of religion; rather, emphasis is placed on those respects in which religions resemble languages together with their correlative forms of life and are thus similar to cultures. . . . This general way of conceptualizing religion will be called in what follows a 'cultural-linguistic' approach, and the implied view of church doctrine will be referred to as a 'regulative' or 'rule' theory" (Lindbeck, 1984, 17-18).

He likewise calls for an "intratextual" approach to understanding religion, in which meaning is immanent: "Meaning is constituted by the uses of a specific language rather than being distinguishable from it. Thus the proper way to determine what 'God' signifies, for example, is by examining how the word operates within a religion and thereby shapes reality and experience rather than by first establishing its propositional or experiential meaning and reinterpreting or reformulating its uses accordingly. It is in this sense that theological description in the cultural-linguistic mode is intrasemiotic or intratextual" (114). As we shall see, this approach conforms nicely to the data we receive in study-ing an exegetical, commentatorial tradition such as the Vedānta .

Lindbeck stresses the importance of the *canon* as a key tool by which a community creates its own identity and positions the world in relation to itself and makes coherent an ongoing exegetical task. To quote him again: "For those who are steeped in [the canonical writings] no world is more real than the ones they create. A scriptural world is thus able to absorb the universe. It supplies the interpretive framework within which believers seek to live their lives and under-stand reality. . . . Traditional exegetical procedures assume that Scripture creates its own domain of meaning and that the interpreta-tion is to extend this over the whole of reality" [117]. To understand Śaṅkara is to understand a prolonged effort to explain and defend a textually framed world view.

Three Key Aspects of the Vedāntic View of Scripture

It is not possible here to enter into a detailed analysis of Śaṅkara's exegetical methods, their underlying world view, and the effects of both on his Vedānta , although this project remains a priority[7] However, the kinds of choices and advantages involved in developing a text-centered and commentary-centered approach to the study of Vedānta can be indicated in a preliminary fashion by attention to three important aspects of the exegetical attitude governing Śaṅkara's work.

First, there is what might be called "the principle of convergence": the Veda is neither fragmentary nor self-contradictory; it can and must be read as a single "intratextual" whole. To be sure, Vedic statements are subject to refined and delicate differentiations in genre and purpose, but nevertheless these parts converge when properly understood and con-tribute to one overall meaning.[8] The Vedāntic position in this regard is of course in large part traceable back to the older *Pūrva Mīmāṃsā Sūtras*, where rules were already articulated to show that the disparate information—scientific, mythological, philosophical, etc.—and layers of traditions annexed to older texts do not detract from the unity of Scripture's message but rather contribute to it in various ways.

Thus, for example, the *Mīmāṃsā* notion of the *arthavāda* was developed with this concern for Scriptural unity as a major concern, as a strategy for including and delimiting the multiplicity of statements of all kinds which are apparent in the Vedic hymns—statements which are by no means all obviously contributory to the regularized performance of the rites. According to this theory, statements found in Scripture are never merely a neutral presentation of information; when read properly, all such statements contribute rhetorically to the formation of a "climate" in which rituals will be confidently and energetically performed.

This control of the material can be accomplished, of course, only at the cost of rereading apparently informational texts which reach in other directions. Even when the Vedānta argues vigorously for the validity of knowledge which is not oriented to action[9]—particularly the knowledge of *brahman*—the basic notion that knowledge can be packaged is accepted. But *arthavāda* in any case affords the Vedāntin a way to handle—and to a large extent ignore—the mythology woven into Vedic accounts.

Second, in Vedānta (but not in Mīmāṁsā)[10] Scripture reliably informs us of supermundane realities, knowledge of which is relevant to our salvation. It gives us valid and useful information about the spiritual framework of our world, those aspects of "reality" which are not knowable through the senses and reason—information we can confidently act on when seeking freedom from the world. Not only are soteriology and cosmology connected; both are connected with the proper exegesis which alone assures us the proper viewpoint. This recognition of the soteriological importance of discerning the right ramifications of a right reading of the texts helps explain Śaṅkara's painstaking insistence on the finest details of Scriptural harmonization.

I wish now to offer an example which illustrates both of these first two points, the convergence of meaning in the Veda, and the Veda's soteriocentric informative function. In *UMS* 3.2 Śaṅkara carefully collates and harmonizes the accounts in the *Chāndogya* (5.3-10) and *Bṛhadāraṇyaka*(6.2) Upaniṣads of the journey of the soul of the deceased. The two upaniṣads are in substantial agreement that there are two paths the soul may take at death: either the path of good works, which leads the sacrificer to the moon, whence he gradually returns to the earth and rebirth; or the path of light, by which the knower of *brahman* goes beyond the moon to *brahman* and does not return.[11] The path to the moon is discussed in detail in *UMS* 3.1, while the other is treated more briefly in 4.3 My concern here is the first of these, since it is here that we are afforded a pertinent insight into the exegetical mentality.

The agreed-upon account of the path is summarized as follows in *UMS* 3.1:

> upon leaving the body of the deceased, the soul proceeds upward enveloped in the water of oblations [3.1.1-6]; the souls reaching the moon are not eaten by the gods, despite apparent textual evi-

dence to that effect [3.1.7; this is also discussed in 1.2.9-10]; when the souls have used up their good works and leave the moon, there remains nevertheless a sufficient residue of those deeds to direct them to an appropriate rebirth [3.1.8-11]; evil men, those who do not sacrifice, do not go to the moon, but are reborn immediately as insects, etc. [3.1.12-21]; souls descending from the moon become in turn joined with ether, air, smoke, mist, cloud and rain, are born as "rice and corn, herbs and trees, sesamum and beans," and finally, when this food is eaten, are born in animal or human form through the eater [3.1.22-27].

Śaṅkara smooths out the details of the two accounts without questioning the reality of this journeying. Notwithstanding his general comments elsewhere regarding the difference between "ultimate" and "everyday" realities, this exegetical care in establishing the reality of the path is to be expected because, first of all, he is concerned with the harmony and coherence of Scripture. If the details of the path seem contradictory and do not inspire confidence, three possibilities present themselves: a. the Veda itself is a confusing and unreliable source for information about what is to be known; b. there is no "real" path—it is simply a fictional, textual reality with no extratextual reference and may take on different forms in different texts; or c. the reader who perceives the contradictions has not yet properly read the text and must now delve deeper. Only the third possibility is acceptable—the first denigrates the text, while the second undercuts the possibility of sure, salvific knowledge and ultimately renders the texts unreliable and therefore useless. The Vedāntins are thus challenged to show that they do understand the purport of what is being said and that they can discover, beyond apparent differences, a harmony which will be evident to the skilled reader. This Śaṅkara does, disposing of each apparent difference, one by one.

In introducing the topic in *UMS* 3.1.1 Śaṅkara explains why *this particular* harmonization is soteriologically important. He says, "In this first chapter [*pāda*] the journey through *saṃsāra* is delineated based on the 'meditation on the five fires' (Chāndogya 5.3-10), to bring about desirelessness; as it says, 'Therefore let him turn away [*jugupseta*] from it' (5.10.8)." Awareness of the temporariness of the pleasures resultant upon actions and the inevitability of return to this world—over and over again—will lead to disenchantment with the world and the old economy of salvation. The knowing person, who has mastered the Veda and therefore has a reliable account of what lies beyond ordinary experience, will objectively assess the limited, ultimately unsatisfying value of the after-death journey and will then want to look for something else, higher and more permanent. He will turn to meditation, using other texts—the "higher" parts of the upaniṣads—for which he is now ready. Because Scripture is reliable and can be exegetically shown to be consistent, one can be guided by it to salvation; here, its true report arouses that aversion which is the beginning of interest in salvation. The mythic framework is used in a controlled fashion, and probably for a purpose more limited than originally intended.[12]

The third tenet of Śaṅkara's commentatorial attitude which I wish to note leads us directly back to my initial remarks about Vedānta's "canon-centered" thinking: for Śaṅkara all aspects of religious experience and thinking about religion are encompassed by Scripture, support it, neither contradicting it nor being contradicted by it. The claim is audacious and needs to be carefully handled if it is to accomplish what the exegete hopes for without becoming improbable or contrary to experience. Scripture cannot be thought to ignore, or leave unaccounted for, any aspect of experience; but neither can an exegete allow Scripture to be dominated by reason or any other extra-Scriptural sources of value. Nor can the exegete entertain the more subtly destructive view that inner experience, reason, and Scripture are several merely juxtaposed domains of discourse and authority. As Lindbeck suggests regarding exegetical theology in general, the exegete is inevitably caught in the tension between trying to describe the world comprehensively in Scriptural terms and falling into the trap of allowing "the extra-biblical materials inserted into the biblical universe" to become "the basic framework of interpretation" (Lindbeck, 118).

The subordination of the world's intelligibility to the Veda is a hierarchically accomplished subordination, and Louis Dumont's description of hierarchy as "the encompassing of the contrary" (Dumont, 1979, 239) is helpful for understanding how everything fits into a Scriptural wo .d view: myth, reason, philosophy, ritual, law, etc., are all among the comple/nentary, included genres of discourse (242) placed within the er :or ,passing domain of the Scripturally structured universe.[13] The follc · ng observations of Dumont are especially pertinent: "At the superior level there is unity; at the inferior level there is distinction, there is . . . complementariness or contradiction. Hierarchy consists in the combination of these two propositions concerning different levels. In hierarchy thus defined, complementariness or contradiction is contained in a unity of superior order. But as soon as we intermingle the two levels, we have a logical scandal, because there is identity and contradiction at the same time" (242).[14]

Scripture's viewpoint constitutes the superior order here, and the domains of reason, mythology, popular religiosity, etc., are included as defined areas within that larger whole. Only if we understand this kind of inclusive encompassment—a Scriptural hierarchization which Śaṅkara accepts—can we make sense of the ways in which Śaṅkara so easily shifts in and out of argument by reason alone, refers to cosmologies and symbols and then seems to abandon them, etc.

The earlier discussed treatment of the upaniṣadic cosmology in the Vedānta is one example of hierarchical encompassment by the text; the older cosmology is preserved intact, but preserved primarily to encourage disenchantment with the world. I wish to sketch the main lines of a further and more important example, pertaining to the role reason plays in Śaṅkara's *Bhāṣya*. As one more included element, reason cannot fully make sense of Scripture's claims and inevitably tries to encompass Scripture, reducing it to something more "rational." Śaṅkara resists this.[15] For him, reason is a servant, carefully disciplined, who is invited into the discussion for certain purposes and subsequently invited to leave again. It is not contradicted by Scripture, nor does it contradict it, but neither can it fully understand and appreciate all that Scripture tells us.

The proper place to begin an inquiry into the properly Vedāntic meanings of "Scriptural reasoning" and "mere reasoning," is with an apparent detour into the systems of rules worked out in the grammatical and ritual schools (in the *śrauta sūtras* and then in the *Pūrva Mīmāṃsā Sūtras*) in order to examine their distinctive "rule-based, legal-reasoning" normativity. To sketch just a few aspects of what will have to be done more fully elsewhere: in the grammatical and ritual schools extremely careful attention was paid to the relationship between rules and the multiplicity of cases on the one hand, and among the rules themselves on the other. The grammarians' articulation of the boundaries of a rule's domain offers us a model for the "logic" of hierarchical, encompassing thinking, a kind of logic that is alternative to a more deductive, "scientific" model of reason.

For example, the exposition of grammatical *paribhāṣās* ("meta-rules") near the beginning of the *Siddhānta Kaumudī*, a medieval grammatical treatise, can be profitably explored when calculating how different kinds of truth claims, rules about morality, etc. are thought to have limited one another in traditional India.[16] One key *paribhāṣā—paranityāntaraṅgā-pavādānām uttaram balīyaḥ*—identifies in sequence four kinds of rule relationships, four kinds of precedence. To render its sense in shorthand form: 1. when rules which are applicable nevertheless seem to contradict one another in the course of the formation of proper grammatical forms, those of the contradicting rules which occur later [*para*] in the text of Pāṇini's grammar take precedence over those occurring earlier in the text [*pūrva*]; 2. *nitya* rules, which always apply when applicable, whether or not other rules are applied, take precedence over other [*anitya*] rules, the application of which does depend in part on how other rules are applied; 3. an *antaraṅga* rule, which applies within a domain more comprehensively covered by another, *bahiraṅga*, rule, is applied before that other rule; 4. an *apavāda* rule specifically makes an exception to another rule and always takes precedence over that rule to which it makes the exception. The less powerful, superseded, and temporarily suspended rule does not cease to be true, nor need it fail to apply elsewhere. So too, I suggest, reason and the other sources of knowledge and guides to behavior which are encompassed by Scripture remain valid within smaller realms of authority. The "logic" of systems such as grammar and Vedānta features such encompassing-encompassed rules, while ordinary inductive and deductive reasoning are included discourses within such larger wholes.

The Mīmāṁsakas are the most thorough of the ritualists in proposing comprehensive rules to guide performance and interpretation; like the grammarians, they calculate the force of various means of knowing in relation to one another. Thus, in *PMS* 3.3.14 Jaimini calculates the authority of six kinds of appeal to textual authority: literal meaning [*śruti*], inferred meaning [*anumāna*], the sense of a passage [*vākya*], coherence of a context [*prakaraṇa*], location within a text [*sthāna*], and names [*nāma*]; it arranges and qualifies their authority using the spatial metaphor of "distance" from some explicit meaning within the text, each of the six being more authoritative—because closer to the literal [*pratyakṣa*] meaning than the one following it. Or, in *PMS* 6.5.54, Jaimini cites the (probably earlier) grammatical rule (cited in Pāṇini as rule 1.4.2) that "what occurs later takes precedence over what occurs earlier." In Jaimini, it refers both to actual sequences of activities in a ritual performance and to moments in the more abstract process by which ectypal rites are understood to be derived from archetypal ones—they are "later" than the model, archetypal rites because derivative, even if not in fact, of later historical derivation.[17] Such Mīmāṁsā rules are directly taken up by Vedānta and often used by Śaṅkara and his school; they too provide part of the frame through which the legitimate role of reason is defined and delimited.

From attention to such grammatical and ritual rules one can profitably move more directly to a consideration of the "logic" of Vedāntic reasoning as drawing on grammatical and ritual sources as well as the meditational texts of the upaniṣads. One can examine, for instance, how an apparently static division such as that between the "higher" [pāramārthika] and the "everyday" [vyāvahārika] levels of experience in fact describes not so much a "real" and an "unreal" realm, but two levels of descriptive comprehensiveness within a single overall explanation of the world: the "everyday" is not a mirage, but an encompassed and—within its domain—legitimate view of what the world is.

But the comprehensive issue of the relation of grammatical, Mīmāṁsā, and Vedānta rules is an area too complex and still too uncharted to be further explored here; I wish instead to jump a bit ahead and sketch a few details of how the encompassment of reason itself is exemplified in Śaṅkara's *UMS Bhāṣya*; and within this also too-large subject, to see how philosophical argumentation is used without being allowed to set the agenda for the whole interpretive project.

Examples abound in the *UMS* of carefully introduced and carefully controlled arguments based on reason alone—arguments valid and usable within defined spheres, but not allowed to set the Vedānta agenda. For example: in *UMS* 3.3.53-4, Śaṅkara proves the existence of a self distinct from the body—which is not declared in the Veda precisely since it is otherwise provable—by appeals to the nature of consciousness itself. Scripture merely presupposes the existence of the self—the purposefulness of Vedic activity depends on it—but it is appropriate at some point[18] for the *UMS* to show us why we should accept the self presupposed by the Veda. Śaṅkara generalizes, putting it this way: "At present we will prove the existence of a Self different from the body in order to establish thereby the qualification [of the self] for bondage and release. For if there were no Self different from the body, there would be no room for injunctions that have the other world for their result; nor could it be taught of anybody that Brahman is his Self."[19]

The proof of the self is simple enough. Śaṅkara first poses the argument of the materialists that the alleged self is nothing but a combination of the elements which make up the body. Since there is no evidence of this self as being anywhere but in the body, it is simplest to assume that it has no separable reality. Śaṅkara's response may be summarized as follows: 1. While it is true that the qualities of consciousness, etc., do appear in the body, it is also true that the body is seen without these qualities, as when for example the person has died. Hence they cannot be identical with it. 2. The body is seen to decay, but not those spiritual qualities. Hence they are not totally dependent on the body. 3. If, as the materialists say, consciousness is the consciousness of the bodily elements, this fact itself proves that it cannot be identical with those same elements. It stands over against them as it thinks about them; since they constitute the body, the self must also be distinct from the body and therefore not entirely dependent on the fate of the body's components. 4. The perception of objects in dreams suggests that the soul is not totally dependent on the body even for perception.

Although the proof as such may be liable to various criticisms, as is any proof, it undeniably merits serious consideration; but what is of interest to me here is Śaṅkara's use of the proof, its "location." First, Śaṅkara has made it clear elsewhere in his commentary that it is not the purpose of *śruti* (the Veda or "sacred Scripture" which is the proper object of Vedānta) to offer philosophical arguments in defense of the self, etc.; reason is quite adequate to the task, which therefore may be left to it; the Veda has no need to enter the discussion directly.[20] What the Veda says may of course have to be defended, particularly regarding its relationship to ordinary experience, since incorrect reasoning and wrong understandings of our experience may lead to conclusions opposed to the Veda or placing the Veda in doubt; but such auxiliary thinking can only confirm the Veda, not supersede or alter it.

The background for Śaṅkara's understanding of the role of argument again lies in the *Pūrva Mīmāṁsā*, where the operative distinction between perception and the Veda, ordinary and Scripturally communicated experience, had been established long before Śaṅkara's time. Jaimini's Mīmāṁsā distinguishes between the *laukika*, that realm of ordinary experience accessible to the senses, and the *vaidika*, that realm of experience accessible through the Veda alone. These "realms" however are not separate "places," since the *vaidika* world for Jaimini is made up entirely of ordinary things: it is the *arrangement* of ordinary things which makes up that which is available only through the Veda. Thus, we do not need the Veda to tell us that there are human beings, rice, fires, and words, and there are no exotic beings mentioned in the Veda which cannot—in theory at least—be found outside it. The Veda rather tells us to arrange them in a certain fashion, and that this special arrangement will constitute a sacrifice efficacious of desired results.

Against this Mīmāṁsā background Śaṅkara's position on philosophy and its arguments can be summarized as follows: The Veda need not be relied on to tell us that there is a self, nor how one is to argue in favor of the self, etc. Such are elements of *laukika* experience, even if arduous thinking is required to clarify just what our experience is. The Veda makes them *vaidika* by telling us what to do with them, where to place them: as we have seen the aversion provoked by the Veda's analysis of the trip to the moon suggests that we transform the human self into the meditating self. The meditations described in the Veda in turn invite the use of reasoning to defend the spiritual nature of the self.

To approach the issue from another perspective: if reason can be subordinated, the dominant position of Scripture can also be used to denigrate a priori other systems, simply by describing them as based on *mere* reason. Thus, in *UMS* 2.2 Śaṅkara refutes in series the view of a set of opponents who do not share the Vedānta's acceptance of the authority of the Veda. These refutations proceed on purely rational grounds, since reason is the only tool available to use in discussion with them. Sāṃkhya, Vaiśeṣika, Buddhist [in three schools], Jaina, Śaiva, and Vaiṣṇava [*pañcarātra*] positions are refuted in succession, in order to show that there are no extra-Scriptural grounds which would make us doubt Scripture.

While *UMS* 2.2 contains much fine argumentation,[21] we may still want to ask about the effect of the Vedānta's hierarchical submission of cosmology, myth, and philosophy, etc., to Scripture's boundaries. When the commentator-theologian reads the world through a Scriptural lens, he or she opts for a particular kind of distortion that is not compensated for merely by subsequent honest, rigorous argument, etc. Thus, for example, when the Vedānta places Buddhists of all sorts among those who argue from reason alone—i.e., rejecting the Vedas—Śaṅkara is of course correct in noting their rejection of the Veda as a means of true knowledge. But he is on more dangerous ground, I think, in equating his notion of reason—a limited tool, encompassed by Scripture—with reason as articulated in a non-Vedic universe: the latter, which simply does not presuppose a Scripture, need not appear so deficient and non-spiritual when it is discovered to operate without such a Scripture. Certainly a Buddhist is not likely to hold that the Buddha's teaching on dependent co-origination, for instance, was the product of mere reasoning; while the Buddhist might agree that there is such an activity as "mere reasoning," he or she would also contend that there is also a reason informed by higher spiritual values—and that the latter reasoning is neither oriented to the Veda nor otherwise deficient. To hold that it had to be thus oriented was of course a Vedānta's prejudgment of the limitations of Buddhism—even before the argument could be begun.[22]

In any case: if we do not share Śaṅkara's Scripturally defined hierarchical world view, we may of course disagree with him; we may disagree with his definition of the role of reason and may take exception to this or that argument he proposes. But if we overlook or discount the importance of the fact that he is subordinating reason to a canon of texts, we will probably miss Śaṅkara's characteristic and distinctive positions again and again. A selective reading of Śaṅkara, if the selection is consciously made, may be justified as a project a modern scholar is interested in; but insofar as we distance ourselves from Śaṅkara the exegete we get further and further away from a full understanding of *him*.

The Attainment of Skill in Vedānta

A different question has now to be faced: once we are willing to take seriously Śaṅkara's exegetical thinking—even if in some respects it goes against the grain of modern scholarship—how do we "enter" his world, getting beyond merely respecting it on the one hand, or replacing it with a modern "improvement" on the other? Can we learn to think as he does, if we are not orthodox Hindus and do not accept the authority of the Veda? Lindbeck is again helpful here. In the course of questioning the possibility of identifying universal norms of reasonableness, he remarks that the issue is not whether such exist, "but whether these can be formulated in some neutral, framework-independent language. Increasing awareness of how standards of rationality vary from field to field and age to age makes the discovery of such a language more and more unlikely and the possibility of foundational disciplines doubtful" (Lindbeck 130). Rejecting likewise the easy alternative of relativism, he goes on to suggest that "reasonableness in religion and theology, as in other domains, has something of that aesthetic character, that quality of unformalizable skill, which we usually associate with the artist or the linguistically competent. . . . In short, intelligibility comes from skill, not theory, and credibility comes from good performance, not adherence to independently formulated criteria" (130-1).

"Skill" is the operative word here, suggestive of the kind of learning that is necessary. For one thing, it catches something of the pedagogical purpose of the Mīmāṁsā and Vedānta systems. The apparent redundancy and complexity of the *sūtra* texts of the two schools testify to their refusal to settle for a few general rules or principles; as the seventeenth-century *Mīmāṁsā Nyāya Prakāśā* shows, even the later manuals of *Mīmāṁsā* never succeed in getting down to exceptionless rules. Both schools insist that through a slow, plodding consideration of a series of ritual cases (in the *Mīmāṁsā*) and upaniṣadic texts (in the Vedānta), one is trained to think and read in a certain fashion, "exegetically," as a *Mīmāṁsaka*. Much as a good legal education includes not only the mastery of the laws, but also of cases argued in the courts, the patient student of the Veda is trained gradually to find in every text and ritual action the underlying *artha*—meaning of words and the purpose of actions—catching it in the flow of the words and "between the lines." That mastery of the rules and their right application, and not just the right answers, is the goal.

The Western scholar who studies these systems necessarily comes with his or her own rules and linguistic and conceptual patterns and agenda, but will also have to become familiar with, and to some extent accept at least tentatively the "local customs," in order to be able to converse with Śaṅkara. He or she will have to be patient with the case method of learning, and will have to master gradually the specific ways of asking questions and connecting data.

The Modern Scholar and Sanskrit Learning

One large question pertains to skill in Sanskrit. Even if we bracket the problem of the reliability of translations and the question of the extent to which any text can be understood in translation, there are still other grounds on which a knowledge of Sanskrit and Sanskrit grammar will help the scholar to *think* in a way more closely akin to Śaṅkara's way of thinking. Edwin Gerow's essay on the grammatical notion of *karma* comes to mind as the best recent example of how the apparently arcane knowledge of Pāṇinian grammar can shed light on broader philosophical and cultural issues. In the final section of his explanation of the meanings of the word *karma* in various Indian systems of thought, Gerow connects the grammatical, Advaita Vedānta and Buddhist understandings of *karma* and concludes that "the notion of karma itself is indeed an inescapable function (and *result*) of the passivization or impersonalization of the Sanskrit sentence" (Gerow, 1982, 112). He shows how Śaṅkara's *advaita* Vedānta articulates meanings of agency and the phenomenal self in a way that conforms to the structure of the Sanskrit language itself. While prudently stopping short of asserting any "behavioral consequence of a grammatical cause," Gerow insists that we can only benefit from exploring the relations between grammar and philosophical theories, "to see in what way their universalizing intellectual structures may illumine each other or shed light on the problems of their formulation" (116).[23]

Learning the peculiarly Indian grammatical-ritual rules which guide the commentators in performing their interpretations is a difficult but rewarding task. It is an acquired skill—and an acquired taste—which can profitably and richly inform how one reads texts; when a system like Vedānta is involved, some familiarity becomes a necessity. To offer but one concrete example, which itself must remain only partially developed here, consider the "fate" of the famous pair of birds described in the *Muṇḍaka Upaniṣad*: "Two birds, friends joined together, clutch the same tree. One of them eats the sweet fruit; the other looks on without eating. On that same tree, the person remains immersed; moaning, he grieves his lack of lordship; when he sees the other, the adored Lord and his glory, his grief departs" (3.1.1-2).[24]

The most common Vedāntic interpretation of the verse is that the birds represent the human person and the higher Self, *brahman*: the human person is immersed in this world, eating the apparently sweet fruits of sense pleasures, etc. The Self, however, looks on as a silent witness, uninvolved, not acting. To turn one's glance toward this Self is to become free and stop looking for pleasures in this world. Śaṅkara in the *UMS Bhāṣya* notes and relies on this sense of the text, both to prove the detached nature of *brahman* in relation to the world (2.3.47; 1.3.7) and to distinguish the lower self, caught in and acting in the world, from the higher, witnessing Self (1.1.4).

But the *Muṇḍaka* text also has another role to play in the *UMS*, when it is placed alongside the following text from the *Kaṭha Upaniṣad*: "The two drinking the truth from what is well-done in this world, the two entered into the cave, the highest, the abode of the supreme" (1.3.1-2). Because this text, like the *Muṇḍaka*, refers to "two," Śaṅkara determines (at 3.3.34) that in fact they legitimately form a single context for meditation and together refer to *brahman* and the human self. This is so, notwithstanding the differences between them, most notably that in the *Muṇḍaka* text one bird is explicitly said to be not eating, while in the *Kaṭha* text both are explicitly said to be drinking. The *Muṇḍaka* is thus allowed to shed a powerful light on the *Kaṭha* text, and affects the way the latter is to be read. This literal contextualization compels the Vedāntins to explore (at 1.2.11) the limits of the meaning of the Sanskrit dual in the *Kaṭha* text—"the two drinking" (*pibantau*)—so as to show that the dual number does not indicate that the indicated pair is alike in all possible ways. I.e., the dual does *not* force us either to exclude *brahman* from the "two"—because it cannot be thought to drink—or to rethink *brahman* as an agent. Hence the *Muṇḍaka* and *Kaṭha* texts can be meditated on together.

One could go further in tracing the "flight" of the *Muṇḍaka* birds, into other commentaries and later texts in the Vedanta tradition[25] and back into an analogous Mīmāṃsā example,[26] but I think the point has been made as to how complex and imbedded in a wider literary context is the full meaning of the *Muṇḍaka* verse. My point is that whatever one's preferences may be in reading the upaniṣads or the Vedānta, it is difficult to claim that one really understands the Vedāntic interpretation of the verse without knowing how and why it is connected with the *Kaṭha* text,

why the discussion of the meaning of the grammatical dual becomes important, etc. One must learn to weave all of this together, in order to understand: one must learn the Vedānta language and enter its "conversation."

This emphasis on learning the language of Vedānta—its content and
rules—can be unexpectedly highlighted by looking at the *pre-upaniṣadic* history of the two birds. For the *Muṇḍaka* verse appeared originally in the *Ṛg
Veda*, at 1.164.20, and as Willard Johnson has shown us,[27] the Ṛg Vedic version of the image most likely presumes the context of a *brahmodya* or "symposium contest" which was a form of debate in which "a [mental] grappling
with verbal formulations evocative of *brahman* . . . peculiar, enigmatic formulations [which] forced them to leave ordinary modes of consciousness to
reach other, enhanced paranormal modes that would permit full visionary
participation in the sacrifice" (Johnson, 1980, 10). In the *brahmodya*, *brahman* is truly *in* the language, not as its object, but as an elusive undertone to
be caught and revealed from the use of language itself. In such a context,
according to Johnson, the image of the birds is really about the *brahmodya*
itself, telling us about the participants themselves: ". . . the initiatory structure of the contest appears all-important. The bird image stresses the active
role of the father or master . . . in the initiatory relationship. Just as the bird
feeds its mate or child, so the master, after participating in the mystery [the
fruit which one bird eats] initiates candidates in the charismatic exchange of
'energy' or 'inspiration' through dialogical exchange" (57).

It seems to me that the Vedānta's exhaustive and exhausting
grammatical and ritual exploration of the Muṇḍaka text can be understood as a grammatically rendered replay of the Vedic *brahmodya*—something of a return to the source, beyond the upaniṣadic passage. The old
brahmodya is gone, and upaniṣadic values have been safely incorporated
into society's larger set of values. By their immersion in the arcane realities of ritual and grammatical thinking, the Vedāntic commentators turn
from the content of language to language's own rules (which are never
separate from ritual's rules) as the locus of language's self-expressing mystery: the play of texts and grammatical forms serves to open up the meaning of the bird image. We should of course not be too quickly enraptured
by the notion of "grammatical/ritual mysticism," and should avoid the
exaggerated notion that the Vedāntins entirely lost interest in content.
Nevertheless it is a great mistake to ignore the play of language and contexts and to extract a text such as the Muṇḍaka from the full range of its
Vedāntic interpretation. If we first attain Vedāntic skill, we can later, as
modern Vedāntins of a sort, enter the field with our own recontextualiza-
tions, selections, etc. To be "Sanskritized" is an aspect of education of the
scholar who would study Vedānta, even if he or she may rightly wish to
think and write in non-Vedāntic discourse as well.

Adhikāra: Who Is Competent to Read These Texts?

Another angle from which to explore the ideal of skill is to attempt a retrieval of the Sanskrit notion of *adhikāra*, as a kind of "reader theory." In its older form in the Mīmāṁsā,[28] *adhikāra* is a notion of appropriateness, the right harmony of a certain element in a certain ritual situation with the other elements in that environment, such that the ritual can go forward. Things, actions, people, and the properties thereof have *adhikāra* and can be "actualized" only in the right convergence of circumstances. The most important application of the term was in identifying persons as having or lacking *adhikāra* for various societal and ritual functions, depending on caste, health, stage of life and ritual initiation, etc. Like everything else, persons are carefully "coded" and integrated into a larger matrix of place and meaning, and socially relevant "marks" such as caste, gender, property, etc., are taken into account.

As is well known, *adhikāra* includes the *an-adhikāra* or non-competence of *śūdras*, women and others to learn the Vedas. Yet even if *adhikāra* cannot be convincingly translated into one or another specific social order, and even if extratextual rationalizations of exclusion linked to *adhikāra* are often repugnant, nevertheless *adhikāra* itself may be legitimately interpreted as the forebear of the modern sensitivity to kinds of readers and readiness for certain kinds of texts. To look at *adhikāra* highlights the kind of preparation necessary to make one skilled in the way Lindbeck has in mind. Not every text is generally and always available for a single manner of scholarly reading, nor is the scholar competent in one area necessarily ready for another. This is a question not just of a certain level of learning, but also of sympathy and ability to understand the "geography" of another culture's intellectual landscape. We need *adhikāra* to study India properly: the well-trained Western comparativist is not necessarily and from the start prepared for the study of all kinds of Indian material. The appropriate convergence of the right kind of reader, right academic discipline, right texts, and right rules for reading must occur before useful understanding can "happen." Otherwise, whichever text is under consideration may remain closed: e.g., the classicist may not be able to understand what a popular ritual drama is all about if he or she ignores anthropological data, while the philosopher who ignores Śaṅkara's status as a commentator may never get beyond a partial, desiccated understanding of Vedānta.

Text, Commentary, and the Rediscovery of Theology

If we are to understand Vedānta we will have to learn a great deal about "canon" and "commentary," including something of how those notions developed in the West; thus, a further qualification for the study of Vedānta is attunement to properly theological discourse. One can usefully consult all kinds of sources—for example, Foucault's remarks on commentary in *The Order of Things* are quite provocative[29]—but nevertheless we will eventually be led back to what in the West we have traditionally called "theology," and will need to be versed in the theological heritage of the West.[30]

The difficulties involved in finding a place for theology may be considerable; beforehand, for instance, certain twists and turns in Europe's history of its academic disciplines will have to be reexamined and reconsidered. Words like "scholastic" and "medieval" may have to be rehabilitated, if only because we are discovering in pre-Enlightenment discourse real allies in cross-cultural understanding. So too, while for various historical and dogmatic reasons historians of religion have generally been eager to distinguish themselves from theologians, and vice versa, and for the most part are not eager to bridge the gap and work together again, efforts at dialogue are necessary.[31] Nevertheless, the effort to "retrieve" theology is worth the trouble, if we are not to reinvent the wheel in learning to read other peoples' ancient texts and commentaries.

Once theology is properly understood and assessed and reincorporated into the larger pattern of the study of religion, it can be fine-tuned as an instrument for cross-cultural work. Smith rightly suggests that with certain modulations the notion of canon can be usefully extended beyond its traditional Christian usage. What is needed now, Smith suggests, are "courses and monographs . . . in both comparative exegesis and comparative theology, comparing not so much conclusions as strategies through which the exegete seeks to interpret and translate his received tradition to his contemporaries."[32]

Although he is right in further suggesting that the historian of religion must abstain from judgments about whether any particular canon is truly revelatory[33]—a Scriptural, all-encompassing world view cannot be judged solely from an outside, historian's perspective—in my view the study of texts by theologians like Śaṅkara does eventually demand of us some consideration of the truth question, in a way that reaches beyond the History of Religions discipline. If canons have stubborn "staying power," and are "durable but flexible tools" which their communities use constantly to reinterpret and reshape their worlds, it is also true that these sacred, canonized texts have an active component too, what might be called a "sacred intrusiveness": they constantly intrude upon and (at least threaten to) reshape the world of the reader, even the "unbelieving" reader, the historian, the scholar. Reading such texts can in some cases rewrite the world in which one reads those texts. To study Vedānta and to work through the upaniṣads with Śaṅkara is to find oneself implicated in the world of those texts, to have one's language enriched with new vocabulary—the common phenomenon of coming to rely on words which resist translation into one's mother tongue—but also complicated with new ways of talking and new rules about right living and the right transformation of reality.[34]

Positively put, this intrusiveness is expressed in the claim that the text indicates the way to salvation. Śaṅkara, in keeping with the pragmatism of his Mīmāṁsā tradition, saw the upaniṣads as soteriocentric and salvific, rendering the world verbal and therefore intelligible, and in the process showing that concordant right action—meditation—leads to salvation. Such assertions are indeed the whole point of the Vedāntic manipulation of myths, symbols, cosmologies, philosophies, and reason. Nor is soteriocentricity unexpected, since the Bible has performed precisely the same function in the Christian tradition.

Today we have no satisfactory scholarly method by which to talk about salvation claims without in effect denying their validity—"I understand what the text is saying but it doesn't apply to me"—and no sufficiently sophisticated way for talking about how texts can be judged as effective or not in shaping views about salvation among those *outside* their original canon-making communities. We have no satisfactory way to talk about—without emasculating them—either Christian evangelization (which is the spreading of the Good News expressed in the text) or the Vedāntic salvific meditation on sacred texts. Nevertheless, if we acknowledge that many religious truth-claims are also text-based claims, and if we attend to the function of canon and commentary regarding the substance and effect of such claims, we may in an unexpected fashion have begun to construct a "comparative soteriology" and even a "comparative study of conversion" to go along with a developing "comparative study of Scripture and commentary."

To conclude: Śaṅkara's Vedānta is a system replete with every kind of religious datum. The study of it raises questions which cannot be satisfactorily answered through partial studies which focus on "myth in Vedānta," or "Vedānta as a philosophy." Whether or not a retrieval of the theological tradition is considered necessary or appropriate, it nevertheless remains an urgent task for comparativists to develop vocabulary and methods more suited to the comprehensive study of a thinker like Śaṅkara.

Notes

1.   The Hindu tradition with its Vedic antecedents provides for the student of religion and culture an enormous wealth of still only partially explored data. The world of O'Flaherty and others has opened for us the world of myth and the complex discourse of mythology; scholars as diverse as Deutsch, Vattanky, and Matilal have contributed greatly to the foundations for comparative or cross-cultural philosophy; the area generally termed "praxis" has been opened up through the increasing study of what Staal has called "science of ritual," and there is a growing collection of documentation on Hindu religiosity in its temple, domestic, and other social forms.

See for example: Wendy D. O'Flaherty's *The Origins of Evil in Hindu Mythology* (Berkeley: University of California, 1976) and *Asceticism and Eroticism in the Mythology of Śiva* (Oxford: 1973); Eliot Deutsch's *Advaita Vedānta: A Philosophical Reconstruction* (Honolulu: University of Hawaii, 1969); John Vattanky's *Gaṅgeśa's Philosophy of God* (Madrās: The Adyar Library and Research Center, 1984); Bimal K. Matilal's *Epistemology, Logic and Grammar in Indian Philosophical Analysis* (The Hague: Mouton, 1971) and *Perception* (Oxford: The Clarendon Press, 1986); J. Frits Staal's essays, "Ritual Meaning and the Origins of Science in India," *Journal of Indian Philosophy* 10 (1982) 3-35 and "Ritual Syntax," in *Sanskrit and Indian Studies Festschrift Ingalls* (Dordrecht: D. Reidel, 1979) 119-42. While the comprehensive study of Vedānta includes topics and requires methods which are not identical with any of what these works include, attention to them is necessary for a complete understanding of Vedānta. So too, of course, attention to wider bodies of historical and anthropological data is also necessary.

2.   The dates for Indian thinkers suggested here are standard; throughout I concur with the dates given by Hajjime Nakamura in *A History of Early Vedānta Philosophy*, trans. T. Leggett et al. (Delhi: Motilal Banarsidass, 1983).

3.   Throughout, my references here will be exclusively to Śaṅkara's Advaita, or "Non-dualist", Vedānta although for the purposes of this essay the differences among the Vedānta schools are not significant. As will be seen, my approach raises issues regarding the Vedānta that have not been attended to previously, but nevertheless a great deal of groundwork on the Vedānta has been done. Thus, Paul Hacker's many groundbreaking studies in early Vedānta are still pertinent (e.g., his "Eigentümlichkeiten der Lehre und Terminologie Śaṅkaras," *Zeitschrift der Deutschen Morgenländischen Gesellschaft* 1950, 246-86, and "Untersuchungen über Texte des frühen Advaitavada," *Akademie des Wissenschaften und der Literatur* 1950, n.26, 1907-2072), while Nakamura's work and Tilmann Vetter's *Studien zur Lehre und Entwicklung Śaṅkaras* (Vienna: De Nobili Research Library, 1979) are important assets when any kind of study of Śaṅkara Vedānta is undertaken. Finally, it must be noted that regarding Śaṅkara I have confined myself to considering his *Uttara Mīmāṁsā Sūtra Bhāṣya* alone. For the text of Śaṅkara and the subcommentaries by Vācaspati Miśra, Amalānanda, and Appaya Dīkṣita, I have used the *Brahma Sūtra Śaṅkara Bhāṣya* with the *Bhāmatī, Kalpataru and Parimala*, ed. K. L. Joshi, 2 vols., (Ahmedabad: Parimal Publications, 1981). For standard reference, I refer throughout not to page number, but to *adhyāya*, *pāda*, and *sūtra*.

4.   This has been recently documented by the work of Vasudha Narayanan and John Carman regarding Rāmānuja's school, which had as a primary goal the fusion of Vedāntic brahmanism not only with the Pañcarātra, etc., but also with the powerful streams of Tamil devotionalism surfacing in the songs of the Tamil-language Alvārs. See Narayanan's *Bhakti and Prapatti in the Srīvaiṣṇava Tradition* (Cambridge: Harvard Studies in World Religions, 1987), and her book coauthored with Carman, *The Tamil Veda: Piḷḷāṇ's Interpretation of the Tiruvāymoḻi*, (Chicago: University of Chicago, 1989).

5.   On this issue, see F. X. Clooney, "The Concept of Dharma in the Mīmāṁsā Sūtras of Jaimini," *Kuppuswami Shastri Birth Centenary Commemoration Volume II*(Madras: Kuppuswami Sastri Research Institute, 1985) 175-87; "Jaimini's Contribution to the Theory of Sacrifice as the Experience of Transcendence," *History of Religions* 25/3 (1986) 199-212; and "Why the Veda Has No Author: Some Contributions of the Early Mīmāṁsā to Religious and Ritual Studies," *Journal of the American Academy of Religion* 55/4 (1988).

6.   Jonathan Z. Smith, in *Imagining Religion: From Babylon to Jonestown* (Chicago: University of Chicago, 1982), 36-52.

7.   Although much of the groundwork in this regard remains undone, foundations are provided by certain older works such as P. M. Modi's *A Critique of the Brahmasūtra (III.2.11-IV) with Reference to Śaṅkarācārya's Commentary*, 2 volumes (Baroda, 1956); Richard de Smet's Gregorian University dissertation *The Theological Method of Śaṅkara* (which unfortunately remains unpublished) and his article "Langage et connaissance de l'Absolu chez Śaṅkara," *Revue Philosophique du Louvain* 52 (1954) 31-74; and Satchidananda's *Revelation and Reason in Advaita Vedānta* (Delhi: Motilal Banarsidass, 1974); and by more recent works such as Wilhelm Halbfass' "Human Reason and Vedic Revelation in the Philosophy of Śaṅkara," in *Studies in Kumārila and Śaṅkara, Studien zur Indologie und Iranistik 9*, (Reinbeck: Verlag fur Orientalistische Fachpublikation; 1983).

8.   As Halbfass stresses (see especially 31, 47-8, 53-4). Thus, he says that for Śaṅkara the Veda is "a complex, differentiated structure of discourse, speaking at different levels and with different voices" (31). The paradigm for the kind of unity at issue is that of the Vedic "branches," *śākhās*; it was enunciated earlier in the Pūrva Mīmāṁsā Sūtras (henceforth *PMS*) 2.4, and also structures the approach to the meditations [*upāsanās/vidyās*] in *UMS* 3.3.

9.   See Murty, 68ff. and *UMS* 1.3.33.

10.   See Clooney, "Why the Veda Has No Author," 1988.

11.   See Deussen's account of the two paths: *The System of the Vedānta*, trans. Charles Johnston (New York: Dover, 1973), 362-66. He concludes that the *Bṛhadāraṇyaka* account is more coherent. See also Nakamura, 524-28.

12.   Much more can be said on the use and reuse of mythic elements in the Vedānta. A striking example is what might be called "remythologization," wherein the Vedāntins apparently reintroduce older mythic elements discarded by the Mīmāṁsakas. For instance, the Vedāntins insist that the gods did have material bodies, despite earlier Mīmāṁsā skepticism in that regard (see F. X. Clooney, "*Devatādhikaraṇa*: A Theological Debate in the Mīmāṁsā-Vedānta Tradition," *Journal of Indian Philosophy*).

13.   Thus too Smith, 55-6, connecting ritual and hierarchical discourse.

14.   In a passage cited also by Smith, 55.

15.   Much scholarly attention has been devoted to the study of the role of reason in Śaṅkara, but as Halbfass points out (op. cit., esp. 29-32), too often this scholarship imports modern, European notions of reason and religion into the study of Śaṅkara. When Halbfass correctly notes that the Indian tradition does not contain anything quite like Greek or Cartesian philosophy, he might have done well to add that in its Patristic and medieval periods—i.e., between the Greeks and Descartes—European thought had quite a bit of the kind of exegetical reasoning one runs into in reading Śaṅkara. As general background, his essay is pertinent here as an excellent and comprehensive introduction to Śaṅkara's position, describing for us Śaṅkara's view of the Veda and the proper context in which his remarks praising and confining reason are to be understood; it deserves a careful reading by all those who would study Śaṅkara. Murty's *Revelation and Reason* is a good resource for Śaṅkara's views, in context.

16.   The *paribhāṣā* on Panini's rule 1.3.11, which *paribhāṣā* is given as rule §46 in the *Siddhānta Kaumudī* of Bhaṭṭoji Dīksita, ed. and trans. S. C. Vasu (Delhi: Motilal Banarsidass, n.d.; original printing, 1906).

17.   This latter example, it may be noted, is interesting because it is used again in later Vedāntic controversies regarding the authority of Scriptural statements in relation to one another.

18.   This "proof of the soul" is occasioned indirectly, in a typically Vedāntic fashion. The preceding discussion (3.3.44-52) of the "fire-altars of mind" mentioned in the *Śatapatha Brāhmaṇa* (10.5.3.3) presupposes that there is a mind in which that construction can occur.

19.   Thibaut's translation. In *UMS* 2.3.16, he offers a similar argument: "The individual soul has no beginning and is not subject to dissolution, since thus only it can be connected with the results of action, as the Śāstra teaches. If the individual soul perished after the body, there would be no sense in the religious injunctions and prohibitions referring to the enjoyment and avoidance of pleasant and unpleasant things in another body."

In answer to the charge that this is an odd place in the text—obscure, hidden deep in the third Adhyāya—to prove the self, Śaṅkara merely says that the author of the *UMS* has chosen this place to prove the existence of a self independent of the body, since he has not done so anywhere else. Earlier discussions of the human self, in the first *pāda* of the *UMS,* were not based on any sūtra and were only indirectly introduced. It is likewise noted that even in the *PMS* there is no sūtra there warranting the important discussion wherein Śabara, in his *Bhāṣya* on *PMS* 1.1.5 proves the existence of a self which is different from the body and therefore able to enjoy the fruits taught by the *śāstra*. In any case it would not be without precedent for an important issue to be treated at a later portion of a text and yet be presumed from the start. Pāṇini's grammatical sūtras, the *Aṣṭādhyāyī* (c. 500 BCE), have no overall linear order, and it is presumed that a grammarian would know all the sūtras before applying any of them. The main goal underlying the Vedānta discussion is to make sure that the undeniably important discussion of the self be *somewhere* properly linked to some sūtra in the *UMS.*

The Vedānta tradition, in its other schools, does not take for granted that this is the place to prove the soul's independent existence. Rāmānuja's approach, in commenting in his *Śrībhāṣya* on the same sūtras, is to ask not, "Does the soul exist independent of the body?" but, "Should we understand the meditating self to be the embodied self, or the self in its 'free' state?" Sudarśana Sūri, commenting on Rāmānuja in his *Śrutaprakāsikā*, notes that this posing of the question is appropriate to the context (unlike Śaṅkara's "purple patch") since it preserves the general question of the relation of "components of meditation" to their properties.

P. M. Modi proposes another view, that the issue is whether or not *brahman* has to be meditated on in some personalized form because of the limited imaginative capabilities of the embodied self; because the self is distinct from the body, it is capable of meditation on unqualified *brahman* (vol. 1., 211, 213).

20.   In *UMS* 1.3.7, Śaṅkara says that texts cannot be thought to tell us something about the human self: "It is nowhere the purpose of Scripture to make statements regarding the individual soul. From ordinary experience the individual soul, which in the different individual bodies is joined to the internal organs and other limiting adjuncts, is known to every one as agent and enjoyer, and we therefore must not assume that it is that which Scripture aims at setting forth."

21.   *UMS* 2.2.18-32 has most recently been surveyed by Gregory J. Darling, in his *An Evaluation of the Vedāntic Critique of Buddhism* (Delhi: Motilal Banarsidass, 1987).

22.   See Fumimaro Watanabe's *Philosophy and Its Development in the Nikāyas and Abhidhamma* (Delhi: Motilal Banarsidass, 1983) esp. 94-106, for instance, on the difference between *takka* and *dhammatakka*—"reasoning that occurs from the knowledge of the four-fold truth or dependent origination"—in early Buddhism (104). Or, when Sureśvara, a disciple of Śaṅkara, concedes to the Buddhists only the *anumānaikacakṣu* — the one eye, of inference (reasoning) — this clearly downgrades the whole, due to a view of *anumāna* as encompassed by reason (Halbfass, 66).

23.   Gerow also quotes (88) Renou's maxim which can serve to summarize this part of the discussion: "*adhérer à la pensé indienne, c'est d'abord penser en grammarien,*" *L'Inde Classique*, vol. 2, §1519.

24.   As translated by Wendy O'Flaherty in *The Rig Veda* (New York: Penguin, 1981).

25.   E.g., the much-later *Vedānta Paribhāṣā* finds the dualism implied in the "two birds" image to be a problem and rules that the *Muṇḍaka* text is to be superseded in true, nondualistic knowledge, by the texts which stress nondualism; according to the author, Dharmarāja Adhvarīndra, the *Muṇḍaka* text merely repeats a dualistic distinction commonly assumed in the world. See the *Vedānta Paribhāṣā*, section 7; it is easily available in the Advaita Ashrama edition of Sanskrit with translation by Swami Mādhavananda (Calcutta, 1983); the *Muṇḍaka* text is referred to on page 199 of that edition.

In a different context again, the fourteenth-century Śrīvaiṣṇava commentator Periyavāccāṉ Piḷḷai rereads the bird image in the context of commenting on the saint Nammālvār's Tamil-language *Tiruvāymoḻi*. In 1.1.3 of that work, Nammālvār describes Viṣṇu as "not this, nor lacking in that, nor in the earth or heavens, nor not in them, neither accessible to the senses nor inaccessible." Periyavāccāṉ Piḷḷai introduces the *Muṇḍaka* text as a kind of gloss, wherein the two birds indicate no longer the self and *brahman*, but the two poles of the divine self. See *Tiruvāymoli*, ed. Krsna Ayyangar Swami (Srirangam: Books Propagation Society, 1975) 1.1 and 1.2, 269. For later Vedāntins and Śrīvaiṣṇavas, such interpretations and glosses become legitimate parts of the symbol's meaning, parts we must take into account in understanding those later thinkers.

26.   To make their point, the Vedāntins borrow a Mīmāṁsā analogy (*PMS* 1.4.23-30) between the "two drinkers" and the so-called *sṛṣṭi* bricks referred to in the section of the *Taittirīya Samhitā* (5.3.4) regarding the construction of the fire altar, because at one point all of a certain group of bricks are referred to as "*sṛṣṭi* bricks," even if technically only some of them merit that name. So too, the argument goes, the "two" are called "two drinkers," even if only one of the two merits that name. Vācaspati Mīsra explains this ritual reference in his comment on *UMS* 1.2.11.

27.   Willard Johnson, in *Poetry and Speculation in the Ṛg Veda* (Berkeley: University of California, 1980).

28.   *Adhikāra* is the primary topic of the sixth Adhyāya of the *PMS*. See chapter 5 of Clooney, (*Thinking Ritually: Rediscovering the Pūrva Mīmāṁsā of Jaimini*) [Indological Institute, University of Vienna: De Nobili Research Institute, vol. 17] for Jaimini's understanding of *adhikāra* and the place of human *adhikāra*—the ability to perform rites, etc., calculated in terms of caste, gender, resources, etc.

29.   Especially 34-44, his remarks on the nature of the world itself as a kind of book, and of commentary as an unending task opening the book; also, in 78-81, his remarks on the breakdown of that world view in the seventeenth and eighteenth centuries, as commentary is replaced by criticism and the "primordial sacred text" is, as it were, unbound.

30.   One will have to become familiar, for instance, with the history of Christian exegesis and the background out of which the modern study of texts developed. de Lubac's *Écriture dans la Tradition* (Paris: Aubier-Montaigne, 1966) puts one in touch with that history, the levels of meaning and "fuller senses" of texts, etc., as does Raymond Brown, in a briefer form, in his essay on "Hermeneutics" in the *Jerome Biblical Commentary*, vol. 2, 605-23 (Englewood Cliffs, New Jersey: Prentice-Hall, 1968). Pheme Perkins' 1987 Presidential Address at the Catholic Biblical Society takes into account the current state of efforts to explain the relation between theology and exegesis (*Catholic Biblical Quarterly* 50.1, 1988, 5-23). Work such as David Tracy's adaptation of the "classic" for theology is also pertinent, e.g., his recent *Plurality and Ambiguity* (New York: Harper and Row, 1987).

31.   See the recent discussion in the *JAAR* between the proponents of the "St. Louis Project" (which had as its goal an exploration of "the relationships between theological studies and religious studies in a manner that might enable the two fields to establish a close working partnership within a coherent undergraduate liberal arts curriculum." [Capps, 1984, 727]) and Ivan Strensky. The somewhat heated debate testifies to both the value and the difficulty of reassessing the theology/religious studies distinction (Walter Capps et al. [*JAAR* 52/4, 1984: 727-57]; Strenski [54/2, 1986: 323-35]; and Capps again [55/1, 1987: 125-26]).

32. 52.

33. 43.

34. To give a minor but proximate example, the successive textual-ritual encompassments which structure the *Uttara Mīmāṁsā Sūtras* have been the primary factor instigating my reluctance to consider myth, philosophy, and praxis separately or by the norms of the generally relied-on disciplines of comparative study. Śaṅkara eventually makes difficult any unquestioned compartmentalization of the data of religion.

References

Clooney, F. X.
   1985 "The Concept of Dharma in the Mīmāṁsā Sūtras of Jaimini." *Kuppuswami Shastri Birth Centenary Commemoration Volume II.* Madras: Kuppuswami Sastri Research Institute, 175-87.

   1987 "Jaimini's Contribution to the Theory of Sacrifice as the Experience of Transcendence." *History of Religions* 25: 199-212.

   1987 "Why the Veda Has No Author: Some Contributions of the Early Mīmāṁsā to Religious and Ritual Studies." *Journal of the American Academy of Religion* 55: 659-84.

   1988 "Devatādhikarana: A Theological Debate in the Mīmāṁsā - Vedānta Tradition." *Journal of Indian Philosophy* 16: 277-98.

   1989 "Finding One's Place in the Text: A Look at the Theological Treatment of Caste in Traditional India," *Journal of Religious Ethics* 17/1:1-29.

   1990 *Thinking Ritually: Rediscovering the Pūrva Mīmāṁsā of Jaimini.* De Nobili Research Series. vol. 17. Vienna: University of Vienna.

   Forthcoming: "Binding the Text: Vedānta as Philosophy and Commentary." In *Texts in Context: Traditional Hermeneutics in South Asia*, edited by Jeffrey Timm. Albany: State University of New York Press.

Darling, Gregory J.
   1987 *An Evaluation of the Vedāntic Critique of Buddhism.* Delhi: Motilal Banarsidass.

Deussen, Paul.
1973 *The System of the Vedānta*. Das System des Vedānta. 1883.
Translated by Charles Johnston. 1912. Reprint. New York: Dover.

Dumont, Louis.
1979 *Homo Hierarchicus*. Translated by L. Dumont, B. Gulati, and
M. Sainsbury. Chicago: University of Chicago.

Gerow, Edwin.
1982 "What is Karma (Kim Karmeti)? An Exercise in Philosophical
Semantics." *Indologica Taurinensia* 10: 87-116.

Halbfass, Wilhelm.
1982 "Human Reason and Vedic Revelation in the Philosophy of
Śaṅkara." In *Studies in Kumārila and Śaṅkara. Studien zur Indologie
und Iranistik*, vol. 9. Reinbeck: Verlag fur Orientalistische
Fachpublikation.

Johnson, Willard.
1980 *Poetry and Speculation in the Ṛg Veda*. Berkeley: University of
California.

Lindbeck, George.
1984 *The Nature of Doctrine: Religion and Theology in a Postliberal Age*.
Philadelphia: The Westminster Press.

Modi, P. M.
1956 *A Critique of the Brahmasūtra (III.2.11-IV) with Reference to
Śaṅkarācārya's Commentary*. 2 volumes. Baroda: private publication.

Murty, S.
1974 *Revelation and Reason in Advaita Vedānta*. Delhi: Motilal
Banarsidass.

Nakamura, Hajjime.
1983 *A History of Early Vedānta Philosophy*. Translated by T. Leggett,
S. Mayeda, et al. Delhi: Motilal Banarsidass.

Renou, Louis, and J. Filliozat.
1953 *L'Inde Classique: manuel des études indiennes*. 2 volumes. Paris:
Imprimerie nationale.

de Smet, Richard.
1953 "The Theological Method of Śaṅkara." Ph.D. diss., Gregorian
University.

1954 "Langage et connaissance de l'Absolu chez Śaṅkara." *Revue Philosophique du Louvain* 52: 31-74.

Smith, Jonathan Z.
1982 *Imagining Religion: From Babylon to Jonestown.* Chicago: University of Chicago.

Thibaut, George.
1962 *The Vedānta Sūtras of Bādarāyana with the Commentary of Śaṅkara.* 2 volumes. *Sacred Books of the East*, vols. 34 and 38. Reprint. New York: Dover.

Myth, Philosophy, and Secularization

Chapter 11

Natural Law: A Study of Myth in a World Without Foundations

Winston Davis

We cannot be all devotion, all praises and halleluyahs, and perpetually in the vision of things above.

—John Locke

Throughout civilized antiquity, nature shared with the gods the onerous responsibility of guiding and policing human affairs. Good and evil were not just "values"; they were objective realities laid down by the gods, or by nature itself. Norms were not just "posited" by people; they did not just "develop" in the course of history. They were discovered as facts about the Way Things Are.

In the West, moral naturalism of this sort took the shape of natural law. Cicero put the idea this way:

The material presented in chapter 11 and chapter 12 was prepared with the generous support of the National Endowment for the Humanities, the Sam Taylor Fellowship Program, and Southwestern University. I would like to thank the members of the Writers' Group, the Post-Modernism Seminar, and the Greek Studies Group of the same university for their criticism of earlier drafts.

True law is right reason in agreement with Nature; it is of universal application, unchanging and everlasting; it summons to duty by its commands, and averts from wrong-doing by its prohibitions. And it does not lay its commands or prohibitions upon good men in vain, though neither have any effect on the wicked. It is a sin to try to alter this law, nor is it allowable to attempt to repeal any part of it, and it is impossible to abolish it entirely. We cannot be freed from its obligations by Senate or People, and we need not look outside ourselves for an expounder or interpreter of it. And there will not be different laws at Rome and at Athens, or different laws now and in the future, but one eternal and unchangeable law will be valid for all nations for all times, and there will be one master and one ruler, that is, God, over us all, for He is the author of this law, its promulgator, and its enforcing judge.[1]

Nearly two millenia of social change and philosophical development separate us from Cicero's doctrine. What sense, if any, can we make of it today? In the two essays prepared for this volume, I deal with natural law as a myth, or more accurately, as a family of myths. Both essays have been written for readers living in societies which are liberal, pluralistic, and semisecular. Celebrated nowadays, with no little hubris, as worlds "without foundations," such societies—or at least their educated élites—tend to be uncomfortable with the concept of myth.[2] Yet, I shall argue, the invisible foundations of these societies are based in large measure on the myths I am about to discuss. In the present essay, I discuss the history of the myth of a normative natural order in the religions of the ancient world—a world that purportedly had "foundations." Then I take up the various forms the myth took in the West. I conclude the essay with some general thoughts on the secularization of the myth, and on the proper relationship between the "discourses" of myth, religion, and political rationality in a world which allegedly is "without foundations."

In my second essay, I continue my analysis of the Western myth of natural law by comparing two very different modes of thought and value which it has spawned. Using the phenomenological concept of "fundamental realizations," I try to rescue what I believe is valuable in this myth. Admittedly, the result is less imposing than the traditional concept of a universal, objective law of nature. It is, in fact, a translation of this "foundational" doctrine into the moral language of a society with convictions but few, or rather wobbly, foundations. In the first essay, I argue for the *restraints* that must be imposed on mythological discourse in modern societies; in the second, for the *recognition* of the ability of myth to generate and sustain basic human values. These essays are therefore intended as companion pieces, but ones with no little tension between them.

What does it mean to say that natural law is a myth? Although scholarship thus far has given us no successful *general* theory of myth, we can at least *roughly* set myth apart from other types of discourse by agreeing to call *anything predicated of the Sacred* a myth.³ Metaphorically speaking, we can think of myth as the movement or liquefaction of religious symbols, and of symbols as the substantive congealments of myth. Consisting of symbols arranged in stories, adventures, or plots (Gk., *muthos*), myth is the religious symbol in action. More concretely, it concerns what the Sacred *does*, or better, what it *did* when the world was young. Hence the predicative nature of all religious myth.

While ancient and medieval philosophers did not distinguish between the myth and the doctrine of natural law, I shall do so for reasons of clarity. By the *myth* of natural law I mean the story of God's creation of certain values "in nature" and—what is nearly the same story—His sanctification of certain relationships, acts, and attitudes as "naturally choiceworthy." ("To create" and "to sanctify" being the primary actions predicated of the Sacred in this case.) The *doctrine* of natural law, on the other hand, is the philosophical articulation of the myth—allegedly by "right" or "sound reason" (Gk., *orthos logos*; Lat., *recta ratio*).⁴

Since natural law is a family of myths, it has a variety of meanings and functions. It has been used to situate humankind ontologically between the sacred beings above and the dumb, irrational brutes below. At the "micro-level," by securing the safety of persons and property, promoting reciprocity and freedom from slander, natural law makes friendship possible.⁵ At the "macro-level," it grounds justice, morality, and social order in the natural order of things. It provides guidance in the bewildering interstices of positive law. As a higher law, natural law functions as the *touchstone* of human justice. From the natural-law point of view, positive law is compelling not because it is commanded by authorities (*ius quia iussum*), but because it participates in justice itself (*ius quia iustum*). Natural law unmasks laws which contradict "natural" human dignity. It exposes "legal crime," a notion which, without a higher law, arguably would not even exist. Natural law is also a way of dealing with the disturbing impunity of unwitnessed or unpunishable crimes—the crimes the owner of Gyges' ring might commit, the atrocities modern dictators actually have committed. After all, why forego illicit gain or pleasure when there is no one to witness our misdeeds? Why behave morally, when we can just as well indulge in profitable, criminal activity with impunity? What, then, can ensure morality in the bedroom, the physician's office, the dark alley, the deserted island? The natural-law answer is mythological: give nature eyes. Let her be lawgiver, policeman, and judge.

The Comparative Perspective

While the idea of a normative natural order was widespread, there are reasons to believe that the Western variant was an unusual, perhaps even a unique, mythological mutation. If so, one can ask whether there was any correlation between the variants of the myth and the sundry outcomes of history. This calls for a brief survey of some of the myth's non-Western versions.

In India and East Asia, the idea that the natural normative order is the creation of personal deities is found primarily at the level of devotionalism and vernacular religion. The thinkers of the "Great Traditions" generally concerned themselves with the impersonal, sacred forces of the universe. The Vedic myths of ancient India related the cosmic order (*rta*) to four castes (*varna*). *Rta* was maintained by the sacrificial activity of the Brahmanic priesthood and was protected (but not created) by the gods Varuna and Mitra. (Like the Homeric Greeks, the Indians believed the gods themselves were subordinate to the cosmic order). In the post-Vedic period, attention shifted to the hereditary duties of the four castes (*varna-dharma*) and the relationship between caste, duty, and moral action (*karma*). While Indian theories of the origin of society sometimes describe a state of nature which existed before government, man in this state of nature was not subject to a natural law. The idea of a social contract was used to introduce the king's obligations towards his subjects; it is never elaborated as a secular theory of civic duties and obligations. It was not concerned with rights, but with the protection of high caste interests.[6] It is also significant that, compared with Western natural law, the Indian concept of nature has remained firmly embedded in its traditional, mythological context.[7]

Without rejecting caste as a *practical* reality, Buddhism denied the relationship between caste and enlightenment and devalued the connections Hindus made between *varna* and *dharma*. Buddhists regard the social order as a purely conventional arrangement, and social differences as merely terminological distinctions. This, however, does not allow us to rank Buddhists with modern "conventionalists" or "constructionists," thinkers who deny the reality of the natural normative order. Buddhists still believe in an eternal *dharma* (both a natural and a moral order) taught, but again not created by the Buddha. As in Hinduism, the Buddhist *dharma* is about duties, not about rights. It represents a normative, not an operant understanding of "nature."

In China, too, the order of nature was generally thought to be self-generating and self-authenticating, not something divinely imposed *ab extra*.[8] Daoists, who favored a life of pure, spontaneous activity (*wuwei*), shunned not only metaphysical speculation ("naming the *Dao*") but also the didactic morality of the Confucians. Confucianism sought to establish the *Dao* in the human community itself, but pragmatically restricted speculation about the ultimate order of things. In the third century BCE, the Confucian scholar Xunzi (Hsün Tzu) speculated that law and nature were merely aspects of one and the same Dao.[9] During the Han period, Confucian moralism was transformed into an ideology sanctifying the social hierarchy. Because abstract speculation was avoided in early Confucianism and Daoism, the most explicit articulation of the idea of moral naturalism came only later, viz., in the early Han when the appendices of the *Classic of Changes* were introduced into the Confucian canon. These works served to combine Confucian morality with the cosmological theory of *yin* and *yang*.[10]

Naturalistic speculation reached a highpoint in Neo-Confucianism, for example, in the thought of Zhu Xi (Chu Hsi) (1130-1200) who equated the principles (*li*) of the natural world with the basic standard for the Five Constant Virtues and Five Relationships. As late as the seventeenth century (and actually until much later), Japanese like Nakae Tōju believed that the stars themselves stay in place thanks to human virtue. As an undifferentiated principle of nature and morality, *ri* [Chinese: *li*] continued to influence Japanese thought nearly until modern times.[11]

One could dilate endlessly on the differences between these traditional concepts of order. Ritual, for example, played a role in the creation and maintenance of Hindu *dharma* and the Confucian *Dao* that would be unthinkable in Daoism or Western thought. On the other hand, the Confucian concept of moral order had little room for guilt, inwardness, and repentance, key elements not only in the morality of the West, but in the Christian salvation syndrome itself.[12] Because *dharma* was linked to the concept of *karma* in Hinduism and Buddhism, its "flow" was from past and present to the future. Events were not "pulled" into the future by a natural "end" established at the Creation as, for example, in Thomism. In both India and China, the concept of the normative natural order seemed to be incompatible with the notions of tragedy or intractable moral dilemmas.

The idea that nature and morality depend on the law of a creator-god can be traced back, before the Bible, to the Babylonian cosmogonic myth (c. 2000 BCE) in which the sun-god, Marduk, imposes his will on the stars or star-gods. In ancient Greece, although the gods punished wrongdoers, they were not generally creators or paragons of morality themselves. The Homeric gods were subject to *moira*, the basic order of things. Even Zeus Nomothetes gave laws to men and the other gods, not to nature. The idea of a natural normative order did make sense to the Greeks, however, at least before the rise of "individualism" and the collapse of the traditional cosmogony.[13] The fragments of the pre Socratics suggest that Greek moral naturalism may have originated by projecting human order upon nature, and not just by assimilating the human world to the a priori order of nature. While the early Greek view was generally quite different from the later concept of natural law, the notion (if not the terminology) of moral naturalism was well known to the Greeks of the classical age.[14] Xenophon, for example, tells us that Socrates believed in an unwritten law given to man by the gods.[15] Observed in the same way in all countries, violation of this law entails its own punishment. Violation of the law of incest, Socrates says, is punished by the birth of children who are "badly begotten." Failure to show gratitude is punished by the loss of useful friends. Although Xenophon does not use the term *natural law*, the idea of a higher law was clearly stirring in his mind.

The Western myth of natural law differed from Asian myths in three fundamental ways. First, compared with the nontheistic or atheistic presuppositions of the Great Traditions of Asia, it is unusual in the importance it assigns to God or the gods.[16] Secondly, while "natural *duties*" were justified throughout the ancient world in terms of a cosmomorphic morality, the West gave birth to a concept of "natural *rights*," sacred entitlements which protected individuals and minorities from tyrannical rulers, oppressive majorities, and "unnatural" laws.[17] Third, it was only in the West that the myth of natural law gave rise to the radical idea that an economy "naturally" flourishes only when the "natural" passions (i.e., self-interest) are set free.[18]

To the historian interested in the consequences of religious ideas, the natural normative order is a frustrating concept. The problem is not just that each tradition offers a variety of contradictory expositions

of the idea, but that the same idea may lead to vastly different historical conclusions or outcomes. This is due, first and foremost, to the
multivalence and ambiguity of religious symbols in general, and secondly to the boundless ingenuity of those who exploit these symbols
for their own ends. We shall see that while, in the short term, the
ambiguity of religious symbols enhances religion's popularity and
rhetorical usefulness, in the long term, it raises serious questions about
religion's general credibility as a moral guide.

In spite of the inherent ambiguity of the religious concept of a
normative natural order, one can treat it as an independent variable and
speculate, as Needham has so brilliantly done, about its impact on civilization's scientific development. One can apply oneself to its consequences for the concepts of moral duty or political rights throughout
the world. One can even study the potential of each system to generate
political quiescence and/or restiveness. But the fact is that it is nearly
impossible for the historian who takes the long view of things to use the
concept of order as a comparative, independent variable. This is not
because religions have no consequences but because, thanks to their
polysemous nature, those consequences tend to be unpredictable. When
we look, for example, at the relation between concepts of moral naturalism and political behavior, it is evident that in all civilizations there is a
tendency for the comfortable and powerful to regard the Way Things
Are as the way they naturally Ought To Be. Everywhere, moral or social
naturalism encourages a pious contemplation of the sacred templates of
the past and fosters a religious ethic based on their "application" to the
present. In spite of the "elective affinities" between naturalism, religion,
and conservatism, on the one hand, and constructionism, secularism,
and an openness to change, on the other, the final picture is anything
but clear. As a theory, moral naturalism has been the foundation of a
wide variety of mutually exclusive regimes, from feudalism and fascism
to liberalism. Laozi (Lao Tzu) in the Zhou (Chou) dynasty, Hayashi
Razan in Tokugawa Japan, and Adam Smith in eighteenth-century
Scotland were all, in spite of their great differences, proponents of "natural" systems. Throughout the world, revolutionaries and reactionaries
alike have claimed to be the executors of natural justice, protectors of
the *dharma*, or recipients of the Mandate of Heaven. Likewise, the
opposite doctrine of political conventionalism (e.g., Social Contract theory), has been used to justify "Machiavellian" or authoritarian regimes,
on the one hand, and democratic, constitutional ones, on the other.[19]
Karl Marx was an opponent of natural law, but so was the Japanese

thinker, Ogyu Sorai, who used his theory to fortify a declining feudal regime. While it is therefore impossible to treat moral naturalism (or antinaturalism) as an independent variable, we can, at least, study the context of its historical transformations. Looked at in this way, it is obvious that the struggle between naturalism and conventionalism tends to break out as a *political* encounter after the collapse of rigidly stratified societies. This typically takes place when trade or migration bring unrelated peoples and myths together, when merchants gain political ascendancy, when markets throw off their fetters, when commerce and contractual relations begin to multiply, when rapid social mobility disrupts the traditional order, or when traditional family-ism gives way to individualism. Developments like these often have profound implications for society's concept of nature. Nietzsche, for example, perceptively notes that in America, where individuals defy hereditary social roles, "all nature ceases and becomes art."[20] What in the long run destroys the foundational myth of a normative natural order is therefore not just Hume's "fork," but the dynamite of history.

Natural Law in Western Thought

Like other ancient peoples, the Greeks associated the justice of society with the order of the universe, attributing and explaining one in terms of the other. While the term *natural law* rarely appears before Philo Judaeus and Cicero, we have already seen that the concept of a normative natural order was as well known in Greece as it was elsewhere in the ancient world. By the time of Socrates, however, the Sophists had succeeded in making the relationship between "law" (*nomos*) and "nature" (*phusis*) highly problematic. *Nomos* came to be associated with things variable, relative, conventional, traditional, or expedient; *phusis* with things universal, necessary, and eternal. With the philosophical lexicon gerrymandered in this way, the term *natural law* became something of an oxymoron. Since *nomos* also meant custom, "natural law" (*nomos phuseōs*) would have signified to a Greek of the Classical Age, a *natural* custom, contrivance, or invention. Perhaps for this reason Plato and Aristotle generally speak not of natural law, but of natural justice.[21] Their ultimate concern was what could be called the "ontology of justice." The (pseudo?) Platonic dialogue, the *Minōs* (315a2), for example, defines law itself as that which aims at "the discovery of *what is*."

Scholarship traditionally has traced natural law back to the Stoics, the first philosophers who decisively transported justice beyond the walls of *polis* and *civitas* and made it apply to *oikoumenē*, *kosmos*, and *phusis* alike. While Helmut Koester argues that the natural law comes from Cicero or Philo and *not* from the Stoics, we have seen that the *concept* (if not the term) antedates even the philosophers of the Painted Porch.[22] Conventional scholarship should therefore not be faulted for attributing to the Stoics a major role in the development of the idea of natural law.[23]

While the attitude of the early church towards law, virtue, and justice was in many ways at odds with the classical tradition, the church finally accepted the pagan myth of natural law, if only in order to fortify her new and unexpected role as a power in This World.[24] Amalgamated with Biblical myth, Christian natural law served as a link connecting classical civic virtue and the "softer" Christian values: faith, love, and eschatological hope. By annexing natural law to its own store of myth and legend, the church provided theologians with perplexing examples of moral dilemmas which stimulated critical (or casuistic) reflection and prevented the doctrine from slipping into ethical absolutism pure and simple.[25] The results were impressive. Troeltsch maintains that the "fiction of natural law" made it possible to speak of a "Christian unity of civilization" as such.[26]

Christian natural law reached its apogee in the twelfth-century writings of the canonists Gratian and Rufinus and in the thirteenth-century teachings of the Dominican friar, Thomas Aquinas. The ascendency of natural law at this time may be due to the fact that medieval jurists believed that law *in general* was something found, not made. Although natural law was not used as a criterion for judging positive law in antiquity, canon lawyers used the doctrine to strike down legislation they thought unjust, unnatural, or inimical to the interests of the church. According to Aquinas, natural law is the participation of eternal law in the rational creature. As such, it can be distinguished from the scriptures or divine law—a distinction the canonists did not make. Its precepts, he believed, are the first principles of practical reason, the content of *synderesis*, i.e. the infallible capacity to recognize moral principles. Thomas's real achievement was to graft the essentially Stoic doctrine of natural law into the general Aristotelian-Augustinian framework of his thought. As though this were not enough, he also introduces an element of (what I call) "operant naturalism" into the doctrine. In Thomas's mind, natural law is not only teleological; it also expresses the "givenness" of man's instinc-

tual life. Following the Roman jurist, Ulpian, Aquinas taught that natural law includes sexuality and other forms of behavior "which nature
has taught all animals." Thus, Thomas's doctrine was simultaneously a
priori, teleological, and descriptive of *de facto* human nature.[27]

Since I shall be dealing with the concept of natural rights in my
second paper, I should point out that this doctrine too had mythic origins. While Antigone justified her defiance of Creon in terms of a
divine law, her action owed more to traditional obligations of kinship
than to political rights in the modern sense of the word. While the idea
of rights may have been foreshadowed in Graeco-Roman natural law, it
becomes explicit only in the middle ages. The notion of property rights
seems to have emerged in the fourteenth century in a struggle between
the papacy and the Franciscans. Alarmed at the radical implications of
Franciscan poverty, Pope John XXII (r. 1316-1334) in his bull, *Quia vir
reprobus*, argued that property (*dominium*) could not be avoided in this
world. The Pope argued—on mythological grounds—that "God's
dominium over the earth was conceptually the same as man's *dominium*
over his possessions, and that Adam 'in the state of innocence, before
Eve was created, had by himself *dominium* over temporal things,' even
when he had no one to exchange commodities with."[28] More than three
centuries later, John Locke was (nearly) to absolutize the notion of
property rights, developing the doctrine far beyond the elementary
teachings of John XXII. But the Pope had taken the first step.

Early Modern Natural Law

The proliferation of treatises on natural law between 1600 and
1750 makes generalization difficult.[29] Cassirer points out that many
Europeans believed that natural law could undo the damage done to the
church by Copernicus, Luther, and Calvin, and that it could "recenter"
man in the cosmos and thus reunite Christendom.[30] But natural law in
the early modern period was also beholden to more mundane events: to
the rise of absolute monarchies, powerful commercial classes, and an
economy based on monopoly, colonies, and slavery. Early modern natural law reflected the emergence of Europe as the center of world power.
Lay scholars, who replaced clerics as the principal authors of natural law
(and economics), bent and twisted the traditional doctrine to accommodate the ambitions of the kings and counting houses they served. Bodin,
Hobbes, and Spinoza implicitly rejected classical natural law when they
exalted the state as the source of all law. Sir Walter Raleigh held that

natural law is known only through human law and that human law is the will of a king who is above all law save God's. Francis Bacon made allegiance to hereditary monarchs a dictate of the law of nature. Aside from the family, the new natural law recognized no social group, no *corps intermédiaire* standing legitimately between the individual and the state.[31] In Germany, natural law was attacked by Luther and made part of the theory of enlightened despotism.[32]

Thinkers of the early modern period argued continually about how society and government first came to be. This was not merely a historical question. By speculating about man in the "state of nature," they hoped to discover a paradigm for *legitimate* society.[33] Like the myth-makers of the past, they assumed that what was first or primordial must be right, true, and good.[34] Self-preservation, a key concept in natural law from its inception, moves to center stage in the early modern period. The preservation of self and self's property becomes not only *the* primordial right, but the fundamental axiom of social theory. In these individualistic theories, man's social nature could no longer be taken for granted. In some cases it was denied; in others it had to be developed, explained, and justified. As the product of a contract made by individuals, society became virtually an accidental arrangement of life. It was no longer regarded as something morally or existentially necessary for the fulfillment of human nature.[35]

While some, like Hobbes and Grotius, tried to create a more secure world by absolutizing the state, nearly all thinkers agreed with Locke that the first responsibility of government was to guarantee the rights of individuals and their property. Natural law therefore became an important weapon in the armory of an ambitious but beleaguered bourgeoisie. Spokesmen for this class were in a delicate position. On the one hand, they wanted to use natural law to preserve property. On the other, they were eager to deny "savages," Indians, slaves, and, later on, the proletariat, similar rights.

Traditional natural law had had an oblique way of raising delicate questions about economic justice. It had taught that all men are equal and that—at least before the Fall—all things had been held in common. What did this mean? Thinkers of the early modern period transformed the *communio primaeva* of traditional natural law into a *communio negativa* which actually removed what little legitimacy communal property had ever had in natural law. According to the new natural law, the alleged "communism" of prelapsarian man was no more significant than the common right of all men to air and water, substances owned by all in a "negative" way. With "acquisitive individualism" dominating social thought, it was no wonder that natural *law* itself came to be subsumed under, or dissolved into, a theory of competitive, natural *rights*. As Wolff put it, "whenever we speak of natural law (*ius naturae*), we never intend the law of nature, but rather the right which belongs to man on the strength of that law, that is naturally".[36]

In the natural law of the early modern period one can also discern the beginnings of a utilitarian theory of social exchange.[37] Samuel Pufendorf, for example, taught that man is a creature who *can* be sociable (*animal sociabile*), but who is not naturally (at birth) a social creature (*animal sociale*). What makes him sociable and cooperative? Fear of hell will not do the trick; it is too remote. As Pufendorf puts it, marvelously understating the problem, divine vengeance "walks with slow foot."[38] Thus, man becomes a social creature in order to gain the assistance of his fellows and thereby preserve his life. In other words, sociability is a utilitarian technique which helps man overcome his vulnerability in the state of nature. "In order to be safe, he [man] must be sociable."[39]

Towards a Secular, Empirical, Natural Law: The Work of Hobbes and Hume

Myths can be attacked, weakened, or demolished from two directions: from within and from without. The external destruction of a myth hardly needs explaining. Hitler, Stalin, and Mao have shown the world how it is done. Internal secularization is more interesting. Internally, myths are sometimes underminded by their own inherent rationality. Throughout the development of natural law, we find thinkers elaborating the doctrine of natural law while simultaneously chastening the myth itself. St. Thomas himself may have had a secularizing impact on the doctrine, at least on the canonists' understanding of it. By divorcing natural law from divine law (i.e., scripture), linking it instead to eternal law, he made it possible to draw a relatively clear line between the law of nature and the Biblical legends associated with it. When Suarez, Hugo of St. Victor, Arriga, and Hugo Grotius insisted that natural law would be valid even if there were no God (or if He lost interest in humankind), they were, willy-nilly, laying the groundwork for a more secular understanding of the doctrine. Nevertheless, philosophers of natural law continued to make copious use of Christian myth.[40] In spite of the distinction he made between divine and natural laws, Aquinas used the scriptures to lay out his own religious theory of natural law. Grotius ramsacks the scriptures in search of proof-texts. Even Hobbes, in spite of his probable atheism, taught that natural law was equivalent to the Golden Rule and the Second Table of the Decalogue, and insisted that its precepts derived from Jesus Christ, the prophets, and the apostles. Nevertheless, in spite of these omnipresent Biblical citations, a studied, theological disingenuousness begins to creep into the theory of natural law. Hobbes, Locke, and Spinoza not only cite scripture; they manipulate it to carve out political and philosophical spheres free from the power of religion. Thus, the piety of early modern natural law tended to conceal a staunchly humanistic, secular spirit.

Hobbes' teaching is a good, though perhaps extreme, example of the internal secularization of the doctrine. Hobbes radically broke with tradition by declaring that man in the state of nature did *not* know the law of nature.[41] Natural laws are merely "convenient [i.e. utilitarian] Articles of Peace."[42] They are not laws but a set of "hypothetical imperatives."[43] In his own words, they are "Conclusions, or Theoremes concerning what conduceth to the conservation and defence of [people] themselves."[44] Since there can be no law without an authority to enforce it, natural law can be a law only if it is *thought to be* the command of God. By putting his case this way, was Hobbes trying to steer natural law in the direction of a *theological* utilitarianism? Should one, as Hampton suggests, obey the natural law simply in order to avoid spending eternity in hell?[45] I think not. Hobbes believed that the "natural punishment" incurred by breaking the law of nature applies only to this world. "Intemperance is naturally punished with diseases . . . negligent government of princes, with rebellion; and rebellion with slaughter."[46] The rules that a person "ought to endeavour Peace," "that men performe their Covenants made," "that every man strive to accommodate himselfe to the rest," etc., are therefore only this-worldly, utilitarian precepts.

While nature herself impels man to find a way out of the war of all against all, the ultimate solution is not a natural one. After all, it was nature that created the problem of social disorder in the first place by placing destructive passions in the human heart. The solution to the problem of disorder therefore lies not in nature but in various conventions in the service of self-preservation, i.e., in the social contract and various useful rules (*tendentiously* called "natural law").[47] The foundations of Hobbesian "liberalism" are therefore purely conventional. Why then is God necessary? It seems to me Leo Strauss is probably right.[48] Only by concealing his teaching under the wraps of myth could such a timorous man living in such a dangerous age dare to execute such a radical attack on the traditional laws of nature.

Thinkers in the early modern period were not content to secular-
ize the concept of natural law. They also wanted to give it new content.
Skeptics were determined to base social institutions on the "real" workings of the human heart, not just on man's duties vis à vis some transcendent, and probably illusory, ideal.[49] If Hobbes and Locke developed
the idea of natural law only to undermine it, actual demolition was left
to people like David Hume. Hume joined Hobbes in attacking the
god-like role of "right reason" in traditional natural law. He made
nature depend on passion, custom, sentiment, taste, imagination, and
habit, and thereby divorced it from reason and final causes. He argued
that since moral choices are ultimately made by the passions, reason is,
and ought only to, be their slave.[50] Morality therefore was largely a subjective affair "more properly felt than judged of."[51] The most telling
argument that Hume made against doctrines like natural law was that
they falsely draw normative conclusions from statements of fact. By
drawing attention to this simple distinction Hume drove his celebrated
"fork" straight into the heart of the theory of natural law. Nature is as
indifferent to the ranking of good and evil as it is to the distribution of
cold and heat.[52] Nothing therefore "can be more unphilosophical than
those systems which assert that virtue is the same with what is natural,
and vice with what is unnatural."[53] Hume's attack on the traditional
doctrine of natural law did not, of course, spell the end of natural law
as such.[54] Rather, it marks the ascendency of a new, operant concept of
nature. No longer driven by reason and teleology, nature would henceforth be known in the givenness or behavior of things, in their sheer
operancy. In ethics, this meant that more attention would have to be
given to the passions since they seemed to offer the best explanation of
human nature and moral behavior. Basil Willey's epigram sums up the
state of affairs nicely: before Hume "Nature and Reason go hand in
hand; after him, Nature and Feeling."[55]

Myth, Reason, and Political Responsibility

The idea of natural law is attractive for several reasons. By amalga-
mating morality and the myth of Creation, classical and medieval natural law satisfied the universal urge of humankind to "objectify" its
morality. As Creation, nature became the arena of divine purpose and
salvation. Far from being "red in tooth and claw," nature-as-Creation
acquired a beneficient, magisterial demeanor. As Creation, man could
say of nature what nature would blush to say of herself: that she is good

and beneficent, and that her laws are an inexhaustible reservoir of moral precepts. For thousands of years the myth of God the Creator seemed to secure the life, reason, and society of man the creature. As long as man was God's "property," no one could hope to kill the innocent, rob the rich, despise the poor, or destroy the earth with impunity. One might as well slay the cattle of Hyperion! Natural law therefore was probably the last widely shared ethic in Western civilization to treat society, practical reason, and morality as "objective" realities. According to natural law, neglect of the common good was an act contrary to nature.[56] One can therefore think of natural law as a rational myth seeking "to safeguard the *possibility* of knowledge," as Friedlander has said of Plato's use of myth.[57] The knowledge allegedly safeguarded by the myth of natural law was the proposition that morality and social institutions have real, transcendent foundations. They are not just the products of tribal lore, local knowledge, human concoctions, or wishful thinking.

For millenia natural law has had its critics as well as its advocates. Among its ancient critics were Plato's "Callicles" and "Thrasymachus" and other proponents of the doctrine that "might makes right."[58] Some of the late Sophists, Skeptics, and Epicureans taught that justice was purely conventional. Among Christian theologians, fideists, nominalists, and extreme voluntarists have shown little interest in the doctrine. Augustine did little with it. Occam and Duns Scotus actually undermined it. *Quattrocento* humanists and lawyers showed more interest in civil law. Protestant reformers, who replaced the *natura vulnerata* of Catholic theology with the gloomy doctrine of *natura delecta*, were in no position to develop a thorough-going natural law. High Church Anglicans showed more interest, primarily because natural law seemed to be a moral resource which could be used to cool down England's "hot Protestants."

In spite of the attractiveness of the doctrine, belief in natural law today is limited to traditional Roman Catholics and a handful of philosophers who seem eager to strip the doctrine of its remaining mythological integuments. Since the beginning of the eighteenth century, natural law has gradually been "deontologized" and transformed into a less metaphysical, "deontological" theory based squarely on obligations and rights.[59] It was in the nineteenth century that natural law met some of its most formidable opponents. The degeneration of the French Revolution into a Reign of Terror was the occasion for the initial opposition. Throughout Europe—especially in England—the reaction was: "if *this* is what natural law and natural rights lead to, let us have none of it!" Secondly, there was the rise of nationalism. Natural law, like its first cousin, the law of nations (*ius gentium*), is international in outlook. In the nineteenth century, the universalism of natural law seemed rather quaint and out of place. Nationalism replaced Man with Men—just as feminism in our own time has changed Man into Men and Women. As Joseph de Maistre put it, "I have seen Frenchmen, Italians, Russians, but as for Man, I declare I never met him in my life."[60] In many ways, Nietzsche spoke for many of his generation when he declared that "nature is always value-less, but has been *given* value at some time, as a present—and it was *we* who gave and bestowed it."[61]

In the United States, slavery was a constant embarrassment for the advocates of natural law. With both the advocates and the opponents of abolition appealing to the doctrine, critics were left wondering whether natural law—hallowed though it was in national memory—had any validity at all.[62] In Europe, natural law was also coming under philosophical attack. Bentham and the utilitarians would have no truck with it. Savigny and Von Ranke elaborated the doctrine of historicism as a radical alternative to natural law and other "Napoleonic ideas."

We have seen that even before this, in the early modern period, natural law virtually destroyed itself by giving birth to a purely "empirical" theory. The philosophical speculation of the seventeenth and eighteenth centuries gave rise to an operant or physiocentric naturalism, i.e. a tendency to look for nature in the passions ("natural sensations"), in happiness, or in actual behavior, not in human or social ends as such. Life itself, Hobbes said, is only "Motion." In the fear of violent death, he found a "motion" which actually could *compel* men to be prudent. The revolutionary implication of operant naturalism was this: since the "laws of motion" were made to include *all* human behavior, a genuinely empirical natural law would have to cover not only fear, but greed, vanity, ambition, and other passions previously thought to be *sins*. Thus, a strictly empirical natural law seemed to include "the law of sin which dwells in my members" (Romans 7:23) and the *fomes* (sinful inclinations) of medieval scholasticism. "Kicked upstairs," final causes were assigned to a vague, utilitarian deity, and ultimately forgotten. Traditional natural law had recognized the role of the instincts but had subordinated them to final ends. Descriptions of human nature were thereby controlled by the prescriptions of teleology and theology. In some of the new theories, however, prescription became ancillary to the description of "drives." In effect, empirical natural law allowed Ulpian's physiocentric drives to throw off the teleological constraints St. Thomas had imposed upon them. Hereafter, the theory was to be concerned with causes and effects, not with ends and ultimate reality. Social Darwinists soon took advantage of this philosophical *dénouement* and turned their own version of the "war of all against all" into a natural law in its own right. Married to economism, this biological notion later had profound effects on the social policies of the capitalist world. I shall have more to say about this in the following essay.

Antiessentialism, one of the major premises of modern thought, has turned a host of philosophers against natural law. An "enemies-list" in modern times would have to include romantics, logical positivists, Marxists, instrumentalists, pragmatists, emotivists, existentialists, not to mention most of the leading social scientists of the twentieth century. Many of these critics have tried to resolve the dilemmas of moral naturalism by transforming nature into history, art, or culture. Social scientists in particular tend to reduce nature to a culturally generated artifact.[63] While anthropologists like Clifford Geertz recognize the importance of such cultural symbols as "extrinsic sources of information" transcending the tribe, few would grant to these symbols the ontological density claimed by natural law.[64] Among sociologists, the term *natural law* "conjures up a world of absolutism, of theological fiat, of fuzzy, unoperational, 'mystical' ideas, of thinking uninformed by history and by the variety of human situations."[65] Relativistic sociologists like Max Weber who believe that conflicting life- and value-spheres are beyond rational mediation are, as Leo Strauss points out, prime enemies of the law of nature.[66] Sociologists like Durkheim, who admit that "the social realm is a natural realm," have entirely untraditional ideas about nature and her laws.[67] Nature for them has become a statistical average. In modern jurisprudence, historicism and constructionism have greatly weakened the claims of natural law. Even Supreme Court justices like Holmes and Black have openly repudiated the idea.[68]

The concepts of nature and natural law are riddled with contradictions. Antigone—if she belongs in our story at all—believed the burial of her brother, Polyneices, was the mandate of a heavenly law; Zeno and Chrysippus taught that the natural attitude toward death and burial is one of complete indifference. Aristotle, the Scholastics, Grotius, and many Americans believed that slavery was natural; the Sophists and the Stoics taught that it was unnatural. Cicero taught that it is not *contra naturam* to kill a tyrant; Grotius said that it was. Sir Robert Filmer legitimated absolute monarchy on the basis of natural law; John Locke's argument against Filmer rested on similar grounds.

Grotius taught that the high seas were international waters; John Seldon, at the prompting of two kings and the Archbishop of Canterbury, demonstrated that, by nature, the North Sea was English. The Stoics tell us that there is no incest in nature; Catholic natural law teaches that all sexual relations outside of celibacy and monogamy are unnatural. The Stoics taught that all men are naturally equal. Most pre-modern thinkers and poets however regarded nature as the foundation of an all-embracing social and moral hierarchy.[69] Thus, throughout its long history of use and abuse, nature has aided and abetted nearly every kind of social system or scheme: gerontocracy, Hindu caste, feudalism, socialism, utopian communities of all sorts, physiocracy, Adam Smith's "system of natural liberty," and even Henry George's land tax.

Some would argue that natural law is a myth—"nonsense upon stilts" as Bentham said—merely because it is contradictory. But, while defiance of the law of non-contradiction is the mark of many myths, an idea surely can be contradictory without being mythological. In this essay, I have treated natural law as though it were a mythological package wrapped in the extravagant metaphors of nature and law and tied together with the rather thin string of logic. I have dubbed the result a myth not because it is contradictory, but because it is something "predicated of the Sacred." If contradictions do not make natural law a myth, they do limit its credibility and usefulness. They suggest that the concept of nature no longer can provide the kind of guidance civilization needs to master its own social and moral agendas.

Contemporary debates over surrogate parenting, abortion, euthanasia, the blessing of homosexual marriages, and the "harvesting" of human tissues continue to turn on arguments about what is and what is not "natural." But the "nature" involved in cases like Stearn vs. Whitehead (the "Baby M" case) often rests on a subjective or rhetorical confusion of the categories of the natural and the familiar, on the one hand, and the unnatural and the unprecedented, on the other. The problem is compounded by the contradictory logics of law and technology—medical technology in particular. Technology is constantly outrunning legal precedents for the simple reason that it is in the business of creating the unprecedented. Some technologies clearly do need to be regulated and restricted. Few people today would want to put themselves in the position of the sturdy burgers of Basel who in 1474 burned a rooster alive for the "heinous and unnatural crime" of laying an egg.[70] After all, who knows when the rooster of technology will lay a golden egg?

Conclusions

My approach to natural law has been basically historical, a fact that would not sit well with Leo Strauss and some of the other defenders of this allegedly "timeless" doctrine. But commitment to a historical world view does not, in itself, imply an indifference to the claims of philosophy. As a matter of fact, I would argue strongly for the autonomy of philosophical reason, and consequently, for the need to make a clear distinction between myth—even a "rational myth" like natural law—and reason itself. What is more, the history of natural law, as I understand it, demonstrates the need to *subordinate* myth to reason in the public domain. In the present "laid-back" age of postmodern, ecumenical good will, such an attitude toward myth may seem to be rather old-fashioned, rationalistic or even grumpy. A brief explanatory digression is therefore in order.

Communication among human beings depends on the mastery not only of vocabularies, general syntactical rules and the social context of each "language game," but also on the ability to recognize the *boundaries* of various, culturally defined domains of discourse. While few are able to articulate the precise differences between, say, common sense, science, philosophy, ideology and myth, culturally fluent individuals are expected to recognize the relative positions of these domains on the cognitive map of their society and wend their way between them with some measure of skill. Since different societies divide the world into different categories, the boundaries between discourses will vary widely. While the discourses of simpler, more traditional societies abound in expansive homologies and multivalent symbolisms which seem to defy discourse-boundaries, the boundaries between the discourses of modern, complex societies sometimes must be more tightly drawn. In the Western democracies, for example, explicit boundary lines between the discourses of religion and government were drawn up by the *philosophes* and Founding Fathers of the eighteenth century. The result has been the creation of relatively autonomous and, I would say, *felicitously secular* political domain throughout the modern West.

In this essay, we have seen that natural law is a mythical concept and that political action based upon it is ultimately religious in provenance. If so, direct use of natural law in public discourse would seem to be a serious violation of the separation of church and state. I would therefore like to conclude this essay by crafting in a simple piece of "philosophical legislation." I would like to "move" that the Academy reaffirm the distinction, and the tension, between myth and practical rationality. While the relation between the two cannot be asserted as simplistically as it was in the eighteenth century, we must be careful not to formulate it in a way that would lose sight of what the Enlightenment (and the American Founding Fathers) accomplished: the simultaneous *toleration* of rival religious claims and the *amiable separation* of those claims from the decision-making processes of the state. I make this "motion" because of the dangers posed by the opposite policies of recklessly merging religion, myth and political reason, on the one hand, and separating them in an absolute way, on the other.

Today, two groups in the Academy seem eager to "transcend" the wisdom of the *philosophes* and the Founding Fathers. On the one hand, there are the proponents of (what could be called) "libertarian isolationism," i.e., the idea that all cultures or "language games" are valid and mutually incommensurable, and that all rational attempts to define the common good are illicit. On the other, we have the advocates of "merger mania," i.e., people who seek to blend or fuse philosophy, politics, rhetoric, and mythology in a single, coherent *Kultur* which supposedly will supersede our present "foundationless world."

As *chic* and powerful as these movements are at the moment, both advocate courses of action which are politically mischievous. While libertarian isolationists sound innocent enough (e.g., Jean-François Lyotard's *dictum* "Let us play . . . and let us play in peace") their insistence that all language games are autonomous and incommensurable denies the necessarily "transludic" (game-transcending) function of practical reason, and thereby its role in the oversight of society in general.[71] Libertarian isolationists fail to see 1) that "game players" (if that is all citizens are!) share *common corridors*, if only to move from one "game room" to another, and 2) that sometimes people play different games in the same room. And there, of course, is the rub. It is precisely the *common* use of time and space that make transludic rules necessary. If the games people play are, say, those of myth, politics, and law, and if people choose to play these games at the same time and in the same space—say, in a political election—someone will need to prioritize the rules of one game vis à vis those of the others. Since the seventeenth century, Western society has learned that under these circumstances the wisest course is to give priority to the rules of religious toleration and the separation of church and state. While even the reason that devised these rules *can* become tyrannical, there is no reason to believe this *must* be the case.

If libertarian isolationists overestimate the autonomy of language games, the advocates of merger mania do not take the irreducible differences between the discourses of myth and political reason seriously enough. While the walls between these discourses may not be as thick as the thinkers of the Enlightenment thought them to be, they are not as thin as some in the Academy (and Church) would have us believe. Nevertheless, many in the vanguard of anthropology, hermeneutics, and religious ethics deliberately disregard the caesurae between modern and premodern thought and try to "transcend" the boundaries between the discourses of science, religion, myth, and philosophy. The result is a leveling of the distinctions between field-workers and informants, interpreters and texts, philosophers and myth-makers. As Clifford Geertz put it, "We are all natives now."[72] This dictum is not, of course, all bad, especially if it helps distribute humility more broadly. But, applied to the problem of myth and philosophy, it has some troubling implications. By collapsing anthropology's own etic/emic distinction, Geertz *could* be interpreted as putting reason and myth on an equal footing.

French scholars have added to the confusion. Approaching the matter quite differently from Geertz, the *savants* of structuralism treat myth as a cerebral exercise, a way of analyzing abstract, intellectual puzzles. Some "postphilosophers," "poststructuralists" and "deconstructionists," on the other hand, want to reduce reason and philosophy to myth or rhetoric. Many of these thinkers firmly reject the suggestion that discourses sometimes need to be prioritized—especially if, in the resulting hierarchy of "language games," science, reason, or philosophy were ever to be ranked *above* religion, rhetoric, or myth. Such a conclusion would immediately be rejected as a "Western" or "élitist" prejudice, or, to use Lyotard's word, a form of "terror."

In a society like our own, can social or political thought in general rest on the myth of natural law? To put the question in contemporary jargon: can natural law guide us in our "transludic" arrangement of "language games?" Libertarian isolationists would definitely say no, merger maniacs might say yes—both making up their minds for what I believe are the wrong reasons. Contrary to the libertarian isolationist, I believe the occasional (and limited) prioritizing of discourses is mandatory for the well-being of societies which are democratic, pluralistic, and "without foundations" simply because we do play some of our "games" in the same space and time. Against the merger maniac, I would argue that in a pluralistic society the imposition of mythogenic norms in the public domain is a violation of the constitutional separation of church and state. Liberal societies can endorse *only* those myths which are nebulous and inclusive, e.g., myths belonging to (what today we call) "civil religion"—and even *they* can be notoriously problematic. Before religious ideas and practices can become part of the canon of a civil religion, their *specific* elements must be cast aside. Primary religious colors must be blended with pastels. Sharp theological corners must be ground down and turned into smooth and slippery curves.[73] The American civil religion, for example, cannot endorse the veneration of the Blessed Virgin Mary, even when the President is a Roman Catholic. Such symbols do not belong among the "generic brands" of religious practice associated with the worship of the *deus americanus*.

Does natural law qualify for a role in the American civil religion? Not as long as it bears the specific marks of its mythological past or entails specific mythogenic policies. While natural law can be suitably vague and platitudinous, it can also be as sharp as revelation's own "two edged sword." In spite of its origins in the church and the multicultural *oikoumene* of the Graeco-Roman world, the pluralism of the modern world has ironically transformed natural law into a sectarian dogma. As the property of specific religious groups it is no longer a *common* moral asset or resource. Under these circumstances, I would argue that it is better to struggle for justice and human rights knowing that they are human artifacts, and therefore fragile, than to take refuge in them as though they were natural realities, and therefore invincible.

Notes

1.   *De Republica* (3, xxii, 33).

2.   I use the expression "a world without foundations" to depict as vividly as possible the fundamental structural dilemmas of societies which are at once, liberal, pluralistic, and secular. Philosophically, a foundationless world is one in which philosophers (rightly or wrongly) emphasize "the contingency and conventionality of the rules, criteria, and products of what counts as rational speech . . . the irreducible plurality of incommensurable language games and forms of life, the irremediably 'local' character of all truth. . . . " (Baynes, *After Philosophy*, 3-4). Sociologically, the term can also be used for the conviction of many thinkers (Machiavelli, Marx, and Nietzsche among them) that society rests not on an integrated or consistent set of values (e.g., "*the* central value system" of structural-functionalism), but on competing obligations and contradictory priorities.

Constitutional government may provide a common framework for this kind of society, but not objective foundations. It is true however that even in "worlds without foundations," vague religio-patriotic sentiments—especially those inherited from earlier societies and world views—often create the *belief* or *illusion* that such foundations exist.

3.   By the Sacred, I mean not only Rudolf Otto's *mysterium tremendum* or Mircea Éliade's solemn "ontophanies" and "kratophanies," but also religious experiences of a lighter, magical, humdrum, or happy sort. On the weaknesses of the general theory of myth, see Kirk, *Greek Myths*, 13-29.

4.   I refrain from distinguishing between "true" and "false" doctrines of natural law. From my perspective, all are members of a mythological family consisting of several branches. I should note however that philosophers dedicated to one particular branch of natural law are often reluctant to recognize the legitimacy of others. In the West, conservative and/or Catholic scholars, for example, refuse to call the doctrine of the early modern period natural law at all. (See, for example, the works by Strauss, d'Entrèves, Rommen, and Crowe.) As Gierke put it, this doctrine "was no law at all: it only sailed under the name of law like a ship under false colours, to conceal the bare piratical idea of power" (*Natural Law*, 97).

5.   See MacIntyre, *Whose Justice?*, 180. In general, friendships were to classical social thought what "small groups" are to modern sociology: the basic building-blocks of society itself.

6.   Ghoshal, *A History of Indian Political Ideas*, 550-52.

7.   Ghoshal writes that there is a "striking contrast between the closely reasoned method of Grotius and his successors which is independent of Biblical history and tradition, and the popular, almost story-telling, style of the Indian writers in the background of the cosmological and mythological ideas of their respective sects" (ibid., 539).

8.   Needham, *Science and Civilization* 2, 582.

9.   Hsün Tzu, *Basic Writings*, 125-26.

10. For the impact of the theory *yin* and *yang* (and natural morality in general) on Chinese government and legal practice, see Bodde and Morris, *Law in Imperial China*, 3-51.

11.   Craig, "Science and Confucianism," 133-60.

12.   See Fingarette, *Confucius*, 18-36.

13.   See Adkins, "Ethics and the Breakdown..."

14.   Sophocles, in *Antigone* and *Ajax*, speaks of a divine or heavenly law (the law of decent burial) which legitimately overrides the decrees of the state. While this is often cited as one of the earliest references to natural law in the West, Arthur Adkins ("Law Versus Claims") has shown that what is involved in these passages is not a "higher law" but a "conflict of claims." Thus he effectively removes Sophocles from the history of natural law.

15.   *Memorabilia* (4, iv, 19-25).

16.   In Judaism and Islam one also finds a "personal" God who creates the world and imposes a moral or social law. But the absence of nature as an abstraction inhibited the development of natural law. Moreover, since both religions were based on *sacred* law, a "law above the law" would have been a redundant, if not a blasphemous idea. Although Jewish rabbis speculated about the "Seven Commandments for the Descendants of Noah," the idea becomes part of natural law only in Christian circles, e.g., in the thought of the English antiquarian, John Selden. Medieval Jewish political philosophy was therefore interested in rational, but not natural, law (Lerner, "Moses Maimonides," 196). Thus it seems that the idea of a higher law arises only in cultures where law has been secularized or devalued to some degree (as in Christianity), or where it has been subjected to a moral or political critique (as in Greek thought).

17.   Thus, when Americans today say that their political rights are "God given," they are speaking out of a tradition which is both political and mythological. (By saying this, I do not mean to belittle this tradition which has made abiding contributions to our fundamental concepts of liberty and justice.)

18.   Although there are elements of this in Confucianism, in China the idea of a natural economy generally implied no more than the physiocratic notion that land is ultimately the source of all value.

19.   Maruyama (*Studies*, 189-273) gives outstanding Japanese examples of these contradictory possibilities.

20.   *Gay Science*, 303.

21.   See Morrow, "Plato and the Law of Nature" and Wormuth, "Aristotle on Law."

22.   See Koester, "Nomos Physeōs." The mythological nature of these theories is obvious. Philo identified *physis* with the Hebrew myth of Creation and *nomos physeōs* with *Torah*. God was the "author," "promulgator," and "enforcing judge" of Cicero's natural law. Like other natural law theorists, Cicero does not draw a line between *mythos* and *logos* of his doctrine. Rather, the one flows into the other.

23.   Chrysippus, for example, brings together nearly the same cluster of ideas assembled by natural law itself: nature, universal law, right reason, and divinity. See Diogenes Laertius 7, 128.

24.   It is often said that Romans 1:18ff and 2:14ff were the first Christian statements of natural law. What we have here is not natural law but a theory about a "natural Torah," a primordial revelation of divine will that renders even the Gentile "without excuse" (*anapologetos*) when he stands before the judgment seat of God. Even if these passages are not construed as natural law, they obviously made it much easier for the church to appropriate the pagan notion later on.

25.   Foremost among these dilemmas were questions about divine justice itself. How could natural law (and Christian sensibilities) be reconciled with a God who ordered a man to sacrifice his own son (Gen. 22), who allowed the patriarchs to practice polygamy, told Hosea to commit adultery (Hos. 1:2; 3:1), instructed the Jews to steal (Ex. 3:21; 11:2; 12:35), permitted divorce (Deut. 24:1-4), and allowed an angel to tell lies (Tobit 5:18)?

26.   See Troeltsch, *Social Teachings* 1, 160. Troeltsch believed that the Fathers had divided natural law into an absolute law applicable to the world before the Fall, and a relative one in effect thereafter. Before the Fall, the absolute natural law forbade war, slavery, and private property. After the Fall, the same institutions were recognized, tolerated, or legitimated in terms of the *just* war, *justice* to slaves, and the *common use* of private property. (Perhaps this is why Troeltsch thought that "as a scientific theory," natural law was "wretchedly confused" (ibid., 1, 153ff.). It seems to me, however, that the contrast the Fathers usually made was between an unchanging natural law and *new human institutions* which had to be introduced after the Fall. "Ambrosiaster," Augustine, Gregory the Great, Isidore of Seville, and Ambrose all looked upon government, private property, and slavery as institutions sanctioned not by natural law, but by the Fall. Following the jurists, some of the Fathers distinguished between natural law (*ius naturale*) and the law of the peoples (*ius gentium*), attributing all compromised institutions to the latter.

27.   It was a priori since it included such precepts as "do good and avoid evil" (which he classified, together with statements like "a whole is greater than a part," as *per se notum*).

28.   "God's relationship with the world was paradigmatic for these writers [of the theory of natural rights]: isolated, with no comparable being with which to exchange his possessions, God nevertheless had property in the world, and man could in this respect resemble his maker" (Tuck, *Natural Rights*, 22 and 29).

29.   A thorough-going discussion of natural law during this period would include such names as J. G. Heinecke (Lat., Heineccius), Jean Barbeyrac, Christian Thomasius, Johannes Althusius, Samuel Pufendorf, Hugo Grotius, Emmerich Vattel, John Selden, Richard Cumberland, Nathanael Culverwel, Christian von Wolff, and many others. One would also have to include Thomas Hobbes and John Locke under this rubric even though the thrust of their work leads to the "operant naturalism" of empirical natural law.

30.   *Myth of the State*, 169.

31.   See Gierke, *Natural Law*, 62ff. Free towns, hospitals, villages, universities, and guilds could justify themselves only in terms of private or Roman law. According to Bodin, all of these groups were the creatures of the sovereign. Hobbes (*Leviathan*, 375) groused that corporations were but "lesser Commonwealths in the bowels of a greater, like wormes in the entrayles of a naturall man."

32.   After the rise of romanticism and historicism, German Protestants abandoned the idea completely. This has led some religious conservatives to argue (quite tendentiously, I think) that since fascism ultimately filled the vacuum left by natural law, only a revival of natural law can save the world *from* fascism.

33.   As Rousseau put it: "Man was born free, and he is everywhere in chains. . . . How did this transformation come about? I do not know. *How can it be made legitimate?* That question I believe I can answer." *The Social Contract*, 49; my emphasis.

34.   One must be cautious about accepting the idea put forward by Mircea Eliade and other historians of religion that religion universally establishes the moral or social order in terms of what took place in "primordial time." In China, for example, Confucius preferred to follow the precedents established by the Zhou (Chou) rather than those of the two earlier dynasties (*Analects* 3, 13; see

Schwartz, *The World of Thought of Ancient China*, 63-67). In none of the relevant Ciceronian or Stoic passages which I have examined is the myth of primordial man (or the Golden Age) explicitly linked with natural law. This was primarily a Christian contribution. Natural law, like all mythology, has had a tendency to establish its claims by concentrating on *extreme* cases. One of the old chestnuts of traditional natural law was the "plank of Carneades" (two-drowning-men-fighting-over-plank). Focusing on the *temporal* extreme ("in the beginning"), early modern natural law theorists devoted extraordinary attention to the "Protoplasts" (Adam and Eve), the patriarchs, and the original state of humankind. Some were also concerned with "spatial" extremes, e.g., tales about "wild Peter," cannibals, savages, men on deserted islands, or, in the unauthorized colonies of the Americas (see Dudley and Novak, *The Wild Man Within*). About all such arguments Leo Strauss acidly remarked: "the extreme situation does not reveal a real necessity" (*Natural Right and History*, 196, n. 39). But Strauss was thinking about necessity in philosophy, not in myth.

35.   See Rommen, *The Natural Law*, 81, 95 et passim.

36.   Cited in d'Entrèves *Natural Law*, 62.

37.   This too was foreshadowed in the classics. Xenophon, for example, has Socrates speak of a utilitarian law of repaying favors (*anteuergetein*) (*Memorabilia*. 4, iv, 24). Pufendorf (*De Officio*, 209) cites a similar sentiment in Seneca (*De Beneficiis* 4, xviii): "It is by the interchange of benefits (*beneficiorum commercio*) alone that we gain some measure of protection for our lives . . ."

38.   Pufendorf, *De Officio*, 105.

39.   Ibid., 19.

40.   Duncan Forbes (*Hume's Philosophical Politics*, 41-58) cites the work of Francis Hutcheson, Richard Cumberland, George Turnbull, Heineccius, Pufendorf, and Barbeyrac to show that Grotius by no means gave the coup de grâce to the religious theory of natural law.

41.   If this were true, natural law could not be an *eternal* law inscribed in the hearts of all men. No wonder Cumberland, Locke, and Pufendorf scurried to bring it back into the state of nature, albeit in a much weaker form.

42.   *Leviathan*, 188.

43.   Hampton, *Hobbes*, 89-92.

44.   *Leviathan*, 217.

45.   *Hobbes*, 89-92.

46.   *Leviathan*, 406-7.

47.   A century later, a similar transformation of natural law would be seen in the jurisprudence of Sir William Blackstone (*Commentaries*, Intro., Sec. 2). According to Blackstone, God has made us so "that we should want no other prompter to inquire after and pursue the rule of right, but only our own self-love, that universal principle of action . . . [God] has graciously reduced the rule of obedience to this one paternal precept 'that man should pursue his own true and substantial happiness.' This is the foundation of what we call ethics or natural law. . . ."

48.   *Natural Rights*, 166-202 and *Political Philosophy of Hobbes*, passim.

49.   Hirschman, *Passions*; for an excellent example see Hume, *Dialogues*, 221.

50.   Hume, *Treatise*, 415.

51.   Ibid., 470.

52.   *Dialogues*, 212.

53.   *Treatise*, 475.

54.   Hume did agree that one could use the term *natural law* in philosophy, but only in the trivial sense which makes it the product of a naturally "inventive species" (*Treatise*, 484). Similar attempts to reconcile artifice, design, or convention with nature have been suggested by other conservative thinkers, e.g., Plato (*Laws*, bk. 10, 889ff), Edmund Burke ("Art is man's nature," *Works*, vol. 6, p. 218), Shakespeare, ("The art itself is Nature," *The Winter's Tale* 4, iv, 97) and Pope ("All Nature is but Art, unknown to thee," *An Essay on Man*, ep. 1, 289).

55.   *Eighteenth Century*, 110.

56.   Cicero, *De Officiis* 3, vi, 30.

57.   *Plato*, 182.

58.   After considerable debate among the ancients Sophists, supporters of natural law advertised their doctrine as a radical *alternative* to the idea that might makes right. It is ironic, therefore, that some of its defenders have made so much of "natural punishment," as though some *natural* might could make right.

59.   John Rawls (*A Theory of Justice*, 114-17), for example, defines "natural" duties deontologically as those applying "to persons generally," or as holding "between persons irrespective of their institutional relationships." (Nevertheless, he still grounds them in an "original position" which has some of the trappings of myth.) Many modern philosophers who seem to support natural law (e.g., Ronald Dworkin and John Finnis) have actually espoused positions compatible with its philosophical opposite, legal positivism. (See Weinreb, *Natural Law and Justice*). For some, natural law is simply a synonym for rational juristic principles. In nearly all of these cases, the myth of natural law has been denatured and secularized.

60.   Cited in Becker, *The Declaration of Independence*, 279.

61.   *Gay Science*, 242.

62.   See Becker, *The Declaration of Independence*, 247ff.

63.   No better example of this can be found than the replacement of ("natural") sex by ("cultural") gender in some brands of feminism.

64.   *Interpretations of Cultures*, 92.

65.   Selznick, "Natural Law and Sociology," 154.

66.   *Natural Rights and History*, 36-78.

67.   Durkheim, *Selected Writings*, 253.

68.   In Adamson v. California (1947), Black wrote that natural law actually degrades "the constitutional safeguards of the Bill of Rights." Modern jurisprudence tends to replace natural law with such carefully worded paraphrases as "the fundamental principles of liberty and justice in free government," or "the concept of ordered liberty." Similarly, Benjamin Cordozo discovered in the "interstices of the law" not natural law, but "what fair and reasonable men, mindful of the habits of life in the community and of the standards of justice of fair dealing among them ought in such circumstances to do" (Sigmund, *Natural Law in Political Thought*, 116 and 107).

69.   See Shakespeare's *Troilus and Cressida* I, iii, 85-134, for a marvelous example of the hierarchical concept of society's natural foundations.

70.   Needham, *The Grand Titration*, 329.

71.   For Lyotard's opinion, see Baynes, *After Philosophy*, 70. Whenever reason is applied to language games other than its own, it becomes—we are told—a form of "terror." Actually, Lyotard's position seems to be a polymorphously perverse mixture of the "do your own thing" of the "laid back" 1960s and the "look out for number one" of the neoconservative 1980s. (See Baynes, 1-18.)

72.   *Local Knowledge*, 151.

73.   Hence the vital role of platitudes and the structural significance of ambiguity in the development of civil religions.

References

Adkins, Arthur W. H.
    1982 "Law Versus Claims in Early Greek Religious Ethics." *History of Religions* (Fall, 1982), vol. 21, 222-39.

    1985 "Ethics and the Breakdown of the Cosmogony in Ancient Greece." In *Cosmogony and Ethical Order*, edited by Robin W. Lovin and Frank E. Reynolds, 279-309. Chicago: University of Chicago Press.

Baynes, Kenneth, James Bohman, and Thomas McCarthy, eds.
    1987 *After Philosophy: End or Transformation?* Cambridge: MIT Press.

Becker, Carl L.
    1958 *The Declaration of Independence*. New York: Vintage Books.

Blackstone, William.
    1979 *Commentaries on the Laws of England*. Chicago: University of Chicago Press.

Bodde, Derk, and Clarence Morris.
    1967 *Law in Imperial China*. Cambridge: Harvard University Press.

Burke, Edmund.
1803-1827 *Works*. London: Rivington Edition, vol. 6.

Cassirer, Ernst.
1969 *The Myth of the State*. New Haven and London: Yale University Press.

Craig, Albert.
1965 "Science and Confucianism in Tokugawa Japan." In *Changing Japanese Attitudes Toward Modernization*, edited by Marius B. Jansen, 133-60. Princeton: Princeton University Press.

Crowe, Michael Bertram.
1977 *The Changing Profile of the Natural Law*. The Hague: Martinus Nijhoff.

d'Entrèves, A. P.
1979 *Natural Law*. London: Hutchinson Co.

Dudley, Edward, and Maximillian E. Novak, eds.
1972 *The Wild Man Within: An Image in Western Thought from the Renaissance to Romanticism*. Pittsburgh: University of Pittsburgh Press.

Durkheim, Emile.
1972 *Emile Durkheim: Selected Writings*, edited by Anthony Giddens. Cambridge: Cambridge University Press.

Fingarette, Herbert.
1972 *Confucius: The Secular as Sacred*. New York: Harper and Row.

Forbes, Duncan.
1985 *Hume's Philosophical Politics*. Cambridge: Cambridge University Press.

Friedlander, Paul.
1958 *Plato: An Introduction*. New York: Harper Torchbooks.

Geertz, Clifford.
1973 *The Interpretation of Cultures*. New York: Basic Books.

1983 *Local Knowledge*. New York: Basic Books.

Gierke, Otto.
1950 *Natural Law and the Theory of Society, 1500 to 1800*. Translated by Ernest Barker. Cambridge: Cambridge University Press.

Ghoshal, U. N.
1966 *A History of Indian Political Ideas*. Oxford: Oxford University Press.

Hampton, Jean.
1986 *Hobbes and the Social Contract Tradition*. Cambridge: Cambridge University Press.

Hirschman, Albert O.
1977 *The Passions and the Interests: Political Arguments for Capitalism Before Its Triumph*. Princeton: Princeton University Press.

Hobbes, Thomas.
1982 *Leviathan*. Harmondsworth: Penguin.

Hume, David.
1947 *Dialogues Concerning Natural Religion*. Edited by Norman Kemp Smith. Indianapolis: Library of Liberal Arts.

1985 *A Treatise of Human Nature*. Edited by L. A. Selby-Bigge. Oxford: Oxford University Press.

Hsün Tzu (Xunzi).
1966 *Hsün Tzu: Basic Writings*. Translated by Burton Watson. New York and London: Columbia University Press.

Kirk, G. S.
1983 *The Nature of Greek Myths*. Harmondsworth: Penguin.

Koester, Helmut.
1968 "Nomos Physeōs: The Concept of Natural Law in Greek Thought." In *Religions in Antiquity*, edited by Jacob Neusner, vol. 14, 521-41. Leiden: E. J. Brill.

Lerner, Ralph.
1966 "Moses Maimonides." In *History of Political Philosophy*, edited by Leo Strauss and Joseph Cropsey, 181-99. Chicago: Rand McNally Co.

MacIntyre, Alasdair.
1988 *Whose Justice? Which Rationality?* Notre Dame: University of Notre Dame Press.

Maruyama Masao.
1974 *Studies in the Intellectual History of Tokugawa Japan*. Tokyo: Tokyo University Press.

Morrow, Glenn, R.
1948 "Plato and the Law of Nature." In *Essays in Political Theory Presented to George H. Sabine*, edited by Milton R. Konvitz and Arthur E. Murphy, 17-61. Ithaca: Cornell University Press.

Needham, Joseph.
1956 *Science and Civilization in China*, vol. 2, 518-83. Cambridge: Cambridge University Press.

1969 *The Grand Titration: Science and Society East and West.* Toronto and Buffalo: University of Toronto Press.

Nietzsche, Friedrich.
1974 *The Gay Science.* Translated by Walter Kaufmann. New York: Vintage Books.

Pufendorf, Samuel.
1927 *De Officio Hominis et Civis Juxta Legem Naturalem, Libri Duo.* Translated by Frank Moore, vol. 1, Latin text; vol. 2, English translation [by Frank Gardner Moore.] New York: Oxford University Press.

Rawls, John.
1971 *A Theory of Justice.* Cambridge: Harvard University Press.

Rommen, Heinrich A.
1955 *The Natural Law: A Study in Legal and Social History and Philosophy.* Translated by Thomas R. Hanley. New York and London: Herder.

Rousseau, Jean-Jacques.
1986 *The Social Contract.* Harmondsworth: Penguin.

Schwartz, Benjamin I.
1985 *The World of Thought in Ancient China.* Cambridge: Harvard University Press.

Selznick, Philip.
1963 "Natural Law and Sociology." In *Natural Law and Modern Society*, edited by John Cogley et al., 154-93. Cleveland: World.

Sigmund, Paul E.
1971 *Natural Law in Political Thought.* Cambridge: Winthrop Publishers.

Strauss, Leo.
1953 *Natural Right and History.* Chicago: University of Chicago Press.

1963 *The Political Philosophy of Hobbes: Its Basis and Its Genesis.* Chicago: University of Chicago Press.

Troeltsch, Ernst.
1960 *The Social Teachings of the Christian Churches.* Translated by Olive Wyon. New York: Harper Torchbooks.

Tuck, Richard.
1979 *Natural Rights Theories: Their Origin and Development.* Cambridge: Cambridge University Press.

Weinreb, Lloyd L.
1987 *Natural Law and Justice.* Cambridge and London: Harvard University Press.

Willey, Basil.
1953 *The Eighteenth Century Background: Studies on the Idea of Nature in the Thought of the Period.* New York: Columbia University Press.

Wormuth, Francis D.
1948 "Aristotle on Law." In Konvitz and Murphy (see Morrow), 45-61.

Xunzi, see Hsün Tzu.

Chapter 12

Natural Law and Natural Right: The Role of Myth in the Discourses of Exchange and Community

Winston Davis

Destroyed, the dharma destroys; protected, it protects.

—Manu

My first contribution to this volume seemed to begin and end on a "rationalistic" note. I discussed the myth of natural law—defining myth as anything predicated of the Sacred—and called for its exclusion from political discourse together with all other nonvacuous myths (i.e., myths with patently religious "payloads"). In the present essay, I continue my investigation into the contradictory implications of the myth of natural law, focusing specifically on the conflict it has generated between the political rights of liberal societies, on the one hand, and the socio-economic rights of socialist or welfare states, on the other. In other words, I am concerned with the "mythogenesis" of two discourses which dominate and divide Western social thought. The first, stressing the *invincible* nature of economic law, I call the "discourse of exchange." The other, which insists on the *inviolable* dignity of persons and the *integrity and solidarity of society itself*, I call the "discourse of the community."

An outcropping of seventeenth- and eighteenth-century thought, the discourse of exchange rests on the semisecular, empirical natural law which I described in my previous essay. We have seen that this theory was the harbinger of individualism, utilitarianism, and an operant (as opposed to a teleological) naturalism. The discourse of exchange is concerned above all with the efficiency, productivity, and preservation of assets. Following Hobbes, it accents the safety rather than the dignity of persons. Following Locke, it emphasizes the natural rights of property, sometimes at the expense of the socio-economic rights-claims of the unpropertied classes. Because of its belief in free or unfettered markets, the discourse of exchange prefers big business to big government and chooses to speak of the *public* good rather than the *common* good. While the discourse of exchange flourishes today in the economic wing of the Academy, it cannot be equated with economics *tout simple*. It also influences research in various schools of biology, sociology, anthropology, psychology, and political science.

The discourse of the community, on the other hand, is concerned with the integrity of social groups and the *general* rights—socio-economic *as well as* political—of the individuals who make up those groups. It claims to be the voice of the community itself, including those at the margins of society—the poor, the disabled, the vulnerable, and the disenfranchised. It seeks to contain markets which threaten the community and to expand the role of government when and where markets fail to meet social needs. It bases its agenda not just on the *public* good but, more boldly, on the *common* good.

This paper is divided into two sections. In the first part, I discuss the role of natural law in the discourse of exchange. In the second, I take up the discourse of the community as it has developed in the Roman Catholic Church, a denomination with important ties to the natural law tradition. We shall see that there are serious differences between these discourses and the myths of natural law they presuppose.[1] Although I deal with the secularization of natural law in the first part, the reader should bear in mind that in *both* sections of this paper we continue to deal with the philosophical and practical implications of a myth.

I shall argue that the inviolable dignity of human beings taught by the modern Roman Catholic Church is a fundamental mythogenic "realization" which embodies virtually the whole of natural law. Examination of the idea of dignity will open up a discussion of the importance of religious realizations for the concept of human rights. This discussion I hope will add new dimensions to the "rationalistic" perspective of my previous paper.

The genius of the religious notion of human dignity is its ability to present the core of natural law as a "fundamental realization" about the human condition. Let me explain. A realization is the discovery of a reality which already exists or which has been, and is, given to us. Broadly speaking, realizations are always "traditional." They are, in effect, pluperfect perceptions about our "being in the world." Thus, when we "realize" something about X we are noticing that our past perceptions about X still hold. Some of these perceptions—those which concern things a person should know already, or should know in all cases—are normative. It is a normative realization that we hope to instill in a child when we scold him saying, for example, "don't you *realize* it's wrong to steal!" While some realizations are trivial and mundane, others are profound, shattering and fundamental—e.g., the realization of what it means, or costs, to be a parent, or what we meant when we promised to be faithful "til death us do part." Fundamental realizations break in upon us like divine disclosures, sometimes in the interstices of everyday life, at other times more predictably in life's crises.

Religious systems are built upon our fundamental realizations. Indeed, they "play upon" them the way a harpist's fingers run over the strings of her instrument. Actually, the relationship is more complex. From the historian's point of view, realizations are not simply "given." While religion presupposes our deepest realizations, it also helps to create them. It devises the basic instruments of realization, our "souls." It arranges fundamental realizations in Salvation Syndromes, and inscribes them on our souls and on our "culture" (i.e., the sum total of all fundamental realizations) alike.

While fundamental realizations can be powerful, all-encompassing "kratophanies" or "ontophanies," their consequences can be surprisingly nebulous. Religious experiences, in particular, often obligate but fail to guide, orient but set no specific agenda. Nevertheless, in a "world without foundations," an ethics or social theory based on fundamental realizations may be as "foundational" as can be expected.

In this paper we must inquire whether the fundamental realization of human dignity can transcend its own mythological origins and offer a multicultural society specific, legitimate guidance. I do not wish to imply that I am committing myself *philosophically* to a mythogenic account of human dignity. Since people often "realize" they are no longer bound by realizations they once held sacred, fundamental realizations cannot be regarded as the philosophical loadstones of the moral life. I should emphasize, therefore, that I am using the word *realization* only as a *phenomenological* concept which, hopefully, can help us understand the relationship between our mythological and political discourses. Our inquiry therefore is really an investigation into what goes on "before philosophy."

The Discourse of Exchange

Since the seventeenth century, economic trends have been thought to be as irresistible as gravity and as predictable as clocks and other mechanical devices. Whatever his analogy or root metaphor, the economist-merchant has generally believed that the forces of the market were self-regulating and that the flow of profits into his own pockets was as natural, and as irreversible, as the movement of the tides. Indeed, so strong was his faith in economic naturalism that his analogies took on religious dimensions. The laws of economics became laws of nature; the laws of nature, the laws of God. The nineteenth century, however, had a profoundly secularizing effect on all of this. On all fronts—in philosophy, jurisprudence, and economics—natural law came under attack. While economists continued to talk about natural laws, they now implied nothing more substantial than Montesquieu's "necessary relations" or Alfred Marshall's "statements of tendencies."[2] By the end of the century, James Bonar could say with confidence that there was "general agreement among modern economists that an 'economic law' cannot mean a precept."[3] In this way a purely secular discipline of economics began to emerge from the mythogenic discourse of exchange. Reacting against centuries of ecclesiastical interference in business affairs, the economics of the mercantilist period was often decidedly amoral and antireligious.[4] Thomas Wilson has the merchant in his *Discourse upon Usury* (1584) say that the activities of merchants must not be "over thwarted by preachers and others, that can not skill [know] of their dealings."[5] The unknown author of *Britannia languens* (1680) declares that "no *Statutes*, Nay, or *Preaching*, though never so *learned* or *florid*, can prevail with necessitous men."[6]

The mercantilists began the secularizing of economic thought by dismantling the idea of the common good and the traditional, organic model of Christian society. Joyce Appleby notes that in their writings a fissure appeared between society and the economy, as well as between traditional morality and economic reflection. She points to the "disentangling" of the "economy of sales and exchanges from the moral economy of production and sustenance,"[7] and maintains that it was the "*differentiation* of things economic from their social context that truly distinguishes the writings of the so-called mercantilist period."[8] She also draws our attention to the fact that in the works of people like Thomas Mun, economic concepts were being generated "which moved independently of the specific, the personal, and the concrete. For the first time economic factors were clearly differentiated from their social and political entanglements."[9] These and other basic differentiations—between society and economics, exchange and consumption, the concrete and the abstract, the moral and the profitable—were anything but accidental. They emerged from the very heart of the historical processes that were creating a market society and, with it, new "sciences of man."[10] They suggest that the theory of the market society was based not only on the secularization of traditional social thought, but on its "deethicization." As Albert O. Hirschman put it:

> To deal usefully with the relationship between morality and the social sciences, one must first understand that modern social science arose to a considerable extent in the process of emancipating itself from traditional moral teachings.[11]

Later, under the influence of positivism, moral *epochē* became the regnant spirit of the social sciences, the touchstone of social scientific professionalism. In the case of economics, ethical indifference was also related to a prolonged exposure to (or belief in) the "mechanism" of the market itself. An economy which works in a purely automatic or mechanical way can be affected by no amount of thought—ethical, philosophical, or religious. Conceived as a juggernaut of pure "motion," the self-regulating market simply pulverizes questions about the *legitimacy* of property, wealth, and power under the massive weight of its own operant naturalism.

Adam Smith and the Secularization of Natural Law

There was only one word in the vocabulary of early modern Europe ready to assume the herculean task of justifying the new world of unbridled competition, the word *nature*. In 1675, Roger Coke wrote

"I will never believe that any man or Nation ever will attain their ends by forceable means, against the Nature and Order of things."[12] The early economists used the word *natural* of phenomena and relationships that seemed to be automatic, necessary, or predictable. Their principal strategy was to ground economic nature in *human* nature. Human nature, for all intents and purposes, could be reduced to the "motions" of the heart, especially to self-interest. By making self-interest the mainstay of their explanatory strategy, economists released the passions from the obloquy from which they had suffered in traditional social thought. More important, however, was the economists' belief in the inevitability of the passions. Because people predictably maximize their own gains, the concept of self-interest seemed to impose order on the otherwise irrational activity of markets. Economic activity had finally become rational and predictable, a fit object for science.[13]

Adam Smith made three epochal contributions to the discourse of exchange:

1. He generated interlocking theories of economics and morality, both based on an operant concept of nature.

2. He protected his economic system from conscious interference by demonstrating the efficiency of the "obvious and simple system of natural liberty," and by outlining a theory of morals in which conscious reflection on social or moral issues (ethics) was nearly redundant.

3. He imposed on these essentially secular systems a religious legitimation and theodicy. Like Locke, he brought property and piety together by skillfully weaving into his social theory the myths of providence and natural law.

Since nature was the unquestioned commonplace of the age, Smith did not have to tell his readers what he meant when he called justice, prices, and the market system itself "natural." In the eighteenth century that was too obvious to explain. Because he ordered his lectures on natural theology to be destroyed after his death, it is difficult to relate the naturalism of his economics and moral theory to his concepts of God and Providence. However this may be, the six revisions of *The Theory of Moral Sentiments* (henceforth, *TMS*) give one the impression of a thinker working increasingly in a secular mode.[14]

Although Smith was deeply influenced by the natural economics of the physiocrats, he was critical of the philosophical school of natural law. Like other thinkers of the Scottish Enlightenment, he opposed speculation about the "state of nature" and the "social contract." He rejected the subordination of morality to theology and was more interested in the historical development of positive law than in the discovery of a law for all ages. Believing that nature works from within, i.e., upon man's operant nature, Smith was critical of traditional theories of natural law which imposed obligations on the individual adventitiously, or from without.[15] Here, however, one encounters an enormous tension or contradiction that runs throughout Smith's works. In spite of his commitment to operant naturalism, his system was, as Viner put it, "partly providentialist and teleological, and is so expressly, deliberately, and repetitively."[16] Indeed, it could hardly have been otherwise since British social thought in the eighteenth century was still "soaked in teleology."[17] Smith therefore created what, paradoxically, could be called a "teleological system of operant naturalism," i.e. a synthesis of theory, fact, and general providence. This he achieved, as the physiocrats did, by assigning to God (the Divine Utilitarian) responsibility for the system's long-term success, and to human beings—i.e., to their self-interest and thirst for "approbation"—immediate action therein. The system was summed up in Smith's celebrated image of the "invisible hand."[18] It is clear from his reference to "the invisible hand of Jupiter" in his essay on "The History of Astronomy" that Smith wanted to use the phrase as an expression for the great *regularities* of nature.[19] Although it was a powerful religious symbol in its own right, the "invisible hand" was therefore an alternative to the magical or theistic notion of a Deity who uses His "arbitrary will" to intervene in history "for some private or particular purpose."[20]

According to Smith, morality evolves out of (what we would call) social interaction. One does not act morally simply by rationally observing and applying given, a priori principles. Like Hume, he assigns to reason a secondary, corrective function in the cybernetic hierarchy of moral controls.[21] While Smith places severe restrictions on moral reason, reason still plays a role in his system.[22] In certain circumstances, the voice of the "spectator" seems to be the voice of reason itself.[23] Upon occasion, the rational conscience can become a "more forcible motive" and even "a voice capable of astonishing the most presumptuous of our passions."[24] In the end, however, the efficacy of reason and abstract justice rests upon their ability to serve our vanity and our unquenchable thirst for approbation. One might even say that through Smith the "licentious system" of Bernard Mandeville has triumphed at last![25]

Mention must also be made of the role of natural law in Smith's theory of jurisprudence. In *TMS*, Smith tells us that his general rules of morality could be regarded "as the Laws of the Deity."[26] He virtually equates natural law with equity and contends that the goal of positive law is to approximate "natural jurisprudence."[27] The crucial passages, however, are found in his early lectures on jurisprudence where he equates natural right with the views of the impartial spectator.[28] Here, the reader seems to be referred to the *intersubjective* theory of conscience developed in *TMS*. Smith therefore seems to reduce natural law to the sense of equity established by an informed social consensus. In some ways, his natural law seems to play a role similar to Hobbes's "convenient Articles of Peace."[29] I would contend that, like the latter, Smith's natural law is not natural law at all. At least it is not traditional natural law. Smith's natural law is, at best, a would-be "antidote to subjectivity," i.e. the subjectivity of his own theory.[30]

By this point it should be obvious how secular his system really is, in spite of its theological trimmings. Moral behavior is now under the immediate control of an ideal spectator made, not in the image of God, but of one's fellows. Smith replaces the harmony between man and nature with a "concord" between human beings.[31] For the naturally choiceworthy life he substitutes a life which is socially praiseworthy. In contrast to the a priori precepts of traditional natural law, Smith's general rules grow out of a posteriori, social experience. Smith's morality was therefore an empirical, psychological, sociological, aesthetic theory—all of these adjectives seem to apply. Morality "works" not merely because people observe and apply abstract moral rules; it "works" because of our natural (passionate!) desire for approval.

Smith's natural system of economics and morality raises a number of philosophical and practical problems. Critics quickly perceived that his impartial spectator was incapable of the transcendental, critical functions of true conscience. While the "science of morals" created by Smith and other eighteenth-century figures was a monumental contribution to social psychology, one pays a heavy price for *substituting* social scientific speculation for ethics per se. As socially constructed phenomena, reason and the spectator-conscience cannot tell us how to act in a world which has lost its innocence. Since conscience for Smith is merely a part of the givenness or "operancy" of nature, it can be duped whenever society itself is led astray. Smith does not seem to have imagined that the world could ever become so corrupt that, in the name of decency, conscience could no longer be trusted. But what kind of conscience would one find in the "breast" of the worker in Smith's own "pin factory?" Thanks to the machine-like monotony of his life, the pin operative has become

> as stupid and ignorant as it is possible for a human creature to become. The torpor of his mind renders him, not only incapable of relishing or bearing a part in any rational conversation, but of conceiving any generous, noble, or tender sentiment, and consequently of forming any just judgment concerning many even of the ordinary duties of private life. Of the great and extensive interests of his country, he is altogether incapable of judging. . . .[32]

Should we allow the unfortunate miscreants of the pin factory a voice in the moral decisions of society? Should we let them vote? Would they vote their conscience? Could their conscience be trusted to do the good? Do they even have a conscience? .If the answer to these questions is negative, one is forced to ask whether Smith's theory of conscience is compatible with any worthwhile theory of industrial democracy. Corruption aside, Smith's moral theory would also be discomfited by a society which had become so pluralistic that it could not reach a consensus concerning the objects of its own approbation. In short, the problems of corruption and pluralism remind us that Smith's impartial spectators are products of the social world and, as such, can be expected to provide no better moral guidance than what is currently esteemed by that world.

Distributive justice is another problem for Smith's theory and the discourse of exchange built upon it. In a word, there can be no such thing if the distribution of goods and services is completely left to the market. Bowing to Smith's theory of laissez faire, liberal society has deliberately removed a whole range of social issues from its political agenda.[33]

While Smith's system may avoid the problems caused by a moral or intentional economics—primarily by taking social items off the agenda—his theo-economics leaves God in a vulnerable spot. In the first place, as Smith himself recognized, God is apt to become redundant as the advance of civilization renders people less disposed to explain nature in terms of those invisible beings engendered by "the fear and ignorance of their rude forefathers."[34] Secondly, if Smith's beneficent system were to result in massive distress, even after the rules of fair play had been scrupulously followed, *only God could be blamed*. Fortunately, God disappeared from economics before He could be brought to account.

Smith's greatest philosophical mistake—the greatest of early economics—was the confusion of the powerful, automatic, impersonal, and
anonymous forces of the market with the forces of nature *tout simple*.
While Smith did not invent the world-machine or the notion of a natural economy, his work added great luster to both ideas. Whatever reser-
vations he may have had about natural theology, his work lent renewed
credibility to the theological idea that an economic system of such perfection could only have been designed by a benevolent, divine Artificer.

Although I cannot go into the development of the discourse of
exchange after Smith, I should point out that the discourse of the
community developed, in part, as a reaction to the utter ruthlessness
of the concepts and practices of the subsequent devotees of exchange.
I have in mind, for example, the use of the notion of the wages-fund in
classical economics to keep wages low and the raw "survivalism" of the
Social Darwinists. To many of the critics of capitalism, the economics
of natural law seemed to be simply an ideological device for the
exploitation of the working classes.

Natural Law in the Discourse of the Community

Until recently, the social teachings of the Roman Catholic
Church seemed to many to be the ideology of a religious community
in league with the dictators and *hacendados* of Europe and the Third
World. In 1931, Pius XI acknowledged in *Quadragesimo Anno* (124)
the widespread criticism that the "Church and those proclaiming
attachment to the Church favor the rich, neglect the workers and have
no concern for them. . . ." Today, this situation has changed radically,
thanks primarily to a growing awareness that by the year 2000 the
majority of Roman Catholics will live in the Third World. Church
leaders have not only been exposed to socialist critiques of capitalism;
many have learned their theology by living in impoverished *barrios* and
church-founded *comunidades de base*. But the point of view of the
church and "liberation theology" cannot be understood simply as a
Christian reading of Marx. For decades, the social teachings of the
church have been moving in a more progressive direction. In this
development, the myth of natural law played no small role.

I would like to look briefly at the social teachings of the church
as they developed from *Rerum Novarum* (1891) to the *Pastoral Letter
on Catholic Social Teaching and the U.S. Economy* issued in 1986 by the

National Conference of Catholic Bishops (USA). What is striking in these documents is the role played by the concept of human dignity. According to Leo XIII, "No one may with impunity outrage the dignity of man" (*Rerum Novarum*, 57). The "growing awareness of the exalted dignity proper to the human person" is associated with rights and duties which are "universal and inviolable" (*Gaudium et Spes*, 26). A government which violates these rights is declared completely lacking in "juridical force" (*Pacem in Terris*, 61). The position of the church was summarized succinctly by Maritain when he wrote:

> The dignity of the human person? The expression means nothing if it does not signify that by virtue of natural law, the human person has the right to be respected, is the subject of rights, possesses rights.[35]

I would like to argue 1) that human dignity has become the basic axiom of the social teachings of the Catholic church, 2) that it functioned initially as a holophrastic expression for natural law itself, and 3) that the church has used it as a semantic or hermeneutical device to move from a traditional concept of natural law to a modern theory of natural rights.

The Catholic concept of dignity is closely related to solidarity and the common good, concepts harking back to the traditional Christian version of the organic model of society and to the medieval concept of natural law. Human dignity can only be fully realized "in community." Without it, there can be neither justice nor peace (*Mater et Magistra*, 215). Dignity ensures that people are to be treated as ends and not as means (*Pastoral Letter*, 28). While dignity is rooted in man's own morality, reason, will and work, its ultimate ground is God. God is the source of the vitality of any society which is "well-ordered, beneficial, and in keeping with human dignity" (*Pacem in Terris*, 37). Here we come back to our main concern. Since God Himself has bestowed dignity upon human life, dignity is originally, in my terms, a mythical notion.[36]

In some ways, Catholic social teachings in the period between 1891 and the present are impressively consistent. The various themes of traditional natural law continue to appear, among them the emphasis (just noted) on dignity, solidarity, and the common good. Church documents repeatedly have stressed the organic nature of society, just prices and wages, and even (until recently) *recta ratio*.[37] The emphasis on "the just ordering of goods" (e.g. *Mater et Magistra*, 176) seems to be an echo of the hierarchical class-ranking of goods taught by theologians since Augustine—much to the dismay of economists.[38] Since *Quadregesimo Anno*(1931), the principle of subsidiarity has been another common theme. Like "intermediary institutions" (declared by *Rerum Novarum* (72) to be "permitted by a right of nature"), subsidiarity was put forward as an alternative to the extremes of bureaucratic centralism and socialism.[39] Criticism of both ends of the political and economic spectra—laissez faire capitalism and communism—has also been a fairly consistent pattern.

Changes in the church's social teachings, however, seem to outweigh these continuities. Recent papal teachings have displayed a remarkable openness to pluralism, toleration, and the complexities of international relations. Pope Paul VI openly confessed that "it is difficult for us to utter a unified message and to put forward a solution which has universal validity" and that "The same Christian faith can lead to different commitments" (*Octogesima Adveniens*, 4 and 50). Compared with its traditional teachings, the church today gives greater scope to the concept of rights, including the religious rights of non-Catholic minorities. It has a new appreciation of the importance of "structural" or "institutional" sin, i.e., sin that transcends the will of the individual. The outright condemnation of socialism has been replaced with a more open attitude allowing even for the "socialization" of property.[40] While the Aristotelian and Thomistic conviction that property should be owned privately but used in a public way has generally prevailed, the church is now interested in the co-determination (*Mitbestimmung*) and co-ownership by workers and capitalists of the means of production.[41] Strikes, once forbidden (*Quadragesimo Anno*, 94), are now allowed (*Gaudium et Spes*, 68). Charity, traditionally given out of one's superfluity (*Rerum Novarum*, 36) is now to be given "not only out of what is superfluous" (*Gaudium et Spes*, 88). The encouragement of friendship, harmony, and cooperation between capitalist and working classes has given way to a new emphasis on the active participation of all people at the great economic "workbench."

A careful reading of church pronouncements also reveals a subtle shift in their *mythological* foundation. We have seen that the concept of dignity has been used as a code word for natural law itself. From the beginning, the church's doctrine of human dignity has rested not only on natural law but on the Bible, in particular the myths of Creation, Covenant, Incarnation, and Redemption. Again and again, the dignity of man has been traced back to his creation "in the image of God." The myth of Creation is also used to legitimate the dignity of human labor. Jesus the carpenter conferred an "eminent dignity on labor when at Nazareth he worked with his own hands" (*Gaudium et Spes*, 67). Popes from Leo XIII through John XXIII were explicit in their use of the natural law doctrine. After John, however, a shift in emphasis can be seen. While dignity and humanism remain central themes in papal teaching, the explicit use of natural law begins to wane. In recent documents, human dignity seems to have become shorthand for a *Biblical* view of man and society, or at least, for the church's interpretation of the Biblical view.[42] This remarkable revival of the role of scripture in the social teachings of the church may be a reflection of a growing dissatisfaction with the traditional notion of natural law in theological circles.[43] Whatever its cause, the concept of human dignity seems to have functioned as a catalyst enabling the church to retreat from the rational myth of natural law while reaffirming the (relatively) irrational Biblical myths of "salvation-history."[44] Thus, the church seems to have first "demythologized" its concept of dignity and then "remythologized" it.

Dignity and the Economy

Some advocates of the discourse of exchange regard hunger and starvation as part of the legitimate operancy or naturalness of the economy. This does not sit well with Catholic natural law. As Arthur Okun puts it, "Starvation and dignity do not mix well."[45] The church's teaching about dignity and the new humanism have therefore become linchpins in an overall critique of the economy. Value is not to be measured simply in terms of supply and demand. The value of work ultimately is determined by "the fact that the one who is doing it is a person" (*Laborem Exercens*, 6). The ideal economy is one which encourages the free and active participation of each and every "subject." The "subjectivity" of work demanded by the church is intended as a barrier preventing the commodification or alienation of labor—if I may use Marxist terms studiously avoided by the Vatican itself. This too harks back to human dignity: "a citizen has a sense of his own dignity when he contributes the major share to progress in his own affairs" (*Mater et magistra*, 152; see also *Pastoral Letter*, 61). The "subjectivity" of labor is also rooted in Catholic humanism: the economy must be "*worthy of man*" (*Redemptor Hominis*, 15).

Human dignity stands at the very heart of the American bishops' recent assessment of the U.S. economy: "*Every economic decision and institution must be judged in light of whether it protects or undermines the dignity of the human person*" (*Pastoral*, 13).[46] Thus the *Pastoral* seems to reflect the criteria John Paul II laid down in *Redemptor Hominis* (15)

for determining legitimate economic progress, namely the question
whether in any course of action

> man, as man, is becoming truly better, that is to say more mature
> spiritually, more aware of the dignity of his humanity, more
> responsible, more open to others, especially the neediest and the
> weakest, and readier to give and to aid all.

The question to be asked of any economic proposal is therefore not whether
it will result in "having more," but in "being more" (*Redemptor Hominis*, 16).

While the Catholic hierarchy has been reluctant to impose specific
economic nostrums on its worldwide flock, it also knows that it owes
the faithful more than platitudes. In general, the economic policies rec-
ommended by the church fall no farther to the right than the welfare
state, no farther to the left than Democratic Socialism. It favors a state
active in the protection of private property and human rights in general.
The magisterium has consistently condemned the "errors of individual-
ist economic teaching," on the one hand, and the "economic dictator-
ship" of the socialist economies, on the other (*Quadragesimo Anno*, 88).
It has roundly condemned "economism" fixated on such "objective"
measures of economic growth as the GNP, insisting that "the economic
prosperity of any people is to be assessed not so much from the sum
total of goods and wealth possessed as from the distribution of goods
according to norms of justice" (*Mater et Magistra*, 74). It attacks systems
in which "dead matter comes forth from the factory ennobled, while
men there are corrupted and degraded" (*Quadragesimo Anno*, 135).

The most radical element in the Catholic position is its concept of
rights. Expanding the notion far beyond the limits set by the thinkers of
the seventeenth and eighteenth centuries, the church regards human
rights as "the minimum conditions for life in community" (*Pastoral*, 17)
or more precisely, the "prerequisites for a dignified life in community"
(ibid., 79). One might therefore think of the Catholic concept of rights
as a system of *dignity-thresholds*. Conceived in this way, the barrier
between rights and entitlements is removed, so that rights come to
include nearly all of the amenities of the welfare state. What traditionally fell to charity (and the use of one's "superfluity") has now become a
matter of justice. Far from being abstract or static entities, rights *expand*
as society's spiritual and material strength grows. The list of rights is
therefore long and growing. *Pacem in Terris* says that

> every man has the right to life, to bodily integrity, and to the
> means which are suitable for the proper development of life; these
> are primarily food, clothing, shelter, rest, medical care, and finally

the necessary social services. Therefore a human being also has the right to security in cases of sickness, inability to work, widowhood, old age, unemployment. . . . (11)

By the natural law every human being has the right to respect for his person, to his good reputation; the right to freedom in searching for truth and in expressing and communicating his opinions . . . and he has the right to be informed truthfully about public events. (12; see also *Gaudium et Spes*, 26)

The attitude of the church toward the poor also seems to have changed. At the end of the last century, one senses in its teachings a certain distance from the poor, perhaps even an apprehensive attitude toward them. *Rerum Novarum* (66), for example, frets that the minds of the poor are "inflamed and always ready for disorder." Since the meeting of Latin American bishops in Puebla, Mexico in 1979, the church has been speaking about a "preferential option for the poor."[47] The "option" is not seen as something done *for* the poor, but as a policy to enable or allow them to become active "subjects" in the economy themselves. Today the church regards poverty as "a violation of the dignity of human work" (*Laborem Exercens*, 8). Poverty is a violation of a basic human right, the right to employment (*Gaudium et Spes*, 26).

The Myth of Human Dignity

While Greek thinkers helped to illuminate the concept of honor (*timē*), philosophy in general has shied away from the problem of human dignity. Traditionally, philosophers have explained man's dignity in terms of his ontological position, i.e., the place assigned to him on the "Great Chain of Being." Man, we are told, finds himself above the other animals but below the angels. He is more rational than the dumb brutes and shares the spiritual nature of angels and the Deity. Even Pico della Mirandola, who located man's dignity in his freedom, ultimately judged what man does with his free (and therefore indeterminate) nature in terms of a fixed Christian and Neo-Platonic hierarchy of being.[48] After Descartes, when philosophy began to give priority to the knowing subject, the ontological concept of dignity was replaced with the subjective notion, respect. Still, neither dignity nor respect was a lively philosophical issue. Those who discussed human dignity tended to reduce it (*nolens volens*) to a subjective regard for another's abilities, achievements, status, or honor. Hume rejected the idea that dignity was based on comparisons of ontological rank, or as he put it, on "any fixed unalterable standard in the nature of things" or "an idea of perfections much beyond what he (man) has experience of in himself."[49] Dignity is determined only by comparing "the different motives or actuating principles of human nature."[50] Other philosophers have tried to explain human dignity in terms of a person's inherent freedom to choose. One thinks of Kant, for example, who taught that autonomy is the basis of human dignity (*Würde*).[51] People with dignity are people in charge of their own lives.

The problem with the Kantian position is that it potentially excludes the poor and the disabled, i.e., people who manifestly are *not* in charge of their own destinies. The position might even be understood (or misunderstood) to imply that insofar as rights rest on dignity, and dignity of free choice and self-reliance, only people who are able to choose have rights. Michael Novak and his neo-conservative colleagues have tried to modify the Catholic teaching on human dignity along these lines by insisting that dignity "implies *self-reliance*, the responsibility of every free person for his or her well-being."[52] The danger here is obvious. If dignity is equated with self-reliance, it soon becomes an achievement. Some people will have it; others will not. Robert E. Goodin brings up the case of a paraplegic who, "utterly at the mercy of natural necessity, still suffers an 'indignity' when the nurse examines him in the public ward of the hospital without drawing the curtain."[53] This example raises serious questions about the rights of those who have no voice in the community, who are not self-reliant, or who cannot consciously or autonomously articulate their own decisions. What rights do guest- or migrant-workers, resident aliens, citizens of occupied territories, convicts, the mentally ill or disenfranchised really have? If we believe they have rights, what is the basis for our belief?

The weakness of the philosophical approach to dignity suggests that the concept has deeper origins and roots. This, in effect, is what the church itself is saying when it says that the dignity of man comes from God. Man's dignity is part of the heritage of Creation. "It is He that made us, and we are his; we are his people, and the sheep of his pasture." Dignity is one of the fruits of Redemption. As the ancient Christian saying has it: "Call no man vile for whom Christ has died." These (and other) statements of faith indicate that human dignity is not merely something deduced from philosophical principles; is a "fundamental realization" of the human condition disclosed in religious or mythic terms. Convictions of this sort can be clarified, but not established by philosophical discourse.

One reason we are unclear about dignity is that we confuse it with honor and honorable accomplishments. Dignity actually resembles honor in many ways. In the vernacular, a person who acts "with honor" is virtually the same as one who acts "with dignity." But the dignity described by the church is vastly different from honor. It is an ontological structure; honor is merely a psycho-social achievement. While dignity is given and discovered in the human condition, honor is something "agonistic." It must be won. Honor is a matter of opinion, hierarchy, a measure of status, machismo, or prestige. It is, or may be, hereditary and varies according to race, class, age, sex, and occupation.[54] As such, it reflects the structure and values of society itself. Not only is dignity not agonistic; it is even compatible with the "soft" virtues of humility, trust, and love. Honor is built on competition; dignity on an ethos of acceptance and respect. To shame or dishonor someone is to throw down the gauntlet; to trample on his or her dignity is to violate a taboo. Since dignity has to do with *being* it is not merely an Aristotelian *hexis* or a Rylean "disposition."[55] There is, accordingly, a vast difference between the Christian concept of dignity and the "dignified behavior" of some modern thinkers.[56] It is as far removed from the dignity of the liberal social planners who reduce it to "feeling good about yourself" as it is from the neo-conservatives who treat it as "self-respect" or "self-reliance."[57] Since dignity (as Christians understand it) is part of the very being of a person, it can neither be gained nor lost. What can be gained or lost is one's *respect for* the dignity of another—and for the rights dignity entails. But that is a completely different matter.

Why are children, the poor, the weak, and the sick the touchstones of human dignity and social justice? Because, the church might say, their dignity is so fragile that only God himself can uphold it. They are the embodiment, indeed the incarnation, of the dignity of *all* people. In their daily life the poor reenact involuntarily the voluntary self-emptying of God in Christ. For this reason they symbolize the human condition itself. In the words of a celebrated nonbeliever, poverty is a "sphere of society which claims no *traditional* status but only a human status . . ." It "can only redeem itself by a total redemption of humanity."[58] In other words, human dignity must be real here or it will be real nowhere. It is only when we take the vulnerable seriously that we realize the importance of the relationship between dignity and rights—for human dignity is the mythogenic prerequisite of human rights. To attribute rights to a being without dignity would be like putting a crown on the head of a commoner. Dignity, then, is what makes people worthy of the rights they have.

The Discourses of Exchange and Community Compared

The contradictory nature of the myth of natural law which I discussed in my first paper becomes apparent again when we look at its application to economics. Some of the Stoics thought that private property was contrary to nature. Aquinas held it to be an "addition" to natural law. Leo XIII went beyond Aquinas and declared private property to be "according to" nature. Locke nearly absolutized the "natural rights" of property. Or, take the example of interest-bearing loans. According to Aristotle and the medieval church, interest was "unnatural." William Petty, however, spoke of taking "simple *natural* Interest."[59] Max Weber and Werner Sombart believed the *pre*capitalist economy was "natural."[60] We have seen that Adam Smith taught that, rightly understood, Europe's new "commercial society"—what we today call capitalism—was a system of "*natural* liberty." While Smith's theory of nature leads to *free markets*, the twentieth-century Roman Catholic church deduces from *its* theory of natural law (and human dignity) the need for *contained markets* and the legitimacy of periodic *interventions* to ensure respect for a wide variety of social and economic rights. In short, our survey of the discourses of exchange and community serves, once again, to underscore the contradictory conclusions one can draw from the myths and doctrines of natural law.

Conservative advocates of the discourse of exchange have responded to the new progressive stand of the church with bitter protest. Word of the "radical" nature of the American bishops' *Pastoral* made conservatives so nervous that a self-appointed "Lay Commission" appeared (even before the *Pastoral* was published) to make sure the bishops took account of the "American experience" in their deliberations.[61] Conservatives were comfortable with the traditional, liberal distinction between rights and entitlements; the former guaranteeing the security of persons, holdings, and political rights, the latter being (in their eyes) merely ill-advised concessions to the grumbling masses. They argued that since entitlements cost money, more attention should be paid to the morality of production. The critics minced no words. P. T. Bauer complained that the papal position "buttresses and encourages envy and resentment," that it is "supported by bogus arguments," that "the Pope has lost all contact with reality, both in what he says and what he ignores," and that the Catholic position is "un-Christian," "immoral," and "incompetent." Finally, in a nasty *ad hominem*, he declares that the position of the church is the work of clerics "who have lost their faith."[62]

Among the more serious charges which critics bring against the social program of the church is the claim that it will impose intolerable or unfair costs on the community as a whole. It goes without saying that the maintenance of dignity-thresholds is a costly business. An impoverished society would be able to provision only the "liberal" rights of the eighteenth century, i.e. the safety of persons, property, political participation, and judicial rights. Conservatives, however, fail to realize that even *these* rights can be costly. In this country, for example, millions of dollars and thousands of lives could be saved every year if courts and police departments were allowed to disregard the judicial rights of drug pushers, murderers, and thieves. The fact is that rights of all sorts are expensive, their neglect more costly still. Cost alone therefore does not help us distinguish between rights and entitlements. Having said this, it is important to recognize a point made by conservatives: distribution and consumption are not the only economic issues which are moral problems. One must also deal with the morality of production, efficiency, and productivity. Moral neglect of these economic imperatives is also costly. In short, the cost of neglecting either distribution or production makes the ongoing "dialogue" between the advocates of exchange and the community a moral, political, and economic obligation.

There are at least three points on which the discourses of exchange and community are in fundamental disagreement. Since these disagreements stem from the ambiguity and contradictions in the myth of natural law itself, their political resolution is not easy.

First, the Catholic position on natural law is obviously a religious one, whereas classical economics evolved into a secular academic system. While there is no reason to doubt the sincerity of Adam Smith's belief in Providence, there is also no reason why it could not be replaced by a belief in the inherent order of the economic system and a purely secular theodicy that says, in the face of failure, "just wait, things will be better."

Secondly, classical economics is based on an ontology of individualism. It presupposes a world in which individual actors provide and purchase individual goods and services. The logic of the market is therefore indifferent or hostile to any a priori hierarchy or grouping of values, whether by government or some higher authority. Since the liberal market society has no Archimedean fulcrum for the weighing of values, everything depends on the subjective choices of the individual. This contrasts strongly with the Catholic "interventionist" position which teaches that society itself has a responsibility to judge and rank at least some goods and services and to provide others which the market cannot afford. A moral society must have not only a public good; it must have a common good as well. Contrary to Bentham, pushpin is *not* as good as poetry.

The third difference between the two discourses has to do with the neo-natural law concept of operancy or behaviorism. In the previous chapter, I pointed out that operant naturalism is "Ulpianism" without any teleological restraints, i.e., Ulpianism gone wild. This is why the church has repeatedly criticized the Enlightenment's concept of nature and the "materialism" of modern economics.[63] As the American bishops put it, "there is no word for dignity in the vocabulary of materialism" (*A Statement on Man's Dignity*, 32). The church therefore seeks to replace the inevitability of neo-natural law (the natural "motions" of the passions) with the inviolability and sanctity of human dignity. This, however, puts the church on a collision course with the theory of "natural" or "self-regulating" markets. It is not enough to trust that Providence will transform "private vices" into "publick Benefits" *à la* Mandeville. "Economic development must remain in man's determination . . ." Competition and free trade therefore cannot be the sole norms of commerce and international relations (*Populorum Progressio*, 58). More immediate norms must come into play that will "minister to the dignity and purpose of man" (*Gaudium et Spes*, 29).

The Role of Myth in Political Discourse

Today, as a "politics of values" threatens to edge out a "politics of issues," religious groups of all sorts are frantically competing for the public ear. In such an atmosphere, an understanding of the legitimate role of religion in public discourse is vitally important for the health of the republic. I conclude this essay, therefore, as I did my previous one, with some thoughts on the place of myth in a pluralistic society said to be "without foundations."

In a curious way, our argument has come full circle and returns to ontology. It is an "ontological taboo" that one violates when one desecrates the dignity of another human being, not just a cultural ideal. But we do not end up in exactly the same place where we began, i.e. with a cosmomorphic or cosmogonic morality. A phenomenological analysis of the myth of natural law suggests that the being or nature presupposed by morality is not Being as such, but an *ontology mediated by culture,* an "ontology of finitude," as Paul Ricoeur might say.

There has always been a weak and a strong interpretation of natural law. The strong interpretation expects great things from the doctrine. It holds that the immutable principles of natural law can be expressed as substantive maxims or foundational principles which can be directly applied to concrete political situations. It teaches that accommodation and modification take place only between principles and their concrete application in the world, not between principles themselves. The strong interpretation of natural law sometimes takes the shape of a fundamentalism which looks on its own principles as apodictic, nondialectical truths. Ironically, while the strong interpretation obviously is deeply moral, it tends to remove *ethical* convictions from the arena of philosophical and political negotiation. By absolutizing the deliverances of natural law, it makes it difficult to weight the claims of one (mythogenic) value against another.[64] For example, the church has vindicated the claims of the poor of the Third World in the name of natural law, but condemns birth control, a necessary component in the struggle against poverty, on the same mythological grounds. The nonnegotiable nature of mythological axioms also constrains discussions about abortion and homosexuality within the church.

The weak interpretation is more realistic about what one can expect from fundamental, mythogenic realizations. It insists that natural law can have a real influence only when it is mixed with positive law and political wisdom in concrete situations. It expects natural law to provide basic guidelines but not specific rules. To use a modern analogy, the weak interpretation treats natural law (and all other fundamental realizations) as though they were the "disk operating system" (DOS) of a computer, i.e., the basic program which enables the computer to "read" other software. Insofar as it does not manipulate data the way other software does, DOS is a *limited* program. It is *fundamental* only in the sense that other software will not work without it. In a similar way, the weak interpretation of myth recognizes the importance of the fundamental realizations of religion for secular life and does not reject them simply because they sound platitudinous or vague.

One might say that the *strongest* case to be made for natural law is the *weakest* interpretation. I have argued that the realization of human dignity makes people worthy of the rights they enjoy and makes recognition of those rights obligatory. While some claim they can deduce a definite set of rights from natural law, it seems to me that the number and nature of rights will always be a matter of legitimate debate, even among those who espouse natural law positions. Like DOS, the "realization" of human dignity only prepares us for more specific "programs," or in this case, for more specific rights. But there seems to be no specific list or limit to the rights implicit in the concept of human dignity *per se*.[65]

Although dignity ultimately is a mythogenic concept, it is sufficiently secular to function as a legitimate value in public discourse. The problem is not its right to public space, but whether, in that space, it will play anything more than a rhetorical or ideological role. Political partisans of all stripes can appeal to the dignity of the human person in nearly any debate. The church has argued the case for social democracy on the basis of the dignity *of the poor*. Conservatives, on the other hand, are apt to argue that *only those who work* have dignity and that respect for the dignity of persons puts *limits* on even the benevolent interventions of the state.[66] Ethicists who argue against euthanasia rest their case on the *dignity of life*, while those who support a patient's "right to die" hold that a person has a right to *die in dignity*. Dignity could likewise be used both to support and to condemn abortion, capital punishment, food stamps. gay rights, single sex marriages, and a host of other issues.

Another fly is dropped into the ointment by those who insist that, as dignity-thresholds, rights should *multiply* as the economy expands and that the moral community should "avoid all premature closure of the sphere of rights."[67] Critics are sure to argue that, if this is the case, the number of rights must *decrease* when the economy contracts. Surely we are not ready to say of our rights what we say of the deceased in the Funeral Office—"the Lord gives and the Lord has taken away!" This would be putting God in the same vulnerable spot in which Adam Smith left Him.

Are we then back where we began? Are we forced to distinguish between indispensable political rights and dispensable social entitlements? Has the idea of dignity-thresholds failed to put the matter of social welfare under the rubric of justice after all? Are we still "saddled" with the concept of charity? In short, has the concept of dignity-thresholds clarified the concept of rights at all?

I raise these questions not to condemn the idea of rights as dignity-thresholds, but to call for further elaboration of the idea by those committed to the "preferential option for the poor." A carefully nuanced concept of rights based on the realization of the inviolability of human dignity *could* have decisive advantages over the traditional liberal concept of rights. Even if, as Baum suggests, rights can be founded more securely on the concept of the common good than on dignity as such, the realization of the dignity of the human person is necessary for determining who is, and who is not, worthy of rights. All rights in the early modern theories of natural rights were deduced from the primordial right of self-preservation. If human dignity and/or the common good were accepted as the basis of all rights, there would be no need for any "primordial right." This, in turn, would help to absolve rights from the charge commonly made against them: that they are merely the protected turf of a capitalist individualism which is acquisitive, privileged, and antisocial. The solution to this nagging problem might ultimately lead to a reconciliation of our ideas of rights, duties, virtue, and the common good, a reconciliation which manifestly is *not* possible in the early modern theory of natural rights. Until such a comprehensive theory of the common good appears, social theory and political practice will best be served neither by dismissing mythogenic values in a peremptory way, nor by expecting more guidance from them than they, by their nature, can provide.

Notes

1.   The study of these political and mythological antinomies provides an opportunity to correct the tendency of conservative apologists who emphasize the compatibility of Catholic and Anglo-Scottish natural law. While some papal positions (e.g., *Rerum Novarum* 14, 15, and 23) are redolent of the Lockean doctrine, I shall argue that the natural law of the Catholic church is fundamentally different from that of the Anglo-Scottish tradition.

2.   Schumpeter, *History of Economic Analysis*, 537.

3.   *Philosophy and Political Economy*, 194.

4.   Eli F. Heckscher, *Mercantilism* 2, 286-302.

5.   *Discourse*, 250.

6.   J. R. McCulloch, *Early English Tracts on Commerce*, 376.

7.   Joyce Oldham Appleby, *Economic Thought and Ideology*, 52.

8.   Ibid., p. 26. My emphasis. Appleby's use of the word *differentiation* is significant, especially since the secularization of Western society is largely the result of a growing differentiation between sacred rationales and secular institutions. Secularization seldom implies simply the disappearance of the Sacred as such.

9.   Ibid., p. 41.

10.   See Albert O. Hirschman, "Morality and the Social Sciences: A Durable Tension," 21; William Letwin, *The Origins of Scientific Economics*, 158-59; Walter Weisskopf, *The Psychology of Economics*, 15.

11.   "Morality and the Social Sciences," 21.

12.   Cited in Appleby, op. cit., p. 242.

13.   The relatively leisurely pace of English economic development encouraged the view that economic behavior was a natural, not a historical phenomenon. On the Continent, where capitalism appeared more suddenly, its historical nature was perceived more quickly.

14.   Adam Smith, *Moral Sentiments* (henceforth, *TMS*), appendix 2.

15.   *TMS*, 329ff; Adam Smith, *Jurisprudence* (hereafter, *LJ*), 93.

16.   Jacob Viner, *Providence*, 79. Others deny the specifically religious connotations of the invisible hand, e.g. Henry J. Bittermann, "Adam Smith's Empiricism and the Law of Nature," 719, and Nathan Rosenberg, "Adam Smith and Laissez-Faire Revisited," 24. For a corrective to these views see Alec Macfie, "The Invisible Hand of Jupiter," 595-99.

17.   Viner, *Providence*, 60.

18.   In his two major works, Smith does not use the "hand" image in exactly the same way. In *TMS* (184-85), the "hand" functions to restore the Stoic ideal of natural equality. In *The Wealth of Nations* [(henceforth, *WN*), vol. 1, 456] it is used to explain how each individual, by employing his capital for his own ends, ironically increases the annual revenues of the whole society.

19.   In *Essays on Philosophical Subjects* (hereafter, *EPS*), 49.

20.   "History of Ancient Physics," *EPS*, 116 and 113.

21.   "Reason cannot render any particular object either agreeable or disagreeable to the mind for its own sake." In fact, "nothing can be agreeable or disagreeable for its own sake, which is not rendered such by immediate sense and feeling," *TMS*, 320.

22.   "The reasonings of philosophy, it may be said, though they may confound and perplex the understanding, can never break down the necessary connection which Nature has established between causes and their effects," *TMS*, p. 293.

23.   "It is reason, principle, conscience, the inhabitant of the breast, the man within, the great judge and arbiter of our conduct," *TMS*, 137.

24.   *TMS*, 137.

25.   *TMS*, 308-13.

26.   *TMS*, 161.

27.   *LJ*, 134; *TMS*, 340-41.

28.   *LJ*, 17 and 459.

29.   Like Hobbes's Articles of Peace, Smith's general rules have their utilitarian payoff: "Without this sacred regard to general rules, there is no man whose conduct can be much depended upon," *TMS*, 163.

30.   Stephen T. Worland, "Adam Smith," 11.

31.   "Though they will never be unisons, they may be concords, and this is all that is wanted or required," *TMS*, 22.

32.   *WN*, 782.

33.   See Worland, "Adam Smith," 23. It is significant that Smith follows the well-established custom of distinguishing between justice and "perfect right," on the one hand, and charity and distributive justice, on the other. Smith allows the poor to beg for charity. He does not let them make claims on the rest of society in the name of justice, *LJ*, 9.

34.   "History of Astronomy," *EPS*, 50.

35.   Jacques Maritain, *Christianity and Democracy*, 144-45.

36.   I must point out again that I continue to use the term *myth* in a technical way and that when I call human dignity a "myth," I am not trying to impugn its reality or importance.

37.   *Recta ratio* becomes a stumbling block for a church struggling with "pluralism in self-understandings." Reduced to a plural (*rectae rationes*), the traditional notion of right or sound reason loses its "punch." See David Hollenbach, *Claims in Conflict*, 118-24.

38.   Jacob Viner, *Religious Thought and Economic Society*, 55-61.

39.   The principle of subsidiarity states that nothing that could be done at a lower level of society should be done at a higher level. An intermediary institution is one which stands between the state and the individual, e.g., the church, monastic orders, confraternities, guilds, unions, charitable foundations, and other voluntary associations.

40.   *Laborem Exercens* (14) makes an important distinction between government ownership and socialization, the latter applying only to those situations in which "the subject character of society is ensured, that is to say, when on the basis of his work each person is fully entitled to consider himself a part-owner of the great workbench at which he is working with everyone else."

41.   John T. Pawlikowski (in *Justice in the Marketplace*, Byers, ed., 171) notes that the Second Vatican Council "did not posit any direct link between private property and natural law. In other words, no Catholic may argue, according to II Vatican, that private property is an inherent right of every individual. This is significant because it opens the door for Catholic participation in more socialist models of government."

42.   Pawlikowski (in *Justice in the Marketplace*, Byers, ed., 200) notes that by the time of *Populorum Progressio* (1967) "Catholicism is no longer seen as tied to a social system based on natural law. There is considerable difference between Paul VI and the perspective of John XXIII in *Pacem in Terris*, where the natural law argument predominated."

43.   See Charles E. Curran, *New Perspectives*, 1976.

44.   I use the terms *rational* and *irrational* here in their technical, Weberian sense.

45.   A. M. Okun, *Equality and Efficiency*, 17.

46.   Emphasis in the original.

47. In their recent *Pastoral* (16), the U.S. bishops speak more cautiously about a "*fundamental* option for the poor." *Octagesima Adveniens* (23) speaks of "the preferential *respect* due to the poor" (my emphasis).

48.   *On the Dignity of Man*, 3-34.

49.   David Hume, "Of the Dignity or Meanness of Human Nature," 81 and 83.

50.   Ibid., 84. The dignity Hume is concerned with is not, however, the kind of dignity which can be predicated of all human beings. It is an achievement similar to honor (and therefore the opposite of "meanness").

51.   *Foundations of the Metaphysics of Morals*, 54.

52.   *Toward the Future*, 5. My emphasis. Novak's reduction of dignity to self-reliance is similar to Charles Murray's treatment of dignity as self-respect (which he equates with "earning one's own life" or "measuring up"). Since the neo-conservatives treat dignity as "an indispensable good that cannot be given," they ultimately have nothing in common with the Catholic tradition which teaches that dignity was given to humankind at the Creation. (See Charles Murray, *In Pursuit of Happiness and Good Government*, chap. 6, "Dignity, Self-Esteem, and Self-Respect," 112-31.)

53.   *Political Theory and Public Policy*, 83.

54.   See Julian Pitt-Rivers, "Honor."

55.   Gilbert Ryle, *The Concept of Mind*.

56.   B. F. Skinner, for example, treats dignity as behavior that will accumulate and preserve "credit." Dignity, in other words, is an achievement. (See his *Beyond Freedom and Dignity*, especially chap. 3, "Dignity," 44-59.)

57.   Charles Murray, *In Pursuit of Happiness*, 129. I have no quarrel with those who stress the importance of self-respect and self-reliance in a well-ordered society. I question only their *substitution* of these notions for human dignity.

58.   Karl Marx, "Contribution to the Critique," 64.

59.   *Economic Writings*, vol. 1, 48. My emphasis.

60.   "The pre-capitalist man was a natural man, man as God made him. . . . His economic activity . . . springs quite easily from human nature." Werner Sombart, *The Quintescence of Capitalism*, 13.

61.   The Lay Commission included such luminaries as William Simon (former Treasury Secretary), J. Peter Grace (of W. R. Grace & Co.), Alexander Haig, and Claire Booth Luce. Its report, *Toward the Future* (op. cit.), was largely the work of Michael Novak, a lay theologian associated with the conservative American Enterprise Institute.

62.   "Ecclesiastical Economics: Envy Legitimated," in *Reality and Rhetoric*, 73-89.

63.   E.g., *Mater et Magistra*, 63; *Pacem in Terris*, 5-6.

64.   The ancient and medieval doctrines of natural law were based on rational presuppositions, i.e., "that man is intelligent; that reality is intelligible; and that reality, as grasped by intelligence, imposes on the will the obligation that it be obeyed in its demands for action or abstention" (John Courtney Murray, *We Hold These Truths*, 113). One wonders whether Catholic teaching on dignity, which as we have seen has moved away from natural law *proprie dictu* to a more scriptural or "Protestant" footing, is not in danger of becoming less amenable to "right reason" and of degenerating into a kind of Biblical intuitionism.

65.   Taking the opposite tack, David Hollenbach (*Claims*, 197) argues for the acceptance of "the full set" of liberal and social rights on the grounds of their interrelatedness. Unfortunately, the (undeniable) relatedness of people's claims is no argument for regarding them as rights. Against Hollenbach (and mainstream papal teachings), Gregory Baum ("Catholic Foundation of Human Rights," 8) and John A. Coleman ("Catholic Human Rights Theory," 349-55) contend that other concepts, such as the common good, provide stronger foundations for rights than the notion of human dignity. See also the helpful bibliographical study by Joseph L. Allen, "Catholic and Protestant Theories of Human Rights," 347-53.

66.   In addition to the work of Charles Murray already cited, see Stanley I. Benn, *A Theory of Freedom*.

67.   Hollenbach, *Claims*, 141.

References

Allen, Joseph L.
      1988 "Catholic and Protestant Theories of Human Rights." *Religious Studies Review* (October 1988), vol. 14, no. 4, 347-53.

Appleby, Joyce Oldham.
      1978 *Economic Thought and Ideology in Seventeenth-Century England.* Princeton: Princeton University Press.

Bauer, Peter T.
      1984 *Reality and Rhetoric: Studies in the Economics of Development.* Cambridge: Harvard University Press.

Baum, Gregory.
1979 "Catholic Foundation of Human Rights." *The Ecumenist* (1979), vol. 28, 6-12.

Benn, Stanley I.
1988 *A Theory of Freedom*. Cambridge: Cambridge University Press.

Bittermann, Henry J.
1940 "Adam Smith's Empiricism and the Law of Nature." *Journal of Political Economy* (October 1940), vol. 48, no. 5, part 2, 703-34.

Bonar, James.
1966 *Philosophy and Political Economy*. New York: Augustus M. Kelley.

Byers, David M., ed.
1985 *Justice in the Marketplace: Collected Statements of the Vatican and the United States Catholic Bishops on Economic Policy, 1891-1984*. Washington: United States Catholic Conference.

Coleman, John A.
1984 "Catholic Human Rights Theory: Four Challenges to an Intellectual Tradition." *Journal of Law and Religion* (1984), vol. 2, 343-66.

Curran, Charles E.
1976 *New Perspectives in Moral Theology*. Notre Dame: University of Notre Dame Press.

Goodin, Robert E.
1982 *Political Theory and Public Policy*. Chicago: University of Chicago Press.

Heckscher, Eli F.
1934 *Mercantilism*. Translated by Mendel Shapiro. London: George Allen.

Hirschman, Albert O.
1983 "Morality and the Social Sciences: A Durable Tension." In *Social Science as Moral Inquiry*, edited by Norma Haan, et al., 21-32. New York: Columbia University Press.

Hollenbach, David.
1979 *Claims in Conflict: Retrieving and Renewing the Catholic Human Rights Tradition*. New York: Paulist Press.

Hume, David.
1985 "Of the Dignity or Meanness of Human Nature." In *Essays Moral, Political, and Literary*, 80-86. Indianapolis: Liberty Classics.

Kant, Immanuel.
1959 *Foundations of the Metaphysics of Morals*. Translated by L. W. Beck. Indianapolis: Library of the Liberal Arts.

Letwin, William.
1964 *The Origins of Scientific Economics*. Garden City: Doubleday.

Macfie, Alec.
1971 "The Invisible Hand of Jupiter." *Journal of the History of Ideas*, vol. 32, 595-99.

Maritain, Jacques.
1986 *Christianity and Democracy* (and) *The Rights of Man and Natural Law*. Translated by Doris C. Anson. San Francisco: Ignatius Press.

Marx, Karl.
1972 "Contribution to the Critique of Hegel's *Philosophy of Right*: Introduction." *The Marx-Engels Reader*, edited by Robert C. Tucker, 2nd ed., 16-25. New York: Norton.

McCulloch, J. R., ed.
1856 *Early English Tracts on Commerce*. London: Political Economy Club.

Mirandola, Pico della.
1940 *On the Dignity of Man*. Translated by Charles Glenn Wallis. Indianapolis: Bobbs-Merrill.

Murray, Charles.
1988 *In Pursuit of Happiness and Good Government*. New York: Simon and Schuster.

Murray, John Courtney.
1964 *We Hold These Truths: Catholic Reflections on the American Proposition*. Garden City: Image Books.

Novak, Michael.
1984 *Toward the Future: Catholic Social Thought and the U.S. Economy (A Lay Letter)*. New York: Lay Commission on Catholic Social Teaching and the U. S. Economy.

Okun, A. M.
 1975 *Equality and Efficiency: The Big Tradeoff*. Washington: Brookings.

Petty, William.
 1899 *The Economic Writings of Sir William Petty*. Edited by C. H. Hull. Cambridge: Cambridge University Press.

Pitt-Rivers, Julian.
 1968 "Honor." *International Encyclopedia of the Social Sciences*, vol. 6, 503-11. New York: Macmillan and Free Press.

Rosenberg, Nathan.
 1979 "Adam Smith and Laissez-Faire Revisited." In *Adam Smith and Modern Political Economy*, edited by Gerald P. O'Driscoll, Jr., 19-34. Ames: Iowa State University Press.

Ryle, Gilbert.
 1984 *The Concept of Mind*. Chicago: University of Chicago Press.

Schumpeter, Joseph A.
 1954 *History of Economic Analysis*. New York: Oxford University Press.

Skinner, B. F.
 1972 *Beyond Freedom and Dignity*. New York: Alfred A. Knopf.

Smith, Adam.
 1981 *An Inquiry into the Nature and Causes of the Wealth of Nations*. Edited by R. H. Campbell and A. S. Skinner. Indianapolis: Liberty Classics.

 1982 *Essays on Philosophical Subjects*. Edited by W. P. C. Wightman and J. C. Bryce. Indianapolis: Liberty Classics.

 1982 *Lectures on Jurisprudence*. Edited by R. L. Meek and P. G. Stein. Indianapolis: Liberty Classics.

 1982 *The Theory of Moral Sentiments*. Edited by D. D. Raphael and A. L. Macfie. Indianapolis: Liberty Classics.

Sombart, Werner.
 1967 *The Quintescence of Capitalism*. New York: Howard Fertig.

Viner, Jacob.
 1972 *The Role of Providence in the Social Order*. Princeton: Princeton University Press.

1978 *Religious Thought and Economic Society*. Durham: Duke University Press.

Weisskopf, Walter.
1955 *The Psychology of Economics*. London: Routledge & Kegan Paul.

Wilson, Thomas.
1925 *Discourse upon Usury*. Edited by R. H. Tawney. London: B. Bell and Sons.

Worland, Stephen T.
1983 "Adam Smith: Economic Justice and the Founding Father." In *New Directions in Economic Justice*, edited by Roger Skurski, 1-32. Notre Dame and London: University of Notre Dame Press.

INDEX